During the years before the First World War, the realignment of world powers resulted in agreements concluded in 1904 and 1907 between Britain, France, Russia, and Japan. John Albert White terms this a Quadruple Entente, a more accurate and complete description than the more commonly used Triple Entente, which omits Japan. His more inclusive view leaves undisturbed the conception of Europe as the center of political gravity, but at the same time calls proper attention to the enhanced role which Japan had won through her victories in the Sino-Japanese and Russo-Japanese wars and by careful management of her entry into the larger family of nations. This wider perspective on the crucial pre-war years shows how, in its political context as well as its geographical terrain and its general impact, the First World War was a world war in every sense.

Transition to global rivalry

Transition to global rivalry

Alliance diplomacy and the Quadruple
Entente, 1895–1907

John Albert White

CAMBRIDGE
UNIVERSITY PRESS

Published by the Press Syndicate of the University of Cambridge
The Pitt Building, Trumpington Street, Cambridge CB2 1RP
40 West 20th Street, New York, NY 10011-4211, USA
10 Stamford Road, Oakleigh, Melbourne 3166, Australia

First published 1995

Printed in Great Britain at the University Press, Cambridge

A catalogue record for this book is available from the British Library

Library of Congress cataloguing in publication data
White, John Albert.
    Transition to global rivalry: alliance diplomacy and the
Quadruple Entente, 1895–1907/John Albert White.
        p.   cm.
    Includes bibliographical references and index.
    ISBN 0 521 47445 0
    1. Europe – Politics and government – 1871–1918.   2. Triple Entente.
1907.   I. Title.
D397.W48   1995
940.2′87—dc20   94-42294 CIP

ISBN 0 521 47445 0 hardback

To
Joyce Tate White

Contents

List of illustrations

List of maps

Preface

The focus of this narrative is the era which was ushered in by the rise to world stature of Germany, Japan, and the United States, by the victory of Japan in the war with Russia, and by the concurrent shift in the balance of power out of which there emerged a "diplomatic revolution." This gave rise to the formation of a Quadruple Entente composed of Britain, France, Russia, and Japan. The immediate object of this coalition was to achieve general stability by creating a counterpoise to the Triple Alliance consisting of Germany and Austria-Hungary, and Italy. While Germany and Japan both had contributed to the deterioration of the existing order, Japan had ultimately found it advantageous to adhere to and support the new international system.

This account is both a parallel and a sequel to my *The Diplomacy of the Russo-Japanese War* published in 1964 by Princeton University Press. Both deal with aspects of the major political transformation of the era, the "diplomatic revolution." The rivalry of the two coalitions became one of the primary factors leading to the first world war. Earlier accounts of this mutation have described the new coalition as a "Triple Entente," i.e., an association of Britain, France, and Russia. This, however, did not adequately take account either of the character of the contemporary international order or of the role in its creation of either Russia or Japan. It is the object of this account to incorporate these aspects of the current conditions and to portray the shifting relationships of the principal participants and the nature of the political environment this created.

The characterization of these proceedings in a correct perspective requires taking into account some of the major world developments which influenced the international outlook during this period. One of these, the event which was central to the theme of this study, was the Anglo-Russian rivalry as it unfolded in the contested region of Central Asia and the Indian frontier, particularly as it was modified by the developments of the period which saw the shift in the balance of power. Closely related to this was the dynamic growth and expansion of German power and influence on the European continent, on the oceans of the world, and in the Middle and Far East. Also related to this change in the international balance of power, particularly with respect to Russia and her colonial interests, was the role of Japan, a newcomer to the company of world powers. After having first opposed the existing order in the Far East by upsetting the existing balance of power there, Japan had joined and supported the new order.

This intensifying struggle portended not only a further extension of the great power conflict into Asia but a reaction to it in those regions. It was an era in which western style nationalism came to play an increasingly more important part in the life of that area of the world and in which this reinforced indigenous tendencies toward ethnic and cultural self-assertion as well as political self-determination. Accordingly, an appropriate allotment of attention has been directed to those regions which, in addition to Europe and its eastern and southeastern margins, were claiming an increasing share of consideration from the makers of foreign policy in London, St. Petersburg, and elsewhere.

A factor which has made a reconsideration of this subject particularly appropriate is the circumstance that the last full treatment of it in English was in 1939 when Rogers Platt Churchill published *The Anglo-Russian Convention of 1907*. This was before the archives of Britain, France, and Japan had been opened for these years. It was also before these nations as well as the Soviet Union had opened and published additional source materials which have made possible a much more comprehensive understanding of this period and its implications for subsequent events.

More recently several studies have been made in closely allied fields. One of these was by Ian Nish, *The Origin of the Russo-Japanese War*, London, 1985. Another was by Anatolii Venediktovich Ignat'ev, whose previous publications have also encompassed the decade following his present work. His *Vneshniaia politika Rossii v 1905–1907 gg.* [The Foreign Policy of Russia, 1905–1907], Moscow, 1986, deals with the Anglo-Russian agreement in the context of the major diplomatic events of these years.

A work dealing more specifically and extensively with the subject is that of Alevtina Fedorovna Ostal'tseva, who has also written several articles on the subject. Her *Anglo-russkoe soglashenie 1907 goda; vliianie russko-iaponskoi voiny i revoliutsii 1905–1907 godov na vneshniuiu politiku tsarizma i na peregruppirovku evropeiskikh derzhav* [The Anglo-Russian Agreement of 1907: The Influence of the Russo-Japanese War and the Revolution of 1905–1907 on the Foreign Policy of Tsarism and on the Regrouping of the European Powers], was published in Saratov, 1977. Like Ignat'ev, the author has used a considerable number of Soviet sources and in this respect at least has supplemented all available non-Russian versions of the subject. She has also had access to both Russian and foreign published materials.

A further incentive for reexamining this subject has been provided by the recent course of events in the Middle East, one of the principal geographical centers of interest of this study. Developments culminating there in the late 1970s have given the present a discernible sense of continuity with the earlier period. The rise of a powerful Muslim religious movement and, following the departure of the Shah of Iran, the accession to power of Ayatolla Ruholla Khomeini and his successors emphasize the continuity of the struggle for national identity which was so prominent a factor in Iran in 1906.

An expression of special appreciation must be made to a number of persons and institutions which have helped in special ways to make available the materials used in this study. These include the University of Hawaii which has generously made it possible through its existing facilities as well as special purchases and inter-institutional loans to have access to a considerable portion of the necessary materials. Many of these were made accessible with the able assistance of Mrs. Patricia Polansky, the Russian Librarian, who also prepared the bibliography. In Britain the Public Record Office Library, the Foreign Office Library, and the India Office Library liberally permitted me the use of their extensive collections. In the United States the library resources of the University of California at Berkeley and of Columbia University were kindly made available to me.

Special mention must also be made of the contribution to this endeavor on the part of the Rockefeller Foundation which generously helped to make possible access both to the archival and library resources of Japan and to those of Britain. The British collections include those noted above as well as those at Cambridge University and the Royal Archives at Windsor Castle, the latter made available through the intermediary of my late colleague and friend, Professor Arthur J. Marder. The use of the ample and uniquely significant papers of Sir Arthur Nicolson, the First Lord Carnock, was made possible with the help of Miss Violet Conolly of the British Foreign Office and with the special permission of his son, Sir Harold Nicolson. These papers were then in the Foreign Office Library.

The valuable resources of the Japanese Foreign Office were used with the permission and help of Mr. Kurihara Ken and the kindly guidance of Mr. Oyama Azusa, the grandson of Marshal Oyama Iwao. My colleagues and friends, Professor Yong-ho Choe, who made possible my use of some of the materials relating to Korea, and Professor John J. Stephan and

Professor Robert Valliant who kindly read the entire manuscript and made valuable suggestions, are responsible for many of the positive features of this study.

The simplest and most convenient practices have been adopted in the composition of the narrative. The standard systems of romanization and transliteration have been used. Also, since the Russian events had to be coordinated with those of other nations, all Russian dates, unless otherwise indicated, are given in the new style. Finally, the use of the name Persia rather than the currently more accurate Iran has been adopted in the narrative as a matter of convenience. Since all contemporary references and materials use Persia and since the subject matter deals with a period preceding the Iranian adoption of the present usage, this seemed to be a reasonable simplification.

A brief chronology of the formation of the Quadruple Entente

1896

Jan. 3   Kruger telegram (Emperor Wilhelm to President Stephanus Johannes Paulus Kruger of the South African Republic)

June 3   Russo-Chinese alliance

Sept. 8   Contract signed for construction and operation of Chinese Eastern Railway

Sept. 9   Briner timber concession (N. Korea) signed

1897

June 20   British Diamond Jubilee anniversary celebration

Nov. 14   Germany occupied Tsingtao

Dec. 19   Russia occupied Port Arthur

1898

Jan.   Salisbury sought accommodation with Russia

Mar.   Russo-Korean Bank opened

Mar. 28   German naval law passed by Reichstag

Apr. 4   American China Development Company concession for Hankow–Canton railway

May 1   US defeated Spanish squadron at Manila Bay

June 11   Central Asian Railway reached Tashkent

July 1   China lease of Weihaiwei to Britain

July 6   Sino-Russian supplementary agreements on leased territory and South Manchurian Railway

Dec. 18   First Russian train reached Kushka Post on Afghan frontier

Dec. 30   Lord Curzon reached Bombay to become viceroy of India

1899

Jan. 23   British–Kuwait (Sheikh Mubarak) mutual guarantees

Apr. 28   Anglo-Russian (Scott-Murav'ev) agreement on spheres in China

July 12   Russia made Dalny a free port

Sept. 6   First Hay "open door" notes

Nov. 27	German preliminary agreement for a Konia–Persian Gulf railway
Dec. 26	Extension of prohibition on railway construction in Persia to 1910

1900

Jan. 20	Russian loan to Persia
Feb. 14	Sailing of merchant ship Kornilov from Odessa to Persian Gulf announced
Mar. 31	Russian–Ottoman railway agreement on Black Sea region
June 12	Second German naval law
July 3	Second Hay "open door" notes
Oct. 16	Anglo-German "Yangtze agreement"
Nov. 12	Lansdowne succeeded Salisbury as minister of foreign affairs
Nov. 22	Russian consulate opened in Bombay
Dec. 14,16	Franco-Italian (Barrère–Venosta) correspondence on African interests

1901

Feb. 8	Russian condition for withdrawal from Manchuria presented to China
May 28	William Knox D'Arcy concession granted for oil exploitation in Persia
Sept. 7	Boxer Protocol concluded
Nov. 7	Li Hung-chang died

1902

Jan. 30	Anglo-Japanese alliance concluded

1903

Mar. 5	Bagdad Railway created in final concession
Mar. 8	First passenger train reached Dalny
Apr. 22	British cabinet decision against participation in Bagdad Railway
July 28	Japanese government sounded out Russian government on opening negotiations
Aug. 12	Viceroyalty of the (Russian) Far East established
Aug. 28	Witte dismissed as minister of finance
Oct. 8	United States and Japan concluded treaties with China for opening for commerce of towns in Manchuria (Mukden, Tatungkou, and Antung)
Oct. 28–31	Lamsdorf in Paris (possibly discussed prospective Anglo-Russian and Russo-Japanese agreements)
Nov. 16	Curzon departed Karachi for Persian Gulf tour (returned Dec. 7, 1903)

1904

Jan. 1	British proposals to Russia – last before war
Feb. 10	Third Hay "open door" notes
Apr. 14	King Edward discussed Anglo-Russian relations with Izvolsky in Copenhagen
July 28	Russo-German commercial treaty revised and renewed
Aug. 12	Birth of Aleksei Nikolaevich, heir to the Russian throne
Oct. 13	Lamsdorf instructions for the new minister in Teheran, A. N. Speyer
Oct. 21–22	North Sea incident (Dogger Bank)
Nov. 25	Anglo-Russian agreement to submit the North Sea incident to an international committee which met Dec. 22, 1904–Feb. 25, 1905

1905

Jan. 13	Fourth Hay "open door" notes
July 24	Björkö agreement signed by German and Russian emperors
Aug. 12	Anglo-Japanese alliance renewed
Aug. 28	First All-Russian Muslim Congress at Nizhnii Novgorod (Gorky) during the fair
Sept. 27	Anglo-Japanese alliance published
Oct. 30	Imperial manifesto on Russian government reorganization
Nov. 25	Loicq de Lobel proposal for a railway into northeastern Siberia to connect with North America

1906

Jan. 1	Orenburg–Tashkent railway opened for regular traffic
Jan. 12	British general election
Jan. 15	Algeciras Conference begins (to Apr. 7)
Feb. 10	First British dreadnought launched
Apr. 6	Witte formally notified of German decision against granting a loan
Apr. 16	Franco-Russian loan agreement signed
Apr. 21	Revised Franco-Russian military convention signed in Paris
May 12	Izvolsky became minister of foreign affairs
May 28	Nicolson reached St. Petersburg as ambassador
June 21	Stolypin became chairman of the Council of Ministries
July 20	Wallace went to St. Petersburg (remained until late November)
July 20, 25	Aehrenthal letters to Goluchowski proposing concert of the three eastern monarchies
Oct. 7	Persian Majlis opened by Shah

Nov. 16	Bülow, in Reichstag speech, accused powers of "encirclement"

1907

Feb. 18	Last phase of Russo-Japanese negotiations started
Feb. 20	Russian proposals regarding Persia to Britain and Germany
May 15	Anglo-Spanish and Franco-Spanish exchange of notes concerning status quo in western Mediterranean–Atlantic coastal area
June 10	Franco-Japanese agreement concluded at Paris
June 13	Russo-Japanese railway demarcation in Manchuria
June 22	New regulations for Persian Discount and Loan Bank approved by Russian Emperor
July 30	Russo-Japanese treaty concluded
Aug. 3–6	Russo-German conference at Swinemünde
Aug. 31	Anglo-Russian agreement concluded
Oct. 29	Russo-German protocol guaranteeing their territorial status quo in the Baltic
Nov. 2	Treaty of Christiania (Oslo) guaranteeing integrity of Norway
Dec. 13	Russian ministerial conference in which Izvolsky requested reaffirmation of the treaty of August 31 with Britain

Abbreviations

AHR	*American Historical Review*
AHY	*Austrian History Yearbook*
AMRR	*American Monthly Review of Reviews*
APG	*Archiv für Politik und Geschichte*
BD	Great Britain. Foreign Office. *British documents on the origins of the war, 1898–1914*, 11 vols., London, 1926–38
BFSP	*British and Foreign State Papers*
BIHR	*Bulletin of the Institute of Historical Research*
BM	*Berliner Monatshefte für Internationale Aufklärung*
BSOAS	*Bulletin of the School of Oriental and African Studies*
CDS	Alexander [Aleksandr Feliksovich] Meyendorff, *Correspondence de M. de Staal, 1884–1900*, 2 vols., Paris, 1929
CHJ	*Cambridge Historical Journal*
CID	Committee of Imperial Defence
CJH	*Canadian Journal of History*
CMRS	*Cahiers du Monde Russe et Sovietique*
CR	*Contemporary Review*
CSPSR	*Chinese Social and Political Science Review*
DDAM	France Ministère des Affaires Etrangères. *Documents diplomatiques, affaires du Maroc, 1901–1905*, Paris, 1905
DDF	France Ministère des Affaires Etrangères. *Documents diplomatiques, Français (1871–1914)*, 2nd series, 14 vols., Paris, 1930–55
EHR	*Economic History Review*
FO	Foreign Office. Great Britain
GJ	*Geographical Journal*
GP	Germany Auswärtiges Amt. *Die grosse Politik der Europäischen Kabinette, 1871–1914*, 54 vols., Berlin, 1922–27
H	*History*
HJ	*Historical Journal*
HZ	*Historische Zeitung*
IG	India Government

IO	India Office
IOL	India Office Library
ISSR	*Istoriia SSR*
IZ	*Istoricheskie zapiski*
IZh	*Istoricheskii zhurnal*
JBS	*Journal of British Studies*
JCEA	*Journal of Central European Affairs*
JCH	*Journal of Contemporary History*
JFO	Japan. Foreign Office
JMH	*Journal of Modern History*
JRCAS	*Journal of the Royal Central Asian Society*
KA	*Krasnyi arkhiv*
LA	*Living Age*
LS	*Letopis severa*
M	*Mizan*
MAS	*Modern Asian Studies*
MES	*Middle Eastern Studies*
MM	*Militärgeschichtliche Mitteilungen*
MN	*Monumenta Nipponica*
MVHR	*Mississippi Valley Historical Review*
MZ	*Mezhdunarodnaia zhizn*
NAR	*North American Review*
NC	*Nineteenth Century and After* (now *Twentieth Century*)
NGB	Japan. Foreign Office *Nihon Gaiko Bunsho*
NV	*Novyi Vostok*
PC	Harvard University Committee on Regional Studies *Papers on China*
PCAS	*Proceedings of the Central Asian Society*
PHR	*Pacific Historical Review*
PP	*Past and Present*
PRGS	*Proceedings of the Royal Geographical Society*
PRO	Public Record Office
Protocols	Japan. Foreign Office. *Protocols of the Peace conference between Japan and Russia*
PSQ	*Political Science Quarterly*
QR	*Quarterly Review*
RDM	*Revue des Deux Mondes*
RF	E.A. Preobrazhensky and B.A. Romanov (eds.), *Russkie finansy i evropeiskaia birzha v 1904–1906 gg.*, Moscow, 1926
RH	*Russian History*
RHD	*Revue d'Histoire Diplomatique*

R-IV   USSR Central Archives. *Russko-Iaponskaia voina; iz dnev-*
            nikov A. N. Kuropatkina i N. P. Linevicha, Leningrad, 1925
SEER   *Slavonic and East European Review*
SR   *Slavic Review* (formerly *American Slavic and East European*
            Review)
SV   *Sovetskoe vostokovedenie*
TRHS   *Transactions of the Royal Historical Society*
USFR   United States. Dept. of State. *Papers relating to the foreign*
            relations of the United States
VI   *Voprosy istorii*
VLU   *Vestnik Leningradskogo universiteta Seriia istorii, iazyka i*
            literatury

1   Portents of conflict

Rivalry and power

The decade of international readjustment which reached a climax in 1907 was characterized by national ambitions and political processes which portended not only fundamental change but also discord and conflict on a global scale. The emerging diplomatic order which was manifestly intended to bring about an accommodation to the new conditions was so different from the prevailing diplomatic pattern that it came to be recognized as a diplomatic revolution. The driving force in the creation of the new strategic-political structure was the emergence as regional and then world powers of Germany and Japan and, in the longer view, the United States. The principal leadership, however, which led to the diplomatic restructuring was provided by Britain, then the only actual world power.

The British motive for undertaking this mission was of course the security of the empire. However, since one of the principal threats to imperial security was the recessive role Britain had been forced for decades to play in the perennial Anglo-Russian rivalry, some alleviation of this situation was considered of the greatest importance. This antagonism had for decades defied all attempts to find a mutually acceptable solution and therewith the means of establishing a stable frontier in western Asia to protect India.

But with the expansion of German and Japanese influence and power and the corresponding intensification of international rivalries, Russia was increasingly drawn into the broader world conflict and diverted accordingly from her strategic rivalry with Britain. This in turn brought about a measure of amelioration of the British strategic preoccupation with Russia. The essential consequence was that by August 1907 not only had Britain and Russia succeeded in concluding a relatively equitable agreement but France and Japan had become associated with it in what formed the Quadruple Entente. Anglo-Russian rivalry had been, with the help of an altered global milieu, suspended rather than terminated.

The new diplomatic era was ushered in both by the revision and regrouping of existing patterns and practices and by the extension of the diplomatic network to less explored aspects of world relationships. The Mediterranean agreements, which had provided a link between Britain, Austria, Italy, and Spain and between these countries and the Triple Alliance as a means of preserving the status quo in the Mediterranean and the Middle East, were terminated in 1897 by British withdrawal.

This was also the year in which Germany began announcing her new economic and strategic expansion in the Middle and Far East and on the oceans of the world. This evidence of German ambitions and plans also evoked fears that should the Austro-Hungarian Empire disintegrate in case of the death of Emperor Franz Joseph, Germany might be able to annex part or all of it and form a greater German empire reaching across Europe from the Baltic to the Adriatic Sea. The latter region would give Germany possession of the Austrian naval base at Trieste and make it possible for Germany to become also a major Mediterranean sea power.

It was this fear which inspired the St. Petersburg visit in August 1899 of Théophile Delcassé, the French minister of foreign affairs. His objective was to change the basis of the Franco-Russian alliance from reliance on the duration of the Triple Alliance to the principle of the balance of power. The German plan to expand into the Middle East by means of the Bagdad railway, since it affected the vital interests of both Britain and Russia, was one of the factors which ultimately helped to moderate the antagonism between these rivals and to direct it against Germany.

The British and Russian Empires were, at the beginning of the twentieth century, the largest and most expansive existing domains touching both Atlantic and Pacific oceans but, in an age of increasingly rapid communications, the means of spanning these great distances was comparatively time consuming. The British Empire, while historically and fundamentally a maritime power, had nevertheless significant relationships with continental areas. Consequently, it experienced some significant disadvantages inherent for a sea power in the contemporary growth of land powers both in metropolitan and overseas regions.

Britain's maritime routes passed through or near some unavoidable narrows such as the Turkish straits and the Suez Canal *en route* to significant portions of the empire, passages which were becoming increasingly endangered by rival claims and demands. The imperial commitments also included continental frontiers in Canada, South Africa, and western Asia. The last of these had for decades been a mobile frontier where Britain had tried with only limited success to stem the tide of the Russian advance through Central Asia toward India and the Persian Gulf. This enduring Anglo-Russian rivalry became a diplomatic tradition which other powers, and in particular, Germany, were able to take for granted when making strategic plans.

The Russian Empire, fundamentally a land power, had been, in considerable part because of her inadequate transportation, defeated in the Crimean war by Britain and France. Since then, however, Russia had tried to revitalize her antiquated governmental and social structure and in the process had considerably expanded the transportation network. Railways were projected toward the frontiers in Europe to meet the German challenge, in the south to meet the British challenge more effectively, and in the Far East to meet the Japanese challenge. Still, the demands of the Russo-Japanese war found the Pacific frontier ill-equipped with adequate means of transportation to support a war at such a distance from the European center of the empire. In fact, a continuous railway line wholly on Russian territory did not reach the Pacific until 1916.

The more recently developed empires, Germany and Japan, matured with the support of effective governments, strong political drives, forceful military components, and operable transportation systems. These two nations had emerged on the international scene comparatively late and were conscious of being latecomers in what was already a highly competitive world order. As a consequence they felt the need to use every opportunity to compete for "a place in the sun" before it was too late, i.e., before the best opportunities had been appropriated. Both these nations, however, enjoyed the advantage of sharing access to the Russian frontier in the west and the east. Consequently, this made it possible for them to impose upon Russia a coercive influence often by intended or fortuitous cooperative action. Furthermore, since Russia was also a major participant in the world balance of power this permitted Germany and Japan an opportunity to exercise a unique influence on the development of world affairs.

It became, in fact, the national policy of Germany to seek to alleviate the pressure on her own eastern frontier, thus leaving her free to deal with her other European neighbors, by encouraging Russia to pursue her interests in Asia without concern about her western frontier, the very borderland which in fact caused Russia the greatest apprehension. In a parallel action, Japan, in her own national or regional interests and without any necessary coordination with Germany, could take similar advantage of Russia's widespread multinational frontier and difficulty in defending it.

The German Empire, a product of a military supported unification plan, was located in the center of Europe and while it was strongly nationalist in political bent, it included Poles, Danes, and other nationalities and was, above all, traditionally a descendant of an earlier German empire. It suffered from its founding days a consciousness and apprehension over "encirclement" and of competitiveness with its neighbors. Its already ample internal railway network at the time of the founding of the empire became a point of departure for the extension of a railway through Austria and the Balkans to Constantinople. From there it was projected as the Bagdad railway to the Persian Gulf. This was a route which, by a fortunate coincidence, would assure the minimum possibility of an encounter with the British navy. Even though this route gave unimpeded and relatively uncontested access to the most significant of the German imperial enterprises, Germany also laid the foundations for a navy which effectively challenged the British naval, colonial, and commercial establishments there and elsewhere.

The Japanese Empire was a nation with a unifying cultural and political identity. Unlike Germany, Japan had to approach its intended colonial objective, with which it also had cultural ties, by sea before it could initiate political and military proceedings and before it could begin the railway construction which was part of its imperial program. Its notable advantages were the proximity of the intended imperial territories compared with the remoteness of its rivals, leaving it relatively free to act independently. These were advantages in some ways comparable to the German overland route to her intended objective.

This situation proved very valuable to Japan when in the early years of the twentieth century the international storm broke over Russia's refusal to withdraw her military forces from Manchuria. Supported by the Anglo-Japanese alliance, Japan was able to command virtually uncontested access to Korea and Manchuria and to rely on the neutrality of her prospective challengers, permitting her to settle her score with Russia on her own terms. In this way, Japan, with this windfall of diplomatic cooperation by Germany and other powers, was able to reduce substantially the prestige and power of a principal rival, Russia, and to undermine Russia's ability to involve on her own behalf other competitors of Germany and Japan.

The interaction of forces such as these helped to bring about the diplomatic revolution of 1907 and with it a more competitive international order. To the existing Triple and Dual Alliances and the Anglo-Japanese alliance was added a group of agreements known as ententes, all formed as sequels to the Anglo-Japanese alliance during or after the Russo-Japanese war and known as the Triple Entente. However, the role and significance of Japan in the creation of the conditions which brought about these four accords, in joining with Britain to help form a new balance of power, and in playing a direct and major part in shaping the last three agreements, make it more reasonable that these should be known as the Quadruple Entente. These agreements were the Anglo-French, Franco-Japanese, Russo-Japanese, and Anglo-Russian ententes. The Anglo-Russian entente came last, not because it was the least important but because Britain was in the vanguard of the movement to affiliate these nations and Russia needed British support in building cooperation with Germany and Japan.

It is significant that the agreements which composed the Quadruple Entente evolved in response to a perceived strategic necessity rather than to preconceived or preconcerted attitudes or objectives. In fact, all the signatories of these agreements had at one time or another been directly or indirectly associated diplomatically with the Triple Alliance or had seriously contemplated such an affiliation,

The fundamental objective of the first of these four, the Anglo-French entente, was to render difficult or improbable a combination of Germany and Russia against either of the two signatories. Although both France and Russia had continued for some years to consider the possibility of concluding also an understanding with Germany, the Franco-Russian alliance completed in 1894, became for both allies their accepted diplomatic mooring. In fact, however, an important element in Russia continued either because of personal or political preference or of a sense of security to favor a close tie with Germany.

Sergei Iul'evich Witte himself had favored such a choice but as circumstances changed he came to see a Russian association with the entente powers as a more practical solution to Russia's problem. That it was nevertheless wise to continue to maintain correct relations with Germany was demonstrated during the Anglo-Russian negotiations when Germany was kept informed of their progress.

Britain was not so fortunate as to have even this choice. Until the conclusion of the Anglo-French entente in 1904, with the exception of the indirect assistance given Britain's involvement with Russia by the Anglo-Japanese alliance, she had made no direct progress toward overcoming the impediment of the protracted Anglo-Russian rivalry in western Asia. The Anglo-Russian conflict, one of the most prolonged embroilments in modern diplomatic or colonial rivalry, had emerged as an ingredient in world affairs during the half century preceding the Crimean war. In the course of the succeeding four decades, as the Russian frontier moved southward, it was, however, markedly transformed, becoming greatly intensified not only in competitiveness but particularly in the antagonism it evoked.

This mutation was to a considerable degree brought about by the relatively rapid absorption by Russia of Central Asia, an aggressive defensive movement encompassing more than 450,000 square miles.

1. Nikolai Fedorovich Petrovsky, sent to Sinkiang as consul in 1882, became consul general in 1886

Russia became by this southern movement an immediate and trouble-some neighbor of Persia, Afghanistan, and of Chinese Turkestan [Sin-kiang]. These latter regions constituted a natural protective rampart for British India, the focal point and symbol of British power and prestige in Asia. Britain, with an empire based on seapower, had, accordingly, acquired another land frontier and beyond it a rival for this invaluable heritage whose strength consisted largely in land power.

Political and strategic pressures, aimed ultimately at British India, were exerted even before these Russian and British frontiers had become so nearly coterminous. With the extension of her domain to the mountain frontier, Russia had reached an apparently invulnerable bridgehead from which she could with maximum immunity threaten India. Behind this rampart she deployed military forces and constructed railways, develop-ments which the British saw, in the perspective of the decades-long Russian advance, as evidence of aggressive intent. Accordingly, the achievement of a common frontier with the border states of Persia and Afghanistan opened another and for Britain a more challenging phase of the relentless and menacing aspect of the Russian forward movement, transforming it into a more direct and intensive Anglo-Russian encounter.

As the Anglo-Russian zones of antagonism grew closer the rivalry became more intense and the question of the security of the highly prized Indian dominion more insistent. At the same time, for Russia it raised the question of the security of what had become the southern part of her own realm. British fear was stimulated not only by the Russian advance toward India, but also by her own unpreparedness to meet a possible Russian military encroachment. Britain was also distressed by the possibility of another and perhaps more widespread and more effectively organized Indian mutiny. Such an uprising might be encouraged by the appearance, in fact or prospectively, on or near the frontier of an apparently victorious Russian military force, inviting an Indian uprising.

The Russians on their part saw the British raj in nearby India as more than just another threat on or near their southern border. It was not like the opposition they had already encountered from either the nomadic hordes or the unstable and often turbulent urban-centered states of Central Asia. These tribal and oasis people had been protected largely by their distances from more dynamic neighbors and by harsh geographical conditions on their frontiers. India, ruled by a European power of worldwide dominion and with unknown ambitions and military poten-tial, could, it was at first feared, become a base of operations from which to threaten the Russian frontier, to block Russia's southern advance, and thus to create there a perpetual challenge.

While the principal focus of Anglo-Russian discord remained in the region north and northwest of the Indian frontier the emergence in the 1890s of Germany and Japan as significant forces in international affairs intensified the general rivalry and extended it westward into central Europe and eastward into the Far East. Russia, a continental nation with potentially vulnerable frontiers, sought security in the west by diplomatic affiliation and by a concentration of military forces. In the east she endeavored to strengthen her own frontiers against what she saw as a threat from Japan by trying to convert Korea and contiguous portions of China into a territorial barrier under her own control and by obstructing the Japanese efforts to establish a foothold on the Asian mainland.

The final three agreements, the principal subject of this study, constituted the fundamental settlement of the Russo-Japanese war and issues raised by it and were signed within a period of less than two months in 1907. A comparison of these three agreements with those inaugurated by Britain in 1903 but not concluded shows clearly how the international community had been altered in the intervening years. The Anglo-German negotiations of 1903, a revival of the British attempt to reach an understanding on some significant phase of the global rivalry of these powers, centered on the Bagdad railway question, had failed because there was not the will and the readiness, given the options then available, to accept an accommodation. The Bagdad railway issue must, therefore, be considered as one of the issues which interposed between the Triple Alliance and the entente nations.

This was also the opinion of Friedrich Rosen, a German Foreign Office official familiar with both Middle Eastern and current European affairs. It was he who was sent to Paris to make arrangements for the proposed Algeciras conference. Since Witte opposed Russian participation in the Bagdad railway scheme, it seems likely that this may have influenced his ultimate support of a pro-entente position.

The Anglo-Russian negotiations of 1903 were suspended at the outbreak of the Russo-Japanese war. However, at the time of their interruption the significant questions concerning the division of Persia into spheres or zones, the control of the Seistan region, and the status quo in the Persian Gulf had not been settled. It is significant that these three issues were of vital importance to both parties and that in 1907 all three were settled to the advantage of Britain.

Finally, the Anglo-French negotiations of 1903 were in fact preliminary to the Anglo-French entente of 1904 and to increasingly closer cooperation between these two nations as the tension with Berlin and Tokyo, especially the former, became more acute. The anxiety associated with the termination of the war and the acrimony generated by the

Algeciras conference drew Britain and France closer together than the term entente implied and helped to bring about their cooperation in fashioning the final three agreements of 1907.

Britain's new course

The British government, by the turn of the twentieth century, faced not only prolonged rivalry with Russia but other challenges as well, most recently the consequences of the war in south Africa. These sobering circumstances soon brought the British government to a thorough reconsideration of its foreign policy, in particular to a renewed emphasis on the traditional principles of British foreign policy in the light of the current world situation.

One of the foremost of these fundamental principles and the one from which Britain had departed in the late 1880s in order to associate herself with the Triple Alliance through accords with Austria, Italy, and Spain, known as the Mediterranean agreements, was the balance of power.[1] The equilibrium both of Europe and of the broader geographical milieu in which the British Empire existed had been disturbed by the emergence of Germany as a competitor rather than an ally both in Europe and overseas. A return to the balance of power in which the British Empire could find security would have to correct this distortion by giving appropriate attention to future domestic, imperial, and foreign relations. A policy must be sought which would reduce the vulnerability of the nation and the empire to the present and, in view of the current adverse trends, to the future dangers and pressures.

Another of the basic principles by which it was expected that British foreign policy would be guided was the significance of naval power, a factor which was influenced by the current state of Franco-Russian naval power and, especially after 1901, the realization of the implications of the new German naval policies. Germany, in the late years of the nineteenth century, had projected three interrelated programs comprising: the expansion on a worldwide scale of her naval power, the reinvigoration of her role in the Middle East by the projection to the Persian Gulf of the Bagdad railway, and the inauguration of a new strategic-commercial undertaking in the Far East. The last of these plans was intended to grasp the opportunity provided by the intervention of France, Germany, and

[1] Godfrey Davies, "The pattern of British foreign policy: 1815–1914," in Robert L. Schuyler and Herman Ausubel, *The making of English history*, New York, 1952, pp. 604–605; G.H. Bolsover, "Aspects of Russian foreign policy, 1815–1914," in B. Pares and A.J.P. Taylor (eds.) *Essays presented to Sir Lewis Namier*, London, 1956, pp. 320–356; Lillian Penson, "The new course in British foreign policy, 1892–1902," *TRHS*, XXV (1943), 121–138.

Russia which had forced Japan to retrocede to China the areas she had won in the war of 1895.

All aspects of the new German goals would be likely to have a considerable impact on both the national and the imperial interests of Britain. The naval buildup, however, would have special significance for Britain. Whether one accepted as intended literally the most defiant aims expressed in Berlin or assumed that the German government was using forceful language because it was anticipating stubborn competition on the part of Britain, the scale of German naval plans was bound to be a significant challenge to the dominant position of the British navy on the seas of Europe and of the world.

Since the object of the fleet, Admiral Alfred Peter Friedrich von Tirpitz had written to the Emperor, was to neutralize British sea power its major strength must be in battleships rather than cruisers.[2] It is clear that the Anglo-Japanese alliance, concluded five years later with a growing naval power, was to have at least one very useful function. It was hoped in London that it would relieve the British navy of part of its naval obligations in Far Eastern waters and thus leave Britain free to give greater attention to the region "between Heligoland and the Thames."

A third principle which was intended to be a part of the new operational strategy was expressed in a document dealing with defense. "Our plans," the memorandum stated, "must aim at the defense of the Empire as a whole." The defense of only Great Britain and Ireland, entirely apart from the duty owed other areas, would be economically disastrous. "The maintenance of sea supremacy has been assumed as the basis of the system of Imperial defense against attack over the sea," and remains so.

Having stated that a purely defensive posture was insufficient, that railways had considerably reduced the value of sea power, and that Britain could not under present conditions effectively carry on offensive operations against both Russia and France, the writer showed that none of the available avenues of attack on Russia were really possible for Britain. He noted finally that besides the protection of the British homeland, there was India. "Here alone can a fatal blow be dealt us," he stated, undoubtedly unaware of how precisely this coincided with some Russian views expressed in the immediate post-Crimean war years, asserting that only in Central Asia could Britain strike an effective blow against Russia.

[2] Alfred Peter Friedrich von Tirpitz, *My memoirs*, 2 vols. London, 1919, I, 69–79; Paul Michael Kennedy, "German world policy and the Alliance negotiations with England, 1897–1900," *JMH*, XL, no. 4 (Dec. 1973), pp. 608–609; Jonathan Steinberg, *Yesterday's deterrent. Tirpitz and the birth of the German battle fleet*, London, 1965, pp. 125–148, 209; Jonathan Steinberg, "The Copenhagen complex," *JCH*, I, no. 3 (July 1966), 29; William L. Langer, *The diplomacy of imperialism, 1890–1902*, 2 vols. New York, 1935, 1951, II, 430–442.

This must be prevented, the British memorandum stated categorically, by keeping hostile forces back from the (Indian) frontier.

A fourth principle, essentially an aspect of the third, was characterized, in an era of the emergence of the world-wide presence of Franco-Russian power and of other new centers of power outside of Europe, by the endeavor to help support British imperial interests by diplomatic partnerships with nations whose interests were similar or at least parallel with those of Britain.

The conclusion by Britain and the United States on November 18, 1901 of the Hay–Pauncefote treaty dealing with the Panama Canal area was one of these arrangements. It signified the decision of Britain to strengthen her international position by leaving to some extent the defense of her interests in the western hemisphere to the United States. This was at the time when Britain, in a significantly parallel case, was also seeking the cooperation of Japan in providing through the Anglo-Japanese alliance "a margin of superiority over Russia and France in the Far East."[3] Both these bargains helped make it possible, even without augmenting her existing forces, not only to enlist the support of the United States and Japan in protecting her interests in two significant areas of the world but also to strengthen the British naval presence in the Far Eastern, Mediterranean, and home waters.

Britain had been forced in the summer of 1901 to make another crucial and roughly parallel decision which led to the alliance with Japan. This had to be decided, as in the case of the diplomatic restructuring in the western hemisphere, at a time when her attention and strength were distracted by the Boer war while her principal rival, Russia, was enjoying the added advantage of China's weakness resulting from the outbreak of the Boxer uprising. Her choice of a diplomatic partnership at that time, considering the current official outlook in London, would undoubtedly have been an undertaking either with Germany or with Germany and Japan. However, Lord Salisbury was reluctant to commit the country to so critical an undertaking while Germany on her part wanted Britain to accept outright the responsibility of affiliation with the Triple Alliance.

In the end, Britain's first serious diplomatic partnership, aside from that with the United States, was formed with Japan. In fact, the outcome of the Sino-Japanese war had disclosed the weakness of China and, from the British point of view, had brought into serious question her effective-

---

[3] J.A.S. Grenville, "Great Britain and the Isthmian Canal, 1898–1901," *AHR*, LXI (Oct. 1955), 48, 51, 55, 69; J.H.S. Grenville, *Lord Salisbury and foreign policy: the close of the nineteenth century*, London, 1964, pp. 370–389; S.F. Wells, "British strategic withdrawal from the Western Hemisphere, 1904–1906," *Canadian Historical Review*, XLIX, No. 4 (Dec. 1968), 335 ff.

ness as a rampart against the Russian advance. Even then, in 1895, while Britain was still far from ready to commit herself to an alliance, she had decided to brave the ill-will of the triple intervention powers, France, Russia, and Germany, by refusing to join them in their determined but risky venture of insisting that Japan retrocede her wartime gains to China.

The absence of Britain from the intervention coalition was apparently not well understood by the Triplice and, since they perceived it as an element which might bring about the failure of their maneuver, they not unexpectedly disapproved of it. The reasons for this stance are, however, comprehensible in the context of existing British policy and of current conditions.[4] In the first place the considerable doubt that Japan would readily acquiesce in the Triplice demands raised for Britain the fundamental question if not the impossibility of committing a democratically elected and responsible government to such an unknown and risky future contingency.

There were also issues arising specifically from current conditions. One of these was the conceivable consequence of the Triplice idea of trying to induce Japan to accept Taiwan as a reward for her victory over China in lieu of the Liaotung peninsula, the intended Japanese beachhead in Manchuria. This would place a disappointed and resentful rising power strategically on Britain's maritime route to her commercial sphere of interest in the Yangtze valley. A successful intervention, moreover, could be highly detrimental to China, possibly leading to her further weakening and even dissolution. This would further diminish her role as an expanding British market and completely eliminate her as a barrier to a Russian advance.

It was also obvious that a successful intervention would be, from the British point of view, all too beneficial not only to Russia but to the Franco-Russian alliance as well. This was a factor which in itself, in view of the current state of British relations with France and Russia, would probably have ruled out British support for the intervention. In addition to their partnership with the Triplice which included Germany and France, Russia also played a significant role in helping to make both Manchuria and Korea increasingly unavailable to Japan. The Chinese

---

4 George Alexander Lensen, *Balance of intrigue: international rivalry in Korea and Manchuria, 1884–1899,* 2 vols. Tallahassee, FL, 1982, I, ch. 12, 13; Kimberley's Cabinet Report to the Queen, Apr. 23, 1895, in Kenneth Bourne, *Foreign policy of Victorian England 1830–1902,* Oxford, 1970, pp. 433–436; A.L. Popov (ed.), "Pervye shagi russkogo imperializma na Dal'nem Vostoke (1888–1903 gg.)," *KA,* LII (1932), 67–75, 78–83; Aleksei Leont'evich Narochnitsky, *Kolonial'naia politika kapitalisticheskikh derzhav na Dal'nem Vostoke, 1860–1895,* Moscow, 1956, pp. 676–690, 699; Sergei Iul'evich Witte, *Vospominaniia. Tsarstvovanie Nikolaia II,* 2 vols. Berlin, 1922, I, 38–40; Chirol (Peking) to Holstein, June 21, 1895, in Norman Rich and M.H. Fisher, *The Holstein papers,* 4 vols. Cambridge, MA, 1963, III, 523–524.

Eastern railway, intended to win Manchuria economically and strategically for Russia, was a joint Franco-Russian venture approved by China on June 3, 1895.

Franco-Russian control of the economy was also expected in the case of Korea where French advisers were placed in advisory positions in the post office, the legal department, and the arsenal. In addition, a French company, the Cie de Fives-Lilles, was granted a concession to construct a railway from Seoul to Uiju, a point on the Yalu river and on the Manchurian border. It was from Uiju that Japan planned to link the Korean railways with those of Manchuria. This would mean that the strategic position of this proposed North Korean railway appeared to insure it potentially the role of vanguard either for Russian penetration into Korea or for Japanese penetration into Manchuria.

Finally it was, of course, self-evident that the intervention was bound to be detrimental to Japan, the only nation which appeared ready and able to oppose Russian expansion, at that time a primary objective of British policy. Clearly, in view of the incipient power struggle then emerging in the Far East, diplomatic restraint with respect to the Triplice intervention appeared in London as the wisest policy.

The most realistic and desirable of the options available to Britain as a means of coping with the Russian advance in northeast China appeared, accordingly, to be one attainable through an affiliation with Japan. This prospect emerged from the experience of finding common ground with Japan on an important issue and from the advocacy of a common goal by interested and influential persons. Together these factors helped to create an alignment in opposition to Russian expansion. The common ground was the firm opposition of both Britain and Japan to the extension of Russian occupation further into and beyond the borders of Manchuria. Specifically, Britain objected to Russia's apparent intention to make Manchuria a point of departure for a projection of her influence if not also her ascendancy into intramural China.

Japan at the same time saw the occupation of Manchuria as itself a threat to the integrity of Korea which was in turn seen in Japan as a threat to her own national integrity. Among those in Britain who advocated an affiliation with Japan were: Lord Lansdowne, the minister of foreign affairs, and Lord Selborne, the first lord of the Admiralty. In Japan the supporters of an alliance included Baron Komura Jutaro, the minister of foreign affairs, and Baron Hayashi Tadasu, the minister in London.

One of the alternate diplomatic options which appeared at first to offer a means of bringing Britain and Japan together was the so-called "Yangtze agreement." This was an accord concluded by Britain and Germany on October 16, 1900. Japan adhered to this treaty on October 29 on the assumption that it entailed a restraint on the Russian advance, particularly in Manchuria. The agreement also gave Japan a fully equal association in a treaty with two of the major European powers.

Even though Chancellor Bülow announced on March 15, 1901 that for Germany the treaty did not apply to Manchuria, Japan continued to see the agreement as at least a forerunner of an understanding with Britain giving these same assurances. Furthermore, Britain and Japan, having in mind their common purpose of reducing Russian influence in the region were able to work together during the settlement of the Boxer episode which was concluded by the foreign powers on September 7, 1901. At this time further Anglo-Japanese negotiations were already in progress.

Another diplomatic strategy tried by both Britain and Japan was the attempt to restrain Russian expansion by agreement directly with Russia. The case for this plan was made for Japan by Viscount Ito Hirobumi whose ultimate objective was not basically different from that of his opponents in the government who opposed his strategy for achieving it. Until he became aware of the readiness of Britain to reach an acceptable agreement with Japan, he had doubted that such an outcome was possible. Also, he had objections to forcing Russia to come to terms by reaching an understanding with Britain, not only because he considered it in fact unattainable but also because it was supported by a military group including Generals Yamagata Aritomo and Katsura Taro and he feared that this approach might lead to war, as in fact it did.

In pursuit of his goal, Ito reached St. Petersburg on November 5, 1901 and, during his sojourn there, he held discussions with Count Vladimir Nikolaevich Lamsdorf, the minister of foreign affairs, and others. The results were disappointing for Ito because both Lamsdorf and General Aleksei Nikolaevich Kuropatkin, the minister of war, agreed that the firm grip on Korea which Ito wanted for Japan would constitute a threat to Russian interests in neighboring Manchuria.

Nevertheless, two aspects of these negotiations are of special interest. In the first place, they revealed the central issues which divided the two nations and over which they fought three years later. Secondly, even though Ito's personal initiative failed, negotiations with Russia were continued in 1902 and reopened in 1903 with renewed determination and with the full realization in Tokyo that this Japanese maneuver might lead to open hostilities.

Meanwhile, the other strategy, the endeavor of Britain and Japan to solve the problem by combining against Russian expansion, had been inaugurated. The process had an informal beginning on July 31, 1901 when Lord Lansdowne held a conversation with the Japanese minister, Baron Hayashi. At this time he suggested that, in the light of Russian expansion in Manchuria and its implications for China, they consider a course of action regarding the balance of power in the Far East.[5]

Lansdowne was able to use ideas drawn from a memorandum written a few days before by Sir Francis Bertie, the head of the Asiatic Department of the Foreign Office. By November 5 Lansdowne had a draft agreement ready for cabinet consideration. Baron Komura Jutaro, recently appointed minister of foreign affairs in the Katsura ministry, also had a memorandum prepared by December 7, 1901 delineating the advantages of a Japanese alliance, with Britain rather than Russia. The Anglo-Japanese alliance was concluded on January 20, 1902.

After the failure of Ito's diplomatic mission in St. Petersburg and the assumption of leadership in foreign affairs by Komura, the negotiations proceeded with considerable dispatch since the interest of the two participants were similar enough to make joint action feasible. Those then in power in each nation favored an alliance and were accordingly gratified that the other alternative, a separate bargain of each of the parties with Russia, had been avoided. Such an outcome would probably have reduced the value of an Anglo-Japanese agreement as a means of blocking Russia. Certainly, had Ito succeeded in his mission in St. Petersburg, it was feared in London that the British position in China would have been seriously weakened.

Even though both Britain and Japan wished to use the alliance to strengthen their resistance to any further Russian advance in China their reasons were different. Britain wanted to reinforce the political-geographical status quo while Japan wanted freedom of action to permit her to establish her own continental domain. The Anglo-Japanese alliance, with this difference, gave both parties what they wanted. In addition, the solidarity of the alliance provided an almost certain guarantee that France would remain neutral, a condition which was further assured by the Anglo-French entente, finally concluded in April 1904. Furthermore, since Germany had no interest in defending the Russian stake in the Far East, her neutrality seemed assured.

Thus, the Anglo-Japanese alliance established a strong probability that Japan would be able to use the opportunity of the uncompleted Russian railway to strike while her advantage was at its maximum. Her incentive was the correction of what she saw as the unfairness of having been forced to retrocede to China the benefits of her victory in 1895 only to have these advantages appropriated by the powers which had earlier combined to force their retrocession.

The Anglo-Japanese naval agreement which had been reached during

[5] Ian H. Nish, *The Anglo-Japanese alliance. The diplomacy of two island empires, 1894–1907*, London, 1966, pp. 153–157, 382–385.

the negotiations was embodied in a separate diplomatic note rather than in the agreement itself, thus preserving the secrecy of the arrangement.[6] Both Britain and Japan had experienced the menace of the French and Russian navies, the latter particularly as allies, to their naval power. Lord Selborne, the first lord of the Admiralty, in a memorandum of September 1901, had shown that British naval forces in Far Eastern waters were outnumbered in battleships by the combined forces of France and Russia by a ratio of nine to four. If Britain were to combine forces with Japan, he noted, the two fleets would outnumber the French and Russian battleships in the Far East by eleven to nine. This advantage could give British commerce in that region the necessary margin of protection. In addition, however, by 1902 the growth of the German maritime forces had convinced the British Admiralty that Germany had in mind a possible naval war with Britain.

This also emphasized the need to supplement the naval forces in the Mediterranean and especially in home waters. Both Britain and Japan sought in their agreement to balance the naval power of potential rivals in their respective regions and to discourage as much as possible the further construction and maintenance of this expensive defense component by combining their naval power.

Britain, nevertheless, refused to guarantee the assignment of a specific number of ships to Far Eastern waters. She chose rather to retain freedom of action in order to maintain a sufficient balance of naval power in the regions most exposed to the growing German navy. It was, however, understood that Britain would retain a number of ships in the Far East sufficient to outnumber any other maritime combination. The destruction of the Russian fleet in the Russo-Japanese war eased this problem for both Britain and Japan.

Diplomatic alternatives

The British government, in pursuit of objectives similar to those it had sought through the Anglo-Japanese alliance, took the next step when it embarked in 1903 upon three additional diplomatic ventures. The current circumstances demanded some restructuring of the national defense establishment and the time appeared suitable for such an undertaking. The Anglo-Japanese alliance had by January 1902 alleviated to

---

[6] George W. Monger, *The end of isolation, British foreign policy 1900–1917*, London, 1963, pp. 11–12; Paul Michael Kennedy, *The rise and fall of British naval mastery*, New York, 1976, pp. 210–214; Arthur J. Marder, *The anatomy of British sea power. A history of British naval policy in the pre-dreadnought era, 1880–1905*, New York, 1940, ch. 21; Nish, *The Anglo-Japanese alliance*, pp. 353–358.

some extent the pressure on the British position in the Far East and, in a more general sense, had at least potentially tipped the diplomatic-strategic balance against Russia. The ending of the Boer war the following May had relieved Britain of the burden of an unpopular war, costly in material resources and in prestige. The experience had emphasized the importance of strategically selected alliances in the current competitive world.

Since assuming the office of viceroy of India in January 1899, Lord Curzon had forcefully and frequently called the attention of the London government to Russia's persistence, especially during the British pre-occupation with the South African war, in undermining the British position in Tibet, Afghanistan, and especially Persia as elements of her continental rampart protecting India. In November 1902 the British government had conducted a survey of the security of its position in Persia and the Persian Gulf. The findings provided ample grounds for pessimism and the conclusions called for a cautious policy which fully recognized the strength of Russia's position and took account of the urgent need for wise preparation for the future.

This ominous state of affairs, the outcome of decades of Anglo-Russian rivalry, was rendered even more threatening when it was realized that Russia's ally, France, had recently constructed a naval base at Bizerta in north Africa. This gave her another base of operations along the route to British India and the Far East. She also had a colonial possession, Indochina, to the east and an historically based claim to transit rights through the region juxtapositional to the Persian Gulf.

This was also the occasion of the tightening of the Franco-Russian bond. During a visit to St. Petersburg of the French minister of foreign affairs, Delcassé, France and Russia had revised their alliance in view of the growing international tensions. In an exchange of letters during August 8–9, 1899, the alliance had been geared to the balance of power in Europe rather than the duration of the Triple Alliance as formerly stipulated.

These reactions to the changing balance of power were supplemented by some modifications in the pattern of international affairs. In conferences between the chiefs of staff in the course of 1900–01 the common Franco-Russian fear of Germany was dealt with. Also, French loans were arranged to facilitate the construction of railways, including the completion of the Orenburg–Tashkent line but especially the reinforcement of the network running westward toward the Russian frontier, the region which the Russian minister of war, Kuropatkin, considered the most vital for national defense. Germany on her part continued to project her Bagdad railway eastward toward the Persian Gulf. All three of these nations had growing navies, competitive with that of Britain. By 1901, however, it was becoming clear that it was the German navy which was emerging as potentially the greatest threat.

The three diplomatic ventures which Britain projected in 1903 were intended, building on the Anglo-Japanese alliance, to make further contributions to British national and imperial prestige and security. Also, having in mind the increasingly vulnerable empire, it was hoped that they would lead to the realization of a more stable and congenial international order.

The first of these was an attempt to achieve some of the benefits to be gained by a diplomatic association with Germany. Since British financial assistance had been requested by Germany with reference to the construction of the Bagdad railway, those benefits were assumed to be obtainable under conditions acceptable to Britain for this purpose.

A conference was held on November 19, 1902 at the British Foreign Office which conducted a general review of the strategic position of Britain in Persia.[7] Among its other findings, it reached the conclusion that: "the most effective check to Russian progress towards South Persia lay in the completion of the railway from Constantinople to Bagdad ... provided we can acquire our proper share in the control of the railway and its outlet on the Persian Gulf."

This was clearly a cue to resume the endeavor of earlier years to seek an association with Germany and it is not surprising that Lord Lansdowne should once more become the chief spokesman for what was visualized as basically a business partnership. There were two general ways in which this could be accomplished, both intended to prevent the British from having to share their predominance in the Gulf with any other single nation. It was hoped that this could be done either by converting the railway from a predominantly German to a truly international enterprise with British participation or by leaving the construction and control of the last section of the railway along with the proposed terminal and port of Kuwait to be carried out by Britain.

Lansdowne was one of those who saw the construction of the railway as inevitable and the solution to both the railway and the Gulf problems as available through the association of Britain with the enterprise. Consequently, he found nothing to lose and everything to gain by pursuing such an association. Lansdowne was also impressed with the significance of Germany in Europe, an arena in which the growth of German naval power was a question of the most pressing importance.

It was estimated that Germany would soon be the second naval power

---

[7] Prince Louis of Battenberg (director of naval intelligence) et al., "The Persian Question," Nov. 19, 1902, issued as a CID paper, Mar. 1904, Cab 6/1.

in the world, that she should by then have achieved excellence in gunnery and in the general training of personnel. Under these conditions it was expected that the centers of naval power on the European continent would have shifted from Toulon and Brest to Kiel and Wilhelmshaven. If one considers the growth of German commerce, naval power, and progress in Ottoman railway construction, it is not difficult to see why many in Britain considered that, where dominance of the oceans of the world was concerned, time for Britain as a dominant sea power was running out.

Lord Curzon, expressing his views at about the same time, opposed Lansdowne's proposal, saying: "As for the German railway, I disagree with the Foreign Office. I would not encourage the City of London to find one penny towards bringing it down to the Persian Gulf."[8] The German attitude, undoubtedly without Curzon's knowledge, had already been expressed in a letter of January 2, 1902 from the Kaiser to the Tsar in which the former stated that British behavior at Kuwait (i.e., British objection to Kuwait becoming a base for the German railway) had shown the enormous advantage of "an overwhelming fleet."

That Germany could not immediately do this (i.e., maintain a fleet sufficiently strong to match Britain in the Persian Gulf), the Kaiser continued, showed the need for the Bagdad railway "which I intend German capital to build." Had it not been for the delays on the Sultan's part, the Emperor asserted, the railway could have been completed and the Russian Emperor could have turned the tables on Britain by sending a few regiments from Odessa down to Kuwait and this would have rendered "even the greatest fleet ... powerless." It was clear, at least in the Kaiser's conception, that at the time when the concession of January 21, 1902 was about to be granted, the Bagdad railway was intended to be an instrument of German national policy, shared by Russia as long as a common goal could be found decisive enough to obscure their obvious differences.

A German memorandum which was transmitted to Sir Charles Hardinge by Valentine Chirol of *The Times* indicated that in the spring of 1903 this view was still firmly held also by the German government.[9] The memorandum, a summary of a forty-page typed document, emphasized that it was "of the greatest importance" that "the control of the Railway at the European seat of the Company and in Turkey should remain German," that "the construction of the line shall be in German hands"; that "close cooperation, in order to promote the interests of Germany,

---

[8] Curzon to Hamilton, Apr. 2, 1902, Lord George Hamilton Papers, IOL, MSS Eur. D 510/10.
[9] V. Chirol to C. Hardinge, Oct. 28, 1903, enclosing précis of a memorandum drawn up in the German Foreign Office, May 1903, FO 78/5322.

should be secured in accordance with a well-considered plan between the Railway interests concerned and the German Foreign Office"; and that "this cooperation should be equally exercised in Germany and throughout the zone of the proposed Railway." Stress was given to the favorable opportunity which German merchants enjoyed not only in Turkey but also in Muslim countries generally and how the visit of the German Emperor to Syria had been instrumental in securing this goodwill.

The memorandum stated frankly that while the Germans were more popular among the Muslims than the other Europeans, they were not popular among the Christians of the Near East, a proposition which was not wholly true since the close German association with the Sultan made them disliked among the wider strata of the people, especially the liberals who disliked the Sultan. This furnished Germany with another incentive, in addition to financial help, for wanting to have the British associated with the project.

The memorandum advocated the spread of the German language among the people of the region, promoting it through textbooks and schools and encouraging local people who learned the language to take positions with the railway or to continue their education in the technical and industrial schools of Germany. Such careful management, the writer foresaw, could make this country a source of raw materials for German industry and a market for her products.

Chirol's comment on this disclosure, in view of German encouragement to Britain to invest in the project and of recent British interest in doing so, was that if Britain were to enter upon any arrangement with Germany over the railway it should concern only full control over the section between Bagdad and the Gulf. Hardinge had some reservations about the genuineness of the document as might be expected from a person so convinced that cooperation with Germany was the correct policy. Nevertheless, Chirol's suggestion that as a condition of participation Britain should acquire complete control of the southern section either from Mosul or Bagdad to the Gulf, distances of 670 and 440 miles respectively, was supported by a Board of Trade memorandum and accepted as a bargaining position.

A similar view of the exclusive German control of the railway, though arrived at by other means, was held by *Novoe Vremia* and by at least some members of the Russian government.[10] The newspaper article stated mistakenly that Britain had consented to assume a share in the financing and management of the railway. It was the opinion of the writer that

[10] No. 109 Scott to Lansdowne, Apr. 16, 1903, enclosing a translation of a *Novoe Vremia* article of Apr. 16, 1903, FO 78/5322; No. 26 Kennedy (Bucharest) to Lansdowne Apr. 22, 1903, FO 78/5322.

although both Britain and France were contributing by far the greatest amount of capital to the enterprise, together well over two-thirds, they were receiving almost no share at all in the direction or management of the company.

It was also held by the same writers that even the kilometric guarantee was ultimately paid at the expense of the bondholders who were principally British and French. The future enrichment of the company and the whole investment would likewise accrue mainly in the same proportion as the shares of capital to Germany. The British minister at Bucharest reported a similar view expressed to him by the Russian minister, M. N. Giers, in behalf of his government. Giers added that Witte, the minister of finance, had advised the Russian banks not to subscribe to the new "obligations" since the Russian government was opposed to them on political grounds.

The final form of the railway agreement between the Ottoman government and the Ottoman Anatolian Railway Company, acting on behalf of the German and French investors, through the Deutsche Bank and the Ottoman Imperial Bank, was concluded on March 5, 1903.[11] This provided for the formation of the Bagdad Railway Company as an extension of the Anatolian Railway Company, a change which was accomplished in April, 1903 and which extended the railway from Konia to the Persian Gulf, a distance of about 1,250 miles. It made the final increment of the railway vital by requiring that the section between Bagdad and Basra be completed before the section from Konia in Anatolia to Bagdad could be opened.

Also, a letter of the same date as the agreement and addressed by the German company to the Ottoman government as required by the latter, ruled out any colonization in the area of the railway line, a practice which earlier German advocates of the railway had stressed. The company did nevertheless propose to assist the Ottoman government in developing irrigation to bring a large tract of arid land under cultivation in the plain around Karaman and Konia.

The British General Staff saw the problems which the completed railway could raise in the Tigris–Euphrates region where Britain had commercial interests. They also foresaw the difficulties this would cause in the Gulf if a terminal port was constructed where Britain had in fact enjoyed a monopoly. Furthermore, in case of a war with Russia, the

[11] J.C. Hurewitz, *Diplomacy in the Near and Middle East*, 2 vols. New York, 1956, I, 252–263; Memorandum by the General Staff with two appendices, Nov. 15, 1904, Cab 4/1; Stanford J. Shaw and Ezel Kural Shaw, *History of the Ottoman Empire and modern Turkey*, 2 vols. London, 1977, II, 120–121, 226–227; Bernard Lewis, *The emergence of modern Turkey*, London, 1962, pp. 180–181; William Ochsenwald, *The Hijaz Railroad*, Charlottesville, 1980.

resulting complications and hazards of defending India could be critical, particularly if Germany also were hostile. It was the British view that whereas the Germans had formerly sought their support in the construction of the railway for political reasons having to do with a desire to restrain a determined Russian opposition, in the more recent period, particularly after Russia's loss of prestige with the inception of the tense situation which soon led to the Russo-Japanese war, Germany had been more interested in British financial help.

Lord Lansdowne prepared systematically for the role which he hoped Britain would play in the construction and operation of the Bagdad railway.[12] He saw the line as a means of providing quicker transmission of mail, of offering an alternative route for the conveyance of troops to India, and since it would shorten travel time to India by three days, of providing a great commercial advantage for all who traveled either way. It would open up new, rich and productive areas.

He also thought that the non-accessibility of Kuwait was not in itself a sufficiently important factor to prevent the construction of a terminus on the Gulf since there were alternate locations which the Sultan could open to the German company. He thought particularly that if the project should be carried out without British participation it would "be a national misfortune."

Lansdowne's preparations were quite advanced by the time the campaign to discredit the project became, in early April 1903, barely a month after the final railway agreement had been concluded, too strong to disregard. Lansdowne had appointed Baring Brothers to manage the British participation and had reached an understanding on the British role, most of it with Dr. Arthur von Gwinner, chairman of the Ottoman Anatolian Railway Company, through Lord Revelstoke (John Baring). Financing was to have been shared in the proportion of 25 percent each by Germany, England and France, with 10 percent apportioned to the Anatolian Railway, a German company, and 15 percent to the minor participating nations.

The three major participants would have eight directorships each while three would be allotted to the Anatolian Railway and the Swiss group. There was to be an increase in the Ottoman tariff, a portion of which would go to support the guarantees of the Bagdad railway. If the new route offered substantial advantages it was to be used for the carriage of mail to India; and assistance would be given for establishing a terminus

---

[12] Lansdowne memorandum, Apr. 7, 1903 (with annexes), Lansdowne, "The Bagdad Railway," Apr. 14, 1903, FO 78/5322; FO to Baring Bros, Feb. 14, 1903, Baring Bros. to FO Feb 25, 1903, FO 800/144; Maybelle Rebecca Chapman, *Great Britain and the Bagdad Railway 1888–1914*, North Hampton, MA, 1948, pp. 53–71.

with proper facilities at Kuwait as well as cooperation in establishing customs arrangements.

The general opposition to British participation in the railway was founded on the anti-German feeling which had been emerging in the country for some time. It was supported by the Euphrates Steam Navigation Company, the Peninsular and Oriental Steamship Company which carried mail to India, St. Loe Strachey of the *Spectator*, Leo Maxse of the *National Review*, T.G. Bowles, MP and others.[13] Maxse led the open attack in early April with the charge that British foreign policy was made in Berlin and that the railway was one of the Kaiser's schemes for aggrandizing German power and prestige in the Near East with the object of making Anglo-Russian rapprochement impossible. The *Spectator* followed this up on April 4 with a similar but more moderate opposition.

It has been asserted that, in spite of the vehemence of these attacks and the validity of their contentions, the most significant opposition came from within the cabinet itself as indicated by Lord Lansdowne who wrote on April 12, 1903 to the prime minister: "But for Joe's bile, the opposition would not be serious."[14] The colonial secretary, Joseph Chamberlain, had already suffered defeat in his quest for the prime minister's position and was at this time seeking support for his tariff proposals and seems to have taken this means of making his influence felt. The subject of British participation in the railway enterprise was taken up in Parliament on April 7 and one of the objections stressed on that occasion was "that it might jeopardize the possibility of Britain's reaching an understanding with Russia over interests in the Middle East."

Bowles, however, emphasized his conviction that the railway was a German project and that it would benefit Germany to the detriment of British maritime commerce. There were objections to the Turkish tariff increase, to the use of the line for mail shipment to India, to government encouragement of the investment of British capital in the enterprise, and to the use of Kuwait for a terminal. The opposition spread to other publications such as *The Times*, *The Economist*, and the *Contemporary Review*. *The Times* on April 22 emphasized what was, in view of the increasingly anti-German mood in Britain, a very telling argument: "that the line was unmistakably German." The sole gainers would be the Germans, the writer emphasized, and possibly the Turks.

It was also on this day, April 22, that the cabinet decided not to accept

[13] Ravinder Kumar, *India and the Persian Gulf Region 1858–1907. A study in British imperial policy*, Bombay, 1965, p. 173; Lord Newton [Thomas Wodehouse Legh Newton]. *Lord Lansdowne: a biography*, London, 1929, p. 254; Chapman, *Great Britain and the Bagdad Railway*, pp. 53–71.

[14] Richard M. Francis, "The British withdrawal from the Baghdad railway project in 1903," *HJ*, XVI, no. 1 (March 1973), 168–178.

Lansdowne's recommendation to go on with the project, a decision which was received the following day with acclaim in the House of Commons. Lord Lansdowne's warning about the establishment by other nations of naval bases or fortified ports in the Gulf followed on May 5, less than two weeks later.

It was also during the next six months that France reached a decision to drop out as a participant in the Bagdad scheme. The decision was clearly based on the final Russian position taken in March under the leadership of Witte, then still the minister of finance, ruling out any railway in that region not available to Russian control or direction, and on the British decision of April not to support the enterprise. The French decision was made in October 1903, much against the wishes of the prime minister, Pierre Maurice Rouvier, and many members of the cabinet but upon the insistence of the foreign minister, Théophile Delcassé.

The foreign minister, while eager not to offend Russia, wanting rather to compete advantageously for her favor, aimed especially at cultivating the growing rapprochement with Britain. The Bagdad railway, with this tacit international approval, was left a wholly German enterprise. This also left the Entente to take root in an increasingly and consciously anti-German international atmosphere. The failure of these negotiations thus marks the Bagdad railway issue as one of the major factors which ultimately divided the Entente nations from the Triple Alliance powers. It is significant that not only Britain but France and Russia as well were among the opponents of the German railway, at least in the case of Britain and Russia, for their own reasons.

The second major British diplomatic endeavor was ultimately to become the achievement of an accommodation with France. It was expected that this might moderate the existing naval rivalry in the Mediterranean and along the maritime route eastward from Suez, reconcile the Anglo-French contention in Egypt and Morocco, and, above all, prepare the way for a settlement with Russia. Alternatively, it was hoped that if Russo-Japanese relations deteriorated there might ensue a mitigation of the Far Eastern discord.

One of the themes on which Lord Curzon and the proponents of the prevailing view at the strategic conference on Persia of November 19, 1902 were in agreement was that the Franco-Russian alliance was, with respect to the British position in the Persian Gulf, an inconvenient combination. This was particularly true, it was asserted, with respect to the known history of cooperation on the part of the allies and the prospect that this might hold true in case of a war with Britain. Even though the Admiralty spokesman at the conference of November 19 had cast doubt on the likelihood that republican France might actually come to the defense of imperial Russia in a war with Britain, it was only a year before that the French press had complained about the drawback of British control in the Gulf and urged cooperation with Russia to secure greater advantages for France.[15]

France, however, had reasons of her own in both the east and the west for wanting an accommodation with Britain. The Anglo-Japanese alliance had exposed her Southeast Asian possessions and her cooperative activity with Russia in Manchuria and Korea to a growing and, especially with the conclusion of the Anglo-Japanese alliance, aspiring Japanese Empire. In the west there were, of course, the crucial question of Alsace-Lorraine as well as the French concern about Morocco, matching to some extent the British concern about Egypt. Above all, the continental strength and penchant for expansion of Germany had given Britain and France serious apprehensions about the Bagdad railway and its future role in the Near and Middle East and about the German navy and its future in European waters and elsewhere.

The message, sent to Berlin in June 1903 by the German ambassador in London that the Anglo-French rapprochement "is the product of a common aversion to Germany," had a considerable foundation in fact.[16] There is no doubt that if one were to substitute the word "fear" for "aversion" this would hold true even before 1903 of both Britain and France. These nations were, however, in the most immediate sense seeking to avoid embroilment with their respective alliance partners, Russia and Japan, in the Far East and to seal their growing rapprochement with an Anglo-Russian accommodation.

Arthur James Balfour at that time still feared Russia more than Germany while Lansdowne considered Russian ambitions in the Far East and in the vicinity of India far more important than the issues then being negotiated with France and in fact agreed in viewing the Anglo-French rapprochement to a considerable extent as a means of achieving an agreement with Russia. Lansdowne hinted quite clearly at this when he wrote that: "A good understanding with France would not improbably be the precursor of a better understanding with Russia."[17]

There were others in the British government who saw a rapprochement

[15] Alan J.P. Taylor, *The struggle for mastery in Europe, 1848–1918*, Oxford, 1954, p. 411, citing No. 34 Delcassé to Rouvier, Oct 24, 1903, *DDF*, IV; John Francis Parr, *Théophile Delcassé and the practice of the Franco-Russian Alliance 1898–1905*, Fribourg, Switzerland, 1951, pp. 110–112.

[16] Christopher Andrew, *Théophile Delcassé and the making of the Entente Cordiale*, New York, 1968, p. 205.

[17] Paul Jacques Victor Rolo, *Entente Cordiale. The origins and negotiation of the Anglo-French agreements of 8 April 1904*, London, 1969, p. 168; Sidney Lee, *King Edward VII: a biography*, 2 vols. New York, 1927, II, 246.

with Russia as of even greater importance. Some feared that without an understanding with Russia not only would an Anglo-French entente be deprived of its full effect but that a German–Russian agreement might emerge instead to the great detriment of the balance of power. Sir Charles Hardinge whose role in bringing about the Anglo-Russian agreement was very important wrote that at the time he had "pressed for the absolute necessity of an understanding with Russia and that the easiest way to achieve this was to arrive first at an agreement with France, the ally of Russia." Finally, a hint that Britain and France were not too far apart in their appraisals of the value of an Anglo-Franco-Russian combination was expressed by King Edward who remarked to Delcassé in July 1903: "Russia is indispensable if Germany is to be kept in awe of us."

The specific issues over which the Anglo-French entente developed were Egypt and, most immediately, Morocco where France feared that an Anglo-German arrangement might shut her out of a region she was determined to control. In June 1901 the French minister of foreign affairs, temporarily disenchanted with Britain because of the Boer war, had been on the point of opening negotiations over Morocco with Germany only to discover that the price for such a settlement would have been in effect a guarantee of the German frontiers, *i.e.*, possession of Alsace-Lorraine, an impossible condition for France.

In July 1901 the French minister in Morocco, G. St. René Taillandier, sent a report to Delcassé urging that something be done about the deteriorating situation and emphasizing that the Sultan of Morocco was surrounded by British advisers, particularly Kaid Sir Harry Maclean, a kind of commander in chief of the Moroccan armed forces. Taillandier thought that it was this report which had been the deciding factor influencing Delcassé to start conversations with Lansdowne.

Britain and France were drawn together over the Morocco affair principally because it was an issue of significant and potentially mutual interest. But even more specifically, they shared the view that it was a matter which needed urgent and immediate attention. The strong rule of the grand visier, Ba-Ahmed, had come to an end with his death in May 1900 and the young and incompetent Sultan, Abd-el-Aziz, was left to deal with an international situation which was more than he appeared able to manage.[18]

In particular, the Sultan found himself pressed for action by the French who were building their North African empire and who had already been

[18] Andrew, *Théophile Delcassé*, pp. 140–145; Eugene Newton Anderson, *The first Moroccan crisis, 1904–1906*, Chicago, 1930, pp. 1–17; Samuel R. Williamson, Jr., *The politics of grand strategy. Britain and France prepare for war, 1904–1914*, Cambridge, MA, 1969, p. 6.

successful in achieving, by means of agreements with Italy, considerable stability for her possessions there.[19] An accord of September 30, 1896 recognized the French protectorate in Tunisia. Another increment was added to French solidarity in North Africa by an Italian–French exchange of letters on January 4, 1901. This was followed on June 30, 1902, two days after Italy had joined Germany and Austria in a renewal of the Triple Alliance, by an agreement which further strengthened both France and Italy in North Africa, the former particularly in Morocco. This agreement also had the practical effect of seriously calling into question the Italian role in and commitment to the Triple Alliance and in this sense also strengthened France.

Although an attempt was made in 1901 to discuss the Morocco issue with Britain, Delcassé foresaw difficulties in reaching an agreement at that time with either Germany or Britain. Not only was he to discover in June 1901 that a settlement with Germany was only attainable at the prohibitive cost of renouncing French claims to Alsace-Lorraine but he still had doubts that Britain would be prepared to deal sympathetically with France regarding such a vital issue. It was at this time that Delcassé turned to Russia for support.

British interests in Morocco were of national and imperial importance. Her tenure of Gibraltar and freedom of navigation through the straits and along the coast of Morocco were crucial to her imperial survival. It was hardly less significant that British commercial relations with Morocco were greater than those of either France or Germany since commercial and strategic access to the country were closely related.[20] In view of the fears and suspicions with which Delcassé had regarded Britain, it is understandable that he questioned the likelihood of achieving a mutually satisfactory arrangement with her.

The discussions which were ultimately to lead to negotiations of an Anglo-French entente were apparently those held in January 1902 between the French ambassador, Paul Cambon, and the British colonial secretary, Joseph Chamberlain. The German ambassador in London reported at this time that he had learned "in strict confidence" that outstanding differences between Britain and France in colonial questions, including Morocco, had been discussed. A month later, Baron Hermann von Eckardstein reported that he had overheard a conversation between the same two and that they had mentioned Egypt and Morocco. By July

[19] Sidney Bradshaw Fay, *The origins of the World War*, 2 vols. New York, 1966, I, 144–147; Luigi Albertini, *The origins of the war of 1914*, trans. and ed., Isabella M. Massey, London, 1952, I, 127–132.

[20] Alevtina Fedorovna Ostal'tseva, "Anglo-frantsuzskoe soglashenie 1904 g. i Anglo-russkie otnosheniia," *Uchenye zapiski Saratovskogo universiteta*, XVI: vypusk istoricheskii (1958), 206.

23, 1902 when Cambon in London approached Lord Lansdowne about the Moroccan question the British foreign secretary seemed genuinely interested. Consequently on August 6 negotiations were resumed with Thailand and Newfoundland entering into consideration. In the course of these discussions Egypt was also added.

Meanwhile, the Sultan's incompetence was exhausting his treasury and stimulating internal disturbances which resulted in attacks on French and Spanish possessions. The Sultan, wanting help in carrying out reforms, acquiring loans, and constructing railways demanded of King Edward that Britain and Germany jointly guarantee Moroccan integrity for a period of seven years and provide financial and material assistance. If this was not forthcoming, he was determined to turn to Germany. It is questionable how much attention would normally have been paid to the Sultan at this time in Berlin since the Germans were still observing the dictum of Caprivi that "Morocco should be maintained as a bone of contention between England and France."[21]

The renewal of Anglo-French negotiations in 1903 was in the immediate sense a consequence of the occurrence in late December 1902 of an insurrection against the Sultan, led by a pretender who was able to inflict such defeats on the government forces as to raise the question of the survival of the dynasty. This produced a situation which could have invited foreign intervention.[22] The immediate dispatch of five British ships to Gibraltar to be prepared to protect British nationals meant that the question was no longer whether Britain would become involved in the incident but in what further way she would become so. The British minister in Tangier, Sir Arthur Nicolson, actively urged that, in the interests of peace and of an opportunity for Morocco to survive as a state, a diplomatic accommodation should be reached.

The diplomatic sequel was also in part a consequence of the realization on the part of Delcassé that the Moroccan question could not be solved in association with Germany.[23] Cambon, in his discussion with Lansdowne, gave considerable emphasis to the necessity for restricting the number of nations which might take part in any intervention and for excluding Germany, a point with which Lansdowne agreed. Furthermore, Delcassé had decided during December 1902 and January 1903 that King Edward, Joseph Chamberlain, and Lord Lansdowne were the makers of British foreign policy and that they were not determined opponents of his Moroccan policy. Finally, negotiations were renewed also in part because of the realization in London as well as in Paris and elsewhere by early 1903

[21] E. Malcolm Carroll, *Germany and the great powers 1866–1914. A study in public opinion and foreign policy*, Hamden, CT, 1966, p. 487.
[22] Monger, *The end of isolation*, pp. 111–112.
[23] Andrew, *Théophile Delcassé*, pp. 195, 197.

that the Anglo-Japanese alliance had not had the effect of eliminating Russian occupation of Manchuria and that, as a result, the threat of a conflict remained very real.

A further element in accounting for the interest in an Anglo-French entente was the fact that the uncertainties of the existing situation gave rise to predictions that in case of war Japan would be defeated and to the prospect that such a development would confront Britain with the choice of intervening on behalf of her ally or of seeing her position in the Far East destroyed. A close relationship with France would provide a means of exerting a moderating influence on Russia, a mission which would have a strong appeal to Delcassé who was already apprehensive about Far Eastern events, the prospect of French entanglement, and the effect this would have on the Franco-Russian alliance in Europe.

Informal conversations were resumed in April 1903 and greatly assisted by the visit of King Edward to Paris during May 1–5 and particularly during the return visit to London of President Emile Loubet of France during July 5–6. The latter encounter was apparently of special significance since the French foreign minister, Théophile Delcassé, accompanied the president to London where he held significant conversations with Lord Lansdowne.[24]

The deteriorating political situation in the Far East, reaching a critical point almost simultaneously with these official visits, provided a convenient occasion for breathing new life into the Anglo-French negotiations. The failure of Russia to carry out her agreed undertaking to fulfill by April 8, 1903 the second stage of troop withdrawal from Manchuria, was a severe disappointment, particularly to Britain and Japan. But the fact that in addition Russia made new demands on China as a condition of withdrawal was seen as additional evidence that Russia had no intention of relinquishing or even discussing her disputed acquisitions.

Furthermore, since the establishment of the new Russian viceroyalty in the Far East was followed on August 28 by the dismissal of the influential minister of finance himself, Witte, who was widely held to be a moderating influence, the Russo-Japanese negotiations, even then in progress, were clearly handicapped from the start.[25] These indications in the spring

[24] E.W. Edwards, "The Japanese Alliance and the Anglo-French Agreement of 1904," *H*, XLII, no. 144 (Feb. 1957), 22–23; Paul Cambon, *Correspondence 1870–1924*, 3 vols. Paris, 1946, II, 156; No. 336 Lansdowne to Monson, July 7, 1903, Great Britain. Foreign Office. *British documents on the origins of the war, 1898–1914*, 11 vols., London, 1926–38, II, 294–297 (hereafter BD).

[25] Andrew Malozemoff, *Russian Far Eastern policy, 1881–1904: special emphasis on the causes of the Russo-Japanese War*, Berkeley, 1958, pp. 224–226, 237 ff.; Sergei Iul'evich Witte, *The memoirs of Count Witte*, trans. and ed., Sidney Harcave. Armonk, NY, 1990, pp. 773–775; Edward H. Judge, *Plehve: repression and reform in Imperial Russia 1902–1904*, Syracuse, 1983, ch. 7; David McCullough, *The path between the seas: the creation of the Panama Canal, 1870–1914*, New York, 1977, pp. 254–269.

and summer of 1903 of the deterioration of Russo-Japanese relations together with the apparent collapse of Anglo-German relations already noted served notice to the British and French governments of the unfavorable trend of events and of the need to take measures leading to the security of their national and international interests.

The third British diplomatic goal and the one from which at this point the most immediate benefits were expected was the conclusion of an agreement with Russia. The clear choice of a partner with whom Britain could most directly share desirable steps toward the reduction of tensions along the borderlands of her most important overseas interests and possessions, especially India but also China, was Russia.

The goal of an agreement with Russia had been unsuccessfully pursued in 1898, reconsidered but dropped as unattainable in 1901, and revived again in 1903 as part of a general attempt, which already included the Anglo-Japanese alliance, to escape from "splendid isolation." Conditions at that time were considered to be more favorable for such a venture than heretofore. Russia's claims to Manchuria and even Korea had in the years since the German offensive in 1897 considerably increased and had acquired the unmistakable characteristics of a desire for permanency. This had in turn generated an increasingly higher level of rivalry. Japan had at first responded to the Russian strategy by an ominously systematic development of her armed forces and by 1902 her naval program was nearly complete and provided her with a potentially dominant maritime position in the Far East.

The British interest in an accommodation with Russia had in a practical sense preceded that with France and had been clearly enunciated by Lord Salisbury in 1898, following the termination of the Mediterranean agreements, and more publicly in 1901 by the British press. St. Petersburg finally appeared to show early symptoms of receptivity by 1902 as the impact of the Anglo-Japanese alliance and of the internal repercussion of depression and revolution began to become apparent. Witte, the minister of finance, was aware that not only external but also internal conditions were rendering Russia less potent as an international force.

The internal warnings of trouble included the agrarian conditions, the growth of opposition among the moderates and in the zemstvos, and the revolutionary challenge. These were among the symptoms of the internal predicament which made Witte wary of a foreign policy too abrasively carried out.[26] The warning included also the assassination of such

---

[26] Witte, *The memoirs of Count Witte*, pp. 699–701; Evgenii Viktorovich Tarlé, "Graf S. Iu. Vitte. Opyt kharakteristiki vneshnei politiki," in his *Sochineniia*, vol. 5, Moscow, 1958, p. 532; John Albert White, *The diplomacy of the Russo-Japanese War*, Princeton, 1964, p. 48; USSR Central Archives. *Russko-iaponskaia voina: iz dnevnikov A. N. Kuropatkina i N. P. Linievicha*, Foreword by M. N. Pokrovsky. Leningrad, 1925, p. 6.

significant members of the government as the minister of education, Nikolai Pavlovich Bogolepov, on February 14, 1901, the minister of interior, Dmitrii Sergeevich Sipiagin, on April 2, 1902, another minister of interior, Viacheslav Konstantinovich Plehve, on July 15, 1904, and the governor general of Moscow, Grand Duke Sergei Aleksandrovich, uncle and confident of the Emperor, on February 4, 1905.

Witte also favored a slower advance in China and in this had the support of the minister of foreign affairs, Count V. N. Lamsdorf, and of the minister of war, General A. N. Kuropatkin. All of these, however, were ultimately overruled and by the summer of 1903 Witte was dismissed from his position as minister of finance and the Russian government was left free to concentrate more and more on the gamble in Manchuria. This only furthered the weakening of the government itself and in the end proved disastrous both for its prestige and power and for its ability to assert itself along the entire length of its extensive frontier.

The Anglo-Russian negotiations so much desired by Britain were in fact initiated at this time by Russia, perhaps to some extent, as has been suggested, as a consequence of the conclusion of the Anglo-Japanese alliance, the ending of the Boer war, the nascent Anglo-French entente, and the German concession in accepting a route for the Bagdad railway further to the south in Asia Minor than previously planned and away from the Russian frontier.[27] The members of the British government, with the notable exception of Joseph Chamberlain, were prepared, after the strategic decisions of November 19, 1902 and in the midst of the pervading fear of a possible conflict, to participate in the Bagdad enterprise and in general to make a renewed effort to come to terms with Russia.

Opportunely, the British ambassador in St. Petersburg, Sir Charles Scott, was able to report on December 25, 1902 an optimistic interview with Count Aleksandr Konstantinovich Benckendorff who was shortly to leave for Britain to take up his duties replacing Egor Egorovich Staal as the Russian ambassador.[28] The conversation dealt with a subject of interest to Russia, the wish to revive after an apparent lapse of some months the discussion of her own proposal of nearly three years before of direct Russian relations with Afghanistan. The overture suggested the possibility of an invitation for a general Anglo-Russian settlement. Benckendorff stated in confidence that the Russian government had no intention of entering into "any new relations with Afghanistan without

---

[27] Grigorii L'vovich Bondarevsky, *Bagdadskaia doroga i proniknovenie germanskogo imperializma na Blizhnii Vostok (1888–1903)*, Tashkent, 1955, p. 483; Oswald Hauser, *Deutschland und der Englisch-Russische Gegensatz, 1900–1914*, Berlin, 1958, pp. 39–40.
[28] Scott to Lansdowne, Dec. 25, 1902, FO 800/139.

the consent" of Britain "whose position with regard to the Ameer they knew ..." and that the delay in answering Britain had been caused by a desire to formulate a suitable proposal as a response. Lansdowne replied with a personal message which reflected his great sense of relief at this apparent shift in the Russian attitude.

The British cabinet responded to the new proposal by giving Lansdowne support for pursuing negotiations with Russia and when Benckendorff reached London it was agreed that they would exchange views on "any subjects in which both Russia and this country were concerned," and that the examination might start with Russo-Afghan relations.[29] The rising cost and difficulty of the defense of Britain's stake in the world, both at home and abroad, gave the cabinet a compelling incentive to act quickly and effectively.

Naval ratios were becoming of increasing concern and since Britain could not, it was held, afford a three power standard as some advocated, the cabinet, in view of the growing power of the German navy, adopted a margin over the two power standard and projected plans for a new naval base at the Firth of Forth.

Lord Selborne, the first lord of the Admiralty, wrote to Curzon on January 4, 1903 that of the three exceptions to the "naval and insular character of Britain, the first two of these, the Canadian frontier with the United States and the frontier with the Dutch republics in South Africa, could be controlled but the frontier with Russia in Central Asia remained a challenge." Furthermore, Sir Arthur Godley of the India Office wrote in February 1903 that: "The reports of the Military and Naval Intelligence Departments clearly show that we have not the material force at our disposal, even if Persia were to break up, to occupy any considerable part of Southern Persia." This reflected the pessimism characteristic of the strategy conference of the previous November.

The need and desire of Britain for an accommodation with Russia and the anticipation of Benckendorff's arrival did not, however, inspire any general optimism. There were, of course, the persistent pessimists such as Lord George Hamilton who held that time was on Russia's side and that Britain was unequal to the task of doing anything more than delaying the Russian advance. Sir Arthur Godley was even more specific. In a letter to Curzon dealing with the crucial subject of Russo-Afghan relations, he wrote, "It seems pretty clear that the system under which we have managed to get along hitherto will not work now that the Russians are fairly established on the Afghan frontier; the Russians can make it impossible, and probably will do so."[30]

[29] Monger, *The end of isolation*, pp. 111–112, citing No. 14A Lansdowne to Scott, Jan. 21, 1903, FO 65/1658.
[30] Godley to Curzon, Jan. 1903, Lord Curzon Papers, IOL, MSS Eur. F111, no. 154.

King Edward, writing to Lord Lansdowne on the important credibility aspect of the same subject, noted the difficulty of accepting any Russian assurance that they would not send agents to Afghanistan. He asked: "How can we also be made to believe that the relations desired will be non-political and that they will deal solely with local and commercial matters on the Frontier?"

The British ambassador, Scott, added an encouraging note when he reported from St. Petersburg in early April an interview with the minister of war, General Kuropatkin. The latter appeared to espouse a view also attributed to Count Lamsdorf, in opposition to a continuation of the existing "distrust, suspicion, misunderstanding between our two countries" (i.e., Russia and Britain) and in favor of an understanding dealing with Asia.[31] These views were in fact, according to one Soviet historian, outcroppings of a fundamental reappraisal of Russian foreign policy having particularly to do with Persia.

The focus for this was a memorandum of April 14, 1903 by Pavel Mikhailovich Lessar who had served in both Central Asia where he had been Russian political agent in Bukhara and in London on the Russian embassy staff and was acquainted with the problems of the Middle East. He asserted that it was necessary to oppose Germany with an Anglo-Russian agreement focused on the railway question in Persia. He advocated the building of a railway system between Europe and India through Central Asia as an alternative to the Bagdad railway. Since the proposed railway could be shorter, it would reduce the Bagdad railway to serving exclusively local needs and thus fail to justify the sacrifice the Germans had made to construct it.

The discussion of this question apparently reached persons in various departments of the government, some in the military and financial ministries being favorable while opposition was more characteristic of the foreign ministry. General Kuropatkin supported the positive view with a proposal of July 28, 1903 in which he advocated that Russia unite the Caucasus railway line with Teheran and the Transcaspian railway with Mashkhad and establish a firm alliance with Britain, convincing the British that Russia had no plan to conquer India.

Witte, the minister of finance, held that while Russia could not stop Germany from constructing the Bagdad line, she could, as Lessar proposed, provide a shorter route between Europe and India through Russia with the Indian network as the final link. But instead of a route

[31] No. 88 Scott to Lansdowne, Apr. 2, 1903, FO 65/1660; A.L. Popov, "Stranitsa iz istorii russkoi politiki v Persia," *MZ*, no. 4–5 (1924), 150–152; Firuz Kazemzadeh, *Russia and Britain in Persia, 1864–1914. A study in imperialism*, New Haven, 1968, p. 489; Seymour Becker, *Russia's protectorates in Central Asia. Bukhara and Khiva, 1865–1924*, Cambridge, 1968, pp. 149–154.

from Ashkhabad through Mashkhad to Seistan as Lessar suggested, Witte preferred a Kushka–Chaman route through Afghanistan. This, Witte thought, would furnish some hope that Britain and Russia could escape from the relations of the past and reach a satisfactory relationship.

In spite of Lamsdorf's apparent acquiescence in this view, he continued to represent, as his directives during the Russo-Japanese war indicate, a continuation of the traditional Russian outlook regarding the Persian situation. This view was also firmly supported by such influential officials dealing with Persia and its environs as Kimon Manuilovich Argyropulo and Ivan Alekseevich Zinov'ev.

The Anglo-Russian discussions began with the Afghan question and by the first of April these were progressing and a beginning had been made with the Anglo-Russo-Tibetan question.[32] Lansdowne's statement of May 5, 1903 to the House of Lords, while providing a warning to both Germany and Russia not to establish any naval bases or otherwise fortified ports in the Persian Gulf, was also a pronouncement of policy contributing one of the conditions on which Britain was ready to come to an understanding with Russia. This point was very forcefully made the very next day when Lansdowne suggested to Benckendorff his hope for an accommodation between the two nations with respect to Persia. The British foreign secretary expressed this hope along with the highly controversial question of spheres of interest in Persia, the issues concerning the Gulf ports, and Seistan.

The British were encouraged during May by news which reached them from other diplomatic fronts. This was, of course, the time of the "emotional reconciliation" of Britain and France, achieved by the triumphant visit of King Edward to Paris and the boost this gave to hopes on both sides of the channel for an Anglo-French understanding. It was also in May that an Afghan agent in Mashkhad told Colonel Whyte, on the authority of a Bukhara trader, that Russian authorities had announced in Bukhara that Russia would shortly have regular trade relations with Afghanistan and that Russian merchants would be allowed to go to Afghanistan for trade purposes.[33] This news was, however, counteracted the same day by an official statement from Kabul to the effect that the prohibition on all trade with Russia through Kabul was to be strictly enforced.

The British attitude at this time could be characterized as being eager to reach a settlement but adamant about certain issues considered vital for the defense of India. Bülow characterized the British attitude as "court-

---

[32] Monger, *The end of isolation*, p. 111; No. 74 Lansdowne to Scott, Apr. 1, 1903 (with three enclosures), FO 17/1746; No. 16A Lansdowne to Scott, Mar. 24, 1903, FO 17/1745.
[33] IG to IO, May 7, 1903, FO 106/7.

ing Russia" out of fear of Russia and wondering whether Britain might go so far as to incite the Japanese in order to soften the Russians and make them more amenable to an accommodation with Britain.[34]

It should also be remembered that by May British anxiety about a possible war had been heightened by the fact that by this time it was clear that the second stage of the Russian troop withdrawal from Manchuria was not being carried out. Instead, the units which should have been withdrawn were concentrated at certain places, 200 at Newchuang, 3,000 at Liaoyang, and others elsewhere, and the British military attaché saw forty or fifty buildings already completed for Russian use and others being built at Liaoyang. He saw no evidence of any intention to evacuate the forces. He thought that Russia feared what Japan might do if they withdrew, that they might even try to force a quarrel with Japan while they still held the advantage. It was also at this time that Maurice Bompard, the French ambassador in St. Petersburg, suggested that the British attitude had made conditions favorable for a settlement since Count Lamsdorf was satisfied that Britain had not envenomed the Manchurian quarrel and British support for the Bagdad railway had just been abandoned.[35]

The resumption of Anglo-Russian negotiations in July was stimulated by the visit of Delcassé to London, by the opening of Russo-Japanese negotiations later the same month, and by a series of events which followed this new and fateful diplomatic departure. It should be remembered that Britain was already engaged in negotiations with France and Russia and that one of the chief incentives for pursuing an accommodation with France was the assistance it would provide in seeking the vital understanding with Russia. It was also feared in London that if Russia were to succeed in bringing about an arrangement with Japan, the value to her of an agreement with Britain would be much reduced if not rendered altogether meaningless.

On the other hand, the uncertainties inherent in the continuing Russo-Japanese relations tended to enhance the value of British support to Russia, particularly since Britain was an ally of Japan. Britain was already willing to recognize "that Russia had special interests in that part of China which adjoined her possessions" but would expect in return "the recognition by Russia of the analogous interests of Great Britain in other parts of the Chinese Empire." This was a concept which, though considered as a last resort by Britain, was then a commonplace among the

[34] Bülow to Holstein, May 15, 1903, in Rich and Fisher, *The Holstein papers*, IV, 274.
[35] No. 79 Bompard to Delcassé, May 21, 1903, in France. Ministère des Affaires Etrangères. *Documents diplomatiques français (1871–1914)*, 2nd series (1901–11). 41 vols. Paris, 1930, III, 343–344 (hereafter *DDF*).

powers in China and thus gives little satisfying support to A. Galperin's interpretation of this British proposal as an invitation to partition China into spheres of influence.[36]

The visit of Count Lamsdorf to Paris during October 28–31, 1903 provided an opportunity for discussions of a possible French role not only in the intermittent Anglo-Russian negotiations but also in the continuing Russo-Japanese negotiations and succeeded in giving a new impetus to the former.[37] Lord Lansdowne had once again asked for French intervention, expressing to Cambon his regrets about what he called an absence of frankness in Anglo-Russian negotiations.

Delcassé reacted quickly to this suggestion as did also Count Lamsdorf with whom Count Benckendorff had met in Paris. Benckendorff, upon his return to London, called on Lansdowne for the first time since August 12, saying that he had seen Lamsdorf in Paris and found him even more friendly toward Britain than when he had seen him earlier in St. Petersburg.[38] The Russian foreign minister had "felt strongly that it was of importance that an endeavour should be made to remove all sources of misunderstanding between the two governments."

A second interview in mid-November was also preliminary in nature.[39] The Russian ambassador had come to lodge a protest against the entry of a British force into Tibet for which sanction had been given on November 6, 1903 to the Government of India by the secretary of state for India. The secretary had found it impossible not to take action in the face of the recent conduct of the Tibetans.[40] Lansdowne had informed Benckendorff during the interview of November 17 that, owing to its geographical position, Britain would also expect an undertaking that Russia would not send agents into that region.

Beyond this Benckendorff did not at first seem to have any specific proposals to make. But after a discussion he said that the matters Lansdowne had referred to grouped themselves into three categories: those concerning China in which Russia had a special interest; those concerning India in which Britain had a special interest; and those concerning Persia in which both were interested.

Benckendorff also explained that Russia did not favor any arrangement which would place north Persia under Russian and south Persia under British influence and while they recognized British predominance in the

---

[36] A. Galperin, *Anglo-iaponskii soiuz, 1902–1921*, Moscow, 1947, p. 181.

[37] White, *The diplomacy*, p. 124; No. 554 Lansdowne to Monson (Paris), Nov. 4, 1903, *BD*, II, 221–222; Henry S. Robinson, "The Franco-Russian Alliance 1894–1904 with special reference to Great Britain," Ph.D. dissertation, University of London, 1965, pp. 511 ff.

[38] No. 307 Lansdowne to Spring Rice (St. Petersburg), Nov. 7, 1903, FO 65/1658.

[39] No. 330 Lansdowne to Spring Rice, Nov. 17, 1903, *BD*, IV, 183–184.

[40] Editorial note, *BD*, IV, 305.

Gulf area, "they [i.e., the Russians] would probably require a commercial debouche in those waters."

British government opinion at this time was very favorable to the concept of a division of Persia into spheres of interest as a means of halting the Russian advance toward the Persian Gulf. Knowing that for the same reason Russia was opposed to such a division, it has been suggested that the breakdown of negotiations during the preceding months was at least in part attributable to the unwillingness of Russia to accept division into spheres of interest in Persia and to concede that Seistan should be included in the British sphere.[41] Russia had no intention at that time either of forswearing direct relations with Afghanistan or of conceding southern Persia to Britain, an arrangement which would have terminated effectively her decades-long drive toward the Persian Gulf.

Since northern Persia was already well under Russian domination and British approval could add nothing, there was no advantage in accepting an arrangement which, under the ostensible pretext of being reciprocal, would grant the south to Britain. Russia did, however, appear to be willing to make some concessions to Britain regarding the southern region. In response to a question from Lansdowne as to whether Russia's having an outlet on the Persian Gulf would mean the acquisition of a harbor and a strategic base, Benckendorff said no.

The most significant negotiations in the period before the Russo-Japanese war took place on November 22 between Sir Charles Hardinge, assistant undersecretary of foreign affairs, and Count Benckendorff.[42] Hardinge spoke "very plainly" to Benckendorff, recalling that British policy in Asia had been to maintain the status quo while Russia had continually trodden on British toes, "pursuing an aggressive policy in China, Persia, and Afghanistan." He said that Lansdowne had heard from both St. Petersburg and Paris "that he [i.e., Benckendorff] would discuss terms for a general settlement on his return to London" and was disappointed that he had no proposals or instructions. Benckendorff did not deny this but said that "Lamsdorf had spoken to him without appreciation of [i.e., the British] attitude at Peking and Constantinople, and said that the moment was riper now for a friendly understanding than at any time during the past twenty years."

Benckendorff started the dialogue with Britain over the subject of Manchuria which, he said, should be discussed as a question in which "Russian interests predominate." He expressed the hope that Britain

[41] Bondarevsky, *Bagdadskaia doroga*, p. 489; Vladimir Mikhailovich Khvostov (ed.), *Istoriia diplomatii*, vol. II. *Diplomatiia v novoe vremia, 1871–1914*, Moscow, 1963, 544.

[42] No. 181/793 Hardinge to Lansdowne, Nov. 22, 1903, *BD*, IV, 184–186; Bondarevsky, *Bagdadskaia doroga*, pp. 383–388; Briton Cooper Busch, *Hardinge of Penshurst: a study in the old diplomacy*, Hamden, CT, 1980, pp. 46–47, 65–67.

would not press Russia too hard for evacuation, the one point on which Britain had been very insistent. He said that there were two parties in Russia, one in favor and the other against evacuation, and that the issue had not yet been decided. He suggested that instead of pressing this point Britain should seek compensation elsewhere.

Hardinge, turning to more specific aspects of the problem, emphasized that Britain felt strongly on the subject of Newchuang which was a treaty port where Britain had important treaty rights and "considerable trade." Benckendorff answered that Russia would certainly be ready to return Newchuang to China, requiring only that an International Sanitary Commission should be appointed and that, "in view of her great interests and the proximity of her frontier," Russia should have a privileged position on the Commission.

Hardinge replied that Britain would expect Russia to fulfill her promises to open other ports in Manchuria and to maintain the open door. Benckendorff responded that he was authorized by Lamsdorf to say that other ports would be opened but asked not to be pressed too hard on the subject of rates and tariffs since "in every country where British and Russian trade competed, British goods drove Russian goods out of the market."

Benckendorff seemed quite willing to grant that Afghanistan and Tibet should be considered as within the British sphere of influence, leaving open the possibility that Russian relations with Afghanistan, while direct, would be limited to purely non-political questions. The Russian ambassador said that it was Lamsdorf's position that the Russian government "had never surrendered the right to have direct relations with the Afghan officials, but had voluntarily never exercised it." Hence, they were entitled to resume such relations. Hardinge wanted it understood that Afghanistan would be guided in her external policy by Britain and that no Russians would go to either Afghanistan or Tibet.

Lord Lansdowne later supplemented this discussion by saying to Benckendorff: "We should expect Russia to recognize in the most formal manner the position of Afghanistan as being entirely within our sphere of influence and guided by us in regard to external policy. Subject to this I [i.e., Lansdowne] was prepared to admit that there might be direct communications between Russian and Afghan officials in regard to matters of a purely local character, and of a non-political complexion" and that this should be only between local officials near the frontier.[43] Russia would have to agree to send no agents into Afghanistan and the Amir would have to agree to all these arrangements. Benckendorff raised no objection to any of these proposals. Count Lamsdorf stated early in

[43] No. 384 Lansdowne to Spring Rice, Nov. 25, 1903, *BD*, IV, 186–188.

1904 that Russia had no intention of sending agents to Afghanistan but Lord Lansdowne did not view this as adequate assurance.

The Persian question, Benckendorff stated, was more difficult. The Russian government, he continued, would not agree to a division of the north and south into spheres of influence because they saw no reason why their commercial development should be limited to the northern part. Hardinge reminded him of his statement to Lansdowne that a commercial outlet on the Gulf would be needed and asked what it was that Russia actually wanted since there was no obstacle to Russia's shipping from Bushire, Bandar Abbas, or some other point on the coast. Benckendorff said that he meant a railway to the south without a naval base, fortifications, or troops to guard the road as in Manchuria.

Asked whether Britain intended a "mare clausum" in the Gulf Hardinge said that he had never heard this suggested. Lansdowne, in his earlier conversation with Benckendorff, had said that, should the existing embargo on railway construction in Persia ever be lifted and the question be raised of a line reaching into southern Persia, Britain would expect to be consulted and to share in an amicable arrangement hopefully giving them control over the southern portion of the line and the southern approaches to the sea.

Hardinge continued with respect to Seistan, remarking that since it was conterminous with the Afghan and Indian frontiers, it was of the greatest importance to Britain and could never be allowed to become subject to Russian predominance. Because it was thus closely related to the defense of India, it must be considered as being within the British sphere of influence. Finally, Hardinge said that the independence and integrity of Persia "had always been a cardinal principle of British policy in Persia" and would probably be affirmed in any diplomatic arrangement. Lansdowne had already emphasized to Benckendorff the British expectation that Seistan should be entirely under British influence and had added the further expectation that Russia would "abstain from interfering with the trade routes leading through it."

Some clue as to the official Russian reaction to the various pressures being exerted from London and Tokyo to evacuate Manchuria was furnished by a *Novoe Vremia* article which stated: "Today they demand the evacuation of Manchuria; tomorrow it will be Vladivostok which we must abandon – as England regards the coast as still part of the Chinese Empire ... and in that case why should not Turkey demand the evacuation of Transcaucasia?"[44] The *St. Petersburgh Zeitung* added an almost plaintive note: "But to abandon Manchuria would be as great a mistake as the sale of Alaska has proved to have been."

44 Enclosure, n.d. FO 65/1660.

Lord Lansdowne had a conference with Count Benckendorff on December 3, 1903 in an atmosphere of increasing Russian unfriendliness. Cecil Spring Rice had reported that this mood applied particularly to such occurrences as "Mr. Balfour's recent reference to the subject of the defence of India, Lord Curzon's tour of the Persian Gulf, the affairs of Seistan, and especially the question of Tibet."[45] He continued: "England is warned that the defense of India will become a far more serious matter if Russia is opposed in the development of her Far Eastern possessions." Spring Rice also noted that the subject of Tibet was much discussed in the press along with the hope that the Tibetans would be able to resist British pressure. *Novoe Vremia* expressed resentment about the British propensity to monopolize the Persian Gulf and stated that if England wished a monopoly of rights in north Arabia she must be ready "to give compensation elsewhere."

Lansdowne discussed with Benckendorff essentially the same matters as in the previous negotiations.[46] Again Lansdowne emphasized that Seistan would be definitely within the British sphere and assured the Russian ambassador that there would be no difficulty in determining the limits of the province. Benckendorff then asked what was to be the position of those Persian provinces which did not adjoin either the possessions of Russia in the north or the southern coast of the country. This introduced into the discussion the concept which was the basis of the third region of Persia under the Anglo-Russian condominium which came to be known as the neutral zone. Apparently unprepared at that time to discuss this issue, Lansdowne replied that this matter would have to be reserved for future examination but that the object of Britain would probably be "to keep those regions open to British commerce and enterprise of all kinds."

Benckendorff also wanted to know whether, if British predominance in the Gulf were recognized, Britain would be prepared "to undertake to erect no fortifications in those waters." Lansdowne answered that he could only offer his own impression on this matter and that he thought that Britain would be content with erecting no fortifications as long as no one else did so. The interview ended with an offer on the part of Lord Lansdowne to consult with others in the government and furnish the Russian ambassador with an authoritative statement of the views of the British government which might be useful for him to take back in January to St. Petersburg. Benckendorff replied that he hoped he would do so. In a dispatch the following day to Spring Rice in St. Petersburg, Lansdowne indicated that he wanted to keep any future negotiations in his own hands

[45] No. 416 Spring Rice to Lansdowne, Dec. 2, 1903, FO 65/1662.
[46] No. 346 Lansdowne to Spring Rice, Dec. 3, 1903, FO 65/1658.

and that he hoped that such negotiations would lead to a successful conclusion as soon as possible.

Lansdowne had by December 17 prepared the draft of a proposal for the Russian ambassador to take with him on his return to St. Petersburg, his departure being expected to be on January 10.[47] The draft dealt with all the major topics which had been discussed recently by the representatives of the two nations, giving emphasis to those demands which Britain had made and taking note of some of the Russian requirements. Afghanistan and Tibet were to be considered within the British sphere of influence while Russia was to send no agents to either place though she might have direct, purely local, relations with Afghanistan if the Amir approved.

Britain continued to insist on a division of Persia into spheres of interest and on the respective rights of the two parties to construct and control railways in their respective zones though she renounced the establishment of any military works on the Gulf "as long as Persia retains her independence." Seistan was, according to the British proposal, to be within the British sphere while Manchuria was to be recognized as a region of predominantly Russian interest though Russian troop evacuation and equal commercial rights there for Britain were required.

Russia may have been moved to be cautious in her present difficult circumstances by what the French ambassador in St. Petersburg called an alarmist attitude in London which had created the impression in St. Petersburg that Britain wanted a war in order that the Tibetan expedition might go forward without having to be concerned about the Russian attitude.

There is also the possibility that the readiness of the British to gamble even to the point of accepting some risk was a consequence of a degree of desperation. Sir Charles Hardinge, one of the central figures in this drama, wrote that he had recognized the Russian hostility then existing toward Britain and the need many in the government saw for an agreement with Russia over the conflicting issues in Asia, "since we are losing ground all the time."[48] He also thought that even the negotiations would have no "prospect of success except on terms that would imply complete capitulation and the entire abandonment of our policy in Asia." There would have been, under conditions more ideal for Russia, some risk in the decision reached in late 1903 to send a British military mission to Tibet. Russia responded with comparative restraint in a communication of January 7, 1904, made by Count Lamsdorf to Sir Charles Scott,

[47] Horst Jaeckel, *Die Nordwestgrenze in der Verteidigung Indiens 1900–1908 und der Weg, Englands zum Russisch-Britischen Abkommen von 1907*, Cologne, 1968, p. 161 (citing dispatch of Dec. 17, 1903, FO 65/1673).
[48] Lord Hardinge of Penshurst, *Old diplomacy: the reminiscences of Lord Hardinge of Penshurst*, London, 1947, p. 84.

stating that the proposal to send Russian agents to Afghanistan had only been dropped for the moment.

As the three pairs of negotiations then still in progress, those between Russia and Japan, Britain and France, and Britain and Russia, reached a crucial stage in late 1903, statesmen in the four capitals were fully aware what was at stake.[49] At the turn of the year 1904 there still seemed some hope that these negotiations might help to preserve the peace. But as the war came on none of the negotiations had as yet succeeded and instead it was the war which tended to control the course of events. The Anglo-French negotiations were in fact the first to achieve their objective because those two parties were committed to seeking a common policy in regard to a number of mutually significant issues including the prospect of war and of its potential outcome.

[49] White, *The diplomacy*, pp. 50 ff.; Admiralty memoranda, May 6, June 8, 1903, FO 46/574; memoranda by A. J. Balfour, Dec. 22, Lord Lansdowne, Dec. 24, Lord Salisbury, Dec. 24, A. C. Dec. 25, 1903, Cab 1/4.

2   The Focus of Hostility

A global perspective

The worldwide rivalry of which Britain and Russia were a part had by 1903 converged in two principal regions, the Middle and Far East, neither offering the contenders a convenient theater of operations for settling their differences. In the Middle East there were three closely interrelated conflicts of which that between Britain and Russia was the most protracted and seemingly the least susceptible of solution. This deadlock, however, was ultimately broken by penetration into the region of Germany, the very nation whose foreign policy was based in part on the assumption that a continuation of an Anglo-Russian conflict was inevitable. Initially, both Britain and Russia tried to make an accommodation with Germany. Russia, however, found this extremely difficult since she was opposed to the very presence in this vital area of Germany as a competitor with such substantial interests and, in view of her own strategic objectives, found an accommodation virtually impossible.

Britain at first saw Germany as a potential ally against Russia but by 1903 she had found that the aims of the two nations were incompatible. In the end it was Britain and Russia which, confronted with this formidable competitor, were able to reconcile their differences. Before this happened, however, Britain and Japan had made common cause in the Far East against Russia and by the close of 1903 actual hostilities between Russia and Japan appeared to be imminent.

The most persistent of Britain's rivals were either along the maritime routes, in the contested colonial areas, or at or near the commercial centers. All of these conditions were characteristic of India, the centerpiece and principal focus of Anglo-Russian rivalry and of British interest in Asia. The Ottoman Empire along with the Turkish straits and Egypt along with the Suez Canal were of particular importance to Britain because they lay along the shortest maritime route to India and the Far East. The Turkish straits had the further significance of being the entrance and exit channel to and from the Black Sea where a major Russian fleet, a potential threat to the route to India, had its home port.

The straits were also one of the most convenient points at which, as long as British sea power remained predominant along this route, the British navy could help to reassure the security of the route by exercising directly some degree of restraint on Russian access to the Mediterranean sea. It was also almost the only point at which Britain could strike with any significant possibility of success at Russia in retaliation for some aggressive action taken elsewhere by Russia. However, toward the end of the nineteenth century this situation changed radically. The southward extension of Russian railways, the conclusion of the Franco-Russian alliance, particularly the naval aspects of the alliance, and the growth of German interests in and near the Near and Middle East, of necessity turned British attention to Egypt and the Suez Canal, an outpost along the imperial lifeline and a strong point for its protection.

The circumjacent regions such as Persia, Afghanistan, and the Chinese territories of Tibet and Sinkiang were mainly significant to Britain as a buffer zone or as a rampart for the protection of India. Persia was strategically the most important part of this buffer region and had, in addition, a commercial importance. With respect to Anglo-Russian relations Persia had a geographical relationship to India comparable to that of Manchuria to the British zone of interest in China. Persia was also significant because it was adjacent to both British India and the southern Russian territories of Central Asia and the Caucasus.

The Persian Gulf was a point of interest for Russia as a maritime route between the Mediterranean Sea and the Indian and Pacific Oceans. This factor became increasingly important as Japan emerged as a growing threat to Russia's access to Vladivostok and to the Manchurian ports and as Germany became increasingly competitive at the Turkish straits and eastward. At the same time, the Persian Gulf continued to be of the greatest importance to Britain because it constituted the final and crucial stage of the maritime route to India and was contiguous to a significant part of the Indian frontier.

Anglo-Russian rivalry had been a factor of importance in this region longer than was the case in the Far East. In an earlier phase it was wholly an Anglo-Russian competition and was concentrated largely in Central Asia. Only after the Russian border had moved southward did the rivalry become so largely centered in Persia and Afghanistan. The common continental border Russia came to share with these countries gave her a unique advantage over Britain which had access to this region only from the Persian Gulf, a considerable distance from the capitals and national centers of gravity of either of these countries.

This state of affairs became still more complicated and more difficult for Britain toward the end of the nineteenth century when the German government began to press forward with its plan to build a railway eastward across the Ottoman Empire to the Persian Gulf, indicating at the same time a strong interest in the economic penetration of the Ottoman Empire and Persia. Henceforth, German expansion in this region posed a danger to the interests both of Britain, whose commercial and strategic relations there were significant and of long standing, and of Russia whose access to the Turkish straits and across Persia to the Persian Gulf was endangered.

The existing intensity of the international rivalry characteristic of the Middle East, beyond that of the Anglo-Russian competition, was somewhat more recent than that in northeast Asia where Russo-Japanese rivalry had been focused on Korea and Manchuria for more than a decade before the Sino-Japanese war. The intense regional competition which followed that conflict alerted both Russia and Japan to the fact that if they intended to lay claim to the desired spoils of Chinese weakness the time to act had come. Russia had already taken steps in this direction by starting the construction of a railway across Siberia and by Witte's "peaceful penetration" of China. Japan in 1895 had lost her first bid to establish herself on the continent when the Triplice of France, Germany, and Russia forced her to surrender her gains in the war with China.

In preparation for the more rigorous phase of rivalry which the new conditions portended, Russia took steps to divest herself of some of the defense requirements on her western frontier. She sought to achieve this by an agreement with Austria, concluded by an exchange of notes in May 1897, which was intended to preserve the status quo in the Balkan region. Russia was in an immediate sense greatly helped in being able to conclude such an arrangement with some confidence in part because her ally, France, by her very location and national interests, could act as a sentinel on Germany's western frontier. Russia was also to some extent able to proceed with some assurance because Germany in any case favored and indeed encouraged an eastward orientation of Russian interests, anticipating that this would ease the pressure on the German–Russian frontier.

The freedom of action which the Austro-Russian agreement permitted Germany was also very timely. Germany had at that point reached an important stage in her "new course." In 1897 the German government had been reorganized with Count Bernhard von Bülow replacing Baron Adolf Marschall von Bieberstein as foreign secretary while Marschall became ambassador to the Ottoman Empire. In his position in Constantinople he was ably assisted by Karl Helfferich and Hjalmar Schacht, both later distinguished in public service, and became the architect of German policy in the Middle East. This was the policy which promoted the Bagdad railway and the continuation of the economic and strategic developments which accompanied it. In November 1897 Germany occupied the Chinese port of Kiaochow in Shantung province, intended as a base for commercial and naval operations. Finally, the first of the naval laws was passed in 1898 which launched a major German naval building program.

By 1897 Russia also needed freedom of action to deal with the challenges of her "peaceful penetration" policy in Asia. In Persia and Manchuria which were clearly intended for ultimate acquisition she nevertheless resisted any general commitment which would acknowledge her aims. However, she adamantly refused to countenance the introduction of competitive spheres of influence which would restrict her own future access to them.

It was becoming amply clear to statesmen of interested countries that Russia's insistence upon the territorial integrity of these regions meant that her goal was to preserve them intact for her own ultimate absorption. Her careful attention to railway and financial operations in these places also clearly had in mind the same objective. In the Ottoman Empire, however, easy access of Britain by sea and of Germany by land made both their activities and her own opposition to them more difficult either to conceal or realize. This forced her to oppose directly and openly the German Bagdad railway plans by disclosing her own objectives.

Anglo-Russian rivalry in transition

Russian interests in Persia and Manchuria were pursued in ways which reflected the disparate regional conditions and the varying strategies considered necessary to achieve the accepted goals. Circumstances in Manchuria were seen as highly favorable for the construction of railways as a means of promoting Russian interests. From the beginning of construction in 1897 to 1905 when Russia officially lost the section of railway south of Kuanchengtze to the victorious Japanese, Russia maintained a policy of expanding her railway network in Manchuria. This eight-year period was characterized also by the continuing concentration of British economic interest in regions south of Manchuria, particularly in the Yangtze valley, and the exclusion of the Japanese from Manchuria. Japan had been held at bay since 1895 when the Triple intervention of Russia, France, and Germany were able to prevent her from realizing her wartime continental gains from the Sino-Japanese War.

The situation in Persia was also a highly competitive one. Even though the major British interest was centered in India, her involvement in Persia was of long standing. Persia was of great importance as a buffer for India against the protracted rivalry with Russia, as a shield for the sea route to

India, and as a commercial center for its own sake. Persia was particularly significant as a means of deterring Russia from promoting commerce there as a basis for the subsequent introduction of political and even strategic influences. In this uncertain environment Russia determinedly refrained from building or permitting others to build railways which might become a conduit for further disadvantageous political or economic competition.

There was, however, a difference of opinion among members of the Russian government as to the value for Russia of railways in Persia and of the ability of Russia to compete with commercial rivals there. Accordingly, surveys and plans for railways testify to the interest which Russia had shown in a possible link between Russia and the Persian Gulf. As already noted, a plan for such a railway line had been submitted on April 14, 1903 by Lessar whose proposal was supported by General Kuropatkin and others. Witte wanted a railway into Persia but not to the Gulf.

Nevertheless, the treaties which Russia forced Persia to sign forbidding the construction of railways in Persia furnish evidence of a consistent policy in practice of opposing railways in Persia. It is equally clear that Russia feared that such railways might be a means of losing the Persian market to her competitors or even of providing a channel for a stronger economic power to penetrate Russia itself over such a railway.

The instrument of Russia's own financial penetration of both Manchuria and Persia was a state-owned bank. This had evolved from the Persian Loan Company, a concession organized in May 1891 by a merchant operating in Persia, Iakov Solomonovich Poliakov. With the assistance of the minister of finance, Sergei Witte, and the director of the Asiatic Department of the Russian Foreign Office, Poliakov was able in May 1894 to convert the loan company into a bank known as the Discount and Loan Bank.[1] This became a model for an institution intended to compete with the British Imperial Bank of Persia, organized in 1889, and for promoting "peaceful penetration" abroad. The same model was again used the next year when the Russo-Chinese Bank was chartered on December 5, 1895, the institution through which the Chinese Eastern Railway was organized the following year.

---

[1] Kazemzadeh, *Russia and Britain*, pp. 272–277; Boris Vasil'evich Anan'ich, *Rossiiskoe samoderzhavie i vyyoz kapitalov 1895–1914 gg. (po materialam uchetno-ssudnogo banka Persii)*, Leningrad, 1975, pp. 5 ff.; Boris Vasil'evich Anan'ich, "Uchetno-ssudnyi bank Persii v 1894–1907 gg." in Akademiia nauk SSSR, *Monopolii i inostrannyi kapital v Rossii*, Moscow, 1962, pp. 275–282; Alfred Stead, "Conquest by bank and railway, with examples from Russia and Manchuria," *NC*, LIII, no. 216 (June 1903), 936–949; Alevtina Fedorovna Ostal'tseva, *Anglo-russkie soglashenie 1907 goda: vliianie Russko-iaponskoi voiny i revoliutsiia 1905–1907 godov na vneshniuiu politiku tsarizma i na peregruppirovku evropeiskikh derzhav*, Saratov, 1977, pp. 26–27.

The Russian Discount and Loan Bank, headed by E. K. Grube, was used to serve not only the expansive objectives of Russia but also the growing financial exigencies of the new Shah and his government. In both ways the economic dependence of Persia on Russia increased. The bank was able to borrow in Paris at 4 percent and lend in Teheran at 6 percent, providing the means to establish its branches and agencies in various parts of Persia.

Access to the country was made much easier by the construction of roads. The principal access route into Persia was the road from Anzali on the Caspian to Teheran which was begun in 1896 and completed in August 1899.[2] Other roads had been started by then to connect Kazvin with Hamadan and Julfa with Tabriz. These projects in turn facilitated other aspects of Witte's development program such as port facilities, aids to cotton production, warehousing and wholesaling establishments, and others.

Joseph Naus, chosen from neutral Belgium, the country which was also playing a part in financing the Franco-Russian railway ventures in eastern China, was invited in late 1897 to organize a Persian customs service on the European model. This helped to provide a national source of income, furnishing, among other things, the means of paying for the Shah's contemplated European trip.[3] This combination of spending for the royal family, foreign loans, and wasteful public expenditures was to become a factor in the revolutionary movement.

Customs stations were established at two of the principal centers of foreign commerce, the province of Kermanshah near the Iraq frontier and in Azerbaijan, omitting the Gulf ports where British commerce predominated. The new system was instituted on March 21, 1899 though it was not until 1902 that the new customs tariff superseded that established by the Turkmanchai treaty of 1828.

Naus worked closely with E. K. Grube of the Russian bank and with the Russian minister in Teheran, Petr Manuilovich Argyropulo. The cooperation of the Belgian officials in the Persian customs service was emphasized by the fact that they employed many Armenians in their work, a practice which annoyed some Persians and Arabs as well as others.

Rivalry in Persia, heretofore largely between Russia and Britain,

---

[2] Rose Louise Greaves, "British policy in Persia, 1892–1903," *BSOAS*, XXVIII (1965), 37; IG Intelligence Summary, Feb 1899, FO 106/1.
[3] Kazemzadeh, *Russia and Britain*, pp. 312–315; Geoffrey Drage, *Russian affairs*, London, 1904, pp. 533–534; A.L. Popov (ed.), "Tsarskaia Rossiia i Persiia v epokhu Russko-iaponskoi voiny," *KA*, no. 4 (53) (1932), 26 (Lamsdorf instruction to A.N. Speyer, Oct. 13, 1904); Edward G. Browne, *The Persian revolution of 1905–1909*, London, 1966, pp. 99–100, 109–111, 136; Henry James Whigham, *The Persian problem: an examination of the rival positions of Russia and Great Britain in Persia with some account of the Persian Gulf and the Bagdad railway*, London, 1903, pp. 159–161.

became much keener in the late 1890s when German railway plans began to be realized. The Bagdad railway was created in a competitive environment and evolved in an even more contentious era. The railway itself was useful to the Ottoman Empire which needed to be able to communicate with the remote regions of a large and widespread empire in order to extend administrative controls to these areas and to defend them against hostile rivals.

Germany, a latecomer in an increasingly competitive world, felt the need to take advantage of every available economic and strategic opportunity. To bring these two interests into effective focus required a communications system which could bring the capital into contact with Bagdad, the Persian frontier, the Persian Gulf, Medina, the Hijaz, and other areas.

The German interest in Kuwait as a terminal for the Bagdad railway was seen as a reality when on January 19–20, 1900 a commission headed by the German consul general in Constantinople, Wilhelm von Stemrich, visited the region and recommended Kathama Bay in Kuwait as a terminus for the railway. He held out to Mubarak, the hereditary Sheikh, ample rewards such as renewed trade and protection against any threat. This was followed in March by reports from the Gulf which indicated that an Algerian engineer employed by the German railway had reached Bahrein to prepare for the arrival of two German merchant ships expected in April on the way to Kuwait with a large number of workmen and materials for building a pier.[4] From the point of view of Kuwait, the closeness of Germany to the Ottoman government was a liability since Kuwait wished to maintain her independent status from Ottoman control. This objective was seen as more easily attained by affiliation with Britain.

The issues which concerned Germany, the need for a railway terminal and the availability of Kuwait, passed a crisis in September–October 1901.[5] German pressure moved the Turkish Sultan to send the Sixth Army from Basra under Ahmet Ferz Pasha who attempted to land a force on Kuwait. The British barred the way claiming a special relationship to Kuwait because of the agreement of 1899 with the Sheikh and this was essentially the end of the matter. The larger and more important question for Britain, however, remained the continued preservation of the British position in the Gulf.

[4] Assistant resident, Persian Gulf to IG, Mar. 29, 1900, FO 78/5102; Briton Cooper Busch, *Britain and the Persian Gulf, 1894–1914*, Berkeley, 1967, pp. 189–192; Jens B. Plass, *England zwischen Russland und Deutschland: Der Persische Golf in der Britischen vorkriegspolitik, 1899–1907. Dargestellt nach Englischem Arkhivmaterial*, Schriftenreihe des Instituts für Auswärtige Politik, no. 3. Hamburg, 1966, pp. 263–268.
[5] Bradford G. Martin, *German–Persian diplomatic relations 1873–1912*, The Hague, 1959, p. 81.

Lord George Hamilton, reflecting over a year later on how well Britain had survived the ordeal, wrote that if she had gone a step further and accomplished the same thing by some form of protectorate over Kuwait, "We should at once have formed against us in the Persian Gulf a combination of Turkey, Russia, Germany, and probably France, and the pressure this combination would have been able to exercise would probably have been exerted in quarters where we have far more vital British interests than in Kuwait, or even the Persian Gulf."

The Russian response to the German acquisition on November 27, 1899 of an exclusive preliminary concession for the construction of a railway between Konia and the Persian Gulf was defensive and counteractive. The minister of foreign affairs, Mikhail Nikolaevich Murav'ev, issued a policy statement on February 7, 1900. This took into consideration not only the Russian reaction to the German achievement but also the British preoccupation with the Boer war and the possibility that this might encourage Britain to yield too easily to the momentum of German success even to the point of foregoing some commercial advantages in Anatolia. Murav'ev was unprepared to concede to Germany any rights or interests in the Ottoman Empire which might contravene Russian interests there.

Murav'ev, in fact, had proposed unequivocal Russian opposition to any major German presence at the straits, on the Black Sea shores or in the Transcaucasian regions of the Ottoman Empire near the Russian frontier.[6] He opposed railway concessions to any foreign power along the southern Black Sea shore. It was recognized by both Russia and Germany that Russia could not actually prevent Germany from acquiring the concession. But Russia proposed without result in the Russo-German negotiations in the spring of 1899 that Germany promise Russia control of the straits in exchange for a Russian agreement not to object to German economic expansion in Anatolia.[7]

Germany, however, would not consider such a proposal and refused to consider any arrangement unless Russia would consider a mutual guarantee of frontiers. This would have involved a guarantee of the Franco-German frontier and thus the issue of Alsace-Lorraine, a proposition which would have been unacceptable to France and would therefore have threatened to dissolve the Franco-Russian alliance. The possibility that

[6] Mikhail Nikolaevich Pokrovsky (ed.), "Tsarskaia diplomatiia o zadachaiakh Rossii na Vostoke v 1900 g." *KA*, no. 5 (18) (1926), 4–11; Andrei Nikolaevich Mandelstam, "La politique Russe d'acces à la Mediterranée au XXeme siecle," *Academie de Droit International. Recueil des cours*, XLVII (1934), 632–635.

[7] Valerii Ivanovich Bovykin, *Ocherki istorii vneshnei politiki Rossii konets XIX veka-1917 goda*, Moscow, 1960, pp. 19–20; Taylor, *The struggle for mastery in Europe*, p. 384; Bondarevsky, *Bagdadskaia doroga*, pp. 212–221.

the failure to come to an understanding might have led to an Anglo-Russian understanding was not considered credible in Berlin and was therefore discounted.

Murav'ev then turned to the Ottoman government for a solution, thinking first of demanding that the government promise not to fortify the Bosphorus in case a final concession were granted for the Bagdad railway as then planned. Meanwhile, however, the Russian government decided to exert pressure on the Ottoman government to agree that no other foreign power should be permitted to build or operate a railway in the region bordering the southern shore of the Black Sea.

This was accomplished by demanding from the Ottoman government the payment of an installment of 57 million francs due on the indemnity assigned by the Congress of Berlin as an alternative to the entire amount assessed by the Congress. According to a British press report, Russia supported her demand by mobilizing some 250,000 troops. The desired agreement was concluded on March 31, 1900 and was known as the Black Sea agreement.[8] This stipulated that in the region between a line running through Ankara, Kaiseri-Sivas-Kharput-Diarbekir-Van and the Black Sea coast the Ottoman government itself would build any necessary railways. If this were not possible, then Russia might do so on the same conditions as those granted in the preliminary agreement to the German group.

The consequences of these two railway agreements concluded by the Ottoman government, one with German financial interests and the other with the Russian government, both within a period of a very few months, was to bring about, at least potentially, a profound change in the international position of the Ottoman Empire. Ottoman territorial integrity, which it had until only recently been the established policy of Britain to protect, as well as the British naval position from which it had once been protected were both finally casualties of the new developments.[9]

A *Novoe Vremia* article, commenting on the altered strategic situation, saw the Bagdad railway as a check on Russia in a very decisive and general

---

[8] Edward Mead Earle, *Turkey, the Great Powers and the Bagdad Railway. A study in imperialism*, New York, 1923, p. 14; Khvostov, *Istoriia diplomatii*, II, 456; Paul Imbert, "Le chemin de fer de Bagdad," *RDM*, 5th period (vols. 1–60, 1901–10), XXXVIII (1907), 659; Hugo Grothe, *Die Bagdadbahn und das Schwäbische Beuernelement in Transkaukasien und Palästina. Gedanken zur kolonisation Mesopotamiens*, Munich, 1902, p. 9; Popov, "Stranitsa iz istorii," 143; No. 30 Marschall to Hohenlohe, Apr. 4, 1900, in Germany. Auswärtiges Amt. *Die grosse politik der europäischen kabinette 1871–1914. Sammlung der diplomatischen akten der Auswärtigen Amptes*, 40 vols. Berlin, 1922–27, XVII, 383–385 (hereafter *GP*).

[9] No. 253 O'Conor to Salisbury, July 18, 1900, No. 280 deBunsen to Lansdowne, June 17, 1902, FO 78/5248.

sense and both the German Emperor and the British government agreed with this view.[10] Another *Novoe Vremia* article of August 1901, perceptively took note of the fact that the very act of German penetration to the Persian Gulf was a threat to the British position there and rendered possible an Anglo-Russian accommodation if Britain were prepared to shift away from the Chamberlain policy of attempted alliance with Germany. The Russian journal pictured the railway as introducing German domination from Hamburg across eastern Europe, Asia Minor and Mesopotamia to the Persian Gulf, separating the Slavic and Latin worlds and thwarting France and Russia politically and economically to the advantage of Germany.

A note written to Eckardstein in January 1900 would have confirmed at least the basic part of these suspicions since it stated that it was German policy to make use of Anglo-Russian rivalry in Asia, keeping both guessing while the German railway was in process of being built toward the Persian Gulf. The writer might have added that this was an eastern and continental counterpart of the breathing space Germany was hoping for while her new battle fleet was even then being prepared for action in the North Sea.

It was clear that the Russian government saw its military situation as considerably impaired by a German railway. Lieutenant Colonel P. Tomilov of the General Staff and several other officers were sent to Asia Minor to investigate the strategic implications of the problem for the Caucasus frontier.[11] Tomilov estimated that the railway would accelerate the ability of Turkey to concentrate the Ottoman V Corps in the Diarbekir region (on the Tigris River near Syria) by two and a half to three and a half weeks and the VI Corps around Erzerum (near the Russian Caucasus frontier) by three to seven weeks. Tomilov saw it as a mistake to allow a German advance into Asian Turkey which would make it possible for Germany to deal a blow to Russia from both the west and the south. This would give both Turkish and German forces relatively easy access to the Caucasian frontier. Furthermore, Tomilov expressed the view that Germany could assume mastery of the straits area and would be able to penetrate into Persia.

The concept emphasized by Tomilov that the railway would permit rapid German mobilization against Russia was noted by a special ministerial conference which met in September 1902. The point was suggested to the conference by the minister of war, General A. N. Kuropatkin. It is an interesting and symptomatic coincidence that this conference should

---

[10] No. 13 Delcassé to Montebello (St. Petersburg), Feb. 5, 1901, No. 201 Prinet (Berlin) to Delcassé, Aug. 18, 1901, No. 29 Bompard to Delcassé, May 23, 1903, *DDF*, I, 83, 430, III, 350–353.   [11] Bondarevsky, *Bagdadskaia doroga*, pp. 225–226.

have been held within two months of the British conference of the following November which considered the strategic factors in the Anglo-Russian conflict. Each appraised its own strategic position in the Middle East and each found the situation depressing from the point of view of its national interests.

It seems, however, far less coincidental that, having both reached pessimistic conclusions, the two nations should, before the end of 1902, have taken the first concrete steps toward an accommodation. These factors give considerable significance to the assertion of Friedrich Rosen of the German Foreign Office that the parting of the ways between Germany and the Entente nations was greatly influenced by the Bagdad railway question.

The Russian conference decided that even though it was impossible to halt the granting of the concession, Russia would definitely not cooperate even though Germany, Britain, and France would probably share the enterprise. It was further determined that Russia would try to prevent new Ottoman trade agreements with European powers, demanding the lowering instead of raising of the tariff: to prevent any Ottoman attempt to raise new taxes; to channel Turkish revenues to the improvement of the administration of Macedonia; and to construct a railway competitive with the Bagdad line. In short, it would be Russian policy to reduce in every way possible the flow of revenues for kilometric guarantees or for regular earnings in support of the Bagdad line.

Persia was not only the region toward which German railway and German financial interests were moving but also the region which Russia was determined to preserve intact for her own enterprise and expansion. One of the measures Russia took to insure the security of her future position there was her attempt to establish a monopoly of the loan market in order to reduce the role of British financial interests and to make a rumored future German bank unnecessary.

To make such a situation a reality, a Russo-Persian agreement was concluded on January 20, 1900 and its heretofore secret terms were disclosed on January 30.[12] Bearing in mind Murav'ev's concept of competing in the Gulf "by encouraging Russian commerce and shipping and developing trade routes," while using the loan "as a weapon in our hands for fortifying our economic position and strengthening the political hold of Russia [over Persia] to the detriment of England," the agreement appeared to be an ideal instrument for this role. It was basically a loan of

[12] Kazemzadeh, *Russia and Britain*, pp. 324–327; David Dilks, *Curzon in India*, 2 vols. London, 1969–70, I, 131–133; Nikki R. Keddie, "Iranian politics 1900–1905: background to revolution," *MES*, V, no. 1 (Jan. 1969), 4–5; Popov, "Stranitsa iz istorii," 143–147; memorandum on Persian government loans, IG Political and Secret Memoranda, C 120.

22,500,000 rubles (about 2,250,000 pounds) at 5 percent payable over seventy-five years. Until the loan was paid off Persia was not to borrow abroad except with Russian permission. The loan was to be used in part to pay off previous loans made to Persia by the British Imperial Bank. It was hypothecated on all the customs except those of Fars and the Persian Gulf, thereby avoiding a clash with British interests.

The Russo-Persian agreement made it a condition of the loan that the existing ten-year prohibition on the granting of concessions for railway construction in Persia would be extended for an additional period of ten years, a stipulation which was made in a memorandum of December 26, 1899 addressed by Murav'ev to the Persian minister in St. Petersburg and approved by the Shah.[13] Even Lord George Hamilton, the secretary of state for India, was moved to admit to Lord Curzon, the viceroy of India, that the Persians had undoubtedly turned to Russia because they could not "obtain similar pecuniary help from this country" and to lay some of the blame on Hicks Beach who, though "an excellent Chancellor of the Exchequer," was lacking in imagination where oriental countries were concerned.

The growing anti-German feeling in Britain was in part a reflection of the degree to which German development had succeeded in concentrating the Anglo-Russian rivalry of the Middle Eastern area, particularly in the Ottoman Empire and Persia. The realization also in St. Petersburg that a more determined competitor had replaced Britain in the Ottoman region and was now poised for action in the economic and railway spheres as well as in the maritime arena of the Persian Gulf had stimulated Russia to respond in a resolute manner as seen by her surprising loan to Persia in 1900. This not only made Britain unusually alert to Persia's constant financial needs but also encouraged her to seek means of warding off similar Russian efforts in the future to monopolize Persian economic life. But Witte absolutely refused to consider any British participation in a loan, even on a joint basis.[14]

A second Russian loan was concluded with Persia on April 4, 1902 and announced in the *Official Messenger* on April 9.[15] The loan was for 10 million rubles (about £1 million) and was signed after Witte withdrew a demand for a concession to build a pipeline from the Baku oil fields to Bushire on the Gulf. Sir Arthur Hardinge, the British minister in Persia at this time, compared the subservience of the Shah in relation to his

[13] Memorandum on Persian railways, June 20, 1911, IG Political and Secret Memoranda, C 120.
[14] Hamilton to Curzon, Oct. 23, Nov. 7, 1901, Godley to Curzon, No. 29, 1901, Curzon 150.
[15] IG Political and Secret Memoranda, C 120; No. 31 Scott to Lansdowne, Apr. 9, 1902, FO 65/1641; Boris Vasil'evich Anan'ich, "Rossiia i kontsessiia d'Arsi," *IZ*, LXVI (1960), 288.

dependence on Russia for funds with that of the Amir of Bukhara and the Khans of Khiva and Kokand in Russian Central Asia.

Russian ambitions in Persia, it was already known in Britain, encompassed the entire country, including the Persian Gulf. Nevertheless, a new dimension of this expansion appeared to have begun in March 1899 when rumors reached London of Russian intentions to seek a naval station in the Persian Gulf.[16] The port of Bandar Abbas came prominently into British speculation even before any Russian ships had actually sailed for the Gulf. This raised the question given the challenge and the complicated situation, of what should be done if Russia were in fact to seize Bandar Abbas as a naval port and as a terminus for a railway. The latter use was confirmed as a possible Russian objective by October 1899.

The Persian government was concerned at this point about a suggestion in the Russian press that a port on the Gulf might be seized while Britain was preoccupied in Africa. Murav'ev, however, in early 1900, expressed the view that the occupation of a port on the Gulf was impractical and would be provocative.[17] Still, further rumors followed of a projected Russian survey for a strategic railway being carried out between Tabriz in northwestern Persia and the Gulf port of Bushire by a party of engineers accompanied by a colonel from the Russian War Ministry. According to the same rumor, this survey was intended to encompass a possible route to Chahbahar, outside of the Gulf.

Even though the Russian foreign minister explained the survey as part of a project having to do with railways in Transcaucasia the denial was not convincing and left the British contemplating a Russian seizure of ports on the Gulf to accommodate prospective railways approaching through both Mashkhad in the northeastern part of Persia and Tabriz in the northwest. To view this as an aspect of the Russian advance, encouraged or hastened by the eastward progress of Germany or by the prospect of Britain and Germany joining their efforts to construct a railway through Persia to India which would cut Russia off from the Gulf, was of course neither consoling nor in itself helpful.

Lord Curzon led the opposition to the idea of permitting the acquisition by Russia of any port on the Gulf backed by a railway connecting it with Russian territory.[18] Russia, he later wrote, wanted such a port for two reasons: "firstly because it means the eventual economic closure of Persia against India and Great Britain, secondly because it means one more point of pressure upon India and our Asiatic Empire. I cannot see why we should connive at either issue." It was well known to those who

[16] Godley to Curzon, Mar. 15, 1899, Hamilton to Curzon, Nov. 28, 1899, Curzon 142.
[17] Martin, *German–Persian diplomatic*, p. 65.
[18] Curzon to Earl Percy, Apr. 30, 1903, Curzon 162.

were to decide this question that Bandar Abbas was the port Russia wanted most and that it was of key importance in the Gulf.[19]

Even though in 1903 the trade of Bandar Abbas was not thriving, it was believed that it could be converted into a flourishing port, particularly if backed by a railway. Furthermore, it was also thought that it could be converted into a first rate naval base. It might, in fact, become a situation even more favorable for Russia than was the case at Port Arthur and Dalny in Manchuria. In such an eventuality, depending particularly on the outcome of the struggle over Kuwait, Britain might be left alone to deal with a very complex and crucial situation and without an equivalent of Japan nearby to help oppose Russia.

These deep misgivings regarding Russian plans and objectives were in the process of materializing as a grim reality even while the political strategy was being discussed in London.[20] The Russian consul at Isfahan (later consul general in Mashkhad), Prince Dabizha, Moldavian by origin, went with two cossacks in early June 1899 to Bushire on the Gulf. Prince Dabizha was a forceful and aggressive man like A. Miller (Aleksandr Iakovlevich Miller?), the Russian consul at Nasratabad in Seistan, the latter also known as an extreme Anglophobe.

Dabizha raised suspicions of collaboration when he stayed in Bushire with the French vice consul, Haji Mirza Hussein. Some days later, however, when Dabizha discussed with the vice consul the purchase of his house for use as a consulate, the matter appeared to have gone beyond suspicion. A good deal was learned about Russian plans by overhearing some of his conversations. All in all there was little doubt as to Russia's long-range intentions regarding the Gulf region. At this time also, a Russian doctor, Dr. Chevanovsky, added to the growing certainty when he came to Bushire and briefly practiced medicine, treating people free of charge and asking questions about local matters; he shortly returned to Russia. Several other Russians visited the Gulf ports, at least two of them sent by the Russian Steam Navigation and Commercial Company of Odessa.

These signs of intent were soon supplemented by more tangible

[19] Henry James Whigham, *Manchuria and Korea*, London, 1904, pp. 60–77.
[20] Kazemzadeh, *Russia and Britain*, pp. 434–444; Bondarevsky, *Bagdadskaia doroga*, pp. 171–172, 194–196; O'Conor to Lansdowne, Jan. 22, 1901, Messrs. Grey, Paul & Co. Bushire to MacKenzie, Apr. 20, 1901, No. 31 Cons. Gen. C. A. Kemball to IG Mar 9. 1901, FO 416/5; Rear Admiral Basquet (Bombay) to Admiralty, Feb. 16, 1900, IG to Hamilton, Mar. 3, 1900, Admiralty to FO Mar. 24, 1900, FO 416/2; Curzon to Hamilton, July 4, 1900, Hamilton Papers, D 510/5; Dilks, *Curzon in India*, I, 118–137; Mikhail Pavlovich Fedorov, *Real'nyia osnovy sovremennoi mezhdunarodnoi politiki; doklad v Obshchestve Vostokovedeniia*, St. Petersburg, 1909, pp. 115–116; Eugene Staley, "Business and politics in the Persian Gulf; the story of the Wönckhaus Firm," *PSQ*, XLVIII (1933), 340.

indications of Russian plans, heralded by demands in the Russian press for a port on the Gulf. This warning very soon materialized when on February 14, 1900 the Russian gunboat *Giliak*, shadowed by the British cruiser *Pomone*, entered the harbor at Bandar Abbas. Other warships followed as the *Variag*, *Askold*, and *Boiarin* visited the Gulf. When the *Giliak* left Bushire on March 21, word was left with the resident at the port that a line of Russian steamers would be started the following year. Since there was then no Russian trade in the Gulf, this caused some foreboding. It was further confirmed in July, 1900 that a steamer line between Odessa and the Gulf would start in the fall, information which the German minister at Teheran confirmed.[21]

The decision to embark upon this undertaking had been made in St. Petersburg after a careful study of the local situation and of the alternatives.[22] A report of British Consul-General John Michell stated that in the summer of 1900, the Grand Duke Aleksandr Mikhailovich had sent S. N. Syromiatnikov (the editor of *Rossiia* who wrote for *Novoe Vremia* under the byline "Sigma") to report on the prospects for trade in the Persian Gulf ports. The investigation lasted from April to September and was followed by a visit to Paris where Syromiatnikov discussed the Kuwait issue with President Emil Loubet of France. He returned to Russia in October and attended a meeting at Yalta where he reported his findings to the Grand Duke Aleksandr Mikhailovich, Witte, the minister of finance, and others.

The report pointed out that there would be a good market in the Gulf region for sugar loaf, kerosene, cotton and woolen goods, grain, and spirits. Return cargoes of rice, dates, and other products could be expected. The report recommended the sending of regular steamers subsidized by the Russian government as well as the establishment of a Russian bank at one of the port towns and of a consulate and vice consulate supported by a strong cossack guard. Syromiatnikov's views later appeared in his brochure, *Ocherki Persidskogo Zaliva*, St. Petersburg, 1907.

Witte acted on this report by appointing a special commission under V. I. Kovalevsky (who in this year was promoted from head of the Department of Trade and Industry of the Ministry of Finance to assistant

---

[21] No. 71 Spring Rice (Teheran) to Salisbury, July 3, 1900, FO 416/4.
[22] Boris Vasil'evich Anan'ich, "Iz istorii Anglo-russkogo sopernichestva v Persii nakanune Russko-iaponskoi voiny (Persidskii zaliv)," *Uchenye zapiski* Leningradskogo gosudarstvennogo pedagogicheskogo universiteta im. A. I. Gertsena, vol. 194 (1958), 232–233; No. 5 Scott to Lansdowne, Jan. 7, 1901 (enclosing reports of Consul General John Michell and British commercial agent in Russia, Henry Cooke), FO 416/5; J. A. C. Tilley, "Memorandum on relations between Russia and Great Britain, 1892–1904," Jan. 14, 1905, Cab 1/4 (hereafter Tilley memorandum).

minister of finance). The agenda of this commission appears to have represented the final stage in the resolution of the much more fundamental question as to how to use the opportunities and challenges presented by the Boer war on the one hand and the incipient menace of Germany on the other for the advancement of Russian interests in Persia.

It is thus clear that the Russian advent in the Gulf at this moment was inspired by a wish to take an important step in satisfying an existing Russian objective in Persia while these two conditions were favorable, and scarcely less clear that the growing German presence in this region was the principal immediate motive. It was decided to pursue a cautious strategy by foregoing the construction of any strategic position or coaling station in the Gulf and to pursue the slower economic route to opposing Britain by stimulating Russian trade and enterprise there and promoting the construction of roads and of postal and telegraph communications. This was the cautious route which Witte continued to follow in the Far East until a more forceful policy was mandated at the urging of his competitors in the Russian government and the course was set which led to the Russo-Japanese war.

It was as a consequence of an earlier decision and of a request to the British government nearly two years before that a Russian consulate was opened at Bombay on November 22, 1900, one of its stated purposes being to promote Russian commerce in India.[23] Vasilii Oskarovich Klemm was appointed as the first consul. The commission acted on another aspect of this plan at a meeting, in December 1900 by recommending the sending of steamers from Odessa to the Gulf ports and the establishment of a Russian commercial bank as well as a consulate at Bushire.

The wish, expressed somewhat later by Joseph Naus, the director general of the Persian Customs, for two small boats with mounted guns for patrolling the Gulf in support of the customs administration, must have been very disturbing news in London.[24] The equally bad news of the conclusion on July 6, 1901 of a Russo-Persian agreement suggested the possibility that it might have provided for the appointment of a Russian assistant director general of the Customs at Teheran and raised the prospect of a Russian succeeding the Belgian Naus to a position which amounted practically to being the Persian minister of finance.

Russian commercial activity in the Gulf began with the first sailing of

---

[23] Memorandum "Russia's Relations with India (1900–1917)," *CAR*, VI, no. 4 (1958), 457 (based on O. F. Solov'ev, "K voprosu ob otnoshenii Tsarskoi Rossii k Indii v XIX–nachale XX veka," VI, no. 6 (1958), 96–109).

[24] No. 68A Hardinge to Lansdowne, Apr. 30, 1901, No. 21A. A. Hardinge (Persia) to Lansdowne, July 7, 1901, FO 416/5.

the *Kornilov* from Odessa, an event announced for February 14, 1901, and continued through the year. The four ships to be used belonged to the Russian Steam Navigation and Commercial Company and ran between Odessa in the Black Sea and Bushire on the Gulf, the latter a possible terminus for a railway from Transcaucasia through Tabriz. The *Kornilov* reached Bushire on March 21 after calling at a number of ports including Constantinople, Port Said, and others and appointing temporary agents at the principal ports. The steamers were subsidized at 50,000 rubles for each voyage and the Russian government immediately lowered the freight rate to Europe by 70 percent, the cost per ton between Basra and London falling from 50 to 15 shillings.

A consulate general was established at Bushire with consulates at Mohammerah, Shiraz, Basra, and Bandar Abbas. The Russian consul general, Nikolai Pasek, invited Robert Wönckhaus, the enterprising German mother-of-pearl merchant at Lingah, to assume the management of Russian commercial interests in the Gulf. Wönckhaus refused, however, apparently because he did not want to work for Russian national interests.[25]

The Russian merchant ship, *Kornilov*, again called at the Gulf ports in October 1901, carrying the items recommended by the Kovalevsky commission, substituting Nobel for Rothschild petroleum but, like the latter, also still from Baku, and returning with a cargo made up almost entirely of dates.[26] Further trips were made to the Gulf in early and mid-1902. Since this was the only passenger line going directly to the Mediterranean, it was predicted that the Russian line might monopolize this branch of the traffic. It was estimated that the *Kornilov* voyage could probably pay for itself and that the 50,000 ruble subsidy would be a clear gain for the owners.

Russian trade in the Gulf apparently did not then go beyond this point though the watchful government of India reported in 1903 further Russian efforts to develop at Bushire an interest in shipping cotton and tobacco to Odessa. The Russian journal, *Novosti* , in 1901 labelled the British control in the Persian Gulf "prejudicial to Russia" and wrote that British and Russian interests there were "completely at variance."

The Persian problem, the unremitting multinational, but especially the Russian and now the German pressure from without, and the internal disintegration, had long been of great concern to the British government.

---

[25] Staley, "Business and politics," 371.
[26] No. 52 Consul Wratislaw (Bosra) to O'Conor, Nov. 18, 1901, enclosed in No. 450 O'Conor (Constantinople) to Lansdowne, Dec. 26, 1901, FO 416/8; Anan'ich, "Uchetno-ssudnyi bank Persii," p. 289.

At the opening of the twentieth century it seemed that, far from being solved, the problem was becoming less capable of solution.

Lord Curzon, the knowledgeable and assertive viceroy of India, writing to Lansdowne with respect to his Persian dispatch of two months before, characteristically penetrated to the core of the problem. After remarking on the fact that Lansdowne had tried twice unsuccessfully to come to terms with Russia, he wrote:

There is no greater fallacy in contemporaneous politics than the idea that England can come to an agreement with Russia over Asia. It is not possible except at the price on our side of surrendering the outlying bulwarks of the Empire. Innumerable British statesmen have made tentative advances in that direction. Every one has been either discouraged or replaced. The reason does not lie merely in the ingrained duplicity of Russian diplomacy, but also in the fact that an agreement of whatever kind means the drawing of a line somewhere to Russian ambitions, and (that) she does not want to set any limit to these whatsoever.

The accuracy of this appraisal was borne out by events, both past and future. Russian pressure on British interests in Asia was not mitigated by Russian goodwill or by the assertion of British force. It was counteracted by a change in the balance of power brought about by a regional intensification of German influence, by the rise of Japan, and by the defeat of Russia in the Russo-Japanese war.

Nevertheless, an attempt was made, in this case not so much to reach an understanding with Russia which would achieve some lasting advantage over her as to plan some way to reach a consensus which would make coexistence with her easier. An opportunity occurred in the latter part of 1902, after the end of the Boer war, for the British government to give careful consideration in a series of special departmental studies to the various assertions and ideas relating to the strategic problems inherent in Anglo-Russian rivalry in Persia.[27] The occasion for the policy review was unrest in Persia which developed in the aftermath of the large Russian loans, raising the prospect that Russia might use the unrest as a reason or excuse to intervene in the country to protect her subjects and property or to "restore order." This would force Britain to consider steps to protect her own national interests.

The disorders, more specifically, were reactions to various policies and activities of the Shah which were considered a disgrace or even a menace to national integrity and independence such as Russian loans but also including Russian road building, the appearance of Russians making railway surveys, and the employment of Belgian customs officers, asso-

---

[27] Kazemzadeh, *Russia and Britain*, pp. 390–396; Keddie, "Iranian politics 1900–1905"; A. Hardinge to Lansdowne, Aug. 27, 1902 (with comments by Lansdowne and Balfour), FO 60/664.

ciated, as in the case of the other undesirable activities, with Russia. The discontent was significant for another reason not yet apparent for it was in fact the beginning of the revolutionary movement. Finally, it presented an unusual opportunity for the British upon whom, because of their opposition to Russia, the clerical leaders tended to look with some favor; they also hoped for some sympathy and even assistance.

The basic paper and starting point of the series of discussions was a dispatch from the British minister in Persia, Sir Arthur Hardinge to Lord Lansdowne who added his comments. To this was added an extensive note by the prime minister, Arthur James Balfour. It was the role of the paper by Balfour to ask basic questions about the British reaction to a possible Russian intervention in the wake of the local disturbances in Persia. Balfour established the basic pattern in part with the epigrammatic formula: "until Russia moves we remain still; as soon as Russia moves in the north we move in the south." The prime minister was asking for views as to the nature of a British response in such an event.

The answers were given in papers prepared by the appropriate departments of the government, the Foreign Office, the War Office, the Admiralty, and the India Office. The papers were discussed at a meeting held at the Foreign Office on November 19, 1902. Generally speaking, these reports and the conclusions derived from them were pessimistic and cautious with respect to the future of British tenure in Persia and in the Persian Gulf.

These conclusions were a disappointment to Sir Arthur Hardinge, the British minister in Persia, who had written the original dispatch which, he hoped, had helped to set the tone for a reappraisal of the situation. Hardinge and the military attaché in Teheran, Major J. A. Douglas, wrote papers which gave a different, far more optimistic, view of the situation.

Lord Curzon, the viceroy of India, was another of those who were generally optimistic and who tried to encourage a more positive attitude about the Persian situation on the part of the London government. It is noteworthy that those more familiar with the environment of southern Asia were more optimistic than those who were less familiar with the region and whose perspective on the Persian problem was largely acquired from the experience of dealing from a distance with Russian activities regarding Persia. The latter were, at the same time, however, those whose responsibilities were concerned with the empire as a whole.

Lord Curzon had wished in 1901 to give some visible and forcible expression of the British presence in the Persian Gulf by making a tour of the region. The government, however, including Lord George Hamilton, the secretary of state for India, had opposed the idea as too provocative. Since then, on May 5, 1903, Lord Lansdowne, a former viceroy of India, had issued in the House of Lords his well-known statement of policy which Curzon was to refer to as "a Monroe Doctrine with regard to the sea."[28] In it he expressed the view that "we should regard the establishment of a naval base or of a fortified port in the Persian Gulf by any other Power as a grave menace to British interests, and we shall certainly resist it with all the means at our disposal."

Lansdowne made this pronouncement in parallel with a positive statement about the promotion of British trade in the Gulf and the disavowal of any intention of excluding legitimate trade there. The statement was also made under circumstances which left no doubt that it applied to Germany as well as Russia. Hamilton, however, was still reluctant to countenance the official visit to the Gulf which Curzon proposed to make as a reinforcement for the Lansdowne statement.[29] Hamilton wrote:

I do not quite see what political advantage is likely to accrue from such a visit ... A visit to the two latter places [Bahrein and Kuwait] would be very distasteful to the Turk, and with your known views as to the policy that we are to pursue in Persia, an inspection of Bandar Abbas and Bushire, I think, is almost certain to provoke on the part of Russia increased pressure at Teheran upon the Shah and his Government.

Lord Curzon was, nevertheless, able to carry out his planned tour in the somewhat more assertive environment of 1903. It was with this object that he left Karachi on November 16, 1903 on the Royal Indian Marine steamship *Hardinge*, a ship named after the governor general of India who had conquered the Punjab in 1847 and whose grandson, Sir Arthur Hardinge, was then the British minister in Persia. Hardinge joined Curzon at Muscat to accompany him on part of the Gulf tour as far as Bushire.[30]

The expedition was accompanied by the naval commander in chief of the East India Station, Rear Admiral G. Atkinson-Willes, and was escorted by the first-class cruiser *Argonaut*, the second-class cruiser *Hyacinth*, the third-class cruisers *Fox* and *Pomone* and at Muscat was joined by three smaller vessels. Curzon visited Muscat on November 18 and 19, reached Shargah on November 21, Bandar Abbas on November 22 and received the governor of the Gulf ports. He visited the nearby islands of Hormoz, Qeshm, and others, went on to Bahrein, stopped at

[28] Memorandum, "Our Policy in Regard to Persia Generally," Mar. 22, 1905, Cab 6/3; Busch, *Britain and the Persian Gulf*, p. 256; Curzon to Hamilton, June 17, 1903, Curzon 162; Ernest L. Woodward, *Great Britain and the German Navy*, Oxford, 1935, p. 148.

[29] Hamilton to Curzon, July 9, 1903, Curzon 162.

[30] Arthur H. Hardinge, *A diplomatist in the East*, London, 1928, pp. 305–318; Lovat Fraser, *India under Curzon and after*, London, 1911, pp. 109–110; IG to IO Jan. 14, 1904, FO 106/8.

Kuwait during November 28–29, Bushire on December 2 and finally returned to Karachi on December 7.

The tour of the Persian Gulf has been called "the crowning event of five years of strenuous and successful endeavor to maintain the position of Great Britain intact against the assaults of other Powers."[31] The expedition itself was, certainly in those waters, an impressive array of sea power, unparalleled, it has been said, since the Portuguese "Governor of India," Afonso d'Albuquerque, was there in 1507. There were speeches and durbars at every important stop, all helping to remind the spectators and listeners of the British Empire and its value for their well being. Speaking to the durbar at Shargah on November 21, Curzon said: "We were here before any other Power, in modern times, had shown its face in these waters. We found strife and we created order. It was our commerce as well as your security that was threatened and called for protection."[32]

Curzon apparently was successful in making a very deep impression, in raising British prestige among people in the Gulf, and in associating British supremacy in India with British supremacy in the Persian Gulf. It is difficult to assess the effect of this tour in St. Petersburg. A recent Soviet writer has stated that the assertion of this "Monroe Doctrine" in the Persian Gulf played a major part in the failure of the Anglo-Russian negotiations in 1903 regarding an accord, an appraisal which is ill-suited to the facts.[33] The term for this event, "Monroe Doctrine in the Persian Gulf," had been used in *The Times* of London on May 7, 1903.

Russian challenge in Manchuria

The relatively sheltered overland approach to the Middle East stood in contrast to the long, exposed German maritime route to these regions and especially to the even longer sea lane to her recent acquisitions in the Far East. There she had also the disadvantage of being a commercial competitor not only of Britain, France, and Russia, as well as Japan in addition to being a competitor of these powers for place and preferment in a declining Chinese Empire.

Sergei Witte, the Russian minister of finance, was strongly opposed to the first German acquisition in China, Kiaochow, on the coast of Shantung province. Expressing a tactical word of warning to a competitor, he told the German ambassador on November 12, 1897, two days before the German occupation of the port, that: "Germany's seizure of

---

[31] Lord Ronaldshay [Lawrence Zetland], *The life of Lord Curzon*, 3 vols. London, 1927, II, 315.

[32] Sir Thomas Raleigh (ed.), *Lord Curzon in India. Being a selection from his speeches as viceroy and governor-general of India, 1898–1905*, London, 1906, p. 502.

[33] Bondarevsky, *Bagdadskaia doroga*, p. 501; Browne, *The Persian revolution*, p. 107.

Kiaochow would force Russia to occupy some other more northerly port, that this would give Japan occasion to consolidate either on the Chinese mainland or in Korea or both, and that this would lead to a Russo-Japanese war."[34] On December 19, 1897 Russia occupied Port Arthur, thereby taking another step toward what many saw as the partition of China and what Witte had predicted would be the road to a Russo-Japanese war.

It was at this point, with both the Chinese and Ottoman Empires in danger of disintegration, as Lord Salisbury, the British minister of foreign affairs, saw the situation, that he turned to Russia seeking an agreement which might help to stabilize the disintegrating empires. He directed Sir Nicholas O'Conor, the British minister in St. Petersburg, to discuss with Witte the possibility of Britain and Russia working together to this end. Salisbury suggested that one of the means the two countries might adopt in working together in China to prevent a further weakening and even the potential collapse of China was an agreement to recognize spheres of interest. He suggested a British sphere in the Yangtze valley and a Russian sphere in the Yellow River valley and northward.

O'Conor received the impression from this inquiry that Russia was indeed interested in a sphere of influence in China but one which would include practically all of north China. During a conversation with Witte on January 22, the minister of finance took a map from the locked drawer of his desk, passed his hand over the northern Chinese provinces of Chihli, Shansi, and Kansu, and said that sooner or later Russia would probably absorb all of that region. Then he put his finger on Lanchow in Kansu and said that the Transsiberian railway would in time have a branch down to that point. He conceded the Yangtze valley to Britain. But O'Conor also learned that the Russian government, and especially the Emperor, was concerned that complications might arise before the completion of the Siberian railway. This suggested that Russia's interest in an arrangement with Britain might be only a matter of temporary convenience.

The British and Russian visions of the future, if comparisons are made before the latter was influenced by the German landing at Kiaochow and while she was still pursuing a policy of "peaceful penetration," appeared, at least in the short run, to have had a great deal in common. However, Salisbury's description of the British view as stated in late March 1898, in

---

[34] Lensen, *Balance of intrigue:*, II, 753 ff.; Witte, *The memoirs of Count Witte*, pp. 276–277; No. 12 O'Conor to Salisbury, Jan. 23, 1898, *BD*, I, 7–8; White, *The diplomacy*, ch. 2; Howard R. Spendelow, "Russia's lease of Port Arthur and Talien: the failure of China's traditional foreign policy," *PC*, XXIV (1971), 149 ff.; John Van Antwerp MacMurray, *Treaties and agreements with and concerning China, 1894–1919*, 2 vols. New York, 1921, I, 127–128, 154–156, 156–158 (other pertinent agreements).

terms far more precise than those employed in statements of two years before which had been intended to encourage Russia to look eastward, give a different impression. "Speaking generally," Salisbury wrote to Sir Nicholas O'Conor, "it may be said that the policy of this country is effectively to open China to the commerce of the world, and that our estimate of the action of the other Powers in the Far East depends on the degree to which it promotes or hinders the attainment of this object."

The policies of other nations, he continued, are to be judged by their impact on the commercial interests of nations interested in trading in China. The British government took the same view of the use made of railways and ports, including those of Manchuria, to which Britain did not object as long as they were used for purely commercial purposes. However, it was evident not only that Russia wanted to use Port Arthur as a naval port but also that this port was so strategically located with reference to the Gulf of Chihli and to Peking itself as to constitute a danger to the national independence of China, a point which Russia had herself made so forcibly to Japan less than three years before.

The political impact on China of the Russian establishment of a naval base at Port Arthur would, accordingly, be very significant. Such an event would be "universally interpreted in the Far East as indicating that the partition of China had begun." Salisbury expressed regret that Russia, which already had an important means of exerting influence upon China through a common frontier dangerously accessible to Peking, should be allowed to acquire another such advantage by the occupation of Port Arthur. This would also give Russia command of the maritime approaches to Peking.

Salisbury had hoped that Witte would be more responsive than M. N. Murav'ev, the Russian minister of foreign affairs, had been to some kind of an accommodation with Britain. But Witte had stated clearly and bluntly the future prospects of the Anglo-Russian conflict in China which had been exposed and aggravated by the German landing on November 14, 1897. Russia, as the British government knew, had been occupied since the Sino-Japanese war in building by negotiations and political pressure various components of her exclusive sphere in the Far East. Then the German landing had induced some members of the Russian government to respond by resorting to more forceful means in order to hasten the progress of her enterprises before increased competition rendered them more difficult or impossible to achieve.

The Russian program in Manchuria, like that in Persia, was predicated on the hope of being able to control the railways and the finances, the latter especially through banks. Hopefully, this would preserve Manchuria intact for future Russian acquisition. While in 1896 Li Hung-chang had refused Russia the right to extend the Chinese Eastern Railway southward from Harbin to Port Arthur, Russia had accepted this as only a temporary set-back.

In the spring of 1897, however, when it became apparent that anti-Russian sentiment was growing among the Chinese and that China, with known British support, was preparing to resume the construction of the railway into Manchuria which had been abandoned when the Sino-Japanese war broke out, Russia responded by pursuing her own railway plans more actively.[35] This applied also to the trunk line running south from Lukouchiao near Peking, a railway which Chang Chih-tung, the viceroy of Hukuang, had planned to build in 1889 with Chinese finances. This program was abandoned during the Sino-Japanese war, after the completion of the 175 miles of railway to Chunghouso, a town 40 miles north of Shanhaikuan. The T'ientsin–Shanhaikuan railway project was revived after the war though the promoters now had to seek foreign financing.

The railway became the first project considered by the American–China Development Company. But by the spring of 1897 the British had to face the prospect that the railway might be financed by a Belgian company behind which stood the Russo-Chinese Bank and the French and Russian governments. The Russian government might in this way be able to reach into the Yangtze valley or even beyond. Consequently, supporting the railway which the Chinese were proposing to build further northward into Manchuria might present the only means of preventing the possibility of total Russian railway control from the northern frontier of Manchuria at least to the Yangtze valley.

An agreement for the financing of the Peking–Hankow railway was concluded with the Belgian syndicate in May 1897 though a final contract was not approved until June 26, 1898. The actual money for the project came largely from France and it had been intended that the Russo-Chinese Bank would be its agent thus giving Russia control of the railway. Opposition, however, prevented this. Meanwhile, the American–China Development Company had received a concession from the Chinese government on April 4, 1898 to complete the trunk line by building the Hankow–Canton section. This line, however, was also acquired by the Belgian interests by an agreement signed July 13, 1900, thus raising the specter of Russian control of the trunk line, not only to the Yangtze region

---

[35] Arthur Lewis Rosenbaum, "The Manchuria bridgehead: Anglo-Russian rivalry and the imperial railways of North China, 1897–1902," *MAS*, X, no. 1 (1976), 42–43, 45–46; Meribeth Cameron, "Chang Chih-tung," in Arthur W. Hummel (ed.), *Eminent Chinese of the Ch'ing period (1644–1912)*, 2 vols. Washington, 1943, I, 27–32.

but to the southernmost part of China. Belgian capital apparently continued to dominate this line until 1905.

Similar plans for "peaceful penetration" characterized Russian policy in Korea.[36] The excessive haste and zeal on the part of Japan in trying to achieve a firmer grip on her Korean acquisitions, followed by the flight of the Korean King to the Russian legation on February 11, 1896, presented Russia with a golden opportunity which she succeeded in squandering over the next two years. In general, the Russian government offered far less than the Korean government had expected, particularly in such vital matters as the training of troops, sending of advisers, and granting of loans.

The special Korean ambassador to the Russian imperial coronation, Prince Min Yong-hwan, remained in Russia for three months and returned with a very discouraging appraisal of what was to be expected of the relationship with Russia. On February 20, 1897 the Korean King returned to his own palace disillusioned with any hope of assistance from Russia. Four days later, on February 24, the Japanese published the Weber-Komura Seoul Protocol of May 14, 1896 and the Lobanov-Yamagata Moscow Protocol of June 9, 1896 to show the insincerity of Russia in having presumably made bargains with Japan which contradicted her obligations to Korea.

Before the acquisition of the concession for the railway outlet through south Manchuria, Russia had considered Korea as an alternate route to the south. Since the Japanese presence in Korea, both in business and settlement, far exceeded that of Russia, Petr Mikhailovich Romanov, the chancellor of the Ministry of Finance and a member of the Board of Directors of the Chinese Eastern Railway and of the Russo-Chinese Bank, had suggested in a memorandum of March 29, 1897 to Witte that Russia seek to remedy this by constructing a railway through Kirin in Manchuria to a port in Korea, a project which, it was hoped, would provide a safeguard against a Japanese seizure of Korea.[37] It was also decided to establish what became known as the Russo-Korean Bank. Kir Alekseevich Alekseev, an official of the Russian Customs Service who was sent to Seoul in September 1897 to investigate various opportunities,

[36] Seung Kwon Synn [Sin, Sung-gwon]. "The Russo-Japanese struggle for the control of Korea, 1894–1904," Ph.D. dissertation, Harvard University, 1967, pp. 191–291; Malozemoff, *Russian Far Eastern policy*, pp. 84–92, 107, 110; Boris Aleksandrovich Romanov, *Russia in Manchuria (1892–1906)*, Ann Arbor, MI, 1952, pp. 108–115; George Alexander Lensen (trans. and ed.), *The D'Anethan dispatches from Japan, 1894–1910. The observations of Baron Albert d'Anethan, minister plenipotentiary and dean of the diplomatic corps*, Tokyo, 1967, pp. 60–66; C. I. Eugene Kim and Han-Kyo Kim, *Korea and politics of imperialism, 1876–1910*, Berkeley, 1967, pp. 85–96.
[37] Malozemoff, *Russian Far Eastern policy*, pp. 91–92.

tried to have himself named superintendent of the Korean Customs instead of the British incumbent, MacLeavy Brown, only to incur the successful opposition of the British, supported by the fleet, which helped to sustain Brown in his position.[38]

The movement to place Russians in some key Korean adviserships was gathering force at this time. Whereas in the spring of 1896 the Russian minister at Seoul, Weber, had given cordial support to MacLeavy Brown, the head of the Korean Customs Administration, his attitude had been criticized by the Russian press as "unpatriotic" and as showing a lack of support for his own government. Russia had sent a military mission to organize the Korean forces and had offered the Korean government a loan of $3 million to pay off a Japanese loan of the same amount.

In the fall of 1897 the efforts of Alekseev to supplant Brown as superintendent of the Korean Customs, thanks to British support for Brown, ended in a compromise. Brown retained his customs post while Alekseev became financial adviser but with the understanding that he would have a key role in Brown's work. By January 1898 the British were complaining that the Russian minister in Peking was trying to oust Claude W. Kinder, the able chief engineer of the railways of North China.

Alekseev had hardly made the recommendation that a fitting place for a railway terminal would be the port of Uiju in northern Korea when the German landing occurred and was followed by the acquisition by Russia of Port Arthur, thus obviating the need for a railhead in Korea. Having achieved a more substantial position in southern Manchuria, Russia was willing to conclude the Rosen-Nishi Convention of April 25, 1898, officially recognizing considerable freedom of action for Japan in Korea for commercial and industrial activities. Nearly two weeks before, on April 12, all Russian military and financial advisers had left Korea and, on the same day, after having been open for business under its director, M. S. Gabriel, only since March 1, the Russo-Korean Bank closed its doors. The way was thus opened for a resurgence of Japanese influence and activity.

A writer in *The Nineteenth Century* for March 1897, eight months before the German landing at Kiaochow, had been prompted by the publication on the previous October 30 in the *North China Herald* of the "Cassini Convention" to take a broad look at the post-war Far Eastern situation.[39] This "Convention" was said to have been a Chinese grant to Russia of extensive railway privileges though it had been considered more

---

[38] Tilley memorandum, Cab 1/4.
[39] Holt S. Hallett, "France and Russia in China," *NC*, XLI (March 1897), 487–491, 494–495; Malozemoff, *Russian Far Eastern policy*, p. 78; Romanov, *Russia in Manchuria*, pp. 99–102.

likely that it was a sketch of desiderata drawn up by Cassini (Artur Pavlovich Kassini), the Russian minister in Peking, before his conference of April 18, 1896 with the Chinese government.

Among the provisions of this alleged convention, it should be noted, was not only the right to build a railway into northern Manchuria, a privilege already granted a month before the *North China Herald* disclosure, but also the right to complete the railway by extending it into southern Manchuria. This would, of course, have conflicted with the Chinese plan to project their own railway northward from Shanhaikuan into that region. The existence of this Cassini Convention as a reality, according to Holt Hallett, the writer of *The Nineteenth Century* article, was taken for granted by many in Berlin and he cited in this relationship the views of the Berlin reporter for the *Daily Chronicle* who, in turn, cited a letter from T'ientsin which had appeared in the *Tageblatt*.

The view of China as seen in these sources was a depressing one for the British reader to contemplate. It delineated a conception of a Russian sphere of interest reaching as far south as the Yellow River. A possible German sphere could extend from the Yellow River to the Yangtze while the region south of the Yangtze would be a British sphere except for the province of Yünnan which, it was assumed, might go wholly to France. Implicit in this idea was the suggestion that if Germany wanted a share she had better act to secure it and that there was no room left for Japan.

Hallett saw the article as signifying that eleven of the intramural provinces of China with the addition of Manchuria, Mongolia, Chinese Turkestan, and Tibet would pass under the influence of "our Protectionist rivals." These regions, he assumed, would be practically closed to British trade while her rivals, Germany, France, and Russia would enjoy their spheres of influence "as close preserves for their mercantile and manufacturing classes."

The likelihood that, in view of these prospects, Russia would respond favorably to Lord Salisbury's proposals was not promising. Britain, in the first place, stood for an open door policy in China in a field in which her principal rivals, except Germany, could only compete by establishing monopolies. These conflicting ambitions had reached an impasse when Britain declined to join the intervention of the Triplice powers but had chosen to support the integrity of China at a time when she controlled 70 percent of China's foreign commerce, a category of business which comprised one-sixth of her own commerce.[40]

The implications of such a scheme were far-reaching. It would have been difficult for Britain to claim a voice in moderating the demands for

---

[40] Walter LeFeber, *The new empire: an interpretation of American expansion, 1860–1898,* Ithaca, 1963, p. 316.

compensation which were likely to follow. It would also have weakened the long-standing Anglo-Chinese community of interests which had theretofore been a stabilizing factor in Far Eastern politics. At the same time, the benefit to Japan during the crucial immediate post-war years would have been destined to remain largely potential, even as late as the Rosen–Nishi agreement of April 1898 which came too late to be of any use to Salisbury in early 1898. Finally, the widespread gains of France and Russia in the Far East followed by the interposition between them of German military power would have made it difficult even to consider a return to an open door policy.

Britain faced a further difficulty in the fact that even her adherence to the open door had been qualified two years before when, in order to turn Russia away from the west she had, like Germany, deliberately tried to direct her rival eastward. Sir Ernest Satow, the British minister in Tokyo, wrote to Admiral Sir Edward Hobart Seymour, the commander of the China station, that he feared Britain's efforts in China's behalf were not destined to be successful.[41] "We gave the whole position away two years ago," he wrote, "when Mr. Balfour declared in a speech at Bristol [February 5, 1896] that there was no objection to Russia obtaining an outlet to the Pacific." Britain had tried to insist that Russia should be contented with a commercial port "but that is not what she wants, which is a naval base."

It is not difficult to understand why, in response to a letter from the Kaiser of May 30, 1898, the Tsar wrote concerning a memorandum Russia had received from Britain containing some tempting proposals for "a full agreement upon all points in which our interests collide with hers."[42] He found the proposals amazing and was suspicious, particularly since Britain had never before made such offers to him. It seemed clear to him that Britain was in need of Russian friendship and wanted to check Russian developments in the Far East. He added that "Without thinking twice over it, their proposals were refused."

The same fate had recently befallen a British overture to Germany and for the same reason. Salisbury's illness and departure from London on March 28, 1898 followed by his continued absence from the diplomatic scene for a month, left open the opportunity for others, especially Joseph Chamberlain, the colonial secretary who was concerned about the security and survival of the empire, to test their hopes for a German alliance as an alternative to Russia.[43] Chamberlain was alarmed by the weakness of

---

[41] Satow to Seymour, Mar. 28, 1898, *BD*, I, 41.

[42] J.D. Bickford and E.N. Johnson, "The contemplated Anglo-German alliance, 1890–1901," *PSQ*, XIII, no. 1 (March 1927), 31.

[43] Grenville, *Lord Salisbury and foreign policy*, pp. 148–176; Zara S. Steiner, *The Foreign Office and foreign policy, 1898–1914*, Cambridge, 1969, pp. 27–28.

Britain in general and, in particular, he feared that France and Russia would join hands against her in the growing crisis in the Far East. Alfred Rothschild and perhaps also Baron Hermann von Eckardstein had acted as intermediaries for the German ambassador in London, Count Paul von Hatzfeldt-Wildenburg, who wished to improve Anglo-German relations.

Chamberlain used the occasion of his meeting with Hatzfeldt on March 9 to propose an Anglo-German alliance. But Baron Friedrich von Holstein saw an alliance with Britain as a liability and considered such a proposal as an effort to embroil Germany with Russia in China. Furthermore, Holstein found no benefit from such a relationship that could compensate for the Russo-German estrangement which it would bring about. Bülow agreed in seeing no advantage in this proposal and was not even moved by the possibility that it might prevent an Anglo-Russian rapprochement; in fact, he thought such an outcome might at least have the advantage of loosening the bonds of the Franco-Russian alliance. Even though some discussions continued through the year, nothing came of the effort.

The negotiations initiated by Salisbury in relation to China continued during the early months of 1898. These encompassed numerous demands being pressed on China by several nations and together brought about a highly competitive relationship among these nations. While the German action at Kiaochow had induced some haste in the agenda of the Russian advance in China, Germany remained formally cooperative though by no means a partner in any military sense. France was more truly a partner of Russia though she was in reality a beneficiary of the Russian advance rather than a contributor to it; her financial role was, however, beneficial both to Russia and herself. Britain and Japan were competitors of Russia, the former in China and the latter in Korea, while the United States was, from the standpoint of exerting pressure on China, largely a non-participant.

When the British saw that their program of an open door for commerce in China was not faring well, they took steps to shore up the most important centers of their commerce. These endeavors came too tardily some said. L. J. Dudgeon, the chairman of the Shanghai branch of the China Association, wrote in October 1898: "We seem to have left the policy of 'Integrity of China' and, walking through the 'Open Door,' to have arrived at the policy of the 'Spheres of Influence.' We think that the long neglect of Chinese affairs by our government . . . has been the cause of an indecisive policy."[44]

---

[44] Dudgeon to Beresford, Oct. 6, 1898, in Charles Beresford, *The break-up of China: with an account of its present commerce, currency, waterways, armies, railways, politics, and future prospects*, New York, 1900, pp. 456–457.

The measures taken by the British government could at best have been only a partial remedy since the number of competitors and, with the exception of Germany, their inability to compete in the open market, left available little more than a partial rescue operation. One of the British measures was to fortify her position by assurances from the Chinese government, a kind of support which, however weak militarily, was at least the same kind of foundation which had been sought for all other foreign rights and concessions. On February 9 and 11, 1898 respectively, the British asked for and received assurances from the Chinese government that the provinces adjoining the Yangtze would not be alienated to any other nation.[45]

London had received a warning of another danger the previous December 22 from the British minister in Peking, Sir Claude Maxwell MacDonald. He had communicated the news that Russia was offering to guarantee, at a very attractive figure, the third indemnity loan, in return for which China was to grant Russia control over all the railways in Manchuria and North China and "that a Russian should be appointed Inspector-General of the Customs when that post becomes vacant."[46]

In response to a British request, the Chinese government also gave assurances that as long as British trade was preponderant over that of the other foreign nations, the position of inspector-general of the Maritime Customs Service would continue to be held by a British subject.[47] The memorandum by Tilley noted that: "These concessions having been secured, both the loan and the understanding with Russia became matters of comparative indifference to Her Majesty's Government and the negotiations [were] dropped." In fact, an Anglo-German agreement was concluded on March 1, 1898 with China, arranging for a loan to China of £16 million by the Hong Kong and Shanghai Banking Corporation and the Deutsche-Asiatische Bank.[48]

The key to the next phase of the negotiations was the conclusion on June 6, between the Chinese administrator of the railways of North China and the Hong Kong and Shanghai Banking Corporation, of a preliminary agreement providing for a loan of £2,300,000 for extending the T'ient-sin–Shanhaikuan railway into Manchuria as far as Hsinmintun near Mukden.[49] Russia protested this on June 7 as a violation of China's

[45] MacDonald to FO Feb. 14, 1898, cited in Tilley memorandum, Cab 1/4; *BFSP*, XCVI (1902–3), 572–573; MacMurray, *Treaties and agreements*, I, 104–105; A.L. Popov (ed.), "Anglo-Russkoe soglashenie o razdele Kitaia (1899 g.)," *KA*, XXV (1927), 111; Nathan A. Pelcovits, *Old China hands and the Foreign Office*, New York, 1948, pp. 216–219.

[46] Pelcovits, *Old China hands*, p. 210 (citing No. 26 MacDonald to Salisbury, Dec. 22, 1897, China No. 1, 1898).

[47] Tilley memorandum, Cab 1/4; Tsung-li Yamen to MacDonald, Feb. 10, 1898, in MacMurray, *Treaties and agreements*, I, 105–106.

[48] MacMurray, *Treaties and agreements*, I, 107–112.

[49] Tilley memorandum, Cab 1/4; Rosenbaum, "The Manchuria bridgehead," 52–53.

commitment and Britain, on her part, kept the door open for negotiations with Russia on the Manchurian railway issue until these finally broke down. Salisbury was hoping to prevent the dismemberment of China or the inconvenience of having considerable portions of it become a Russian preserve and sought to promote these ends by using British claims and Chinese rights in the T'ientsin–Mukden railway as a means of dislodging the Peking–Hankow line from the Belgian-Franco-Russian grip.

A final Anglo-Chinese loan agreement was concluded on October 10, 1898; yet even this left some room for negotiations with Russia. It did, however, continue the practice begun in 1886 of stipulating a British engineer and a European engineering staff. It was the British hope that a revision of this railway agreement could be a diplomatic concession with which an Anglo-Russian understanding might be achieved. This became all the more necessary once the Peking–Hankow railway concession had actually been acquired by the Belgian syndicate.

Pressures from the other powers for concessions or other rights and privileges in China either centered on Russia or were in a general sense associated with her. The Russian government had been considering, since about mid-February, the demands which she finally presented to China on March 3, 1898.[50] Meanwhile, on February 16, apparently in response to a suggestion of January 7 from Murav'ev, Japan presented Russia with some proposals regarding Korea, the essence of which was the desire of Japan to replace Russia as the paramount power in Korea.[51]

Behind the proposals were two grim facts: the warnings of the Russian military attaché that the Japanese were incensed over Russian occupation of the Liaotung peninsula and that they were in a fighting mood over it and the fact that the military balance in the Far East at that time favored Japan over Russia. Following Russian presentation of her demands to China on March 3, agreements were reached with China on March 17, May 7, and July 6 conceding to Russia the right to lease the Liaotung peninsula and to extend the Chinese Eastern Railway to the Gulf of Chihli.[52]

Since the precise relations existing between Germany and Russia were not then known, it was considered of the greatest importance to insure against the rise of a possible "Zweikaiserbund" in the Far East. France had already received ample benefits from the Russian advance in the Pacific region and in April and May received further advantages with respect to railways connecting Indochina with China including Kuangchou Bay.[53] The Japanese achieved part of their desired objective with the

---

[50] Langer, *Diplomacy of imperialism*, II, 470–471.
[51] Malozemoff, *Russian Far Eastern policy*, pp. 108–110.
[52] MacMurray, *Treaties and agreements*, I, 119–121, 127–128, 154–156.
[53] Ibid., I, 124–125, 128–130.

conclusion of the Rosen–Nishi agreement on April 25, 1898 which, on balance, left Japan with an advantage where commercial and industrial enterprises in Korea were concerned.

The seemingly rather solid wall of Russo-German concentration in Shantung and Manchuria, somewhat weakened by Japanese gains in Korea was militarily undermined by the British acquisition of Weihaiwei on the northern coast of Shantung by a grant of July 1 from China. This was by no means a clear-cut asset since it was not considered a good choice for a naval base and was exposed on both sides to potentially hostile German and Russian naval forces. Also, an occupant would be unable to exert any leverage on the next step in Russia's "peaceful penetration" of China, the grant on June 26, 1898 of the right to finance the Peking–Hankow railway to the Belgian Group, supported by the Russo-Chinese Bank and the Russian government.

The outcome of Lord Salisbury's search for an accommodation with Russia was a relative success. This was because the Chinese Empire was continuing as a field for increasingly competitive interests and because Britain had an interest in supporting the Chinese extension of a railway into Manchuria. The line consisted thus far only of the sections from Chunghouso to Hsinmintun and Yingkou, as a basis from which to bargain. The German landing at Kiaochow had inconveniently caught Russia in the process of realizing large gains from her "peaceful penetration" and had not only checked German progress at Kiaochow but had moved her, against the advice of Witte, to respond with force in the seizure of Port Arthur.

This had aroused the resentment of Japan where the memory of a forced surrender of her gains of only three years before was still fresh. Coming at a time when the Russian welcome in Korea was wearing thin, these factors led to the reappearance of Japan as a competitor on the continent. Seeing in these developments the decline if not the termination of the open door in China, Britain ventured to preserve as much of it as she could. In this regard she had particularly in mind her own survival as a competitor in China. She sought and received from China guarantees for her Yangtze valley commercial sphere and for her control over the Chinese Customs.

The Anglo-Russian negotiations, in which Britain sought further guarantees for her Yangtze valley preserve, began on August 12, 1898 between the Russian chargé d'affaires, P. M. Lessar, and the British foreign secretary, Lord Salisbury. While the British regretted to see the disappearance of the open door, they were nevertheless convinced that its most generous days were gone and were generally divided only on the question as to whether Russia or Germany could help most in preserving what remained.

The Russians were divided on the question of spheres of interest. Murav'ev was ready to agree to such a regime while Witte continued to oppose any division into spheres lest his "peaceful penetration" plans should be limited in scope. Neither, of course, wished to have British capital or commerce competing with Russia in any part of China but particularly not in Manchuria. The Chinese had capitulated to the Russians on a significant issue when on July 31, 1898 they had acknowledged that the assignment of the extramural railway line as security for a loan had been a violation of the special protocol of March 27, 1898 [Russo-Chinese agreement on the Kuantung Territory]. Nevertheless the loan of June 6, 1898 was a fact and the vagueness of the language in which these transactions were expressed left the railway loan a valuable British asset in the bargaining with Russia.[54]

After eight months of intermittent negotiations interspersed with considerable hesitation, especially on the Russian side, an Anglo-Russian agreement was concluded by an exchange of notes between the two governments on April 28, 1899. The agreement stated that "Great Britain and Russia, animated by a sincere desire to avoid in China all cause of conflict on questions where their interests meet, and taking into account the economic and geographical gravitation of certain parts of that Empire, have agreed as follows." It drew a line, for purposes of seeking further railway concessions, at the Great Wall of China, a division intended "to consolidate peace in the Far East, and to serve the primordial interests of China herself." Assuming that the English readers saw the word "primordial" as meaning really "fundamental" in the ultimate sense and that the Russian readers saw the word "pervostepennyi" as meaning really "paramount" or "fundamental," this could be seen as an attempt to avoid the more current term "territorial integrity" with all the qualifications of territorial integrity it had come to imply.

The meaning was quite clearly, however, not this at all. For the agreement itself gave the Russians an almost uncontested sphere of interest not only in Manchuria but also in Mongolia and perhaps also in Sinkiang. Also, Murav'ev's wish to have the Russian sphere extend southward as far as Peking was in practice realized by guarantees given to Russia by China on June 1 and July 21 that no power other than Russia would be permitted to build railways north or northeast of Peking.

The continued presence of the British in the construction of the Manchurian railway from Chunghouso to Hsinmintun and Yingkou was seen by the Russians of various views as undesirable and they turned immediately to the task of trying to buy out the British interest. Witte, however, in view of his long range plans for "peaceful penetration" and of

[54] Rosenbaum, "The Manchuria bridgehead," 52–54.

the French financiers who supported him, regretted equally the prospect of losing such opportunities as had already been opened by the Peking–Hankow railway and the Yulinpu–Taiyuanfu line in Shansi.

The Anglo-Russian agreement did not provide, as these realities indicate it was probably not expected by its Russian cosigners to provide, even the limited delineation for which the British had hoped. The Russian press at least was very clear and candid about the questions which might arise in the course of the Anglo-Russian accommodations under the treaty. As though in direct response to Salisbury's words of nearly a year and a half before concerning the absence of formidable differences between the two countries, the *Novoe Vremia* of May 21, 1899 asked the question: "What common object in the sphere of practical politics can there be in Asia for Russia and England?"[55] The answer clearly was none. Two months later, Vladimir Holstrem wrote for the *North American Review* an appeal for Russo-American understanding which was in fact a stinging rebuke to British intentions and strategy.

Holstrem accused Britain of using the "open door" as a slogan to cover what was really a plan of partition and conquest in China as shown by British conduct in the case of Egypt and India. These were strange analogies since Britain had in neither case demonstrated any wish to partition these countries or to divide them with any other nations.

Russian policy, Holstrem continued, was seeking to maintain the integrity of China, and was building the railway in Manchuria and establishing herself at Port Arthur in order to protect China from the advances of Britain and Germany and to stave off the policy implied by the recent appointment of Lord Curzon as viceroy of India. Russia was trying a policy of spheres of influence as a counterpoise to Britain's policy of conquest in China. Holstrem, however, reminded his readers that the American, Gilbert Reid, and the Russian, Prince Esper Esperovich Ukhtomsky, both authors of articles on the Far East, wanted the same thing i.e., a reformed, strengthened, and independent China.

It seems wholly reasonable that in view of the enormous stakes for which this diplomatic game was being played, the American commercial interests which were at issue even though the United States was not one of the main players, and the seemingly innocuous claims made by the principals, that the United States would have responded by trying with such means as she thought useful to strengthen her own position. A British request was made to the United States on March 8, 1898, while Russia was still seeking Chinese approval for her occupation of Port Arthur and before the outbreak of the Spanish–American war, asking

---

[55] Kazemzadeh, *Russia and Britain*, p. 321.

American support for Britain in opposing "preferential treatment" in China.[56]

American interest in this region which lay in what was becoming German and Russian spheres is understandable. American cotton goods, considered "heavier, superior, and cheaper," went largely through the ports of Chefoo and Newchuang to North China and Manchuria. Also, while this accounted for 90 percent of the American sales of cotton goods to China, it constituted 31 percent of the trade at Newchuang,

Russia on her part assumed a benevolent stance toward the United States and made a special effort to prevent the development of too close an American–British cooperation. Cassini, the Russian ambassador in Washington where he could watch events in the light of his experience in Peking, did not really expect the American–British relationship to become anything as serious as an alliance but still thought it needed to be carefully watched.[57] It was especially important, he noted, to observe what the Americans were up to in the Philippines, whether they intended to annex them or whether their holding them might have any implications for the United States as a possible ally of Britain. This was a combination of naval powers which could seriously disturb the balance of power in the Far East.

The generally favorable light in which Russia saw the American retention of the Philippines, in fact, had in mind especially the damage that could be done to the balance of power in the Far East if the islands were to have fallen into the hands of one of the more serious rivals.[58] It was considered worth while to go to some length, as Russia did, to encourage the Americans to think that their commercial future in Manchuria was secure, a point which seemed to be greatly emphasized by an Imperial order of July 12, 1899 making Talienwan (Dalny) a free port.

The open door notes were, as has often been emphasized, in the British tradition. Britain, however, had been forced to a great extent to give up the principle in order to defend her enormous stake in China. It was only reasonable that the United States might take a stand on such an issue since she had a growing commercial stake in a region where the dependability of its future was at that time questionable. It is important also to note that the open door was as much in the American as in the British tradition; it

---

[*] A.L.P. Dennis, *Adventures in American diplomacy 1896–1906*, New York, 1928, pp. 170–171.

[57] Cassini to Murav'ev, June 22, Cassini to Lamsdorf, June 23, 1898, in Edward H. Zabriskie, *American-Russian rivalry in the Far East: a study in diplomacy and power politics 1895–1914*, Philadelphia, 1946, pp. 203–205.

[58] James K. Eyre Jr., "Russia and the American acquisition of the Philippines," *MVHR*, XXVIII (1942), 548–561; Vladimir Holstrem, "Ex Oriente Lux: a plea for Russo–American understanding," *NAR*, CLXIX, no. DXII (July 1899), 6–7; Malozemoff, *Russian Far Eastern policy*, p. 117.

could, in fact, be considered, in the words of a recent writer, "as a codification of the peaceful, liberal expansionist strain in American foreign affairs."[59]

The issuance of the first of the circular notes on September 6, 1899 to Britain, Germany, and Russia, was basically an expression of a hope that the conditions heretofore pertaining to commerce in the ports of China might appeal strongly enough to these nations to induce them to support their continuation.[60] It asked general support for the principles that the treaty ports continue to remain open for commerce in spite of the new spheres of interest, that the Chinese treaty tariff apply as formerly to all shippers except in "free ports," and that harbor dues and railway rates remain the same for all.

The Russian reply indirectly accentuated the same basic differences as those dividing Britain and Russia by ignoring completely the issue of railway rates. At that time it was, of course, only with Russia that there existed any practical railway problem. In fact, the acceptance of Hay's proposal would have been detrimental even to the financial and economic interests in Manchuria represented in Witte's program of "peaceful penetration." Certainly, the request for the observance of the "territorial and administrative entity" of China represented in the Hay circular notes of July 3, 1900, coming at a time when Russia's position in Manchuria was being directly threatened by the growing militant, anti-foreign Boxer movement, seemed an impossible hope.

Yet the United States saw in the perpetuation of the Russian occupation not only the loss of a valuable commercial stake in Manchuria but, as the British and others also feared, the prospect of the extension of this regime to other parts of China. Henry Miller, the American consul who reached his post at Newchuang in 1901, was convinced that Russia had no intention of loosening her hold on Manchuria and that if she did not American trade there would be "annihilated," a view which was widely shared by others who knew the situation.[61]

This is the reason that the United States went beyond the issuance of circular notes. On October 8, 1903, the anniversary of the unfulfilled Russian promise to remove her troops from Manchuria, the United States joined Japan in signing similar treaties with China calling for the opening

[59] Akira Iriye, *Pacific estrangement. Japanese and American expansion, 1897–1911*, Cambridge, MA, 1972, p. 66.

[60] United States. Dept. of State. *Papers relating to the foreign relations of the United States, 1899*, Washington DC, 1900, pp. 132–133 (hereafter *USFR*).

[61] White, *The diplomacy*, pp. 101 ff.; Alexander Hosie, *Manchuria. Its people, resources and recent history*, Boston, 1910, p. 218; Rosen telegram, June 18, 1903, in Anatolii Kantorovich, *Amerika v bor'be za Kitai*, Moscow, 1935, pp. 154–155; Michael H. Hunt, *Frontier defense and the Open Door. Manchuria in Chinese–American relations, 1895–1911*, New Haven, 1973, pp. 64–76, 82–84.

to foreign residence and trade of the Manchurian towns of Mukden, Tatungkou, and Antung. Baron Rosen, the Russian minister to Japan and then ambassador to the United States, saw this as evidence of "complete mutual political understanding and cooperation" between the United States, Britain, and Japan.

The failure of Russia to withdraw her forces from Manchuria by the appointed time was a severe disappointment to all three of these nations, particularly Japan. But the fact that in addition Russia made new demands on China as a condition of any further withdrawal was seen as ample evidence that Russia had no intention of even considering the relinquishment of her disputed gains.[62]

The point in Russia's present course at which this new and fateful direction had been taken was at a special conference on May 20, 1903 presided over by the Emperor. In fact two significant decisions were taken at that conference. The new withdrawal policy, startling enough in itself, had also the effect of annulling the Sino-Russian understanding of April 8, 1902 regarding the evacuation of Manchuria. But in addition a viceroyalty of the Far East was created at the same time. This was affirmed on August 12, the very day on which the Russo-Japanese negotiations were opened.

The new administrative agency was headed by Admiral Evgenii Ivanovich Alekseev, then commander of the naval forces in the Pacific region and of the Kuantung garrison. Since the viceroy had jurisdiction over all military, economic, administrative, and even diplomatic affairs in the Russian possessions east of Lake Baikal, the new organization made diplomatic transactions difficult and protracted. Also, since it was followed on August 28 by the dismissal of the influential minister of finance, Sergei Iul'evich Witte, who was widely held to be a moderating influence, Russo-Japanese negotiations appeared to be handicapped from the start.

The official and definitive Japanese reaction to the Russian strategy in Manchuria was expressed on June 23, 1903 in a policy statement adopted by an imperial conference intended to insure the security of Japanese interests in Korea.[63] The objective was to be achieved by reducing the Russian threat to both Korea and Manchuria. It was determined to accomplish this in spite of the anticipated rise of hostilities. The decision was conveyed to the British government on July 3 by the Japanese minister in London, Baron Hayashi Tadasu. Through Hayashi the

---

[62] White, *The diplomacy*, pp. 60 ff.; David MacLaren McDonald, *United government and foreign policy in Russia, 1900–1914*, Cambridge, MA, 1992, pp. 52 ff.

[63] White, *The diplomacy*, pp. 101 ff.; Ian Nish, *The origins of the Russo-Japanese war*, London, 1985, pp. 158–162; Nish, *The Anglo-Japanese alliance*, pp. 262–266; Monger, *The end of isolation*, pp. 123–127.

British government was reminded that the permanent occupation of Manchuria by Russia would create a condition prejudicial to the interests of both Britain and Japan, interests "the defense of which was the object of the Anglo-Japanese alliance."

The British government was already aware of the seriousness of the Far Eastern situation through its own intelligence sources. It was known in London that the Russian government had a firmer hold on the Manchurian region occupied by its forces than was generally supposed, that the Russians were determined to establish mastery over the region, and that they could doubtless only be induced by force to withdraw.

While the British government had serious doubts about the ability of Japan to deal successfully with this situation, there were some assuring aspects to the problem. There was the knowledge that the United States was committed to the Japanese side, the assurance that Germany would be likely to remain neutral, and a growing hope that the current negotiations with France would prevent that country from supporting Russia. While the situation was, accordingly, a gamble for Britain, the wager on Japan appeared currently to be the only solution to an extremely difficult problem.

3   The emergence of encirclement

Russia at bay

Russo-Japanese hostilities began formally on February 10, 1904 when Japan declared war on Russia. Japan had decided, after long and careful consideration, to challenge the further progress of Russia's absorption of northeastern Asia. The Russians had not heeded the warnings of some of their own better informed and more perceptive observers that Japan was preparing to resist, forcibly if necessary, and, in all likelihood, effectively the Russian advance. Instead, the Russian government had continued to assume that Japan would not contest their steady but progressive absorption of the continental areas which Japan held vital to her security and future well being. They were accordingly divided in their counsels and unprepared for either the determination and vehemence of the Japanese attack or for the compromises that might have avoided war.

The military weakness of Russia, disclosed early in the struggle, soon led to a search for peace. The Japanese government had prepared for the possibility of having to escape from a difficult turn of events in the war by sending as spokesmen Baron Kaneko Kentaro to the United States and Baron Suematsu Kencho to Britain.

Russia, however, had not been able to take such a precaution and there were, accordingly, no established or suggested channels through which peace could be considered in behalf of Russia. Russian relationships with Germany lacked such an identity of interests. There were ties between the two imperial families and relationships between the two governments and the two economic systems. But the countries were essentially competitive and were both concerned about the security of their frontiers. The Kaiser hoped to keep Russia sufficiently occupied with her Asian frontiers to relieve the pressure on the eastern German frontier. He also insisted, foreseeably, that Russia continue the war until victory had been achieved. This was a condition which was seen increasingly as unrealistic both with respect to the security of Russia and to the growing desire for peace.

With the increasing duality of power among the nations, the search for peace and for a new balance of power tended to merge and to render Germany's effort to counteract the endeavor to reconstruct a new balance

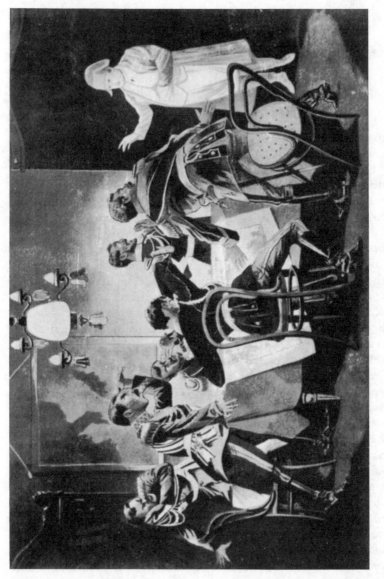

2. The ghost of Napoleon warning the Japanese strategists of the fate of those who invade Russian territory, Russian war cartoon

of power difficult and largely negative. Since Germany was feared because of her growing strength and because of the prospect of upsetting further the balance between the Triple Alliance (Germany, Austria, and Italy) and the Dual Alliance (France and Russia), peace became as much a threat as war to the balance of power.

The Russian foreign policy which had been so important a factor in leading the country into the unfortunate war with Japan was a product of traditional elements as well as miscalculated and mismanaged attempts to deal with new and unfamiliar conditions. It was formulated under influences emanating not only from the Ministry of Foreign Affairs but also from the Ministry of Finance as well as the Council of Ministers and the Emperor or from other sources filtered through one of these institutions. The Foreign Ministry, the conventional source of this policy, was headed during the years 1900–6 by Vladimir Nikolaevich Lamsdorf, a man of considerable ability and of long experience, who had served in senior positions in the ministry for over twenty years.[1]

Because the Russian agreement with Britain was finally concluded only after Lamsdorf's resignation, there has been a tendency to see in his policies an anti-British, even a pro-German emphasis. But this was by no means the case. The Franco-Russian alliance had been transmitted to him from the era of Emperor Alexander III and was the handiwork of his mentor, friend, and predecessor, Nikolai Karlovich Giers, whom he held in great esteem.[2] This alliance was held by Lamsdorf to be the pivot of Russian foreign policy, a guideline which could serve to keep the nation's foreign commitments in balance.

Lamsdorf was devoted to this principle of balance and to the daily tasks required to realize it though he was not at home in the world of the contentious military officers, bureaucrats, and courtiers which characterized the official life of St. Petersburg.[3] He was described by one junior admirer as "short, with a very high forehead and a soft affable manner," with "nothing bureaucratic or imposing" about him. He was seen as a "leisurely, well-bred man of good society," inclined to leave the more abrasive aspects of the bureaucratic process to his friend and close associate, Sergei Witte, the minister of finance. Witte had often supported

---

[1] Russia. *Ocherk istorii Ministerstva inostrannykh del. 1802–1902*, St. Petersburg, 1902, p. 184.

[2] Sergei Iul'evich Witte, *Vospominaniia*, 3 vols. Moscow, 1960, II, 28 n, 112–113; No. 119 Spring Rice to Grey, Feb. 12, 1906, *BD*, IV, 224–225; Eduard Markovich Rozental', *Diplomaticheskaia istoriia Russko-frantsuzskogo soiuza v nachale XX veka*, Moscow, 1960, pp. 229–234.

[3] Andrew D. Kalmykov, *Memoirs of a Russian diplomat. Outposts of the empire, 1893–1917*, New Haven, 1971, pp. 139–140; Mikhail Aleksandrovich Taube [Baron M. de Taube], *La politique russe d'avant-guerre et la fin de l'empire des tsars (1904–1917)*, Paris, 1928, pp. 19, 43.

him and was sorely missed after the minister of finance was dismissed from office in August 1903. Nevertheless, Lamsdorf held firmly to his goals and principles as the test of the North Sea incident of October 1904 showed.

The end of this severe test found Russia safely past the twin dangers which Lamsdorf feared for the Franco-Russian alliance, the threats and offers of friendship of the German Emperor. He told his assistant, Baron Taube [Mikhail Aleksandrovich Taube] as the latter was on the point of leaving for Paris to participate in the international commission which would consider the settlement of the North Sea incident, that in spite of the unfortunate war with Japan, the Anglo-Japanese alliance, or even the North Sea incident itself, he considered the political constellation in the west to be very favorable for Russia. He added that for some persons of importance in Europe Russia's position was like that of a rich bride which none wanted to see fall into the arms of another. Lamsdorf commented regarding his stewardship of the foreign ministry that during his tenure of office he had not and would not advance one step further toward Potsdam than toward Buckingham Palace. He did not mention Tokyo in this context even though the Russo-Japanese rivalry had already led to war.

Lamsdorf's adherence to the Franco-Russian alliance was based not only on national and departmental traditions but also upon a single-minded perception of its benefits to the nation. He courageously defended this stance even after the dismissal of Witte left him without support. Like the minister of finance he regarded as very unfortunate the earlier eastward shift of Russia's responsibilities and commitments. Lamsdorf particularly regretted the aggressive economic and military posture which appeared to him to be driving Russia headlong and unprepared into a clash with Japan. This course had, to be sure, been set before Lamsdorf became minister of foreign affairs. Witte himself, although he had intended a comparatively gradual approach to the Far Eastern expansion, was to a considerable extent responsible for it.

The Russo-German agreement concluded at Björkö in 1905, after the dismissal of Witte, Lamsdorf also saw as unfavorable to the interests of Russia and, along with Witte upon his return from negotiating the Portsmouth settlement, took a strong stand against it. He earned thereby the ill-will of the German government some members of which considered him the wrecker of the scheme.

Both the German press and government mounted a campaign against Lamsdorf similar to that which had helped to drive the French foreign minister, Delcassé, from office, only a month before, in June 1905, This was noted in England where Sir Charles Hardinge, the ambassador to St. Petersburg, wrote that even though Lamsdorf was weak and indecisive, "he is an element of law and order and is, I really believe, well disposed toward us."[4]

Before Lamsdorf became minister of foreign affairs in June 1900 a new and more assertive course had been set for Russia in Asia by Witte, the minister of finance, and others. While Witte agreed with Lamsdorf's concept of a foreign policy balanced between Britain and Germany, he was also interested in expansion in Asia. He saw such growth as possible if it were projected gradually and under relatively non-abrasive conditions, by economic or financial rather than military means.

This did not mean that Witte neglected military force; he apparently did not slight the armed forces to the extent that General Kuropatkin, the minister of war, claimed. And it is also by no means true that Witte saw no relationship between economics and foreign policy. On the contrary, it would be far closer to the truth to say that he wanted to shape foreign policy to fit economic objectives.

Witte laid the foundation for such an economic program in three principal acts between 1894 and 1896. The first of these was the acquisition of the Persian Loan Company in 1894 and its conversion into the Persian Discount and Loan Bank. The second was the Russo-Chinese Bank, the charter for which was signed December 5, 1895.[5] The banks provided a means of economic aggrandizement by the Russian finance ministry under cover of banking institutions that suggested the private financial methods of the other competing powers. The third of these instruments of economic outreach was the Chinese Eastern Railway, the contract for which was signed on September 8, 1896. Along with the bank this provided a far better means of reaching out into the rich provinces of Manchuria and to Port Arthur and Dalny (Dairen) than Russia could hope for in Persia.

Witte's methods and even his achievements were called into question, particularly after his program of economic development faltered around the turn of the century and was replaced by depression. As his critics became bolder they extended their disparaging comments to various other aspects of his program, including foreign affairs. General Kuropatkin, the minister of war, held that Witte's economic program had not only neglected the defense needs of the country but that his development program in Manchuria had overextended Russian defense requirements and unduly burdened the defense establishment in an area of the frontier

---

[4] Hardinge to Lansdowne, Dec. 6, 1901, FO 800/140.
[5] Anan'ich, "Iz istorii Anglo-russkogo sopernichestva," pp. 275–282; Petr Mikhailovich Golovachev, *Rossiia na Dal'nem Vostoke*, St. Petersburg, 1904, pp. 159 ff.; Malozemoff, *Russian Far Eastern policy*, p. 71.

which was, in his view, of far lower priority than the western frontier facing Germany.

The decision which actually brought the Far Eastern situation to a hostile climax was made with the approval and with the recommendation of Murav'ev, Lamsdorf's immediate predecessor, and with the disapproval and opposition of Witte. At a special ministerial conference held on November 26, 1897 the question was considered whether to acquire a port on the Liaotung peninsula, preferably Talienwan (later Dairen). After a discussion it was decided not to acquire any port at that location. However, sometime between the date of the conference and December 11, 1897 this announced decision was reversed. It is not known how this came about, only that the Emperor announced the decision to occupy Port Arthur.[6]

Witte had opposed the project on two basic grounds. He had maintained that such an action at that time would violate the spirit and intent of the Russo-Chinese agreement of June 3, 1896 by which Russia enjoyed her advantageous relationship with China in exchange for protecting China from pressures exerted by the other powers. It could, of course, lead to the dissolution of China. He asserted further that seizing a port would be doing exactly what Russia, along with France and Germany, had prevented Japan from doing in 1895. This, he predicted, would at once deprive Russia of Chinese cooperation and could lead to war with Japan.

It is also true that Russia had seized Port Arthur at the cost of violating one of her own guidelines observed during her territorial expansion: not to acquire any area which was discontinuous with the main body of Russian territory and therefore difficult to defend. Communications with Port Arthur were possible by land only if part of the intervening region of Chinese Manchuria were appropriated or if a railway were constructed to Port Arthur. Choosing the second alternative, the South Manchurian railway which Russia proceeded to construct was already by June 1900 an arena of serious conflict with the Chinese Boxers. Furthermore, the right of Russia to continue freely to construct railways was already being challenged by China and Britain. Likewise, the 1,100 mile maritime route from Vladivostok to Port Arthur passing through the Tsushima strait became increasingly dangerous as the Japanese navy developed.

The six months from August 1903 to February 1904 offered the final opportunity to achieve through negotiation an operable formula for coexistence. Long before the Japanese government had sent its fourth and final set of proposals on January 13 it was clear to those who were able to follow the course of the negotiations that the prospects for peace were not good. In fact, the visit of the Russian foreign minister, Count Lamsdorf,

[6] Malozemoff, *Russian Far Eastern policy*, p. 101; Witte, *The memoirs of Count Witte*, pp. 229–237.

to Paris during October 28–31, 1903 became the occasion for an attempt to clear up some of the points known then to be in dispute.[7]

Baron Komura, the foreign minister of Japan, also saw that occasion as an opportunity to seek a clarification of some of the difficult questions. He hoped that because of the incomplete state of Russian military preparation and of the fact that, by Komura's own estimate, the effective Japanese forces in the zone of operations were nearly double those of Russia, a firm attitude on the part of Japan might induce Russia to take a moderate stand.[8]

There was at the same time the conviction expressed by Baron Komura and apparently held generally by the members of the Japanese cabinet that if mediation were undertaken the Russians would only use the time this would occupy "for the completion of their warlike preparations."[9] Furthermore, Komura saw the real difficulty as lying beyond the reach of mediation, viz., in the often indistinct domain of the factions within the Russian government contending respectively for war and peace. The respite provided by a mediation might, according to Komura's view, only favor the war party. In short, the foreign minister feared that time favored Russia.

This was a point of view which Witte, then holding the largely non-functional office of chairman of the Committee of Ministers, had only recently expressed in the course of an interview with the Japanese minister, Kurino Shinichiro. Since Russia was bound in the end to win the contest with Japan for the mainland of Asia, Witte continued, it would be better in the long run for Japan to be content with a "frontier which Russia could not transgress – that is the sea." Under these assumptions, it would seem wise for Japan to limit severely the duration of any period of mediation in which she and Russia were involved.

A distinct change had, by mid-January 1904, come about in the conduct of the negotiations. The new Japanese proposals of January 13 were drawn from a document entitled grimly "The Final Japanese Proposals for the Russo-Japanese Negotiations regarding Manchuria and Korea." These had been approved at an imperial council held the day before and were met with a different spirit in St. Petersburg, perhaps, as has been suggested, in some way connected with the fact that this was the

---

[7] No. 264 Cambon to Delcassé, Oct. 27, 1903, *DDF*, IV, 66–67; No. 22 Harmand to Delcassé, Oct. 29, 1903, No. 195, Delcassé to Boutiron, Nov. 4, Nos. 283, 284 Cambon to Delcassé, Nov. 11, 1903, *DDF*, IV, 70, 80, 103–105; No. 8 Komura to Motono, Jan. 14, 1904, Japan. Foreign Office. "Diplomatic Correspondence" – letters, telegrams, misc. items.

[8] No. 22 Harmand (Tokyo) to Delcassé, Oct. 29, 1903, *DDF*, IV, 70.

[9] No. 2 MacDonald to Lansdowne, Jan. 7, 1904, No. 10 MacDonald to Lansdowne, Jan. 18. 1904, FO 46/577; memorandum between Mr. Kurino and M. de Witte (interview of Dec. 30, 1904), Jan. 12, 1904, enclosure in No. 27 Scott to Lansdowne, Jan. 20, 1904, FO 65/1678.

Russian new year according to the Russian Julian calendar.[10] Or perhaps, as current proceedings indicate, the government was facing a dilemma between its tenuous assumptions about Japan and the apparent realities. In addition to its untested conceptions about the Japanese, there was the German Emperor's encouragement of these views by which he urged Russia to defy Japan, annex all of Manchuria, and even assert Russian dominance over Korea. In spite of this, the Russian Emperor took what he considered to be a step toward conciliation by requesting the French foreign minister, Delcassé, to undertake personal intervention in the negotiations.

This step may have been taken in response to a special ministerial conference held in St. Petersburg at which General Kuropatkin, the minister of war, and Viacheslav Konstantinovich Plehve, the minister of interior, were said to have given strong support to peace. Kuropatkin had warned that under present conditions a war in the Far East would be more costly and protracted than was commonly supposed and that to secure any decisive results Japan would have to be crushed. But if such an outcome appeared possible, it must be assumed that both Britain and the United States might become co-belligerents on the side of Japan, thus creating for Russia an impossible situation.

Delcassé first broached the subject of a personal intervention on January 13 to Motono Ichiro, the Japanese ambassador in Paris.[11] He told Motono that the Russian Emperor wanted peace and that, after a careful study of the claims of both parties, he had concluded that the points over which discord continued "are in no way of such a nature as to render worth while a great war." The points of difference were, nevertheless, not only serious but fundamental. Furthermore, in contrast with the situation in Russia where the conduct of the negotiations was decentralized and handled partly in St. Petersburg and partly by the Russian viceroy at Port Arthur, Baron Komura kept tight control of the entire process in a way typical of the importance it had had in Tokyo from the first.

In accordance with this policy of firm control of the process, Komura wrote to Kurino in St. Petersburg: "You will be careful not to make any remark or to express any opinion even in your own personal capacity. If he (i.e., Lamsdorf) seeks explanations on any point you will ask for instructions."[12] The attitude of Komura on mediation had been accurately expressed by Baron Hayashi: "Should Russia seek or accept mediation, she would do so simply for the purpose of gaining time in order to

---

[10] White, *The diplomacy*, pp. 121–123; No. 23 Komura to Kurino, Jan. 14, 1904, JFO; No. 33 Scott to Lansdowne, Jan. 21, 1904, FO 65/1678; Maurice Paléologue, *Three critical years (1904–05–06)*, New York, 1957, p. 5 (dates of Jan. 13 and 19); Maurice Bompard, *Mon ambassade en Russie (1903–1908)*, Paris, 1937, p. 46; Nos. 283, 284 Cambon to Delcassé, Nov. 11, 1903, *DDF*, IV, 103–105; Judge, *Plehve*, pp. 170–171; Robinson, "The Franco-Russian Alliance," pp. 509 ff.

strengthen and consolidate her position in the Far East without any desire to come to a complete and permanent understanding on the present questions."

It was against the backdrop of this suspicious and unpromising circumstance that Delcassé received a telegram from London, transferring to him a message from Baron Komura through Baron Hayashi in London.[13] In it Komura suggested that Russia consider these questions: settlements in Manchuria, a neutral zone in Korea, and the territorial integrity of China in Manchuria. He might have added a fourth question – the freedom of Japan to use Korea for strategic purposes.

In his communication to Komura acknowledging receipt of these instructions, Motono took note of Komura's concern over permitting any delay in the negotiations by assuring him of the sincerity of Delcassé in wanting peace and in respecting the wishes of both sides. He noted the enormous French investment in Russia which he estimated at about 10 billion francs and the concern in France that war would cause a drop in value of Russian securities.

The personal intervention in Paris was brought to an end by January 22 and the negotiations were returned to St. Petersburg where Japan's efforts were concentrated on getting a response to her last proposal.[14] But even in St. Petersburg both the official channel through Lamsdorf and the less official channels through Aleksandr Mikhailovich Bezobrazov, Rear Admiral Aleksei Mikhailovich Abaza, and Witte were tried. With the end of personal mediation, Komura instructed Motono to tell Delcassé that the last Japanese proposals were to be considered an irreducible minimum. This pronouncement stunned Motono himself for it closed off the possibility of all compromise with Russia at a time when crucial issues were unresolved.

It seemed at first to be a favorable omen that sole control of negotiations had been returned to Lamsdorf, setting aside the delays and influence of the viceroy of the Far East.[15] This meant that if all went well messages would go directly from St. Petersburg to Baron Roman Romanovich Rosen in Tokyo or at least notification would go to Japan as to when to expect an answer. Unfortunately, when the Russian answer to Japan was ready to send, Lamsdorf told Bompard that Bezobrazov had persuaded the Emperor that it should not be sent without the advice of the viceroy and that it had been transmitted to him.

[11] No. 11 Motono to Komura, Jan. 13, 1904, JFO
[12] Komura to Kurino, Jan. 14, 1904, JFO, *Nihon Gaiko Bunsho*, Tokyo, XLVII, 34 (hereafter *NGB*); No. 6 Lansdowne to MacDonald, Jan. 5, 1904, *BD*, II, 229–230.
[13] No. 13 Motono to Komura, Jan. 16, 1904, JFO
[14] No. 22 Motono to Komura, Jan. 24, 1904, No. 70 Kurino to Komura, Jan. 30, 1904, No. 17 Komura to Motono, Jan. 27, 1904, JFO
[15] No. 18 Scott to Lansdowne, Jan. 26, 1904, FO 65/1684; Bompard, *Mon ambassade en Russie*, p. 48 (Feb. 1).

The most crucial of the unresolved issues and one of great interest to both Britain and Japan was that of recognition of the territorial integrity of China in Manchuria. Delcassé understood fully the seriousness of the issue to both parties but thought that to speak of the independence and integrity of a country to which another power might send and station troops was not a serious position.[16] But neither party agreed with this. The issues for which they were contending were too serious to surrender the prize on such unsubstantial grounds.

Bezobrazov summarized as follows a fundamental Russian contention regarding Manchuria as reported by Kurino:

It was clearly impossible ... after immense expenditure and sacrifice which Russia has incurred in Manchuria, to abandon the Russian interests and enterprises acquired there to the mercy of foreign competition. These enterprises, he added with revelatory candor, could not be developed with any hope of profit if they had to compete on equal terms with the commerce and industry of Japan and other foreign nations ...[17]

Russia was willing, he stated, to recognize the rights and privileges, except for settlements, enjoyed by other powers in Manchuria under existing treaties.

The Japanese government, in a corollary to this fundamental concept, expressed its suspicion that behind the Russian refusal to make any concession that would compromise her existing rights, interests, and future prospects in Manchuria lay the intention to annex the region.[18] Lansdowne expressed the idea aptly in an interview with the Russian ambassador. He asked the ambassador if it were not natural, since Russia was in military occupation of Manchuria and had not carried out pledges to evacuate her forces from it, "that Japan should desire to be protected by a distinct engagement that sovereignty of China was not to be called into question."

A solution was sought in a formula whereby China's sovereignty in Manchuria could be guaranteed by a separate Russo-Japanese agreement or by an agreement among all the powers concerned.[19] But by the time Hayashi had received an answer from Tokyo it was too late for Japan to entertain the idea. The question was a vital one to Japan, not only because of possible loss of benefits from a closed door in Manchuria but also because of the constant and growing menace to Korea. This region, lying

---

[16] No. 16 Motono to Komura, Jan. 17, 1904, JFO; No. 19 Delcassé to Bompard, Jan. 17, 1904, *DDF*, IV, 264–265.

[17] No. 6 Scott to Lansdowne, Jan. 6, 1904, FO 65/1678; No. 11 Komura to Motono, Jan. 15, 1904, No. 11 Takahira to Komura, Jan. 12, 1904, JFO

[18] Delcassé to Cogordan (director of political affairs), Jan. 6, 1904, *DDF*, IV, 220–221; Lansdowne to MacDonald, Jan. 28, 1904, FO 46/580.

[19] No. 31 Lansdowne to MacDonald, Feb. 4, No. 36 Lansdowne to MacDonald, Feb. 8, 1904, FO 46/580.

directly on the frontier, would almost certainly be occupied and monopolized by Russia, giving these frontier territories a common border, a condition each considered threatening. The failure to reach some accord on this issue left it as the principal grounds for the war that followed.

The question of settlements had become a legal and diplomatic issue for Japan as a consequence of the conclusion with China of similar commercial agreements by the United States and Japan on October 8, 1903, the anniversary of the day on which Russia had pledged to have all her forces withdrawn from Manchuria.[20] These compacts provided for the opening up of the Manchurian cities of Mukden, Tatungkou, and Antung for foreign residence and trade. Russia opposed any settlements in Manchuria under these treaties claiming that the treaties were not in existence when she acquired her rights in Manchuria. Furthermore, such settlements, Russia maintained, made possible growing numbers of immigrants to Manchuria, an increasing need for their protection, and thus a progressive encroachment on Manchuria.

The Japanese held that the exclusion of settlements "would be inconsistent with the terms of their new commercial treaty with China, that it implied a serious limitation which would arouse the resentment of Japan, that it would be an obstacle to Japanese immigration to Manchuria, and that, since it applied only to Japan, it would be a serious blow to her amour-propre."[21] However, Japan agreed not to press this issue if she were to receive "equal treatment with another Power which had acquired a similar right of settlement in Manchuria."

A provision prohibiting the use of any part of Korean territory for strategic purposes had survived through the Russian counter proposals in the third exchange dated January 6, 1904. Japan's objection was simply that since there was no such guarantee regarding Russian use of Manchuria, it was natural that it should not exist in Korea. Otherwise there would be no equality of the means of defending established rights and interests. But Lamsdorf found it impossible to see how this provision could be suppressed at a time when Russia had accorded Japan the right to send troops to Korea to suppress disorder and protect her nationals. To do so would be to lose the means of safeguarding the independence and sovereignty of Korea, both of which had been supported by the Anglo-Japanese alliance and the Franco-Russian declaration of 1902 regarding the Far East.[22]

[20] White, *The diplomacy*, pp. 106–107; No. 19 Delcassé to Bompard, Jan. 17, 1904, *DDF*, IV, 264–265. No. 2 Cambon to Delcassé, Jan. 18, 1904, *DDF*, IV, 271–272.
[21] Komura to Motono, Jan. 15, 1904, No. 16 Motono to Komura, Jan. 17, No. 15 Komura to Motono, Jan. 22, 1904, JFO; Henry N. Whitney, "British foreign policy and the Russo-Japanese War," Ph.D. dissertation, University of Pennsylvania, 1948, pp. 116–117.
[22] No. 9 Bompard to Delcassé, Jan. 16, 1904, *DDF*, IV, 259–262.

Lamsdorf also refused to recognize the right of Japan to discuss the outcome of Russian military establishments in Manchuria and thus make it a matter of reciprocity.[23] The issue was stubbornly contested on both sides and was not resolved; it reappeared in the final Russian counter proposals dated February 3, 1904.

The last among the most troublesome issues was raised by Russia's insistence that the part of Korea north of the 39th parallel be observed as a neutral zone. For Russia this would not only have created a convenient buffer area for Manchuria but a shield for the Briner timber concession south of the Yalu River. Yet the Russian government showed signs of willingness to negotiate this issue.

In the counter proposals of December 11, 1903, Russia had specified on the one hand that neither party might send troops into the neutral zone and, on the other, that the Chinese Eastern Railway in Manchuria and the Korean railways might be joined.[24] The Japanese saw in this a contradiction since it would render it impossible for Japan to protect any railway she might build through the neutral zone or, for that matter, to protect any of her rights and interests there. This issue was resolved, however, and did not appear among the final Russian counter proposals.

European counterpoint

One of the most serious immediate consequences of the outbreak of the Russo-Japanese war was the deterioration of Anglo-Russian relations. The apparent irony that the encouraging efforts toward accommodation should so quickly become a casualty of the hostilities with Japan was in reality an understandable outgrowth of the rivalry which the concurrent Anglo-Russian negotiations were attempting to abate. It was also a natural reaction to the Anglo-Japanese alliance, the purpose of which was to dampen the expansive propensity of Russia.

Prince Vladimir Petrovich Meshchersky was one of those who saw in the Japanese attack the result of British encouragement.[25] He stated in the pages of *Grazhdanin* in late January, as the Russo-Japanese negotiations were reaching a climax, that Britain was the real enemy of Russia, the "one irreconcilable and unalterable foe." She had incited Japan to attack Russia to make it easier for her to annex Tibet, the territory of which a British expedition was even then just entering.

Meshchersky urged that Russia reach a peaceful settlement with Japan and concentrate her efforts on thwarting this British plan. "Only those

[23] Bompard to Delcassé, Jan. 18, 1904, *DDF*, IV, 271–272.
[24] White, *The diplomacy*, pp. 353–354; No. 19 Delcassé to Bompard, Jan. 17, 1904, *DDF*, IV, 264–265; No. 16 Motono to Komura, Jan. 17, 1904, JFO
[25] No. 38 Scott to Lansdowne, Jan. 26, 1904, FO 65/1678.

3. London Royal Fusiliers marching through Lhasa

Russians who are tainted with the poison of cosmopolitanism," he wrote, "can fail to recognize that Russia will only have lasting peace in her foreign relations when the moment comes for the struggle with England."

This point was made with equal force in an article entitled, "The Future War between Russia and England" which had appeared in an issue of the *Bakinskie Izvestia* (Baku News) and was sent to London on February 8, 1904 by the British consul in Batum.[26] It stated: "The idea of a war between Russia and England has long since become rooted in the minds of the Russian public. This general view is based on good grounds." The article was even more precise; it stated that "this collision will take place in India and Afghanistan."

Sir Charles Hardinge explained that this desperate view was not shared by the Russian naval authorities who foresaw in a clash with Britain the destruction of the Baltic fleet and the end of any possibility of retrieving the Far Eastern naval situation. This was an interesting forecast of the outcome eight months later of the actual encounter between the Russian Baltic fleet and the British fishing boats in the North Sea.

The surprise which many in St. Petersburg experienced as they

[26] No. 3 Consul Stevens to Lansdowne, Feb. 8, 1904, enclosing article, "The future of war between Russia and England," from *The Bakinskie Izvestiia*, FO 106/8; Busch, *Hardinge of Penshurst*, p. 82.

watched the Japanese assume a determined and then a hostile position in the Far Eastern controversy was undoubtedly the consequence to some extent of a misunderstanding of the issue. Some had failed to take seriously the warnings of General Kuropatkin or General Dean Ivano-vich Subotich that Russia would fight at a great disadvantage on such a distant frontier, of Count Lamsdorf that Russia should not allow a balance of her national power to become redistributed in such a way as to endanger her European flank, or even of Witte who advocated and practiced a slower and less abrasive form of expansion from the southern and eastern frontiers of Russia. Finally, there was the view about which Spring Rice wrote with some slight exaggeration in early February: "Russia has been successful for many years in Asia in the policy of peaceful penetration – especially with England, who raised some ineffec-tual howls, and ran; Japan had no question but one, that is Asia – and did not run. We spoiled Russia and she has taken the consequences."[27]

Russian sensitivity to British comments on the course of the war was also in part a reflection of the awareness of her own inadequacies. Such was the comment made by Mechislav Vladislavovich Rutkovsky, the agent of the Russian Ministry of Finance in London, who in early March described how *The Times, The Financial Times, The Economist* and other British newspapers informed the public. He noted how the press dealt with such subjects as the resources of Japan and the exhaustion of Russian finances and how it warned the public against taking any part in a Russian loan which was expected to be announced immediately.[28]

There was considerable apprehension among some in Russia as to the possible influence of the British press on the French bankers to whom Russia would be looking for a loan. In view of these obstacles, the Russian ambassador in Paris, Aleksandr Ivanovich Nelidov, was even then advising the minister of finance, Vladimir Nikolaevich Kokovtsov, against the large loan of 1 billion francs which the latter saw as necessary and suggesting a postponement of the application for the loan.

The tendency of some in the Russian government in spite of warnings from both Lamsdorf and General Kuropatkin, to underrate the Japanese determination to assert themselves in pursuit of their interests caused them to find Japanese readiness to resist Russian pressure "inconceiv-able." Consequently, after the outbreak of war they blamed Britain or even the United States for inciting Japan to take action and found imaginary instances of British complicity with Japan in the war itself.

[27] Spring Rice (St. Petersburg) to President Theodore Roosevelt, n.d. but probably in Feb. 1904, in Stephen L. Gwynn (ed.), *The letters and friendships of Sir Cecil Spring Rice. A record*, 2 vols. Boston, 1929, I, 394; No. 526 Hardinge to Lansdowne, Sept. 6, 1905, FO 65/1702.

[28] Boris Vasil'evich Anan'ich, *Rossiia i mezhdunarodnyi kapital, 1897–1914*, Leningrad, 1970, pp. 98–101.

These included the report that the British base at Weihaiwei had been the point of departure for the Japanese ships which attacked the Russian fleet at Port Arthur and the accusation of the complicity of Hull fishermen in the imaginary attack of the Japanese torpedo boats on the Russian Baltic fleet in the creation of the North Sea incident.

The impact of this disturbing and openly expressed view in Britain was to generate considerable apprehension and to alert the government to watch with extra care the usual trouble spots such as Central Asia and the course of German–Russian relations. The British military attaché in St. Petersburg suggested that: "If matters go badly with Russia in the Far East . . . it is possible she will look southwards to retrieve some of her lost prestige in what is regarded by many Russians as an easier and more profitable campaign towards India or endeavour by a large concentration of troops to intimidate England into a policy opposed to Japan."[29]

Colonel Napier called attention to the continuing work on the Orenburg–Tashkent railway and the great impact its completion could have on the strength of Russia along the Afghan frontier. He noted the depots being constructed at 200 mile intervals along the line, each with the capacity to provide 1,000 men at a time with hot meals. The significance of this was the subject of a comment made by Cecil Spring Rice in a letter to his sister in which he wrote that while the war with Japan was very unpopular, a war with Britain would be very popular.[30]

The evidence which prompted British apprehension about the Russian attitude was noted also by Japan and Germany.[31] Both Benckendorff and Count Paul Wolff Metternich zur Gracht, the Russian and German ambassadors respectively, noted the growing unpopularity in Britain of the Anglo-Japanese alliance, the British government tending to underplay it in some cases while the newspapers stressed the neutral position of Britain. It is likely that Lansdowne's concern expressed to the American ambassador, that before the end of the war Russia might attempt to appropriate Manchuria completely, a point strongly emphasized in the Anglo-Russian negotiations, was inspired much more by the menace of the anti-British attitude of Russia than by events in the Far East. It was quite clear that the feeling developing in Russia could serve not only as a stimulus to Anglo-Russian conflict but to the development of a German–Russian rapprochement and even, as some feared, to the revival of the Franco-Russo-German triplice of 1895.

The fear which drove the British at that time to let no opportunity pass

[29] No. 12 Napier to Scott, Feb. 18, 1904, FO 65/1678.
[30] Spring Rice to (sister) Margaret, Mar. 3, 1904, in Gwynn, *Letters and friendships*, I, 394.
[31] Whitney, "British foreign policy," pp. 131–147; No. 17 Napier to Scott, Mar. 17, 1904, FO 65/1679; Spring Rice to Louis (Mallet?), Mar. 28, 1904, FO 800/139; No. 234 Metternich to Bülow, Mar. 14, 1904, *GP*, XIX-1, 167–172.

to achieve an accommodation with Russia was noted by Sir Cecil Spring Rice in a letter to President Theodore Roosevelt: "The reason we are doing so is that with the establishment of a strong German navy on our flanks we can't afford to have a life and death struggle in Asia and the Far East. Germany is rapidly acquiring a strong position in Russia."[32] He stressed the importance in international relations of the German navy and, above all, "Unfortunately the crux of the situation is – neither America nor England will consent to compulsory military and naval service. That being so, we can't compete with 'million' armies."

This may have been the fear which inspired some liberal leaders to go so far as to suggest the repudiation of the Anglo-Japanese alliance in favor of a determined effort to come to terms with Russia. The assumption, probably correct, that if forced by some crisis or turn in the war to make a choice between Britain and Russia, France would undoubtedly choose the latter, made it seem prudent in London to endeavor to avoid the need for such a choice.

The climax, though by no means the last, of the British efforts to mollify Russian susceptibilities, came in April 1904 and coincided with King Edward's visit to Copenhagen on the occasion of King Christian's birthday. In the absence of Emperor Nicholas who would normally have been present at such a gathering, King Edward dined at the British legation on April 14 with the Russian minister, Aleksandr Petrovich Izvolsky, already considered by some as the possible successor of Lamsdorf.[33] The King was well impressed with this old school diplomat who had received part of his political education under Prince Gorchakov and appeared to be "a man of generous sympathies, of well-balanced judgement, and harmonious temper" with "a high reputation for honour and integrity."

The King explained to Izvolsky that the Anglo-French entente had been concluded only six days before and was looked upon in London as a step toward a similar accord with Russia, an outcome which was hoped for as soon as conditions permitted. The King, in response to Izvolsky's assertion that the Anglo-Japanese alliance was the principal cause of the war with Japan, minimized the alliance as a factor in this incident. He informed the Russian minister that in May Sir Charles Hardinge would go as the new envoy to St. Petersburg with the specific charge of seeking the earliest opportunity to reach an understanding with Russia similar to the one just concluded with France.

This congenial and conciliatory conversation provided the focus for a

---

[32] Spring Rice to Roosevelt, n.d. but in reply to a Roosevelt letter of June 13, 1904, in Gwynn, *Letters and friendships*, I, 422.

[33] Lee, *King Edward VII*, II, 284–285, 289; No. 176 Lansdowne to Spring Rice, Apr. 22, 1904, No. 188A Lansdowne to Spring Rice, May 4, 1904 (apparently not sent until May 10), *BD*, IV, 188–189, 189–190; Newton, *Lord Lansdowne*, p. 308.

general reaffirmation of the objective until recently pursued of seeking an Anglo-Russian understanding.[34] The King on his return to London and Izvolsky in his report to St. Petersburg followed this interview by discussions of Hardinge and Lamsdorf in St. Petersburg and of Lansdowne and Benckendorff in London. These provided the constructive atmosphere needed for the consideration of such issues as the Anglo-Japanese alliance and the Anglo-French entente as well as current problems such as that raised by the British expedition then proceeding into Tibet.

It was a matter of considerable importance that both Lamsdorf and the Tsar agreed with the King and Lansdowne in seeing the Anglo-French entente as a step toward an Anglo-Russian agreement. Furthermore, the presence of Hardinge, who had visited Copenhagen with the King, in St. Petersburg after May was the best possible guarantee that every opportunity would be used to further the "new course" in British foreign policy looking toward an accord. Hopefully, this would also leave the Russian government as little reason as possible to follow through with the alleged assertion that it had no intention of pursuing further the proposals for agreement elaborated in the course of 1903.

The various efforts to placate Russia appear to have had some results well before mid-year; Hardinge reported that "since my arrival ten days ago there has not been a single attack on England in the Russian press."[35] But this situation required constant watching by the very able ambassador in St. Petersburg. In August he cautioned the British government in London about hasty action against Russian ships of the Volunteer Fleet which were passing the Turkish straits as merchant vessels and then appearing armed on the high seas. Precipitate action might encourage those in Russia who feared the fall of Port Arthur and who would have preferred "to yield to a combination of Britain and Japan" and to gain Herat as an offset to the loss of Port Arthur rather than face defeat at the hands of Japan alone. Hardinge's presence in St. Petersburg and the after-effects of the gathering in Copenhagen were also of great value during the tense days when the crucial North Sea Incident was being negotiated and when final defeat encouraged advocates of desperate measures.

It was also during the early months of the war and while foreign loans

---

[34] No. 256 Hardinge (St. Petersburg) to Lansdowne, May 18, 1904, *BD*, IV, 190–192; Khvostov, *Istoriia diplomatii*, II, 544; Whitney, "British foreign policy," pp. 138–139; Jaeckel, *Die Nordwestgrenze*, p. 165 (citing No. 168A Lansdowne to Scott, Apr. 19, 1904, FO 65/1677); Ostal'tseva, "Anglo-frantsuzskoe soglashenie," 247; Busch, *Hardinge of Penshurst*, pp. 69–96.

[35] Hardinge to Lansdowne, May 25, Aug. 4, 1904, FO 800/139; Consul General C. S. Smith (Odessa) to Lansdowne, Oct. 11, No. 397 Lansdowne to Hardinge, Nov. 3, 1904, FO 418/27; Law Officers of the Crown to Lansdowne, Oct. 29, 1904, FO 418/20; No. 150 Hardinge to Lansdowne, Oct. 25, 1904, FO 65/1729.

were under consideration that the climax of the protracted Anglo-French diplomatic negotiations was reached. The entente was concluded on April 8, 1904, the anniversary of the unfulfilled Russian agreement to evacuate her troops from Manchuria.[36] This was an agreement of great importance to the principals in that the "unexpressed major premise" was clearly the security it provided against Germany, a factor which had acquired greater meaning only with the outbreak of the Russo-Japanese war and the possibility that each of the signatories might be drawn into it on an opposing side.

There was also no doubt that the conclusion of the Anglo-Japanese alliance followed by the war between the Russian and Japanese allies of France and Britain respectively had endangered the Far Eastern position of France. This had provided her with a reason for seeking a rapprochement with Britain, particularly one which would settle their differences over various parts of the world, especially Egypt and Morocco. Their agreement did this in nine public and five secret articles in addition to a Khedival decree concerning Egypt.

The North African aspect of the agreement defined the respective positions of Britain in Egypt and of France in Morocco. France agreed not to require a time limit for the British occupation of Egypt but to leave Britain a free hand there. The annexed Khedival decree created a new set of rules and relationships between the Egyptian government and the bondholders. Also, so far as the French government was concerned, the Caisse de la Dette was shorn of its powers to interfere in the financial administration of the country, leaving the Caisse in the position of a receiving and distributing agency for the bondholders.[37] The Egyptian treasury would thereby be able freely to dispose of its own revenues.

The agreement also recognized the special position of France as a colonial power in Algeria and consequently as the immediate neighbor of Morocco. In this relationship France was accorded the right to maintain order in Morocco and to carry out reforms there, both permitted in order to make Morocco a safer neighbor. It provided that the territory opposite Gibraltar should remain unfortified and that this region should be maintained as a neutral zone. Should this area be in danger of becoming

[36] Joseph J. Mathews, *Egypt and the formation of the Anglo-French entente of 1904*, Philadelphia, 1939, pp. 96–102; Fay, *Origins of the World War*, I, 152–168; Declaration between the United Kingdom and France respecting Egypt and Morocco, signed at London, April 8, 1904, *BD*, II, 385–395; Whitney, "British foreign policy," p. 53.
[37] John Marlowe, *Cromer in Egypt*, New York, 1970, p. 252.
[38] Lyle A. McGeoch, "British policy and the Spanish corollary to the Anglo-French Agreement of 1904," in Nancy Baker and Marvin Brown, Jr. (eds.), *Diplomacy in an age of nationalism. Essays in honor of Lynn Marshall Case*, The Hague, 1976, pp. 209–222; Taylor, *The struggle for mastery in Europe*, pp. 411–417, 420–422 (map p. 416); Cedric James Lowe and M.L. Dockrill, *The mirage of power*, 3 vols. London, 1972, I, 7–9.

separated from the control of Morocco and of passing into the control of any other major power, it should be committed to the control of Spain.[38] By agreement with Britain, France came to a separate understanding with Spain supporting this arrangement which was concluded on October 3, 1904. This has been referred to as the Spanish corollary of the Anglo-French agreement. Spain, by this agreement, received a narrow strip of northern Morocco which was to be observed as a neutral zone.

The opportunity arose immediately after the conclusion of the entente agreement for the adherence of Russia to one aspect of it and thus for bringing into being a rudimentary form of the Triple Entente which was so basic to both the British and French plans. In this case the problem was British need for approval of the Khedival decree by powers other than France which were parties to the Egyptian debt control, and thus the liberation of Egypt from international fiscal controls and the desire of Russia for a guarantee against the British establishment of a protectorate over Tibet.[39]

The opening of the Russo-Japanese war had interrupted the course of what might have been promising Anglo-Russian negotiations. Nevertheless, it was understood that, even though the long-range discussions were suspended, questions that needed more immediate attention would be brought up. One of these was the concern that each had over the intentions of the other in Tibet and especially Russian concern over the advantage Britain had both during the war as well as the more permanent leverage she had because of her direct boundary with Tibet. But the conclusion of the Anglo-French entente and the fact that Russia was both an ally of France and a party to the Egyptian debt commission opened the way for some profitable bargaining on both sides. In dispatches of May 4 and 10, 1904 Britain gave Russia the assurances she desired over her role in Tibet while Russia gave her approval to the Khedival decree, thus making it easier for Britain to become master in her Egyptian house.

The most immediate impact of the Anglo-French entente was unquestionably the need of the contracting parties to reduce the likelihood that, since their respective allies, Russia and Japan, had actually reached the point of open hostilities, one of them would be drawn in and thus fulfill the condition which would engulf the other partner. Count Johann-Heinrich von Bernstorff, counselor of the German embassy in London,

---

[39] No. 188A Lansdowne to Spring Rice, May 4, 1904, *BD*, IV, 189–190, No. 190 Lansdowne to Spring Rice, May 10, 1904, *BD*, IV, 307–309, No. 256 Hardinge (St. Petersburg) to Lansdowne, May 18, 1904, *BD*, IV, 190–192, No. 323 Monson (Paris) to Lansdowne, May 27, 1904, *BD*, IV, 193, No. 224A Lansdowne to Hardinge, June 2, 1904, *BD*, IV, 310; Brodrick to Ampthill, May 20, 1904, Lord Ampthill Correspondence, IOL, MSS Eur. E 233/37; Whitney, "British foreign policy," pp. 141–146; Ostal'tseva, "Anglo-frantsuzskoe soglashenie," 245–250.

had written on October 12, 1903, before the entente was concluded but during the time when the Anglo-Russian and Russo-Japanese negotiations were in progress, that "as far as can be judged from here, if Japan wishes to go to war with Russia at all, the last suitable moment for it seems to have come. They appear to have made up their minds in Tokyo that England is no longer to be regarded as an absolutely reliable friend. . . ." The Anglo-French negotiations during M. Loubet's visit [July 6–9] here have not remained hidden from the Japanese government."[40] Such a situation, he continued, would be likely "to lead the Japanese Government to begin a war with Russia soon, if it wishes to at all."

Both the immediate and longer range perspectives indicated beyond a doubt that the conclusion of the Anglo-French entente was a conscious and coordinated if somewhat disguised endeavor to place restrictions on German freedom of action. It was, as Holstein expressed it, not a prelude to an attack on Germany but a condition capable of limiting her free access to overseas commerce and colonial possessions.[41] "Against France and England," he wrote, "an overseas policy is impossible." Richard Kühlmann, then first secretary of the German legation in Tangier, wrote from that vantage point that as a consequence of the entente "the Egyptian question is dead," a point with which Bülow agreed, adding that this had been carried off so successfully that German prestige had suffered and was in need of a success to balance it.

While German freedom to act within existing circumstances was restricted, it was even more inauspicious that so also was her power to pursue her course toward world power in a more active way through the usual diplomatic and political channels. Kühlmann noted that while the door was closed to the future use of Egypt as a fulcrum for maneuver against Britain and France, the door had been thrown open on the Moroccan question, an issue with which, because of her recent experience in regard to Morocco and German Southwest Africa, Germany was not at the moment in a position to deal.[42]

Kühlmann also took note of another salient feature of the entente, i.e., that it was intended to insure against the risks inherent in the Anglo-Japanese alliance by settling British relations with one of the great powers, "thus nipping in the bud a possible coalition between Germany, Russia, and France" and thereby laying the groundwork for a similar settlement with another, Russia. It was an arrangement which might

[40] Bernstorff to Bülow, Oct. 12, 1903, in E.T.S. Dugdale, *German diplomatic documents, 1871–1914*, 4 vols. New York, 1928–1931, III, 177–179.

[41] Oron James Hale, *The great illusion 1900–1914*, New York, 1971, p. 242; Kühlmann memorandum, Oct. 1, 1904, in Dugdale, *German diplomatic documents*, III, 196–198; Carroll, *Germany and the great powers*, pp. 498–499.

[42] Taylor, *The struggle for mastery in Europe*, p. 421.

coordinate the defensive operations of three armies and three navies, a pattern which Germany was to call "encirclement." The executive committee of the Germany Navy League reacted by meeting at Dresden where they issued a demand for a further expanded naval building program.[43]

The Anglo-French entente was thus instrumental in giving a new emphasis to German thinking about the diplomatic and political aspects of her continental defense arrangements. Discussions of this question tended to center on two general courses of action, both aiming at breaking up or anticipating existing or future attempts on the part of Britain, France, and Russia to maintain or form potentially anti-German coalitions. The plan advocated by the German Emperor envisioned a continental alliance based firmly on a Russo-German understanding.[44]

The Emperor saw the impending war in the Far East as providing a very favorable occasion for this since it would weaken both Russia and France. This could force upon France the choice of either accepting the essentially German terms for joining the Russo-German group to form a continental alliance aimed at Britain or of detaching herself from the Franco-Russian alliance and remaining outside the Russo-German group. The latter could isolate France on the continent and render her weak and at the mercy of Germany. In a heated exchange with Count N.D. Osten-Sacken, the Russian ambassador in Berlin, Emperor Wilhelm disclosed that his eagerness for an alliance with Russia was based on his fear that Britain more than France was the power with which Germany would have to reckon and that to achieve such an alliance he was even ready to sacrifice Austria then and there.[45]

Holstein, on the other hand, saw an alliance with Russia as a danger for Germany. In December 1903 he had opposed neutralizing Denmark and closing the Baltic since the only effect of this would be to protect Russia from Britain, the ally of Japan. To form such an alliance would in his view give Russia the advantage of the strongest military power in the world while exposing Germany to a needless war with Britain without any compensating advantages. In fact, Holstein maintained, no alliance was necessary to take advantage of Russian preoccupation in the Far East. "The indispensable condition for Germany in a Russian alliance was a

---

[43] Albertini, *Origins of the war*, I, 117–138; Frederic A. Ogg, "European alliances and the war," *AMRR*, XXXIII, no. 3 (Sept. 1905), 297–301.

[44] Bülow to Holstein, Jan. 15, 1904, in Norman Rich, *Friedrich von Holstein. Politics and diplomacy in the era of Bismarck and Wilhelm II*, 2 vols. Cambridge, MA, 1965, II, 678–680.

[45] Evgenii Nikolaevich Shel'king [Eugene de Schelking], *Recollections of a Russian diplomat: the suicide of monarchies (William II and Nicholas II)*, New York, 1918, p. 144; Lee, *King Edward VII*, II, 305, quoting *GP*, XIX-2, 360–365.

guarantee of her existing boundaries. But a guarantee of Germany's boundaries meant a guarantee of the Treaty of Frankfurt of 1871," i.e., a guarantee of Alsace-Lorraine against France which could not be expected without first breaking up the existing Franco-Russian alliance.

Germany was notably unable to reach a satisfactory and feasible solution to the problem addressed by these proposed policies. The reaction to this situation on the part of the German military attaché in London, Major Count Bernhard von der Schulenburg, was impressive. He wrote on December 13, 1904: "There need be no fear of an immediate war but little doubt, on the other hand, that war will eventually occur, for England has not forgotten the Boer war. This feeling has popularized the English-Franco Entente, and moves toward an agreement with Russia. It is altogether improbable that friendly relations will again be established between England and Germany. The only remedy against conflict with England lies in union with Russia."[46] In fact, according to one view during the two years between the outbreak of the Russo-Japanese war in February 1904 and the end of the Algeciras conference in the spring of 1906 "German diplomacy staggered from one crisis to another, teetering on the brink of war with no fewer than three great powers, and permanently antagonizing a fourth."

The politics of averting war

Anglo-Russian relations unexpectedly reached a climax when Russia dispatched a fleet from the Baltic Sea to the Pacific war front. This event came closer than any other to extending to Europe the conflict in the Far East and perhaps thereby determining the outcome of the war in the east. The Russian Baltic Fleet, to become known as the Second Squadron of the Pacific Fleet, *en route* from the Baltic to the Far East on the night of October 21–22, 1904, passed near the Dogger Bank, an extensive submarine shelf about 70 by 170 square miles in area and located about 60 miles off the English coast near Hull.[47] Vice Admiral Zinovii Petrovich Rozhdestvensky, the commanding officer of the squadron, had reason to know that there were small fishing craft in this region, that fact having been noted in his sailing directions.

There is considerable uncertainty as to whether the commander steered

---

[46] Steinberg, "The Copenhagen complex," 31.
[47] Irving H. Smith, "Anglo-Russian relations and the Dogger Bank Incident 1902–1905," M.A. thesis, McGill University, 1955, p. 57; J.N. Westwood, *Witnesses of Tsushima*, Tallahassee, FL, 1970, pp. 89–91; Macgregor (Admiralty) to Lansdowne, Oct. 26, 1901, FO 65/1729; No. 66F. Clarke (Stockdale) to Lansdowne, Nov. 1, 1904, FO 65/1730; Thomas Barclay, *Thirty years. Anglo-French reminiscences (1876–1906)*, London, 1914, pp. 254–255; Busch, *Hardinge of Penshurst*, pp. 78–84.

his course directly through this area in order to avoid running too close to the coasts where it was suspected that danger might lurk or whether in the more positive sense, he thought that there would actually be less danger of a suspected Japanese attack if he were to traverse the Dogger Bank area. Whatever impulse or reason may have guided the Russian admiral, his command is said to have been running some 40 to 60 miles off course and if this is true it is difficult to see how an enemy could have conspired to waylay him with such precision as the Russians claim. Nevertheless, under the alleged impression that they were suddenly confronted with Japanese torpedo boats, the Russian ships opened fire on some British fishing trawlers, sinking two, damaging two, and causing a number of casualties.

The Russian squadron moved on southward without stopping to investigate the damage or to offer a word of explanation or apology. The first stop was made at Cherbourg during October 23–24 where French hospitality was enjoyed for the first time and the two destroyer divisions coaled before making a more general halt on orders from St. Petersburg at Vigo, Spain.[48] This order was given in response to the indignant outcry which had by then arisen in Britain and was to reach an intensity beyond all expectations.

The owners of the fishing vessels, with the help of the local member of parliament, Sir Henry Seymour King, had immediately brought their story of the attack to the attention of Lord Lansdowne, Parliament, and the press. The Russian chargé d'affaires, Sergei Dmitrievich Sazonov, and, after his hasty return from the continent, the Russian ambassador, could see clearly for themselves that Lord Lansdowne was not exaggerating when he stressed the seriousness of the situation and urged that something must be done.

Lord Curzon expressed it pointedly a few days later: "We are on the brink of war with Russia. We all hope it may be avoided but the national honour is at stake. In her apparent refusal to realize the seriousness of the case, I read the inevitable consequence of our long series of surrenders to her on every point that has arisen between us for years."[49] This opinion is

---

48 Gordon Blanding Chamberlain, "Japan, France, and the Russian Baltic Fleet: a diplomatic sidelight on the war of 1904–1905," Ph.D. dissertation, University of California, Berkeley, 1972, p. 37; Lee, *King Edward VII*, II, 302–303; "The North Sea Outrage," *Winchester Gazette*, Oct. 24, 1904, "Baltic Sea Outrage," *Daily Mail*, Oct. 21, 1904, Port of Plymouth Chamber of Commerce to Lansdowne, Oct. 24, 1904, G. Goodwin, Secretary of the Spalding Constitutional Club, resolution to Lansdowne, Oct. 25, 1904, all in FO 65/1729; Itakura Takuzo, *Kokusai funso shiko*, Tokyo, 1935, pp. 120–125.

49 Curzon to Ampthill, Oct. 28, 1904, Ampthill E 233/37; Edward J. Bing (ed.) *The secret letters of the last Tsar, being the confidential correspondence between Nicholas II and his mother, Dowager Empress Maria Feodorovna*, New York, 1938, p. 175.

given some corroboration by a view expressed by Emperor Nicholas in a letter of October 26 to his mother, the Dowager Empress Maria Fedorovna, that: "I do not think the English will have the cheek to go further than to indulge in threats. Our own calmness will calm them."

The six days which intervened between the North Sea incident and the characterization of the outcome by Lord Curzon witnessed the development of three related and equally ominous international complications. The original Anglo-Russian embroglio became almost imperceptibly engulfed in two derivative episodes, centering respectively around France and Germany, each looking toward a regrouping of the European powers.[50] The foundation of all three was established on Monday, October 24, when the news which had begun to reach London and the other capitals the day before began to assume an operational form. The British Mediterranean, Channel, and Home fleets were immediately alerted for possible action against the Russian Baltic Fleet. Lord Lansdowne supplemented this by holding a conference with Sazonov, the Russian chargé d'affaires, and telegraphing the first official British reaction to Russia through Sir Charles Hardinge, the British ambassador in St. Petersburg.

These communications conveyed to Russia the essential British reaction to the North Sea events, emphasizing the apparent callousness shown by Admiral Rozhdestvensky in leaving the scene without inquiring as to the damage or offering assistance. These messages also conveyed some basic demands such as those requiring an ample apology, "complete and prompt reparation," and guarantees against a recurrence of such an incident. Sazonov had also offered an explanation which was to become a form of the standard defense, i.e., the alleged culpability of the Japanese.

The occurrence of the North Sea incident and its impact in London had become clear in Berlin and Paris in the course of Monday and Tuesday, October 24 and 25.[51] The incident was seen in these two capitals not only with regard to the respective responsibilities these nations had assumed for the Russian squadron and for providing it with port facilities along its route to the Far East but, particularly in the light of these new circumstances, with respect to the prospective new balance of power which the emergent hostilities portended. The coaling operation was an outgrowth of a recent and more general development of an increasingly closer German–Russian relationship,

While Germany, as the war approached, had assumed an attitude of

---

[50] S. to Admiralty, Oct. 24, 1904, Adm 116/969, The North Sea Outrage; No. 374 Lansdowne to Hardinge, Oct. 24, 1904, No. 174 Lansdowne to Hardinge, Oct. 24, 1904, FO 65/1729.

[51] No. 935 Metternich to Bülow, Oct. 24, 1904, *GP*, XIX-1, 282; Nos. 60, 61, Cambon to Delcassé, Oct. 25, 1904, *DDF*, V, 464–465.

strict neutrality, the manner and amazing success of the Japanese attack on Port Arthur, followed by progressive Russian defeats had brought the German government face to face with an unpleasant reminder that the still incomplete German navy was vulnerable to a similar "Copenhagen" treatment, i.e., an attack on ships in port, at the hands of Britain. At the same time, German interests and possessions in the Far East would be exposed to the Anglo-Japanese combination in case of a Russian defeat.[52]

Two aspects of the British outlook were particularly disturbing to the Kaiser: the tolerant attitude of the British press toward what many believed to be a Japanese attack on the Russian fleet and the report current in Germany that the new British first sea lord, Admiral John Fisher, was an advocate of a "Copenhagen" treatment for the German navy with Kiel as the target.

These conditions turned Germany toward firmer support of Russia and by June 1904 when the Hamburg–American Line concluded an agreement with C. Wachter and Co. of St. Petersburg to supply the Russian squadron with coal, the German government was prepared to face the possible consequences.[53] Not only was coal an "unconditional contraband of war" but supplying 338,200 tons to the Russian squadron at intervals between the east coast of Denmark and the Far East, most of the distance exposed to the British navy, was potentially a hazardous undertaking.

This alleged risk, the reality of which tended to be discredited by information supplied by Metternich from London, was artfully used by the German Emperor in an apparent attempt to draw Russia and France into an alliance with Germany against Britain. The core of this proposed alliance was to be a German–Russian combination since this would make the most effective use of the immediate British threat to the coaling of the Russian ships and, if it succeeded, would be more likely to break up the Franco-Russian alliance than to include France in a German-Russian-French grouping.

The Kaiser had for some time been cultivating the Tsar through correspondence, had been very frank in showing him in which camp his interests lay, and had most recently cooperated in the renewal of an exchange of personal representatives between Berlin and St. Petersburg, a practice which had lapsed in 1891.[54] The German Emperor selected his

---

[52] White, *The diplomacy*, p. 93; Steinberg, "The Copenhagen complex," 31–32; Ruddock F. Mackay, *Fisher of Kilverstone*, Oxford, 1973, p. 319.
[53] Lamar J. Cecil, "Coal for the fleet that had to die," *AHR*, LXIX, no. 4 (July, 1964), 993, 1005; Hardinge, *Old diplomacy*, p. 104; Rozental', *Diplomaticheskaia istoriia*, p. 77.
[54] No. 549 Hardinge to Lansdowne, Nov. 2, 1904, FO 65/1682; Fay, *Origins of the World War*, I, 57–58; Lamar J. Cecil, *The German diplomatic service, 1871–1914*, Princeton, 1976, pp. 67, 127.

personal aide-de-camp, Count Gustav von Lambsdorff, a nephew of the Russian foreign minister, Count V. I. Lamsdorf, to serve as a special military attaché to the Tsar. The latter, in response, sent Colonel V. N. Shebeko to serve in the same capacity with the Kaiser. The *Vossische Zeitung* saw this as "a symptom of renewed warmth between Germany and Russia."

The Kaiser, in a further step toward bringing the two countries into closer accord, telegraphed the Tsar his general plan for a German–Russian agreement on October 27.[55] He repeated a point made three days before by Holstein to the Russian ambassador in Berlin regarding the threat which the English press was then leveling at Germany over the coaling issue. He emphasized the fact that it was Germany and Russia which enjoyed a genuine community of interest, a relationship which he meant to urge upon France, the ally of Russia. Appealing to the Tsar on the grounds that both had reason to fear Britain and Japan, he suggested, at the Tsar's invitation, that they conclude a defensive treaty.

The German military attaché in London, Major Count Bernhard von der Schulenburg, addressed to Bülow an analysis of the tense Anglo-German situation, strongly advocating that Britain be confronted with a firm Russo-German defensive-offensive alliance.[56] The treaty was sent to the Tsar on October 30. The preamble and three articles stated that: its aim was to localize the war; if either were attacked by a European power the other would assist with all its land and sea forces; France would be summoned to assume her obligation under her alliance with Russia; neither would conclude peace except in common; and, finally, it dealt with the coaling problem.

The proposed agreement foundered on the Russian Emperor's suggestion of November 23 that it be shown to the French government before being signed, a request which made the German Emperor furious since he knew that the French government would never accept it as it was.[57] Two factors should be kept in mind with respect to the outcome of this proposal. In the first place, the North Sea incident was, with French intercession, reaching a point at which for Britain and Russia a reasonable settlement of the dispute appeared to be in sight.[58]

Secondly, the Kaiser was not strongly supported in this project by his

[55] Rich, *Friedrich von Holstein*, II, 689–690; No. 816 Bernstorff to Bülow, Sept. 6, 1904, Wilhelm to Nicholas, Oct. 27, 1904, Nicholas to Wilhelm, Oct. 29, 1904, *GP*, XIX-1, 218–220, 303–305; Wilhelm to Nicholas, Oct. 30, 1904, in Herman Bernstein, *The Willy-Nicky correspondence. Being the secret and intimate telegrams exchanged between the Kaiser and the Tsar*, New York, 1918, pp. 75–76.
[56] Wilhelm to Nicholas, Oct. 30, 1904, Schulenburg to Bülow (annex enclosed), Dec. 13, 1904, *GP*, XIX-1, XIX-2, 308, 360–365.
[57] Rich, *Friedrich von Holstein*, II, 689.
[58] Parr, *Théophile Delcassé*, p. 153; Monson to Delcassé, Nov. 27, 1904, *DDF*, V, 553–554; J. Steinberg, "Germany and the Russo-Japanese war," *AHR*, LXXV: 7, 1976–1977.

own government and needed not only a high degree of receptivity in St. Petersburg but also a quick success to carry it off. The Kaiser telegraphed the Tsar on December 21, 1904 that: "We cannot take France into our confidence before we two come to a definite arrangement," and that if the Tsar felt it necessary to consult France beforehand, "then it is better for all parties, to continue in our present condition of mutual independence."[59] It is significant that the Anglo-Russian maritime crisis had passed and it had been agreed to settle the issue by the appointment of an international commission.

The North Sea incident thus presented Delcassé with what appeared from the first to be a choice between witnessing the disintegration of the diplomatic security system established by him and his predecessors or seizing the opportunity of the crisis to move forward boldly toward its completion. Both sides were warned by him that it would require their entire cooperation to avoid serious trouble. He warned the Russian ambassador, A. I. Nelidov, on October 24 that an apology would have to be made without losing any time and invited him to ponder the outcome if the next morning the British fleet should receive orders to fire on the Russian ships as they approached Vigo.[60] Meanwhile, Paul Cambon in London warned Lord Lansdowne that "The Entente Cordiale will not survive a blow against our ally."

Delcassé was aware by October 26 of the essential features of the British demands and of the emphasis Lord Lansdowne had given to the failure of Admiral Rozhdestvensky to show even a minimum of concern for the fate of the fishermen and to aroused British national feeling.[61] He was aware by then also that the Russian ships had touched at Cherbourg and were already effectively bottled up by the British navy at Vigo. Finally, he had been warned by the chargé d'affaires at St. Petersburg of the growing closeness between the courts of Berlin and St. Petersburg and that positive steps should be taken to oppose the German policies there.

The very next day, October 27, a telegram from Admiral Rozhdestvensky not only reinforced the position already alluded to in Russian responses but provided such solid ground as the Russians were able to offer as a basis upon which an Anglo-Russian accommodation could be discussed.[62] Lord Lansdowne told Count Benckendorff quite bluntly that

---

[59] Wilhelm to Nicholas, n.d. but about Dec. 21, 1904, *GP*, XIX-1, 340–341; Keith Eubank, *Paul Cambon, master diplomatist*, Norman, OK, 1960, pp. 92–93.
[60] Paléologue, *Three critical years*, pp. 100–101; Eubank, *Paul Cambon*, pp. 92–93.
[61] No. 60, 61 Cambon to Delcassé, Oct. 25, No. 63 Cambon to Delcassé, Oct. 26, No. 151 Boutiron (St. Petersburg) to Delcassé, Oct. 26, 1904, *DDF*, V, 464–465, 468, 470–472; Rozental', *Diplomaticheskaia istoriia*, p. 273; Paléologue, *Three critical years*, pp. 104–105.
[62] Nos. 66, 67 Cambon to Delcassé, Oct. 27, 1904, *DDF*, V, 472–473; No. 378 Lansdowne to Hardinge, Oct. 27, 1904, *BD*, IV, 15–17; Rozental', *Diplomaticheskaia istoriia*, pp. 277–279.

"the version given by the Admiral was one which would not carry the slightest conviction in this country." He insisted upon a thorough investigation and suggested that consideration be given to an international commission under articles IX and XIV of the Hague Convention on International Commissions of Inquiry. It was to be understood that those found guilty were to be punished.

The suggestion of the use of procedures provided by the Hague Convention was, as Maurice Paléologue noted in his diary, an important part of the conciliatory approach encouraged by Delcassé both in London and St. Petersburg. It had, in fact, a special appeal to the Russian Emperor who had invited the participants to take part in the Hague conference in 1899. The Emperor, in addition to his faith in Rozhdestvensky's assurances, expressed two principal concerns about the British reaction. One was the menacing attitude of the British press which was essentially demanding condemnation and punishment of the squadron officers even before they had been heard; the other was the extensive and highly provocative state of British naval preparedness.

The immediate reaction to the incident in St. Petersburg was quite violently anti-British.[63] Even Count Lamsdorf was deeply stirred by the news of the alleged Japanese torpedo boats and while Hardinge went so far as to doubt that the telegrams were in fact the admiral's reports, he cautioned against underestimating the danger to Britain of the Russian mood which possessed so many in St. Petersburg who might welcome a war with Japan's ally. But calmer moods soon prevailed and the Anglo-Russian storm had subsided by October 28 and the Russian fleet was temporarily safe.

This achievement was registered in a British Admiralty message which went out on October 28 to Vice Admiral Lord Charles Beresford, the commander of the Channel Fleet at Gibraltar.[64] It stated that: "There appears a good prospect of a peaceable termination of the crisis ... Continue to keep touch so far as you can with the whole Russian fleet which now appears to be somewhat scattered but remember how liable they are to night panics." It was also registered in an entry in the diary of Emperor Nicholas for October 29 which indicated that with commitment of the issue to the international commission, the matter was essentially taken care of, at least for the time being.[65] This did not, however, mean that the Emperor had ceased to credit Admiral Rozhdestvensky's version

[63] Hardinge Diary, Oct. 27, 1904, Hardinge to Lansdowne, Oct. 27, 1904, FO 800/140; No. 159 Hardinge to Lansdowne, Oct. 27, 1904, FO 65/1729.
[64] Admiralty to Vice Admiral Beresford, Oct. 28, 1904, Adm 116/969.
[65] Rozental', *Diplomaticheskaia istoriia*, p. 279; Hardinge Diary, Oct. 30, 1904, Sir Charles Hardinge Papers, Cambridge University Library, V; No. 167 Hardinge to Lansdowne, Oct. 30, 1904, FO 65/1730.

of the incident, as Sir Charles Hardinge discovered in the course of an audience he had the following day with the Emperor.

The issue seemed hardly to have been settled when the first of two repercussions caused a temporary crisis in British and, to some extent, in French circles.[66] This was brought about by the departure on November 1, on orders from St. Petersburg, of the main Russian squadron from Vigo under Admiral Rozhdestvensky. The British Admiralty alerted the Channel Fleet in advance of the departure so that the vice admiral of the Channel Fleet was able to report on November 1, that preparations for action were complete. The message continued: "When ordered to act I shall order all Russian Fleet at Tangier into Gibraltar and if disobeyed they will be sunk and I shall proceed to meet Vigo Fleet."

The issues in this encounter were the unscheduled departure and the fact that the officers left behind were not considered to be those "responsible" in the sense of having ordered the action in question. Those left were Commander Nikolai Lavrentevich Klado, the chief of intelligence for the squadron, Lieutenants Nikolai Oskarovich Ott, a flag officer, Veniamin Aleksandrovich Ellis, an ordnance officer, and Shramchenko, a gunnery officer. Excitement over this event soon died down, apparently since it was realized that nothing short of open hostilities could serve as a remedy, and the Russian ships were not overtly shadowed past Tangier. It was clear that, according to Lamsdorf's understanding, those left behind, while not those considered responsible in the sense of being guilty, were those in the best position to testify as to the facts and would be punished if found guilty by the international tribunal.

The second repercussion emerged while the issue caused by the departure of the squadron was still being discussed and was far more serious. It came to light during a conversation on November 4, between Maurice Paléologue and the Grand Duke Pavel Aleksandrovich, the uncle of the Tsar.[67] The Grand Duke revealed the close relations which had recently arisen between the German and Russian emperors and, in particular, the fact that the former had written to Nicholas: "If you have war with England, I will put my fleet at your disposal. And I will force France to come in with us." This information he had received from his brother, Grand Duke Sergei Aleksandrovich, the governor general of

[66] Admiralty to Vice Admiral Beresford, Oct. 31, 1904, No. 89 Admiralty to Vice Admiral, Channel Fleet, Nov. 1, 1904, Adm 116/969; Vice Admiral Channel Fleet, Gibraltar, to Admiralty, Nov. 1, 1904, FO 65/1731; V. Baddeley of Admiralty, note, Nov. 1, 1904, No. 395 Lansdowne to Hardinge, Nov. 2, 1904, No. 196 Hardinge to Lansdowne, Nov. 5, 1904, FO 65/1730; No. 190 Hardinge to Lansdowne, Nov. 8, 1904, FO 65/1731.
[67] Paléologue, *Three critical years*, pp. 112–121; Rozental', *Diplomaticheskaia istoriia*, pp. 280–281; Note Secrète (Paléologue), Nov. 8, 1904, No. 315 Cambon to Delcassé, Nov. 17, 1904, *DDF*, V, 514–516, 535–540.

Moscow, whose wife was the sister of Empress Alexandra Feodorovna and who was to be assassinated only a few months later by the Socialist Revolutionary, Ivan Kaliaev.

Both the message and source were carefully considered and it was decided that the information had to be taken seriously, not only with respect to the collaboration which might have been planned between Germany and Russia but also the aspect of the plan which would seek to force France into compliance and cooperation. It was the first time Paléologue could remember having heard Delcassé refer to Alsace-Lorraine, the sacrifice of which would be final if France were forced into compliance with the German plan. Refusing to support the German plan meant denouncing the Franco-Russian alliance and opposing Germany alone with 840,000 French forces facing 1,400,000 Germans.

The truth of this revelation could also be tested against a conversation which the French foreign minister, Delcassé, had had only two days before with the German ambassador, Prince Hugo von Radolin, in the course of which the latter had recounted the details of a plan very similar to that mentioned by Grand Duke Pavel Aleksandrovich.[68] Radolin's message was essentially that the Japanese victories had made their allies, the British, a threat to Germany, a situation which arose from the fact that the British were jealous of German commercial success. Had it not been for Delcassé, Britain and Russia would have come to blows recently in the North Sea incident.

In a parallel conversation which Radolin had with the Spanish ambassador, Marquis Del Muni, and which the latter reported to Delcassé, the Prince stated clearly that it would be impossible for Germany to stand aside while Japan, encouraged by Britain, made war on neutrals. This would lead to war between Germany on one side and Japan and Britain on the other and this in turn would bring about a Russo-German alliance and a general war in Europe.

Maurice Paléologue was sent to London on the evening of November 5 to discuss this important issue directly with the British government. He presented the story of the dangerous developments through the French Ambassador, Paul Cambon, in four papers stating the substance of the conversations of Delcassé with the German ambassador, of Delcassé with the Spanish ambassador, of Paléologue himself with Grand Duke Pavel Aleksandrovich, and the materials dealing with the discovery of the German plan to attack France through Belgium devised by the chief of the German General Staff, Count Alfred von Schlieffen.[69]

---

[68] Paléologue, *Three critical years*, pp. 109–111; Note Secrète (Paléologue), Nov. 4, 1904, *DDF*, V, 501–503.

[69] Paléologue, *Three critical years*, pp. 45–48, 115–121; Walter Goerlitz, *History of the German General Staff*, New York, 1954, pp. 131–134.

This case, completely convincing to the French government, was placed before the British government through Lord Lansdowne together with the recommendation that both Britain and Russia be warned of the threat and the consequences. Russia should be warned: "You must not think that we would ever join a Russo-German coalition aimed at England"; this was followed by a reminder that France had intervened to Russia's advantage in the North Sea incident. Britain was to be warned that even with the Japanese alliance, Britain ought to be more tactful toward St. Petersburg and thus, "Help us to keep the peace of Europe."[70]

The French role in the affairs of the east-bound Russian squadron not only remained active after the achievement of the success of October 28 but in some respect became more vital than before. Sir Edward Monson, the British ambassador in Paris, sought assurance on October 28 that Delcassé would be lending his good offices to the task of bringing together the two potential adversaries and was assured that he would.[71]

It was under these favorable circumstances that Britain and Russia reached a formal agreement on November 25, 1904 by which they would commit their dispute to an international commission which met in Paris on December 22, 1904. It was, significantly, at just about the time of this meeting in Paris that the Kaiser signalled his disappointment at the Tsar's insistence on informing France before concluding an alliance. A week later the first Russian ships reached French Madagascar and five days after that Port Arthur surrendered. The French gamble must have seemed better than ever in St. Petersburg.

The Russian gamble must, by the same token, have appeared in Paris to be more difficult and risky than ever. The routing of the Russian squadron and the provision of port facilities for it was under the direction of the French "Secret Committee for War Instructions" of which both Maurice Paléologue and Captain de Saulces de Freycinet, director of the First Section of the Naval General Staff, were members. Both of these officials had strongly urged Russia to proceed to the Far East by way of Cape Horn and across the southern Pacific, thus making it easier for France to preserve the appearance of neutrality in the face of almost certain trouble with Japan and perhaps also with Britain.[72]

But the Russian government decided to send its ships the other way, the main squadron, including the four new battleships under Vice Admiral Rozhdestvensky, taking the 16,000 mile route around the Cape of Good Hope, the remaining ships under Rear Admiral Felkerzam taking the

[70] Paléologue, *Three critical years*, p. 118.
[71] Nos. 130, 296 Delcassé to ambassadors of France in London and St Petersburg, Oct. 28, 1904, Monson to Delcassé, Nov. 27, 1904, *DDF*, V, 478, 553–554.
[72] Paléologue, *Three critical years*, pp. 105–106; Chamberlain, "Japan, France, and the Russian Baltic Fleet," pp. 37–39, 53–54, 73–78; Rozental', *Diplomaticheskaia istoriia*, pp. 77–78.

4. The Great Review of Defiance held at Port Arthur, October 8, 1903, held after evacuation

12,000 mile route through the Mediterranean and the Suez Canal to a rendezvous at Diego Suarez in Madagascar. Vigorous Japanese protests to the French government over this breach of neutrality began with the visit of the Russian destroyer divisions to Cherbourg and continued through most of the voyage. "But if we refuse Russia," warned Paléologue, "think of the arguments Germany will extract from this against us."

The international commission which met in Paris on December 22, 1904 to attempt a settlement of the North Sea incident consisted of five principal technically qualified members. Four of these, Vice Admiral Lewis Anthony Beaumont, representing Britain, Vice Admiral Kaznakov, shortly replaced by Vice Admiral Fedor Vasil'evich Dubasov representing Russia, Rear Admiral Charles Henry Davis, representing the United States, and Vice Admiral François Ernest Fournier, representing France, chose a fifth professional member, Vice Admiral Hermann Baron von Spaun, representing Austria–Hungary. The two principals also had legal representatives, the Right Honorable Sir Edward Fry acting for Britain and Baron Mikhail Aleksandrovich Taube acting for Russia. The Russian representative was to have been the distinguished jurist, Professor Fedor Fedorovich Martens, but the latter requested that Taube go in his place.[73]

The international commission was occupied with two kinds of issues. One was technical in nature and was concerned with what had occurred on the night of October 21–22, hence the reason for choosing professional

[73] Taube, *La politique russe*, p. 10.

naval officers as the primary members of the commission. But this "professional" question was itself divided into two parts, the first of which was the contention alleged by Admiral Rozhdestvensky that the Russian squadron was attacked by Japanese torpedo boats sheltered among British fishing trawlers. This assertion was almost impossible to support except by the most implied, oblique, or directly false reasoning and was not believed even by the Russian officials charged with supporting it. The information attributed to Grand Duke Aleksandr Mikhailovich that Russia had indisputable evidence of the presence of Japanese torpedo boats in the North Sea and withheld by Russia on the grounds that its disclosure would only cause further conflict was considered untrue by Sir Charles Hardinge.

It is significant that some Russian officials who were clearly informed about the Japanese torpedo boat story but were not obligated to take administrative action in the affair simply did not believe the story. Professor Martens explained his wish that his assistant, Taube, go in his stead by stating flatly that he did not "believe one word of Admiral Rozhdestvensky's fine story," and did not wish to stake his reputation on defending such a cause.[74] Petr Ivanovich Rachkovsky, the head of the Russian Investigative Police abroad reported to Taube that he considered this Russian story a fraud and Taube himself agreed with this. Further-

---

[74] Ibid., pp. 26–29; Hardinge to Sanderson, Mar. 15, 1905, Hardinge Papers, VI; Charles Louis Seeger, *Recollections of a foreign minister (memoirs of Alexander Iswolsky)*, New York, 1921, pp. 42–43.

more, Aleksandr Petrovich Izvolsky, then the Russian minister in Copenhagen, who had interviewed the originator of one of the stories then
current about the presence in the North Sea of Japanese vessels, also
asserted positively that these stories were untrue.

The fact that the official Russian explanation was so unacceptable and
that Russian conduct was itself "such an inconceivable action," as Cecil
Spring Rice wrote, made it seem "that it must have been by accident, or
from panic, and not from design."[75] Reports of the incident, in fact,
indicate the likelihood that in the confusion the Russians had fired upon
their own ships. This was one of the factors which made it possible for the
commission to accept the explanation urged by the Russians entirely
apart from the credibility of the admiral's story of the Japanese torpedo
boats.

The version which many found more acceptable was in reality a
modification of the story of the torpedo boat attack and was given in a
telegram which the Tsar had sent to King Edward on October 24. It
stated in part: "Having had many warnings that Japanese were lurking in
fishing smacks and other vessels for purpose of destroying our Squadron
on its way out, great precautions were ordered to be taken, especially by
night, whenever any vessels or boats were in sight."[76] The natural
assumption that Japan would want if possible to prevent the Russian
squadron from reaching the Pacific, the dangers of the passage through
the Danish straits and near the viks and fjords of the Scandinavian coast
made fear, nervousness, and disaster fully understandable if not quite
justifiable.

The second main issue before the commission was by far the more
important of the two – the future of Anglo-Russian relations. This was in
reality a projection of the Anglo-Russian negotiations which had been
recessed upon the outbreak of war and had re-emerged on October 25 in a
conversation between Sir Charles Hardinge and Count Lamsdorf.[77]
Hardinge, after pointing out the gravity of the situation and the danger to
peace, and urging full reparations, joined with Lamsdorf in asserting that
the incident "was so grave that peace might possibly be jeopardized
unless he and I made up our minds that war should not under any
circumstances result." They "gave each other a mutual promise and
shook hands over it."

Delcassé, in the spirit in which he had already conducted the negotia-

[75] Spring Rice to Ferguson, Nov. 10, 1904, in Gwynn, *Letters and friendships*, I, 453.
[76] Lee, *King Edward VII*, II, 301; Baroness Sophie Buxhoeveden, *Before the storm*,
London, 1939, p. 270; Karl Friedrich Nowak, *Germany's road to ruin*, trans., W. W.
Dickes, New York, 1932, pp. 275–276; A.A. Mogilevich and M.E. Airapetian, "Legenda
i pravda o Gullskom intsidente 1904 g." *IZh*, no. 6 (1940), 41–52.
[77] Hardinge, *Old diplomacy*, p. 108.

tions with Britain and Russia, continued this theme in a conversation with Taube at the breakfast given on December 20, 1904 for the delegates to the conference.[78] He said that he wished to make the settlement of the North Sea incident a turning point in Anglo-Russian relations, a first step along a common road. Asked if he meant a common road for three, Delcassé replied, "certainly," adding that when the war had ended "we must think about broadening the entente cordiale."

It was thus made clear from the occurrence of the incident and from being reiterated at the inception of the commission that the stakes for which the game was to be played were by general understanding to be sufficiently high to make the technical issues appear relatively trivial, and to render uninviting any inducements to yield to the demands or incitements from Berlin. The commission completed its work on February 25, 1905 and found Admiral Rozhdestvensky guilty and his act unjustified. It held, nevertheless, that his intention was not to commit the act but to protect his squadron. The incident was formally and finally closed when on March 9, 1905 the Russian ambassador handed Lord Lansdowne £65,000 as compensation for the losses suffered by the fishermen.

The most significant outcome of the maritime incident and of the deliberations of the commission was, however, the impact of these upon the balance of power in Europe. A cataclysmic Anglo-Russian naval battle, not only devastating the fleets of the principals but undoubtedly drawing in and at least partially annihilating important elements of the French navy, had been avoided. The alternative to French cooperation on the side of Russia might have been the almost inconceivable case of a deliberate French decision to join forces with Britain against Russia, knowing full well that this could only destroy the Franco-Russian alliance. This would, in either case, have left Germany supreme on the European continent and much closer than she could otherwise have expected to be to her goal of a dominant maritime position,

The other route to the destruction of the Franco-Russian alliance, the formation of the German–Russian alliance under German leadership which could maneuver France into an uncomfortable if not untenable position, was also avoided, thanks at least in part to Delcassé. The success of this strategy was undoubtedly a consequence of the endeavors of Britain and Russia in the recent past to cooperate with and with current endeavors on the part of Delcassé, Cambon, Hardinge, Lamsdorf, and others to use the occasion of the crisis to help insure the success of their diplomatic goal.

The successful avoidance of a major catastrophe had, however, left

[78] Rozental', *Diplomaticheskaia istoriia*, pp. 82–83.

Germany facing a situation quite different from that preceding the crisis and, at the same time, more difficult for Germany than that raised by the Anglo-French entente. Holstein, who was critical of Bülow's policies, had written to the chancellor in July 1904: "For reasons with which I shall not deal here, the prestige of Germany has declined in recent years while our opponents and rivals are about to encircle us."[79]

The fear of encirclement was, of course, associated with the prospect of a projection of the Franco-Russian alliance and the Anglo-French entente to include some closer affiliation of Britain and Russia. After the emergence of an apparently serious peace movement, there was the further prospect that mediation by either Britain or France might add to this triple combination the Anglo-Japanese alliance to form a quadruple alliance or entente. The diligent cultivation during the North Sea incident of an Anglo-Russian accommodation was followed by new rumors and further fragmentary evidence of a movement looking toward a mediated Russo-Japanese peace.

The movement for a mediated peace became quite definite and seemingly practical in the course of November 1904, even before the conclusion of the formal Anglo-Russian agreement on the 25th to commit the North Sea issue to an international commission.[80] The "two Danish sisters," as Bülow termed the Russian Dowager Empress, Maria Fedorovna, and Queen Alexandra of Britain, had corresponded during the crisis on behalf of the improvement of Anglo-Russian relations.

It should also be remembered that this family tie had only recently been emphasized by the birth on August 12, 1904 of a son and heir to the Russian throne, Aleksei Nikolaevich. The christening, held at the Peterhof chapel on August 24, had brought together the godmother, Dowager Empress Maria Fedorovna, and the representative of the King of Great Britain, one of the godfathers, Prince Louis of Battenberg, then the director of Naval Intelligence in the British Navy. Prince Louis was also able to explain to the Tsar and the Russian naval authorities British views on the Russian seizure of British merchant ships, then a divisive issue between the two countries.

President Roosevelt knew by November 11 of the continuing efforts of Britain and France to seek an end of the war and intended to sound out

---

[79] Otto Hammann, *Bilder aus der letzten Kaiserzeit*, Berlin, 1922, p. 33.
[80] Kwang-Ching Liu, "German fear of a quadruple alliance, 1904–1905," *JMH*, XVIII, no. 3 (Sept. 1946), pp. 223–227; Bernhard Heinrich Martin Karl von Bülow, *Memoirs of Prince Bülow*, Boston, 1931, II, 74; No. 333 MacDonald to Lansdowne, Nov. 22, 1904, including a memorandum of T.B. Hohler second secretary of the British legation in Tokyo, Nov. 13, 1904, *BD*, IV, 64–66; Hardinge Diary, Sept. 2, 1904, Hardinge Papers, V; Buxhoeveden, *Before the storm*, pp. 103–106; Robert Y. Massie, *Nicholas and Alexandra*, New York, 1967, pp. 105–107; Busch, *Hardinge of Penshurst*, p. 77.

Japan on this issue. A week later the German embassy in London learned that Lord Lansdowne had been discussing the Japanese peace terms with Baron Hayashi Tadasu, the Japanese minister in London, and was even then trying to reduce them.

Toward the end of November the German Emperor wrote to the Tsar warning him of the British and French "schemes" only to receive word by early December that Russia was not unfavorable to the idea of mediation.[81] Russia had, by this time, passed the stage of enthusiasm for the agreement with Germany, and, with the maritime crisis past, the plans completed for the use of French ports by the Second Pacific Squadron *en route* to the Far East, and Anglo-Russian relations greatly improved, she was in some ways closer to France than to Germany.

The growing interest in seeking peace by mediation raised in Berlin the twofold suspicion that the quest might lead to a quadruple alliance, a prophetic apprehension, excluding and isolating Germany. There was also the growing fear that this might be accomplished in part by a new appropriation of Chinese territory by the allies, again with the exclusion and to the detriment of Germany.[82] Baron Hermann Speck von Sternburg, the German ambassador in Washington and a friend of President Roosevelt, reported that the President's views were far more favorable to Japan than to Russia. He added that in the President's view the former would be more amenable than the latter to cooperation with the western nations and that he did not think that Russia could be trusted. While Roosevelt favored committing Korea to a Japanese protectorate, he wanted to return Manchuria to China under a guarantee of neutrality by the interested powers.

Chancellor Bernhard von Bülow wrote a note to Emperor Wilhelm on December 26 in which he expressed the view that "America and Japan want to share with us the resolution of the Far Eastern question while, on the other hand, Russia, France, and England would like to keep us in ignorance of the current negotiations."[83] He mentioned that the peril of the quadruple grouping would make a greater impression in the United States than the yellow peril, a favorite theme of the Kaiser. Bülow also noted the opportunity for furthering this diplomatic diversionary plan presented by the proposed visit of Viscount Aoki Shuzo, the former foreign minister and minister in Berlin who was known to be friendly to Germany, for the occasion of the wedding of the German Crown Prince Wilhelm. The opportunity was promptly seized upon.

---

[81] Kaiser to Bülow, Nov. 23, Tsar to Kaiser, Dec. 7, 1904, *GP*, XIX-1, 316–317, 323–324.
[82] Liu, "German fear," 229–230; Sternburg, Promemoria, n.d. but enclosed in Bülow to Kaiser, Dec. 24, 1904, *GP*, XIX-2, 547–551.
[83] Bülow to Kaiser, Dec. 26, 1904, *GP*, XIX-2, 400–403.

Baron Friedrich von Holstein supplied the next link in the chain of events by lending his support to the movement aimed at halting a possible assault on the integrity of China.[84] He also urged in a note of December 29 that President Roosevelt be asked to sound out Britain and France on the issue. This would, hopefully, force them to disclose their positions and make a partition scheme impracticable. The request was transmitted to Roosevelt in a note from Sternburg and led to the issuance by Secretary of State John Hay of a circular note addressed to the powers concerned. This was the second circular note issued by Hay during the Russo-Japanese war, the first having been issued on February 10, 1904, just after the outbreak of war. It asked the nations immediately concerned with the region forming the locale of the war as well as others to respect the neutrality and administrative entity of China.

The similarity between the occasions when these two circular notes were issued is striking. Both signalled a threat to the integrity of China. It had been reported on the eve of the Russo-Japanese war that Germany, France, and Russia, the Far Eastern Triplice of a decade earlier, were planning to combine once again against Japan, compensating themselves as before by sharing a further partition of China.

The rumor was given some substantiation by a separate report according to which Russia maintained that Tibet, Turkestan (Sinkiang), Mongolia, and Manchuria were not integral parts of the Chinese Empire. Such an interpretation would not only invite Russia to help herself to these regions but would indirectly encourage at least Germany and France to join in further partitions of China. Furthermore, since this was the time when the Anglo-French negotiations were nearing a successful conclusion, the scheme, if completed, might also have served to halt these negotiations and leave France in effect isolated.

The second of these circular notes was issued on January 13, 1905 in the hope of averting a potentially similar crisis in China. It was once again issued at the request of Germany and in order to sound out the powers on the open door and the territorial integrity of China. The British government readily agreed to respect these principles though the French position was less clear, leaving some doubt in the American President's mind. The crisis appeared, however, to have been temporarily headed off.

It may have been as a means of preventing such recurrent crises by

---

[84] Holstein note, Dec. 29, 1904, Sternburg to President Roosevelt, enclosed in No. 1 Bülow to Bussche-Haddenhausen, Jan. 4, 1905, No. 20 Sternburg to FO Feb. 3, 1905, *GP*, XIX-2, 551–556, 556–557, 567–568; Tyler Dennett, *John Hay from poetry to politics*, New York, 1933, pp. 407–409; *USFR*, 1904, pp. 2–3, 42; *USFR*, 1905, p. 1; Edward B. Parsons, "Roosevelt's containment of the Russo-Japanese War," *PHR*, XXXVIII, no. 1 (Feb. 1969), 26–29; Frederich W. Marks III, *Velvet on iron. The diplomacy of Theodore Roosevelt*, Lincoln, NE, 1979, pp. 65–66.

giving the Far East some stability that William H. Taft, acting as the personal emissary of President Roosevelt, signed a private and secret agreement with Prime Minister and Foreign Minister Katsura Taro on July 29, 1905, five days after the signing of the Björkö treaty which had contained no provision dealing with the Far East. It was also two days after the conclusion of the better known Taft–Katsura agreement. While the Taft–Katsura agreement was an executive "agreed memorandum" which dealt with the Philippines and Korea, the second and less known agreement appertained to the support of Japan in the interest of the larger balance of power in the Far East. This was a principle with which Roosevelt was vitally concerned and which he attentively and helpfully watched emerge from the Portsmouth conference.

The North Sea incident, accordingly, served as a catalyst for bringing into being a further stage of the ongoing diplomatic revolution. The expectation of an Anglo-Russian conflict, long anticipated in Berlin and feared in London, had been tested and found unreliable as a means of manipulating the European balance of power. Instead of eliminating the effective naval forces of Britain and Russia, and undoubtedly those of France as well, Britain was left with all her naval forces including forty-six battleships compared with over thirty-two for France and Russia together, and sixteen for Germany.[85] The Russian navy, however, would soon be largely destroyed by Japan. Thus, instead of impairing or terminating the recently formed Anglo-French entente the incident infused new effectiveness into it to the extent of educing from Berlin the accusation of "encirclement." The fear of encirclement by the joining of the Franco-Russian alliance and the Anglo-French entente through an Anglo-Russian association and adding the Anglo-Japanese alliance to form a quadruple alliance or entente became a more imminent likelihood.

[85] Monger, *The end of isolation*, p. 200; compare Taylor, *Struggle for mastery in Europe*, p. 426.

4   Russia in political recession

Domestic checkmate

The year 1905 began with events so calamitous for Russia as to augur even further misfortunes. The fall of Port Arthur at the very beginning of the year was followed three weeks later by the outbreak of revolution. These signs of a decline in Russian power and prestige set in motion both internal and external demands of rivals wishing to use the opportunity to enhance their own positions at the expense of Russia or of her ally, France.

Internally there emerged demands from the people for a clearer and firmer voice in the affairs of state. A reapportionment of priorities was expressed by Count Witte in his memorandum of October 9, 1905 to the Emperor: "The government should openly and sincerely strive for the good of the state, and not for the preservation of one or another of its forms."[1]

Externally this pattern of decline raised expectations in some quarters for a share in the benefits of Russian defeat. One such desire was expressed by the Amir of Afghanistan who, inspired by the example of Japan, would have liked to rid himself of further Russian pressure by a forceful move against his powerful and troublesome neighbor. It also raised the hopes of the German government for greater freedom of action and a more dominant role in Europe, as unencumbered as possible by the restraints of potential threats of either Russian or French power.

The devolution of Russian power and prestige, in addition to being noted by domestic and foreign observers, was inscribed and perpetuated in the Portsmouth treaty and in due course incorporated into the national foreign policy. Witte, the principal Russian plenipotentiary to the Portsmouth peace conference, returned to Russia in September 1905 with the treaty which constituted the symbol and blueprint for the Far Eastern policy which the Russian government set about fashioning as they made the adjustment to the new conditions. The treaty was regarded in

[1] Geoffrey A. Hosking, *The Russian constitutional experiment; government and Duma, 1907–1914*, Cambridge, 1973, p. 5.

120

influential court and government circles in St. Petersburg as at best premature and at worst totally uncalled for or even disgraceful.

General Kuropatkin, upon preparing to leave the war front, addressed the attachés at his headquarters as follows:

Had we been given more time, and had it been decided to continue the war, I do not doubt that events would have assumed a different character, and that final success would have inclined to our side. But by the will of fate and the decision of our Emperor the war must cease at the very moment when, perhaps, we hold in our hands the means whereby to snatch from the enemy that victory which is so necessary for us and for Russia.[2]

Kuropatkin noted later that he considered the Russian troops better prepared for action than when the war began while the Japanese had reached the limit of their resources. In advocating that the war should continue in order to provide Russia an opportunity to win, Kuropatkin expressed a view which was echoed by many, particularly in the court and government. The real question was whether this could be accomplished by "one more battle" as some hoped. There was also the more pessimistic appraisal which claimed that so entrenched were the two armies that, even if one of them did win a battle, the line could not be moved forward. Like other appraisals, however, Sir Charles Hardinge considered this purely speculative.

Witte himself reflected an attitude of guarded tolerance toward the treaty and a consciousness of the unpopularity of a peace concluded at that time. This was an attitude which he conveyed both in his negative response to his appointment as plenipotentiary and in his view that the document was a necessary evil, meanwhile blaming the war on his opponents. And indeed it was not a treaty of which a nationalist could be proud since it followed upon and reflected a military defeat and in effect prescribed a Russian retreat in foreign policy not only in the Far East but along the entire frontier. The measure of the retreat was delineated in the Portsmouth treaty and in other understandings, culminating in the Russo-Japanese and Anglo-Russian agreements of 1907.

The foreign policy which the Russian government formulated and pursued in the aftermath of the war was, to be sure, not wholly new. It sought, rather, a redistribution of national interests and emphases in order, to some extent, to return to the apportionment which had prevailed before the war. That was a time when the Far East had not yet claimed as large a share of attention as it later did and when the shifts in the world balance of power which had occurred during the intervening period had

---

[2] General Kuropatkin's speech to the attachés who had been stationed with his command during the war in Manchuria, Sept. 28, 1905, FO 65/1703; No. 526 Hardinge to Lansdowne, Sept. 6, 1905, FO 65/1702.

not yet required an equivalent allocation of national strength within the country. The new policy was distinguished from its immediate predecessor not only by its continuing emphasis on Russia's European affiliations, interests, and defense requirements but by a new emphasis on the actual growth not only of German and Japanese but also of British and United States power and stature. It did this by seeking to supplement the existing understanding with France by forming others with Japan and Great Britain, thus ultimately giving final form to the entente diplomatic system.

The entente agreements resembled their counterparts in the opposing alliance system, composed of Germany, Austria-Hungary, and Italy, in that they bore witness to the fact that, even with Japan included in the entente and with a considerable portion of world power having accrued to the United States, the fulcrum of power in world politics remained in Europe. The entente agreements differed, however, from those which converged in central Europe, in that they dealt wholly or in large part with the world beyond Europe. This was basically because, by contrast with the alliance powers, at the time the agreements were formed, the European entente nations had extensive imperial interests and possessions in the extra-European world. They needed to guarantee these not only to insure continued tenure of them but also to provide them the freedom of action in Europe which the tense international situation required.

The colonial guarantees also represented an awareness, often expressed explicitly, of a rising crescendo of national self-consciousness on the part of Asian peoples, encouraged by the Japanese example and advocacy. This was a factor difficult if not impossible to control in the long run and not in itself susceptible of regulation or direction by means of the customary kinds of treaty guarantees. As a consequence, these treaties only vaguely or indirectly disclosed a degree of unexpressed anxiety for the future of colonial possessions in Asia. This was an important clue to the dramatic changes for which the diplomatic settlements could not provide.

Assessing the post-war situation was less difficult than finding a suitable counterpoise to the new balance of forces. The fact was that the balance had shifted in the course of the war to the detriment of Russia and to the advantage of her competitors, Germany, Japan, the United States and Britain. This suggested a grouping based on the long-existing Franco-Russian alliance supplemented by the more recently formed Anglo-French entente and by an Anglo-Russian understanding. Such a confluence of national power might be expected to serve not only as a control over Germany in Europe but also as a counterbalancing force providing a restraining influence over the most detached member of the entente, Japan.

As for the question of relations with Britain and Germany, the Russian foreign minister, Count Lamsdorf, is said to have aimed at a policy of keeping both these nations friendly to Russia and not too friendly to each other. This was a formula which, in the period since Bismarck, had been viewed as a means of guaranteeing the country a maximum degree of independence. The real problems in this respect centered around the precise details of the balance between these two nations and the task of fitting the defense of the Far East into this new combination.

Political and social cohesiveness and general national responsiveness to international conditions were among the characteristics which would, more than ever, determine the capacity of imperial Russia to survive and compete in the emerging world balance of power. It was, however, precisely these qualities which were in the course of being tested and further weakened by war, defeat, and revolution. Russia had lost the war to a considerable extent because of ineffective diplomacy and inadequate railway capacity to support a war on the frontier, reasons similar to those which had accounted for the defeat in the Crimean war a half century earlier. Once again in an even more distant theater of conflict Russia had failed to fashion a coherent policy which would bring into focus her own strength in relation to that of her competitors, this time more imminent and determined opponents.

Witte, until recently the minister of finance, had for a decade been trying to improve the productivity and international economic stature of the nation. His aim had been to bring the country abreast of her more advanced competitors. But while these enterprises had made progress they had raised opposition and by the end of the century had given way to a depression. This in turn had helped to stimulate political and social dissent including strikes; these conditions were aggravated in turn by war, defeat, and revolution. Instead of the expected benefits of the Witte reforms, the empire thus faced the world weakened and divided at a time when her two ambitious neighbors, Germany and Japan, were in a posture of vigorous and successful expansion.

It is ironic that the Transsiberian railway, largely Witte's contribution to Russia's ready access to the Pacific world and to the international rivalries developing there, should become the major supply route line to the Manchurian war fronts. It was there that Russia suffered a defeat of overwhelming proportions and with such fateful consequences. It is also an interesting coincidence that this railway became a major focus of the revolutionary activity directed against the imperial regime at the very time when Witte had been asked to assume a position in the government equivalent to prime minister and thus to assume responsibility for dealing with the revolution.

The revolutionary activity was already in progress by the time Witte assumed this new role in October 1905. The formal breach with the sovereign had taken place on "Bloody Sunday," January 22, 1905. The primary agency for organizing the country-wide strike, the All-Russian Union of Railway Employees and Workers, was formed in April 1905, not to initiate a strike movement but to organize and direct more effectively the movement already in progress.[3] The organizing conference represented the centrally located cities of Warsaw, Vilno, Moscow, and Saratov. With the potential availability of a widely developed railway network reaching all the major regions of the country, its direct and indirect influence was prospectively considerable. The railways were of significant economic and strategic usefulness not only to Russia but also to potential allies or opponents of Russia. Control of the railways or any segment of them would therefore be a valuable means of influencing the course of the development of either domestic or foreign affairs.

Because of its close association with the war, the Transsiberian railway became the object of considerable revolutionary attention and activity. The major center of revolutionary activity in Siberia in 1905 was at Krasnoiarsk, while the principal center east of Lake Baikal was at Chita in Transbaikal oblast. Politically, there was in Siberia a variety of groups, including not only Bolsheviks and Mensheviks, then not as clearly differentiated as later, but also persons labelled Economists as well as Socialist Revolutionaries and, above all, liberals.

The effort, particularly on the part of the Bolsheviks, to sort these out and to give their adherents a leading role, was making some progress by 1906. Such unity as existed by 1905 in the revolutionary movement in Siberia has been credited to the efforts particularly of such persons as Nikolai Nikolaevich Baransky, and to the formation at Tomsk in 1901 of the Siberian Social Democratic Union, said to have been patterned after the Union of Struggle for the Working Class, founded some years before.[4]

The Transbaikal region was also made more susceptible to revolutionary activity by the presence there of such exiles as Ivan Vasil'evich Babushkin and Emelian M. Iaroslavsky (Minei Izrailevich Gubelman), both associated with Chita; students and teachers at Tomsk, Irkutsk, and

---

[3] Henry Frederick Reichman, *Railwaymen and revolution: Russia 1905*, Berkeley, 1987, pp. 159 ff.; John L.H. Keep, *The rise of social democracy in Russia*, Oxford, 1963, p. 178.

[4] Nikolai Nikolaevich Baransky, *V riadakh sibirskogo sotsial-demokraticheskogo soiuza. Vospominaniia o podpol'noi rabote v 1897–1907 godakh*, 2–e izd. Tomsk, 1961, pp. 20–22; Mikhail Ivanovich Matveev, *Studenty Sibiri v revoliutsionnom dvizhenii*, Tomsk, 1966, pp. 59–64; P.T. Khaptaev, *Istoriia Buriat-Mongol'skoi ASSR*, vol. 1, Ulan-Ude, 1954, p. 398; Ostal'tseva, *Anglo-russkie soglashenie*, p. 82.

the schools of various levels throughout Transbaikal;[5] the railway workers, especially the railway shop workers, printers, coal-miners, and others; and the military forces stationed in or moving through the region by railway. It was out of these elements that ultimately there were created soviets of workers' and soldiers deputies at Krasnoiarsk, of soldiers' and cossacks' deputies at Chita, of sailors' deputies at Vladivostok, and of soldiers' deputies at Harbin.[6]

Emelian Iaroslavsky, who was born in Chita in 1878 and had carried on revolutionary work in Chita in the late 1890s, returned there from prison in the spring of 1903 to organize the Union of Workers of Transbaikal which is said to have become the pioneer organization of the Bolsheviks in Transbaikal.[7] The results of the organizational work carried on through 1904 became evident by early 1905 in two areas. One was the organization of the workers of Chita for a railway strike in early February 1905.[8]

Some 1,000 workers were said to have been implicated in strike activities, or about one-fifth of the work force in the railway shops at Chita. The strike had been intended to carry into practice the defeatist position of the Bolsheviks and, as the leaflets proclaimed, to rally the workers against the war. The event was poorly organized and was soon abandoned. The other area of endeavor, extending revolutionary work into the smaller towns, was itself a mere beginning and not until 1906 was there much more than a first step in forming a group of active professionals bringing the revolutionary message to the countryside.[9]

Harbin, situated near the heaviest concentration of troops, was also a busy center of revolutionary activity. Although revolutionary activity had long been carried on there, Bolshevik influences appear to have gained strength there only in November 1905. It was then that the Harbin Workers' Group was organized at the railway shop with its promising concentration of about 3,000 workers.[10] The organization later extended its activities to other parts of the railway, to the workers of the Sungari River boats, and to the flour mill workers at Harbin. The Bolshevik

---

[5] Mikhail Kuzmich Vetoshkin, *Bol'sheviki Dal'nego Vostoka v Pervoi russkoi revoliutsii*, Moscow, 1947, pp. 76 ff.

[6] A. A. Milshtein, "Revoliutsionnye vystupleniia trudiashchikhsia i soldat v 1906–1907 gg. na Dal'nem Vostoke i Vostochnoi Sibiri," in M.N. Tikhomirov, *Sbornik statei po istorii Dal'nego Vostoka*, Moscow, 1958, p. 320.

[7] L.M. Ivanov, A.M. Pankratova and A.L. Sidorov (eds.), *Revoliutsiia 1905–1907 gg. v natsional'nykh raionakh Rossii: sbornik statei*, Moscow, 1955, p. 789; George M. Enteen, "Writing party history in the USSR: the case of E. M. Iaroslavskii," *JCH* XXI no. 2 (Apr. 1986), 321–339.

[8] S. A. Urodkov, "Chitinskoe vooruzhennoe vosstanie 1905 g.," *VLU*, no. 8 (1956), 22–24.

[9] Vetoshkin, *Bol'sheviki Dal'nego Vostoka*, p. 136.

[10] Ibid., pp. 197–199; Rosemary Y.I. Quested, *"Matey" imperialists? The Tsarist Russians in Manchuria 1895–1917*, Hong Kong, 1982, pp. 179–180.

organizers worked persistently to press their creed and program against their competitors. Mikhail Kuzmich Vetoshkin, the author of an account of the events, claimed to have been the only party professional in the Harbin organization, the rest having been workers mobilized specifically for the operation.

Vladivostok, by contrast with Harbin, appears to have been less active as a center of organized revolutionary activity.[11] Even though this was the seat of a garrison and of a naval port, a shortage of party workers may have forced the revolutionaries to focus their efforts in the main areas of troop concentration and military activity. Soviet sources also indicate that competing influences of the Mensheviks, Socialist Revolutionaries, and liberals were factors which delayed their progress. It has been conceded that the liberal-led Union of Unions controlled such workers' activities as there were and that the same group was influential among the lower ranks of the military forces.[12]

The month of October 1905 was, from various political points of view, the culmination of the preceding months of preparation. A general strike apparently began in the formal sense in the early afternoon of October 6, 1905 on the Moscow–Kazan railway when the All-Russian Union of Railway Employees and Workers called for it; after October 10, Moscow was completely shut off. Within a few days the strike encompassed all the major railway lines of the country, thus bringing the business life of St. Petersburg and other important centers to a standstill.[13] The strike at Chita was apparently inspired or urged by Baransky who telegraphed word of its beginning back from Irkutsk to Chita where it began on October 27.[14]

The strike along the Transsiberian railway immediately encompassed the postal and telegraph employees, the machinists, the power station workers, the workers along the railway line and at the depôts, and then spread to the bakers, wine warehousemen, the banks, municipal offices, teachers, lawyers, engineers, and others. By the second day, the 28th, crowds carrying red flags converged on the railway station and tried to plunder the arms warehouse. Although this outburst was to some extent

[11] V. P. Golionko, "Vooruzhennoe vosstanie matrosov Tikhookeanskogo Flota v 1905–1907 gg.," in S. F. Naida, *Voennye moriaki v period pervoi russkoi revoliutsii 1905–1907 gg.*, Moscow, 1955, pp. 281–283; Kh. I. Muratov, *Revoliutsionnoe dvizhenie v russkoi armii v 1905–1907 gg.*, Moscow, 1955, pp. 312–315.

[12] No. 58 Union of Unions of the Ussuri Region, "Appeal to the Ussuri Branch of the Union of Unions with the Call to Support the Demand of the Striking Postal and Telegraph Employees," probably December 1905, in A.I. Krushanov (ed.) *Vladivostok (sbornik istoricheskikh dokumentov, 1860–1907 gg.)*, Vladivostok, 1960, pp. 97–98.

[13] Reichman, *Railwaymen and revolution*, pp. 198, 356–380; Witte, *Vospominaniia*, III, 134.

[14] Baransky, *V riadakh*, p. 64.

suppressed, the movement was renewed on October 31 with strikes, meetings, and demonstrations.[15] The strike was also renewed at Harbin on the morning of November 6 with crowds and demonstrations, some claiming to be celebrating the Manifesto of October 30.

The revolutionaries undertook during November and December to translate the enthusiasm and cooperative experience of the strike movement into a more precise sense of purpose which could lead to the seizure of power. This required building worker-soldier-cossack solidarity, acquired by propagandizing and organizing the military forces. This movement attempted particularly to capitalize on the eagerness of the troops to be returned home since the war was over and to carry this to the point where the necessary coordination could be achieved.[16] Since a military role was also intended for the workers, the weeks of November and December saw the formation of workers' detachments. Arms were provided by plundering military storage depots and the seizure of trains carrying arms. A soviet of soldiers' and cossacks' deputies was formed on November 22, thus at least reaching a stage of integration of these vital groups into the revolutionary program.[17]

The movement culminated on December 20 in another nationwide railway strike and in armed uprisings. Meanwhile, the directors of the revolutionary movement had shown themselves capable not only of building a power structure but of using it. As their strength grew they exerted increasing pressure on General I. V. Kholshchevnikov, the military governor of Transbaikal oblast, to surrender his prerogatives to them and, starting with control of the telegraph, their writ came to run progressively farther and to affect the region more comprehensively.

The effectiveness of the "seizure of power" which the revolutionaries were able to introduce by a combination of their own readiness to take full advantage of every opportunity and of official complicity, either intentional or inadvertent, is confirmed in official government documents.[18] They indicate that the railway was indeed in the hands of the strikers' committees which had a tight control over train movements. They confirm the restraint exercised over telegraphic communications to the point where no official traffic was sent at all. Courier and even foreign

[15] Khaptaev, *Istoriia*, pp. 399–400; USSR Central Archives, *Russko-iaponskaia voina*, pp. 110–111.

[16] Report of the Strike Committee of Irkutsk, Dec. 6, 1905, Report of the Session of the Congress of Workers' Deputies of Chita, Dec, 21, 1905, Report of the Chief of the Irkutsk Gendarmery, Jan 7, 1906, in Khaptaev, *Istoriia*, pp. 400–406.

[17] Urodkov, "Chitinskoe vooruzhennoe vosstanie," 28; Reichman, *Railwaymen and revolution*, pp. 493–514; Keep, *The rise of social democracy*, 1963, p. 263.

[18] Durnovo to Emperor, Jan. 2, 1906, in V. Maksakov (ed.), *Karatel'nye ekspeditsii v Sibiri v 1905–1906 gg.*, Moscow, 1932, p. 50.

telegraphic services had to be used for essential messages, meanwhile leaving the strike committee free to send its communications at will. They also confirm the assertion that the committees exercised considerable control over local administrations on behalf of their objectives. All in all, these features lent a coordinated and disciplined aspect to the episode which was clearly unnerving to some officials.

But this time the imperial regime was better prepared to withstand the attack while the revolutionaries, including locally those of the Chita committee, were lacking in any clear program beyond the seizure of power and were isolated from other regions.[19] The Chita committee fell on January 24, 1906 to the special forces of Lieutenant General Baron Meller-Zakomelsky. Many were arrested and tried, some sentenced to confinement, others to death. Lieutenant General I. V. Kholshchev- nikov, the military governor of Transbaikal, was sentenced to confine- ment in a fortress for a year and four months without loss of rank.

Another focus of revolutionary aspirations and activity which had particularly significant implications for foreign policy was Russian Central Asia and the neighboring Asian countries. Cultural-religious and political responses to foreign rule had long been significant factors in these regions. They had, however, been intensified and in some cases developed new objectives by the impact of the Russo-Japanese war and the revolutionary wave in Russia. The Russo-Japanese war was seen by the people on both sides of the Indian–Russian border region as a testimony to Japanese bravery and strength and to Russian weakness and, by implication, to the doubtfulness of western invincibility.

The Japanese success in itself made a great impact because it not only affected the hopes and thoughts of the leaders but "touched the imagina- tion of the people" who "responded to it with great enthusiasm."[20] The British minister in Persia, Sir Arthur Hardinge, wrote later with respect to the impact of the Japanese victory at Tsushima that "from one end of Persia to the other, a huge weight appeared to have been lifted from men's hearts, and the whole native population breathed again . . . The destruc- tion of the Russian Fleet by an Asiatic power was one of the main indirect causes of that national, if ill-managed, revolutionary attempt to overth- row the ancient polity of Persia."[21]

Furthermore, in their search for a way to duplicate the success of the Japanese in playing, by peaceful or forceful means, an independent role in

[19] Urodkov, "Chitinskoe vooruzhennoe vosstanie," 33–37; Keep, *The rise of social democ- racy*, 1963, p. 263.
[20] Ramparkash A. Dua, *The impact of the Russo-Japanese War on Indian politics*, Delhi, 1966, pp. 22–27; Hardinge, *A diplomatist*, p. 345.
[21] Surendra Gopal, *British policy in India, 1858–1905*, Cambridge, 1965, p. 223; Michael Edwardes, *High noon of empire, India under Curzon*, London, 1965, p. 237.

the world, the Japanese example was seen "as a blow to Great Britain, which represented the West to the Indians." It has also been pointed out that the viceroyalty of Lord Curzon, which had contributed so much to British India but which was not loved by many people, came to a formal end on August 21, 1905, and "marked the apogee of British Indian administration and the beginning of adult Indian nationalism."[22]

The situation of Afghanistan, influenced by the same events, changed markedly during the Far Eastern war, particularly with respect to its northern neighbor. Amir Habibullah had succeeded Abdur Rahman in 1901 and was already inclined to be independent though not unfriendly to Britain. He was also strongly influenced by the Japanese victories over Russia and began to dream of achieving complete independence from Russia by a similar heroic act. When these venturesome thoughts were compared by worried observers in London and Simla with the Amir's actual military weakness, the strategic consequences for India of an unsuccessful military adventure on his part, and the increasing accessibility of Afghanistan to Russia by Central Asian railway, apprehensiveness about the security of India grew.

The awakening movement in Central Asia was expressed in three different ways, all in some way, however, receiving encouragement from the Japanese victory. One was a moderate movement among non-Russian people which sought modernization through reform. The proportion of the Central Asian population touched by this movement was relatively small, and was the more industrious and prosperous part, enjoying a level of material well-being and cultural affluence far above the rest of the population. It was also the segment of society which enjoyed some rapport with the Russians, achieved through facility with the Russian language, adoption of western dress, some modification of the architecture of their houses, and an unusual degree of adaptation of their religious outlook and practices to the pattern of Christian society.

A principal leader of this Muslim movement was Ismail Bey Gasprinsky (or Gaspirali), a Crimean Tatar who advocated the uplift of the people through a reformed education, thus giving the movement the name Jadidist (reformist).[23] Gasprinsky opposed revolutionary methods,

---

[22] Arminius Vambery, *Western culture in Eastern lands. A comparison of the methods adopted by England and Russia in the Middle East*, London, 1906, pp. 89–94.

[23] Edward James Lazzerini, "Jadidism at the turn of the twentieth century: a view from within," *CMRS*, XVI (1975), 245–277; Edward James Lazzerini, "Ismail Bey Gasprinskii and Muslim modernism in Russia, 1878–1914," Ph.D. dissertation, University of Washington, Seattle, 1973, pp. 54–56; Serge A. Zenkovsky, *Pan-Turkism and Islam in Russia*, Cambridge, 1960, pp. 32–33; Alexandre Bennigsen and Chantal Lemercier-Quelquejay, *Islam in the Soviet Union*, Foreword by Geoffrey E. Wheeler, London, 1967, pp. 35–42; Hélène Carrère d'Encausse, "Social and political reform," in Edward Allworth (ed.), *Central Asia: a century of Russian rule*, New York, 1967, pp. 193–196.

at least for Muslims, held that their greatest need was modernization, and maintained that this could best be achieved through Russian goodwill.

The movement which, accordingly, sought accommodation with Russia, was dealt a severe blow by the Japanese victory and the consequent loss of western, including Russian, prestige. It was stimulated however, to renewed effort by the parallel revolutionary movement and, while continuing to seek modernization and to strive for the awakening of a national consciousness, it added a more determined drive for an end to foreign domination and for the realization of social and political reform.[24]

While the earlier accommodation movement in Central Asia had been most prominent among the Kazakhs and was represented by such persons as the Kazakh poet and descendent of the Khans of the Middle Horde, Chokan Chingisovich Valikhanov, the movement developed later in Turkestan and approached the accommodation process with greater sophistication and reserve. The moderates took the first step toward unity at this time with the calling of the first All-Russian Muslim Congress, held illegally on August 28, 1905 at Nizhnii Novgorod, followed by two others held in January and August 1906.[25]

The second movement was popularly based, aimed at non-Muslims, and religious in leadership. It was an outgrowth of the protracted Islamic decline under pressure from the west, a process which contributed to its ranks many landless peasants and other displaced persons. After the Russian conquest, new pressure was added with the introduction of railways, banks and other aspects of a new economy and the movement became specifically anti-Russian. Under the leadership of the Sufi Naqshbandi order the aim was to eliminate the infidel Russian masters. On May 18, 1898 a holy war was declared and directed against a Russian garrison at Andijan under the leadership of a Naqshbandi Sufi, Muhammad Ali Khalfa, but was quickly suppressed.[26]

In 1906–7 the Russo-Japanese war and the revolution again activated the roving bands which, under the leadership of the legendary Namaz Premkulov, who was seen as a protector of the weak and a redistributor of wealth, plundered the Samarkand area. Later the conditions of the first world war and the revolution gave rise to a continuation of the movement which was known as the Basmachi.

The third movement in the southern Russian borderland was almost

---

[24] Hélène Carrère d'Encausse, *Islam and the Russian Empire: reform and revolution in Central Asia*, Berkeley, 1988, p. 178–179.

[25] Richard A. Pierce (ed.), *Russian Central Asia, 1867–1917. A study in colonial rule*, Berkeley, 1960, pp. 255–257; Bennigsen and Lemercier-Quelquejay, *Islam in the Soviet Union*, pp. 14–15; Lazzerini, "Ismail Bey Gasprinskii," pp. 60–67.

[26] Carrère d'Encausse, *Islam and the Russian Empire*, pp. 66–67, 72 ff.; Edward D. Sokol, *The revolt of 1916 in Russian Central Asia*, Baltimore, 1954, pp. 56–72.

exclusively Russian in adherents and outlook and, though it came to include some non-Russians, it gave no thought to improving their position in society.[27] It centered mainly on railways and cities, particularly stations, railway depôts, and repair shops though by 1906 it began to spread beyond the cities into regions more typically indigenous. The political groups such as the Social Democrats, both the Bolsheviks and Mensheviks, as well as the Socialist Revolutionaries, and even anarchists, Zionists and Dashnaks, still cooperated at the beginning. But the Social Democrats were better organized. Their center was at Tashkent where the Bolshevik, M. V. Morozov, had at his disposal a legal Russian newspaper, the *Samarkand*. The Union of Turkestan Organizations of the Russian Social Democratic Workers' Party gave this group its first central organization.

Revolutionary activity began in Central Asia well before the St. Petersburg events of January 1905. The railway workers at Kala-i-Mor near Kushka struck in 1902 and the Russian railway workers of Tashkent demonstrated on May 1, 1904. Central Asia was thus prepared to join in the great strike of October 1905 and did so formally and officially on a signal from the strike committee of Ashkhabad at midnight on the night of October 13–14.[28] The Grand Duke Konstantin Nikolaevich who was then in Tashkent noted on October 26 that the strike appeared to be over and it officially ended the next day only to begin again when the First Tashkent Reserve Battalion and other units mutinied on November 15.

General Dean Ivanovich Subotich, who was sent in early 1906 to take over the troubled city of Tashkent, tried, at a time of administrative weakness, to restore order by appeasing the terrorists and revolutionaries, thus assisting them. When the government began to regain control of the situation, Subotich and his assistant, General V. V. Sakharov, were relieved of their commands. The government never lost complete control of the region and by early 1907 it was once more in command of the situation. There remained, however, a heritage of brigandage drawn from displaced peasants, the experience of some involvement on the part of non-Russian people, and, even though the Social Democrats and Socia-

[27] Pierce, *Russian Central Asia*, pp. 238–240; Carrère d'Encausse, *Islam and the Russian Empire*, pp. 181–188; David Lane, "The Russian Social Democratic Labour Party in St. Petersburg, Tver and Ashkhabad, 1903–1905," *SS*, XV (1964), 340–343; A.F. Iakunin, "Revoliutsiia 1905–1907 gg. v Kazakhstane," in L.M. Ivanov, A.M. Pankratova, and A.L. Sidorov (eds.), *Revoliutsiia 1905–1907 gg. v natsional'nykh raionakh Rossii: sbornik statei*, Moscow, 1955, pp. 678–682.
[28] Anatolii Vladimirovich Piaskovsky, *Revoliutsiia 1905–1907 godov v Uzbekistane*, Tashkent, 1957, pp. 109 ff.; Anatolii Vladimirovich Piaskovsky, *Revoliutsiia 1905–1907 godov v Turkestane*, Moscow, 1958, pp. 181–209; "Iz dnevnika Konstantina Romanova 1905 god," *KA*, I (44) (1931), 139–142; Becker, *Russia's protectorates*, p. 204.

list Revolutionaries had been badly broken, they retained the memory and experience of the "dress rehearsal."[29]

There was another factor which must have had a significant bearing on the readiness of Russia at this time to consider an accommodation in Persia with Britain. This was the situation in Central Asia which, like other parts of Russia, had suffered from both war and revolution. The consequences of these were aggravated by administrative weakness under such persons as General N. N. Teviashev, the governor general of Turkestan, to whom the British military attaché, Lieutenant Colonel Napier, had once referred as "a weak and fussy old gentleman ... sincere only in anxiety to avoid troubles and complications," and whose unfortunate administration ended with his death in the strike of October 1905.[30]

After a short period during which his assistant, General V. V. Sakharov, greatly improved the situation, Teviashev was replaced by General D. I. Subotich whose administration had been called disastrous because, like Teviashev, he tried unsuccessfully to appease the revolutionaries. Others, such as General V. P. Prasalov at Kushka Post were said to have encouraged unpopularity and even rebellion by over-zealous and ill-timed acts. The government, for one reason or another, was unable to deal with a serious situation in which there were crippling strikes, an increase in murder and other crimes, and a general breakdown in public safety, all of which helped to reduce Russian influence and prestige in an essentially colonial society.[31]

The military situation in Central Asia further aggravated the general deterioration. The troop strength of the region had been reduced during the war, apparently as much as 15 percent, and the number of troops there in early 1906 was estimated at 45–50,000 men.[32] The Russian government induced a potentially embarrassing relationship when a request that the Khan of Khiva help by supplying some troops was turned down by the Khan. This was a particularly humiliating experience since the non-Russian people of the region had not been fully integrated as citizens and military service had not heretofore been required of them. More than 50

[29] Carrère d'Encausse, *Islam and the Russian Empire*, p. 186.
[30] No. 4 Nicolson, "Annual Report on Russia," Jan. 2, 1907, FO 371/318 and *BD* IV, 263; No. 579 Hardinge to Lansdowne, Nov. 10, 1904, enclosing Lt. Col. H. D. Napier, "Diary of a visit to Central Asia," Nov. 9, 1904, FO 65/1652.
[31] IG Agent's report on Russian Central Asia, July 7, 1905, Curzon 394; Hélène Carrère d'Encausse, "Organization and colonization the conquered territories," in Edward Allworth, (ed.) *Central Asia: a century of Russian rule*, New York, 1967, p. 159; No. 14 Consul Stevens (Batum) to Grey, June 15, 1906, enclosing a report on Central Asia, FO 371/127.
[32] IO Memorandum on "Affairs on and beyond the North-West Frontier of India" for July 1906, FO 371/128; IG to IO, Nov. 23, 1905, FO 106/11; No. 64 Consul Stevens to Lansdowne, Dec. 9, 1905, FO 371/119.

percent of the soldiers stationed in Central Asia were non-Russian and consisted largely of Poles, Jews, Georgians, and Armenians, especially the last of these. Efforts were made by the predominantly Sunni Muslims to convert the Christian troops, particularly the non-Russians. Many of the latter hated the Russian government and were in sympathy with the revolutionary movement.

The railway system of Central Asia, in addition to its obvious economic purpose and function, had always been an important component of the defensive-offensive structure and plans and continued to serve this role after the war with Japan. The post-war railway plans sought to strengthen the internal military capability of the borderlands with reference to the frontier. With respect particularly to the advance of Russian influence in Persia, it was intended to supplement the Russian economic and strategic gains as prudence and opportunity permitted.

The most significant addition to the communications facilities of the region in recent years was the Orenburg–Tashkent railway line which was formally opened on January 1, 1906 though its southern section between Kazalinsk and Tashkent still had a number of serious defects which needed to be corrected.[33] One of these was the need to move a considerable section of track further away from the Syr Darya river since that river at times overflowed its banks and flooded the tracks. The railway with its 74 stations bridged the 1,500 miles between Orenburg and Tashkent and connected this line with Kushka Post on the Afghan frontier over the additional 450 mile railway southward. The line gave this distant outpost a direct connection with St. Petersburg 3,180 miles away.

This railway gave the country much easier and more direct access to Afghanistan than the Transcaspian line which was indirect and required transshipment at Krasnovodsk. It also obviated any further attempts to navigate the Syr Darya and reduced the traffic on the Amu Darya to purely local traffic. Potential traffic on the Tashkent–Samarkand section was estimated in November 1904 at ten trains each way as compared with twelve trains between Krasnovodsk and Merv on the Transcaspian line.

Other Central Asian railway projects of this period were intended either to complete existing construction, improve economic or strategic relationships with other regions, or project internal railways into Persia.

[33] No. 14 Consul Stevens to Grey, June 15, 1906, FO 371/127; Col. C. E. de la Poer Beresford, "Russian railways towards India," *PCAS*, (1906), 3–5; Anan'ich, *Rossiia i mezhdunarodnyi kapital*, p. 96; Becker, *Russia's protectorates*, pp. 189–190; Ronald Ray Rader, "Decline of the Afghan problem as a crisis factor in Russian foreign policy, 1892–1907," Ph.D. dissertation, Syracuse University, 1965, pp. 142–144; IG to Morley, Feb. 16, 1907, FO 371/321; No. 10 Napier to Spring Rice, Feb. 15, 1906, FO 371/123; No. 40 Napier to Nicolson, June 12, 1906, FO 371/126; No. 579 Hardinge to Lansdowne, Nov. 10, 1904, enclosing Lt. Col. Napier, "Diary of a visit to Central Asia," FO 65/1652.

The railway which would later be constructed as the Turkestan–Siberian line was considered at this time because it would provide direct communications for Russian forces between Central Asia and the Far East and proposals of foreign capitalists to build it were seriously discussed.[34] The southward projection of the Russian railways into Afghanistan or Persia in fact depended upon the unlikely chance that these two neighbors would consent and that some accommodation could be reached with Britain. Extending the railway southward from Kushka Post into Afghanistan to Herat and Kandahar or to Chaman on the Baluchistan frontier was one of these unlikely projects.

Retreat in Persia

The situation in Persia was in some ways comparable, even parallel to that in the Far East. In both cases Russia had sought to achieve ascendancy by "peaceful penetration," by railway and bank in Manchuria and by highway and bank in Persia. In both cases she had been seeking to acquire a region which was considered not just desirable in itself but strategically unique for the fulfillment of Russia's own territorial and maritime development. Furthermore, she was hoping to be able to accomplish this at a time when she could still hope to have one or both as a monopoly. This was particularly important with respect to the Middle East which, while equally desirable, was more important for Russia's competitive prospects. Even if Russia were unsuccessful in maintaining an outlet through Manchuria, she would still have a means of access to the Pacific through Vladivostok. On the other hand, in the Middle East the German advance was not only engulfing the Russian outlet through the Turkish straits but was rapidly advancing in Persia and the Persian Gulf region.

Accordingly, the Russian interest in continuing the advance in Persia was, as both policy and practice since early 1904 had shown, likewise stimulated rather than being in any way daunted by the military reverses in Manchuria. It was held by Moshir ol-Molk, the Persian minister in St. Petersburg, as well as others that in fact the "failure of Russia's attempt to obtain an access to warm water in the Far East could only result in increasing her desire to obtain command of a port in the South."[35] Major H. R. Sykes, in a paper read to the Central Asian Society on March 1, 1905, agreed with this and added that in his view Britain would be unable to prevent Russia from creating a second Port Arthur on the Persian Gulf.[36] It was also to be expected that, having been so effectively

---

[34] No. 40 Hardinge to Grey, Jan. 10, 1906, FO 371/121.
[35] No. 772 Spring Rice to Grey, Dec. 16, 1905, IO Political Dept. X (3653/05).
[36] H.R. Sykes, "Our recent progress in southern Persia and its possibilities," *PCAS* (1905), 18–19 (paper read Mar. 1, 1905).

checkmated at the Turkish straits by the German railway, Russia would leave no stone unturned to prevent either the Germans or the British from outmaneuvering her either on the crucial seaboard of the Gulf or in the heartland of Persia.

The downward course for Russia in the war in the Far East, however, cast a lengthening shadow over her heretofore auspicious and promising enterprises in Persia. The Russian Discount and Loan Bank was the principal instrument of Russian expansion there, acting through its branches at Teheran, Julfa, Anzali, Isfahan, Kazvin, Mashkhad, Nasrata-bad, Rasht, Tabriz, Barfrush, Hamadan, Kermanshah, Sebzevan, and Urmia.[37] The mission of the bank was to acquire concessions, supply loans, finance Russo-Persian trade including shipping to the Persian Gulf, and facilitate road building and transportation. In general, it was expected that this would give Russia a dominant role in the economic life of Persia.

The objective was to seek a clear predominance in Persia over all foreign competitors. One of the activities of the bank was the endeavor to bring under its control all Afghan wool importers, offering to advance them money and to forward their wool to Russia and Europe at a very low rate of interest and commission. This would take the business out of the hands of the Armenian merchants since these would find competition very difficult with a government institution doing business on such a principle.

These various facets of Russian economic policy and practice were, as they had been throughout the advance in Central Asia, a vital step in achieving the political goal of ultimate domination in Persia.[38] The Russian achievement thus far was viewed as the consequence of a protracted process of struggle with Britain for the strengthening of Russian influence in Persia which had been going on since the conclusion on February 22, 1828 of the Russo-Persian treaty of Turkmanchai. It was fixed policy to oppose a partition of the country or the exercise of control over it through a condominium or through the hegemony of any third power. The plan was rather to seek to preserve the territorial integrity of Persia in order to maintain it intact for Russia.

Lord Curzon expressed this relationship aptly when he wrote that Russia was seeking "supreme political influence and unchallenged econ-omic control" within a state which would hopefully be "so weak as to be dependent but not so weak as to fall absolutely to pieces."[39] The

---

[37] A.L. Popov (ed.), "Anglo-russkoe sopernichestvo v Persii v 1890–1906 gg." *KA*, I (56), (1933), 51–53 (report of special conference, June 20, 1901); Popov, "Tsarskaia Rossiia i Persiia," 17 (Lamsdorf Instructions to A. N. Speyer, Oct. 13, 1904); IG to IO Jan. 7, 1904, FO 106/8.

[38] Popov, "Tsarskaia Rossiia i Persiia," 17 (Lamsdorf Instructions).

[39] Kazemzadeh, *Russia and Britain*, pp. 406–407.

government should also, according to Lamsdorf's specifications, be stable in order to be able to prevent internal disorder and preserve order in its border regions.[40]

There was at the same time on Lamsdorf's part a frank recognition, reminiscent of similar statements by British observers, that internal order in Persia was weak. He told a special conference of June 20, 1904 that internal order in Persia was not sound, that conceptions of legality were extremely shaky, and that arbitrary rule was the standard both at the center and at the local level; reforms were badly needed. Thus, for different reasons both Britain and Russia were very concerned about the balance in Persia between survival and extinction as a nation.

The outbreak of war and the consequent attenuation of Russian power in the Middle East required some abatement of the Russian advance in Persia. This encouraged from the very beginning not only a British economic counter-attack but, especially after the successful conclusion of the Anglo-French entente, a renewed British effort to seek an Anglo-Russian accord dealing with Persia. Sir Arthur Hardinge, the British minister in Teheran, noted even before the actual onset of the war a greater readiness on the part of the Russians to discuss the Persian question.[41]

Hardinge's suggestions for such discussions included a negative view on the question of a geographical division of the country into spheres of interest since this would favor Russia by leaving Teheran and the Persian government in her area. He favored a condominium which would give both parties equal influence at Teheran, joint control over financial policy, and a common interest in maintaining the country as a neutral, intermediate state in order to preserve the integrity and independence of Persia as the Austro-Russian agreement had done in the Balkans.

The conclusion of the Anglo-French entente appears to have turned Hardinge's attention to a consideration of this treaty and particularly that part of it which pertained to Thailand.[42] St. John Brodrick, writing at this time to Lord Ampthill, reflected a new optimism with respect to the Persian question. He wrote: "I fancy time is on our side there," and continued, envisioning the favorable effect of further Russian defeats in the Far East.

The Anglo-French agreement established in Thailand a division into spheres of influence which Hardinge suggested as a basis for an Anglo-

[40] Popov, "Tsarskaia Rossiia i Persiia", 17 (Lamsdorf Instructions); Popov, "Anglo-russkoe sopernichestvo," 51; Kazemzadeh, *Russia and Britain*, pp. 458–459.
[41] A. Hardinge to Lansdowne, Feb. 1, 1904 (Curzon?) to Lansdowne, July 19, 1904, FO 800/137.
[42] A. Hardinge to Lansdowne, May 23, 1904, FO 800/137; Brodrick to Ampthill, May 6, 12, 1904, Ampthill E 233/37.

Russian settlement of the Persian question. Lord Lansdowne stated in a covering dispatch accompanying the Anglo-French settlement respecting Thailand: "The distinctive feature ... is that the parties pledge themselves not merely to abstain from poaching on each other's preserves but to do all in their power to further one another's interests."

Hardinge, with a backward glance to the circumstances of 1899, went a step further and suggested that the Russian sphere be extended to include a limited portion of the Persian Gulf coast. He had learned some of the provisions of a secret treaty which he believed to have been formally or informally concluded in that year between Russia and Persia. By this treaty, signed at a time when he deemed British influence to have been at its nadir, Persia had presumably been ready to grant Russia a frontage on the Persian Gulf such as Chahbahar from which she would be able to repel any aggressive movement from India.

The year 1899 was in fact a time when Russia had exerted considerable pressure on Persia to grant various privileges and advantages, including a Gulf port.[43] It was also the year when Curzon heard that the Sultan of Muscat had expressed the fear that this might turn out to be a Russian gain. Furthermore, Lord Salisbury had warned the Persian government on April 15, 1899, well before the start of the Boer war with its debilitating effects on British prestige, against allowing any other European nation to "exercise control or jurisdiction over any gulf port."[44] Nevertheless, Hardinge suggested that the Russian sphere include Mohammerah and a section of the coast eastward to Fars, while the coast from there eastward to Bushire might be within a British sphere. Both nations, he thought, should be asked to agree not to fortify their respective portions of the coast.

Some members of the Russian government, notably the minister of finance, Vladimir Nikolaevich Kokovtsov, and the agent of the Ministry of Finance in Persia, E. K. Grube, favored some limitations on the granting of loans to Persia. By late 1902 Grube had called Witte's attention to the inadvisability of catering to the insatiable financial needs of the Shah, the heir to the throne, and of the government.[45] Kokovtsov, who replaced Eduard Dmitrievich Pleske as minister of finance on February 18, 1904, encountered opposition to his proposed expenditure restrictions from Count Lamsdorf and from the diplomatic establishment.

[43] George Peabody Gooch, "Continental Agreements, 1902–1907," in George Peabody Gooch and A.W. Ward (eds.), *The Cambridge history of British foreign policy: 1783–1919*, 3 vols. New York, 1923, III, 315.
[44] Kazemzadeh, *Russia and Britain*, pp. 324–354; Dilks, *Curzon in India*, I, 118–120; C. Hardinge to Lansdowne, Dec. 30, 1904, in Greaves, "British policy in Persia," 288.
[45] No. 14 Hamilton to IG, July 6, 1900, *BD*, IV, 363–365.

By mid-1904, Lamsdorf had not lost hope in a favorable outcome of the war and was, therefore, not prepared to sound retreat in Russia's forward policy in Persia. He wanted, accordingly, to avoid any hint of a limitation on Russian largess since he assumed that Persia would ultimately fall to Russia in any case, and to refrain from all appearances of readiness to partition the country into spheres of influence lest the Persian government lose confidence in Russia. Kokovtsov, having to deal with the growing cost of the war and the increasing difficulty of securing necessary loans, saw the need to reduce expenditures wherever possible. Yet even he wanted at that time to do so without attenuating Russian achievements and prospects any more than necessary.

The deliberations of the special ministerial conference called on June 20, 1904 to consider Russian economic and financial policy in Persia confirmed to a considerable degree the optimistic views then being expressed in London.[46] It was attended by the ministers of foreign affairs and finance, Lamsdorf and Kokovtsov, the assistant minister of finance, P. M. Romanov, the Russian ambassador in Constantinople, I.A. Zinov'ev, the directors of the State Bank, Sergei Ivanovich Timashev, and of the Discount and Loan Bank of Persia, Petr L'vovich Bark, and three officials of the Ministry of Foreign Affairs in addition to the minister, the assistant minister, Prince Valerian Sergeevich Obolensky-Neledinsky-Meletsky, the senior counselor, Kimon Manuilovich Argyropulo, and the director of the first department, Nikolai Genrikhovich Hartwig. The decision of this theoretically financial question was thus recognized as having a significant political aspect by being committed to this financial-diplomatic group.

The central role of Russian economic policy in Persia was reaffirmed by the conference, particularly that of the bank. The achievement of Russian financial and political dominance in the country was also reaffirmed but some curtailment was to be sought which would decelerate the rate of progress without losing sight of the goal. The expenditure thus far of 32,500,000 rubles in loans in 1900 and 1902, of government outlays through the bank of 11,300,000 rubles and the extension of 10,000,000 rubles in credits had considerably advanced the Russian position in Persia but the great outlays for the wars, the poor condition of the Persian government which rendered it a bad risk, and the difficulty of competing financially and commercially with Britain required a reconsideration of the program.

The solution proposed, while retaining existing opposition to a division into spheres of influence, was a condominium with another foreign power

---

[46] Boris Vasil'evich Anan'ich, "Krizis ekonomicheskoi politika tsarizma v Persii v 1904–6 gg." *IZ*, LXXIV (1963) 247–250; Anan'ich, *Rossiiskoe samoderzhavie*, pp. 108–111.

or the hegemony of a third power, the actual recognition of a division along a line drawn through Isfahan. It was suggested that Russia concentrate her commercial and financial activities north of this line since this was the area already most developed by her, most accessible, most promising for the future, and least complicated by foreign rights and competition. But even in the north no new enterprises would be undertaken unless they were of some real advantage and even among these preference would be given to those which could contribute to the achievement of predominance over foreign enterprises.

Since the Persian budget had an annual deficit of some 3 million rubles and handled loans wastefully, loans had a relatively restricted immediate value for Russia and would, consequently, be abandoned except where a definite advantage could be seen for Russia. The conference concluded that Russia would decline as much as possible Persian requests for financial help, would make loans of money only if it were of the greatest political and economic importance to do so and if it had sufficient guarantees. The Russian government would seek no unprofitable concessions but would rather develop and improve existing Russian enterprises such as bank activities, roads, transportation, and, while continuing to oppose railway construction in Persia, would nevertheless participate as heretofore in the expansion of the telegraph network supplementary to road building.

Count Lamsdorf wrote a set of instructions on October 13, 1904 for the new Russian minister in Teheran, A. N. Speyer [Aleksei Nikolaevich Shpeier].[47] These were written to fit the difficult current circumstances but they stressed the traditional need to preserve the territorial integrity of Persia in order to retain it as an area for Russian activity. He directed Speyer to seek a close union of Russia and Persia but cautioned that the present was not a favorable time to think of an alliance with the Shah's government since Russia did not at that time have sufficient strength in Asia to support such a relationship.

Although the Persian Cossack brigade, a unit formed with Russian help and under Russian control, was a force for stability in Persia, Lamsdorf wrote, there was still an urgent need to support the authority of the central government both at the center and in the border regions. The opportunity should be sought for appointing Russian officers to train the Persian army but not in such a way as to create the impression that reforms were to be carried out systematically, since Russia did not wish a "complete revitalization of that country." Lamsdorf also charged Speyer with reinforcing the authority of the central government in the border regions, with trying

[47] Popov, "Anglo-russkoe sopernichestvo," 49–55; Kazemzadeh, *Russia and Britain*, pp. 457–468; Anan'ich, "Krizis ekonomicheskoi politika tsarizma," pp. 250–252.

to control the brigands on the Transcaucasian border, with strengthening the hand of the government and of Russian influence in general in Seistan, and with extending the latter into Baluchistan.

The German presence in the Ottoman Empire had an even more immediate and unequivocal impact in Persia and on the vital Anglo-Russian interests there than was the case with Egypt. The German ventures which had long been heralded by the eastward advance through Turkey of German railway and other economic interests, finally made their appearance in Persia in the wake of a rumored German loan to the Persian government in 1906.[48] These plans included the construction of a branch of the Bagdad railway project into Persia, the establishment of a bank, a role in the economic rehabilitation in the country with a view to creating "a future market and source of raw material," and the founding of a steamship connection with a Persian port.

The rumored loan was an outgrowth of the same kind of financial difficulty which had long plagued the Persian monarchy. In this case it had its inception in the pressing need of the grand vizier or prime minister, Eyn od-Dowleh, for a means of sustaining himself in office and of staving off bankruptcy for the country.[49] This had led Persia on December 1, 1905 to ask Britain for a loan of £800,000 stating that if this were not granted Persia would be forced to turn to Russia for a third loan of £1,500,000 on certain political conditions. It later became apparent that still a third possibility being considered was a loan from Germany, the condition being the granting of a charter for a bank.

Consequent Russian readiness to consider cooperation with Britain in making a loan to Persia was a complete reversal of her attitude at the time of the last loan in 1902 and was to become characteristic of a new Russian approach to the Persian question.[50] The reasons for this Russian attitude included the need for British support in dealing with Germany at the Turkish straits and in Persia itself as well as in dealing with Britain's alliance partner, Japan, the last of these requirements intended to achieve security for her Far Eastern–Pacific frontiers. But a further reason for those concerning Persia was the growing revolutionary movement with its demands for a constitution and a national assembly or majlis. These

---

[48] Popov, "Tsarskaia Rossiia i Persiia," 13–14; Kazemzadeh, *Russia and Britain*, pp. 464–467.

[49] Martin, *German–Persian diplomatic*, p. 92.

[50] No. 252 Grant Duff to Lansdowne, Dec. 2, 1905, IO 233, 1906; Erskine memorandum, "Current events in Persia," IG Political and Secret Memoranda, C 121 (hereafter Erskine memorandum); Dawson Phelps, "Izvolskii and Russian foreign policy, 1906–1910," Ph.D. dissertation, University of California, Berkeley, 1931, pp. 113–114.

demands were the expression of a national feeling which had long been anticipated and about which concern had often been expressed.[51]

Specific objectives of the national movement had been delineated by the reformers Sayyid Jamal ad-Din al-Afghani and his successor, the Egyptian, Muhammad 'Abduh. With the conclusion of the British tobacco concession on March 8, 1890, the movement became actually devoted to violent protest against the granting of concessions to the infidel Christian nations.

A working alliance was brought about at that time between the religious leaders, some of whom were based abroad in the Shi'ite shrine cities of Iraq, and the liberal and radical elements of the population. These people were strongly influenced by the religious aspect of the movement and by the fact that the issue concerned tobacco, an article of widespread use. But the reality of this outburst was, in its most recent phase, a development of incalculable and potentially dangerous significance for Russia.

The movement was in 1905 and 1906 specifically aimed at the prime minister, Eyn od-Dowleh, and at the foreign domination with which he and the Shah were associated, in particular, Russian loans and tariffs. It was also influenced by the victory of Japan over Russia and emphasized nationalism in the sense of "true independence." This called for the building of a modern, cohesive state capable of defending the country against foreign inroads and of achieving prestige abroad for Persia.[52]

It was clear that such a development could terminate, even more effectively than the ambitions of either Britain or Germany, Russian hope for a frontage on the Persian Gulf and could cause Russia to see the alternatives in a new light. These appeared to be: greater support for the Persian monarchy which opposed this program from within or greater cooperation with Britain in the expectation that sharing the country with that nation might help to rescue some of the gains of the past, especially in northern Persia. If neither Russia nor Britain demonstrated the degree of partiality toward Persia sought by those influenced by this concern for the integrity and true independence of the country, it was thought that there could emerge a movement to turn for help to the nation which some saw as

---

[51] Phelps, "Izvolskii and Russian foreign policy," p. 102; Gwynn, *Letters and friendships*, II, 95.

[52] Rouhollah K. Ramazani, *The foreign policy of Iran. A developing nation in world affairs*, Charlottesville, 1966, pp. 82–86; Browne, *The Persian revolution*, pp. 117–119; J. M. Hone and Page L. Dickinson, *Persia in revolution. With notes of travel in the Caucasus*, London, 1910, pp. 54–67; Kazemzadeh, *Russia and Britain*, pp. 241–282; Nikki R. Keddie, "The origins of the religious-radical alliance in Iran," *PP*, no. 34 (July 1966), 170–180.

being free from the taint of being currently engaged in acts supposedly constituting an affront to the nation's integrity – Germany.

The auspicious advances made during 1906 by the Persian constitutional movement could easily have been interpreted as a foretaste of greater successes to come. The movement was formed from a number of strands including a liberal group opposed to the Qajar dynasty, an antifeudal group among the peasants, a movement among the clergy and others strongly opposed to the west, and a Social Democratic group called the Ejtemayun Amiyun, founded in 1904 in Baku among the many Persian workers there, some of whom were active in Persia. The movement reached a climax in December 1905 with a large-scale public demonstration opposing the prime minister, demanding reforms, in particular, representative institutions, and seeking refuge in the Royal Mosque.

The Shah agreed in early January 1906 to establish a representative assembly which, however, following the grant of a constitution on August 5 and of a legislative body consisting of a Majlis and a Senate, turned out to be more consultative than legislative in form and function. Nevertheless, the Shah duly opened the Majlis on October 7, 1906; its life was ended on June 23, 1908 by the Russian-led Cossack Brigade.[53]

The characteristic institutions and political commitment of Britain and Russia to support these creative attempts came into focus at this point and were tested, not for their inherent value or their ability to impart political or social benefits but for their ability to force acceptance of their programs. It is noteworthy that in August 1906 some 14,000 Persians took refuge in the British legation and that the new institutions of the country were British in conception. The Russians, at the same time, saw their own fortunes bound up with the monarchy in opposition to these institutions. Russia was the more dependable supporter of her internal allies and in 1909 she supported them by a military invasion.

Nevertheless, a parallel and more immediate and urgent reason for Russian readiness to cooperate with Britain was that at the very time of the reemergence of the recurrent financial difficulties of Persia there occurred a near collapse of the Russian financial and economic program in Persia.[54]

---

[53] Bennigsen and Lemercier-Quelquejay, *Islam in the Soviet Union*, pp. 50–60; Russia. Ministry of Foreign Affairs. *Sbornik diplomaticheskikh dokumentov kasaiushchikhsia sobytii v Persii s kontsa 1906 g. po 31 dekabria 1911 g.*, St. Petersburg, 1911–17, I, 1–4; Ivan Alekseevich Zinov'ev, *Rossiia, Angliia i Persiia*, St. Petersburg, 1912, pp. 23–27; Browne, *The Persian revolution*, p. 122; Spring Rice (Teheran) to Grey, Oct. 12, 1906, FO 800/69.

[54] Editorial note, *BD*, IV, 356; John A. Murray, "British policy and opinion on the Anglo-Russian entente," 2 vols. Ph.D. dissertation, Duke University, 1957, pp. 307–308; Ivar Spector, *The first Russian revolution: its impact on Asia*, Englewood Cliffs, NJ, 1962, pp. 42–49.

The Russian Discount and Loan Bank, an arm of the Russian ministry of finance and long an instrument of Russian expansion policy in Persia, had by 1903 acquired control of all major Russian financial and commercial enterprises in Persia. Consequently, the sharp decline in the financial position which followed in the wake of the Russian defeat and the outbreak of revolution was reflected in a comparable decline in the Russian position in Persia. The straitened circumstances of the Persian government were as before the core of the problem, while its current distinctive feature was the fact that Russia's reduced financial condition made it impossible to supply the needed funds. As a result, the curtailment of the Russian economic program went considerably further than the change necessitated by the stringency enjoined earlier in the war.

Such a predicament at a time when, in addition to other circumstances inauspicious for Russia as noted earlier, a competitive German financial interest in Persia, observed with due interest in London, was indicating to some the urgency of a full turn toward Britain.[55] The advancing German presence had by 1906 begun to reach Persia and the Persian Gulf. Although the Russian government had actively opposed the German plans from the start, the railway project had moved steadily ahead and while Russia had been unable to stop it she had slowed or blunted its progress whenever possible. This had been the case in 1900 when she had forced the Ottoman government to agree to allow no railway construction near her Black Sea coast without consulting Russia.

Zinov'ev, the Russian ambassador in Constantinople, had learned in March 1902 of a German plan to connect Bagdad and the Shi'ite holy cites of Karbala and Najaf with Khaneqin on the Ottoman–Persian frontier and had warned that the capture of the pilgrim traffic by this means would be a blow to the Persian economy.[56] It was also learned from Naus, the Belgian head of the Persian customs, that a German–American railway syndicate, thought by some to be a German scheme using the syndicate as a front, was interested in building a connection between the Bagdad railway and Khaneqin for which it had Turkish approval in the railway concession of 1903. The syndicate was said also to have in mind a line to Teheran with options to build a branch to Mohammerah, eventually to be extended to Mashkhad and to the Transcaspian frontier of Russia.[57] Russia was equally alarmed about the possibility of an extension into Persia of the British Quetta–Nushki line.

The growing pressure from Germany was discussed at a special

[55] Anan'ich, "Uchetno-ssudnyi bank Persii," pp. 306–314; Popov, "Anglo-russkoe soper-nichestvo," 60–61.

[56] (Private) Nicolson to Grey, Sept. 12, Nos. 220, 221 Sept. 14, 1906, *BD*, IV, 242, 391.

[57] Kazemzadeh, *Russia and Britain*, p. 592.

ministerial conference held on September 20, 1906 at which a policy of agreement with Britain and of the division of Persia into spheres of influence was advocated by Izvolsky. Kokovtsov called attention to the decline of Russian political influence, the impossibility of Russian domination of all of Persia, the fact that Britain was firmly entrenched in the south, and to the German threat approaching from the west along the route of the Bagdad railway.[58]

In October, the very next month, Izvolsky sought during a visit to Berlin to dissuade the German government from entering the railway field in Persia, maintaining that Russia's relations with Persia were basically geographical and mentioning an agreement contemplated with Persia which would specify that no concessions for railways, telegraphs, or highways were to be built in Persia without a Russian understanding.[59] The response he received from the German Foreign Ministry was that German consent to such an agreement would be easier "if Russia should not work against the Bagdad railway." It was not in fact until 1911 that a Russo-German understanding was reached regarding the Persian railway issue. Meanwhile, however, the Hamburg–American Line had established shipping services between Europe and the Persian Gulf and, for the pilgrim traffic, between the Gulf and Mecca.[60] The first of these ships, the *Canadia*, had reached the Persian Gulf in August 1906.

The possibility of a German loan to Persia and the plan to establish a German bank were closely associated and were in turn related to the extension of the Bagdad railway to Persia and other aspects of promoting German business and influence. Furthermore, a German role in the country had long been welcome to the Persian government as a means of offsetting and mitigating the immediate and persistent influence of Britain and Russia. The Persian government, at the time the first large Russian loan was under consideration, had tried in vain to encourage a German loan, offering as an inducement a concession for a railway from Khaneqin to Teheran, the former point to be connected with the Bagdad line when it reached Mosul, the option for the Persian sector to expire on November 11, 1900.[61]

Word of this reached Russia. A rumor was heard in Teheran in May 1906 to the effect that a loan of 25 million marks was being made by Germany to Persia on condition that Germany receive: (a) a coaling station on the estuary of the Shatt-el-Arab; (b) a concession for a road

[58] A. Hardinge to Lansdowne, Aug. 16, 1905, FO 800/137.
[59] Firuz Kazemzadeh, "Russian imperialism and Persian railways," in Hugh McLean (et al. ed.), *Russian thought and politics*, Karpovich memorial volume. *Harvard Slavic Studies*, IV (1957), 365–366.
[60] Phelps, "Izvolskii and Russian foreign policy," pp. 112–113.
[61] Martin, *German–Persian diplomatic*, p. 107; Earle, *Turkey, the Great Powers*, p. 108.

from Kermanshah to Khaneqin; and (c) the right to establish a hospital and college at Teheran under German control. The agreement was said to have been worked out at Constantinople through Naus, the Belgian head of the Persian customs service.[62] At the same time, Naus was reported to have been at Constantinople and to have had frequent conferences with the German ambassador, Marschall von Bieberstein, "who proposed to him a Berlin loan in return for certain concessions to Germany."[63]

The prospect of German concessions in Persia remained throughout 1906 in the indefinite area of rumor and unfulfilled proposals and yet recurred often enough to retain a touch of reality sufficient to remind Britain and Russia of an outcome which they both dreaded. The question of a German bank arose in a straightforward manner in June 1906 when the German government informed Russia that it was considering such a possibility, adding that this meant no turn toward political aims, only a means of developing its commerce and industry.[64] The following month, July, a rumor was heard that a Belgian loan was under consideration and though this was denied by Naus, a check revealed that he had contacted the Belgian capitalist, Amplain, regarding a loan to Persia of £2,000,000, secured on the Persian customs, the latter already heavily hypothecated.

It was clear that Germany wanted to establish her financial and economic presence in Persia and, as the Russians and British had before, saw the bank as a means of inaugurating this program. It was also understood that the severe Persian need for a loan presented an opportunity for achieving the most important of these desiderata. The plan for a branch of the Deutsche Bank in Persia did not materialize until after 1907, partly because of the disturbed conditions within the country and partly because of the successful Anglo-Russian efforts to prevent it.

A recessive loan market

The significance, through defeat and revolution, of Russia's decline in national and international stature was brought into high relief when, with considerable difficulty, she sought help in winning the war and in repairing the resulting damage by making foreign loans. The situation was further emphasized by the realization that her own deterioration affected the prestige and political effectiveness of her ally and principal financial supporter, France. Also, Russia's retrogression had increased proportionately the power and influence of her opponent, Japan, which

[62] Martin, *German–Persian diplomatic*, pp. 70–71.
[63] Erskine memorandum; No. 131 Grant Duff (Teheran) to Grey, May 9, 1906, IO 2764, I, 1904.
[64] No. 89 Spring Rice to Grey, May 12, 1906, *BD*, IV, 383.

had acquired easier access to the international loan market. This had enhanced greatly her chances of victory and of a favorable peace settlement and, accordingly, more agreeable post-war regional relations. Germany, Russia's most serious rival, had not only acquired a much enhanced strategic position but, herself a source of international loans, was able to influence the availability of loans from other sources and thus to exert considerable influence on the post-war development of Russia.

The problems which had to be resolved or examined during the early months of 1906 in order to reach a meaningful consensus included first of all those generated in Russia as consequence and aftermath of the Russo-Japanese war. These were especially the revolutionary upsurge and the financial crisis of December 1905 which threatened the country with financial bankruptcy. The solution of the financial problems, a significant contribution to domestic tranquility, and the maintenance of an acceptable foreign image, was pursued wherever loans were available. They were sought in France and Germany which were already a part of the international financial community for Russia, in Britain which had as yet only been advocated as an element in this system, and in the United States with which no significant financial tie appeared in prospect.

The other problems included especially those generated as a consequence of the increase of German and Japanese power incident to and as a consequence of the Russo-Japanese war. This threatened the proportionate weakening of the Franco-Russian alliance and the destruction of this alliance and of the Anglo-French entente. These problems included the Morocco question and the larger issues which were to challenge Europe at the impending Algeciras conference. Closely associated with these must be considered the fear on the part of Britain and France that the conference might reveal a militant and aggressive Germany. To balance this, appropriate preparatory steps were even then being taken to meet such an emergency. These included a reform of the British land forces and the assurance of full Russian support for France at Algeciras which had been required as the price of a regular loan.

It was ironic that Count Witte should have been the very one who gave such emphasis to the need for a loan that he became thereby instrumental in helping to bring Russia into a closer diplomatic association with Britain and France.[65] For it would have been Witte's first choice, as it had long been the fixed policy of Count Lamsdorf, to have steered a diplomatic course for Russia over the next quarter of a century equally independent of an Anglo-French or a Franco-German association. Had he found a wholly independent course unattainable, however, he would, at that time,

[65] Phelps, "Izvolskii and Russian foreign policy," p. 111; Martin, *German–Persian diplomatic*, pp. 120–136.

with equal certainty have chosen the latter. Some of the letters Witte wrote from mid-December 1905 preparatory to asking for the largest Russian loan to date under the worst possible conditions were highly optimistic and consequently as unrealistic as the ex-finance minister's outlook appeared to be on the diplomatic prospects.

While the situation in Russia was deteriorating, Witte wrote to Rouvier in Paris and Bülow in Berlin, seemingly under the assumption that no other channel of information was open to either, conveying the impression that order was in reality being established in Russia and that Kokovtsov would soon be visiting them to discuss a matter of common interest.[66] He wrote also to the Rothschilds both in Paris and London asking in the same optimistic tone for their help as though he had not recently been told that the treatment of Jews in Russia had ruled out their financial support; this was again their response.[67] James Rothschild of the French branch of the family, however, told Rouvier in mid-January that he also considered the proposed Russian loan to be an evasion of Russian law and thus financially immoral.

Vladimir Nikolaevich Kokovtsov, the Russian minister of finance, left St. Petersburg for Paris on December 30 accompanied by the secretary of the Ministry of Finance, Lev Fabianovich Dorliak, and prepared to wage a major campaign for the loan which Russia sorely needed.[68] He was met in Paris by the Russian financial agent, Artur Germanovich Rafalovich, and by the French banker who represented Russian interests, Edouard Noetzlin.

Noetzlin immediately dashed Kokovtsov's hopes for a loan by advising him that "only the French government could prevail upon the representatives of the banks to change their decision" by giving them assurances that they would not lose their money. After an interview with Maurice Rouvier, the president of the Council of Ministers, which Rafalovich had arranged for January 3, and in discussions which followed, it was clear that the French government was not then ready to give such approval.[69]

The reasons given for the French attitude were the internal conditions

[66] Pavel Nikolaevich Efremov, *Vneshniaya politika Rossii (1907–1914 gg.)*, Moscow, 1961, p. 51; Witte, *Vospominaniia*, III, 226–227.
[67] Witte to Rouvier, Dec. 15, Witte to Bülow, Dec. 15, 1905, in Boris Aleksandrovich Romanov (ed.), "K peregovoram Kokovtsova o zaime v 1905–1906 gg." *KA*, III (X) (1925), 7–9.
[68] Witte to Rothschild (Paris), Dec. 15, Witte to Rothschild (London), Dec. 15, 1905, in Romanov, "K peregovoram Kokovtsova," 9–10; Bertie (Paris) to Grey, Jan. 12, 1906, FO 371/121; Kokovtsov Report, Jan. 24, 1906, in E.A. Preobrazhensky and B.A. Romanov (eds.), *Russkie finansy evropeiskaia birzha v 1904–1906 gg.*, Moscow, 1926, p. 263 (hereafter *RF*); Cyrus Adler, *Jacob H. Schiff*, 2 vols. New York, 1928, II, 133.
[69] Vladimir Nikolaevich Kokovtsov, *Out of my past: the memoirs of Count Kokovtsov, Russian minister of finance, 1904–1914, chairman of the council of ministers, 1911–1914*, ed. H. H. Fisher, Stanford, 1935, p. 90–92.

in Russia, the Franco-German conflict over the Morocco issue, and the consequent need of France for strong support from Russia. It was held that such support would be more likely to be forthcoming if the loan were withheld until later. Witte's stress on the urgency of the loan created in some quarters the suspicion, and in others the conviction, that he wanted the loan before the meeting of the Duma in order to avoid having either the loan or his own freedom of action in using it become dependent upon that body.[70] Witte may, for quite practical reasons, have wished to avoid becoming prematurely dependent upon a new and untried organ of government which could reasonably require some time to grasp the seriousness of the nation's condition and grow into an understanding of its functions. He was, in any case, clearly confronted with the urgency of a severe financial crisis and with an indisputable need to restore order in a disrupted society.

These were considerations which Witte had stated before the Russian Finance Committee in mid-December, stressing that if the revolution could be suppressed within the next three months the finances on hand would be sufficient. But if the disturbances continued, stronger measures would have to be taken and at greater expense. This was the nadir of Russia's poverty and need, he held, expressing a judgment which has been sustained by a recent study.[71] Contemporary observations also substantiated this appraisal.

A report of the British director of military operations dealing with disaffection in the Russian military forces provided both a view of the basic and vital question of public order and of the impact which this must have had on British thinking.[72] Even though the memorandum listed nineteen known mutinies in the Russian army or navy during November 1905 and twenty-one during December and pointed out the situations in which the government had uncharacteristically granted demands in basic matters such as the reduction of the term of service from seven to five years, the writer found no final proof that the military forces would be unable or unwilling to support the government in case of need.

There were other indicators of social and political maladjustments cited such as the growth of population, the increase in the available labor force, and the accompanying problems. Agrarian unrest, however, was one of the most significant symptoms of trouble in predominantly rural Russia. General Dmitrii Fedorovich Trepov, palace commandant and

[70] No. 106 Kokovtsov to Witte, Jan. 3, No. 1 Kokovtsov to Witte, Jan. 6, 1906, *RF*, pp. 239–241; No. 4 Rouvier to Boutiron, Jan. 5, 1906, *DDF*, VIII, 443–445.
[71] Tarlé, "Graf S. Iu. Vitte," 555–556.
[72] "Iz dnevnika Konstantina Romanova 1905 god," *KA*, I (44) (1931), 149; Bovykin, *Ocherki istorii vneshnei politiki*, pp. 50–51; Witte, *Vospominaniia*, III, 225.

himself a landowner, testified to the severity of the rural situation when in October 1905 he stated that he would be ready to give up half his land if he could retain the other half.[73]

A report made for Nicolson by Sir Donald Mackenzie Wallace dealt in some detail with the peasant question, giving emphasis to the disturbances of 1902 and especially those of late 1905 and early 1906.[74] Wallace noted the change in leadership and strategy from the Socialist Revolutionary sanctioning of burning landlords' property to the Social Democratic strategy of organizing for longer range political objectives such as strikes and the lowering of rents. Even in October 1906 when he wrote the report, Wallace found it impossible to predict where the widespread spirit of insubordination in the countryside could lead. Petr Arkad'evich Stolypin, the minister of interior, was only slightly less pessimistic when he told Nicolson in July that while there was a severe crisis, the country was not on the verge of being "mastered by the revolutionary forces."

It was therefore with some reason that Witte continued to stress the disturbed conditions of the country during January as he urged a loan without delay. In spite of the obvious Russian weakness, Witte was able to satisfy the skeptical Rouvier of adequate Russian support to the extent of granting him an advance of 1 million rubles on January 11, 1906.[75] This was done in part by hints of withdrawal of support from the French in favor of Germany but mostly by personal assurances of support given by the Tsar and reiterated at times when guarantees counted. Russian support of France at the crucial Algeciras conference, once given, was sustained throughout.

Kokovtsov, after receiving this smaller advance, addressed a report to the Finance Committee dated January 24, 1906 dealing with his recent experience in seeking a loan.[76] He noted that Russian credit, having survived the severe reverses of the war, had now fallen abroad and panic reigned over Russian investments in the stock market at home and abroad. Also, he found the conditions of the money market at present

[73] Director of military operations to F.O, July 13, 1906, memorandum, "Dissatisfaction in the Russian Army," FO 371/126.

[74] Harry T. Willetts, "The agrarian problem," in George Katkov, et al. (ed.), *Russia enters the twentieth century*, London, 1971, p. 127.

[75] No. 729 Nicolson to Grey, Nov. 1, 1906, enclosed in the Wallace report, No. 412 Nicolson to Grey, July 2, 1906, FO 371/126; Roberta Thompson Manning, *The crisis of the old order in Russia: gentry and government*, Princeton, 1982, pp. 46–49; Willetts, "The agrarian problem."

[76] René Girault, *Emprunts Russes et investissements français en Russie 1887–1914*, Paris, 1973, pp. 434–435; Nos. 13, 14, 15 Boutiron to Rouvier, Jan. 8, 1906, *DDF*, VIII, 476–477; Sergei Aleksandrovich Korff, *Russia's foreign relations during the last half century*, New York, 1922, pp. 22–23; Kokovtsov to Ivan Pavlovich Shipov (minister of finance), Jan. 11, 1906, *RF*, p. 248; Bertie to Grey, Jan. 12, 1906, FO 371/121; No. 64 Spring Rice to Grey, Jan. 16, 1906, FO 371/122.

unfavorable for Russia, indications being that the German market had practically been ruled out and that the house of Rothschild, which had hitherto handled Russian finances, had now declined this service because of the condition of the Jews in Russia.

This situation was rendered all the more difficult by the recent death of the director of the Credit Lyonnais, Henri Germain, the direction thus being left in the hands of the elderly and less experienced Andrei Mazerat, as well as younger men. The French, both in government and finance, had urged that the new loan be international and this meant looking to American and British banks to share it. At the moment everyone's attention was absorbed by the conference at Algeciras and with what many believed to be the inevitability of war with Germany.

The direct participation of Germany both in the Russian search for an international loan and in the European quest for a new diplomatic arrangement gave Germany a potentially decisive share in determining the future course of Russian development. The Russian need for funds to rehabilitate the country, the reluctance of lenders to risk investments in a situation as prone to revolutionary upheaval and the determination of Germany to drive as hard a bargain as possible with her rivals made all these features inconveniently interdependent for Russia.

Consideration of a Russian loan had remained a constant ingredient of the stormy international atmosphere throughout the Algeciras conference and had given rise to pressures on Russia not only from Paris but also from Berlin.[77] Ernst Mendelssohn-Bartoldi, the German financier who handled the Russian accounts, usually through Arthur Fischel, wrote to Kokovtsov in late February that he saw the situation within Russia as much improved from the standpoint of the money market and was therefore more optimistic with respect to the granting of a loan.

But Mendelssohn saw the need for both France and Germany to make concessions and hoped in particular that the Russian government would try to persuade France to accept the current German proposals. Since it was at this point in the Algeciras conference that the two sides had reached what appeared to be a serious impasse, which was only broken on March 3 by a crucial vote, the difficulty of what Mendelssohn was asking can be realized.

Mendelssohn himself apparently held views on this question which differed from those of the German government, the institution which would ultimately have to approve any action taken regarding the Russian loan.[78] He seems to have thought that the "abnormal role of Algeciras"

---

[77] Kokovtsov Report to Finance Committee, Jan. 24, 1906, *RF*, pp. 253–264.
[78] Mendelssohn-Bartoldi to Kokovtsov, Feb. 25, 1906, *RF*, pp. 272–273; Holstein to Bülow, Mar. 25, 1906, in Rich and Fisher, *The Holstein papers*, IV, 402.

was being given too decisive a part in determining the outcome of the Russian loan question. He hoped that financial help would be given to Russia in order to aid in bringing about the termination of revolutionary activities, to reap the benefits of good relations between Germany and Russia developed during the Russo-Japanese war, and to avoid the prospect, already imminent, of closer Anglo-Franco-Russian relations.

The German attitude so pointedly expressed by Mendelssohn constituted for the Russian government not only a warning that Germany might not follow through with her promised share in the Russian loan but also a hint that the rivalry which already characterized the conference at Algeciras might also influence the course of the loan negotiations.[79] Noetzlin, the central figure in Russian access to the most available sources of credit, those in France, had come incognito at Witte's invitation to St. Petersburg during February 15–20 when the general outline of the loan had been elaborated.[80] Mendelssohn's telegram of March 3 apprised Witte of his own imminent visit to St. Petersburg and he had used the same communication to urge once again that the French be encouraged to accept the German proposals.[81]

It was during this visit in late March that Mendelssohn sought to assume German hegemony in the international loan then under consideration, a plan which had been partly elaborated the previous October during Fischel's visit to St. Petersburg but which apparently failed because it had been prematurely divulged. Even though Witte urged Noetzlin to seek first to establish a loan commitment with either Fischel or Mendelssohn, the French banker, perhaps in view of this financial rivalry and of the political reasons which were more understandable to his own government than to Witte, retained his own priority, placing Paris and London ahead of Berlin in pursuit of the loan.

Raymond Poincaré, the minister of finance in the recently appointed French government, who had at first appeared to be a more exacting guardian of the French money market than his predecessor, announced to Rafalovich, the Russian financial representative, on March 26, his conditions for the Russian loan.[82] These conditions were that the Moroccan issue must be settled in a way very favorable for France, otherwise the

---

[79] Bernard F. Oppel, "Russo-German relations, 1904–1906," Ph.D. dissertation, Duke University, 1966, p. 193.

[80] Witte to Rafalovich, Mar. 17, 1906, *RF*, p. 282.

[81] James William Long, "The economics of the Franco-Russian Alliance, 1904–1906," Ph.D. dissertation, University of Wisconsin, 1968, pp. 155–156; Girault, *Emprunts Russes et investissements*, p. 439; Witte, *Vospominaniia*, III, 229; Bovykin, *Ocherki istorii vneshnei politiki*, p. 53.

[82] Mendelssohn to Witte, Mar. 3, 1906, *RF*, p. 274; No. 39 Bompard to Bourgeois, Mar. 29, 1906, *DDF*, IX-2, 752–755.

French government could not support the necessary credit operations in France; secondly, that the loan must be entirely constitutional and would have to be used only to liquidate the expenses incurred during 1905–6. It was understood that the conditions which had led to the suspension of the loan operations on March 12, 1905, the revolutionary disturbances, would have to have reached an acceptable stage of pacification.[83]

The crucial point in resolving the first of these two preconditions was the decision reached at the meeting of the French Council of Ministers on Saturday, March 31, 1906.[84] It was determined that progress at Algeciras was sufficient to warrant allowing Poincaré to give the signal to French financiers and the Russian government to proceed with the loan negotiations.

The fulfillment of the second condition, assurance of the constitutionality of the loan, was accomplished independently by both the French and Russian authorities. An Imperial Russian Decree of April 10, 1906 gave the Committee on Finance the right to determine the time and conditions for a loan and the right to handle all credit operations. This action was later approved by the Duma and the State Council.

Witte also transmitted on April 13 the report of Professor F. F. Martens who held that the loan was entirely constitutional because: it was the right of the Tsar to conclude foreign loans in order to meet pressing needs; the Duma would have no retroactive power in financial matters, the current loan being intended for a period preceding that when the Duma would have any jurisdiction; Article VI of the Fundamental Laws which, when effective on May 6, would ordain that "credits for payment of debts of the Empire, as well as other obligations, contracted in the name of the State cannot be reduced."[85] Consequently, no future government could legally act retroactively on a law of this kind. These conclusions agreed substantially with those of the French government and were considered acceptable. This view regarding the right of the existing government to conclude a loan was in effect the position taken by the Constitutional Democrats (Kadets), the group which was to win the largest number of seats in the first Duma.

There was of course no legally enforceable guarantee which could place any realistic restraints on a future government controlled by the liberals

[83] Long, "The economics"; Rafalovich to Nelidov, Mar. 26, 1906, in F.V. Kelin (ed.), "Novye dokumenty ob Alzhezirasskoi konferentsii i zaime 1906 g.", *KA*, I (44) (1931), 163; Noetzlin to Witte, Mar. 26, 1906, *RF*, pp. 285–286.
[84] Andrew, *Théophile Delcassé*, p. 246; A.L. Popov (ed.), "Zaem 1906 g. v doneseniiakh russkogo posla v Parizhe," *KA*, no. 4–5 (10–11) (1925), 422 (Nelidov report on French attitude, Mar. 23, 1906).
[85] Poincaré to Nelidov, Mar. 31, Nelidov to Lamsdorf, Mar. 31, 1906, in A.S. Erusalimsky, "Rossiia i Alzherirasskaia konferentsiia," *KA*, XLI–XLII (4–5) (1930), 54–55.

or on a revolutionary government which could guard against the unpredictable prospects which many feared both in Russia and beyond the frontier. This aspect of the question left Britain with a difficult choice. Her participation in the loan was seen as a means of establishing closer relations with Russia. But there was also concern that it might be resented by the Russian people soon to be represented by the Duma and thus in the longer run worsen those relations. On the other hand, by not participating, a solution which would have been favored by many in Britain, the government would risk irritating the present Russian government. This could disrupt the French loan to Russia and thus leave the door open for the triumph of a German loan plan.

As some had anticipated, after the conclusion of the loan there was talk in St. Petersburg of boycotting French goods and even of attacking the British and French embassies. In the immediate aftermath of the convocation of the first Duma, however, there seemed less reason for such concern about the impact of the loan.[86] While the reforms had not fulfilled the expectations of those who had urged radical change, it was clear at least that the granting of the loan ahead of the convocation of the Duma had not induced the imperial regime to withhold a charter granting far more widespread participation than had ever before been the case.

The prospect of concluding a loan without the consent or approval of the Duma provoked, during the period when the new charter was imminently expected, some bitter feelings which were only to be aggravated when the publication of the Fundamental Laws and the actual initial experience with the Duma revealed that the hopes of many had been raised far too high.[87] Some members of the Russian Constitutional Democratic party and, with the help of Anatole France, the president of the Société des Amis du Peuple Russe et des Peuples Annexés and a close friend of Jean Jaurès, were able to visit the French minister of finance, Poincaré, and others, asking that the loan be denied. These included the Constitutional Democrats, Prince Petr Dmitrievich Dolgorukov and Vasilii Alekseevich Maklakov, the latter, in company with S. E. Kalmanovich and Count Nesselrode, also visiting Georges Clemenceau.

The campaign against the loan in France was also carried on by Maxim Gorky whose appeal, "Do not give money to the Russian government,"

---

[86] Long, "The economics," 178–180; Witte, *Vospominaniia*, III, 241; Kokovtsov, *Out of my past*, pp. 110–111; Anan'ich, *Rossiia i mezhdunarodnyi kapital*, p. 182; No. 284 Spring Rice to Grey, Apr, 25, 1906, FO 371/122; Hosking, *The Russian constitutional experiment*, p. 11; Spring Rice to Grey, Apr. 12, 18, 1906, FO 800/71; Thomas Riha, *A Russian European: Paul Miliukov in Russian politics*, Notre Dame, 1969, p. 115.

[87] Lothar Schultz, "Constitutional law in Russia," in Katkov, *Russia enters the twentieth century*, p. 45; Chirol to Nicolson, Sept. 6, 1906, in Sir Arthur Nicolson (Lord Carnock) Papers, PRO FO 800 (336–381).

was first published in *Krasnoe Znamia* in April, 1906. This journal was edited by Aleksandr Valentinovich Amfiteatrov, a Russian exile and friend of Jean Jaurès who had reached Paris after escaping from Siberia. Amfiteatrov also addressed a letter to Jaurès saying that the loan would chain the French bourgeoisie to the Russian throne.[88]

A few weeks after the loan had been granted the French government, in view of the strong Russian reaction against the loan and against the French, reversed its position and urged the Russian government to come to terms with the Duma not only because of the existing financial situation but also of such future loans as might be needed.[89] The dismissal of the Duma on July 22 was said to have had an effect on the market "like a clap of thunder." Again the hope was expressed, this time by Noetzlin, that a more friendly attitude be shown the newly enfranchised elements by the government.[90]

The fact that Noetzlin, instead of starting with Fischel or Mendelssohn as Witte had urged, began the international loan negotiations with the British and American bankers called forth a strong protest from Mendelssohn.[91] In a note to Witte expressing his dissatisfaction, Mendelssohn complained that Noetzlin had treated Germany as though she were a second rate power. When Witte called Rafalovich's attention to this, the financial agent telegraphed Witte on April 2 that the loan negotiations were already under way and included Arthur Fischel, Mendelssohn's representative. Noetzlin and Lord Revelstoke, the latter representing the house of Baring, had their first general meeting on April 3 in London.[92] There was apparently no discernible evidence at that time that Russo-German relations were within two days of a serious breaking point.

Witte wrote to Mendelssohn on April 4 that it would be impossible to delay the loan even, as the German financier had hinted, while further consideration was given to industrial orders.[93] Nevertheless, to conclude a loan without Germany would be very unfortunate both financially and politically since it would signify to the whole world the rapprochement of Russia with a political grouping which did not correspond with the interests of either Russia or Germany.

[88] Spring Rice to Grey, Feb. 16, 1906, FO 800/71,; James William Long, "Organized protest against the 1906 Russian loan," *CMRS*, XIII (Jan.–Mar. 1972), 25 ff.
[89] Aleksandr Valentinovich Amfiteatrov, *Franko-russki soiuz i 9-oe ianvaria: pis'mo k Zhanu Zoresu*, Geneva, 1905.
[90] No. 261 Bertie to Grey, June 29, 1906, FO 371/126.
[91] Noetzlin to Kokovtsov, July 28, 1906, in Fedor Aronovich Rotshtein (ed.), "Perepiska V. N. Kokovtsova s Ed. Netslinym," *KA*, IV (1923), 132.
[92] Rozental', *Diplomaticheskaia istoriia*, pp. 205–206; Noetzlin to Witte, Mar. 12, Witte to Noetzlin, Mar. 10, Noetzlin to Witte, Mar. 26, 31, 1905, *RF*, pp. 277, 285–290.
[93] No. 101 Cambon to Bourgeois, Apr. 7, 1906, *DDF*, IX-2, 814–815.

Such a move, in fact, would separate Russia and Germany even more than had been the case when they had drawn apart and failed to realize the principle proclaimed at Björkö. Then on the same day, Bülow, reflecting an attitude which must have arisen with the resentment felt in Berlin two weeks before when Cassini's instructions to the Algeciras conference were revealed, notified Mendelssohn that he would refuse to authorize the participation of Germany in the loan and on the following day, April 5, Mendelssohn relayed this word to Witte.[94]

Witte commented on this startling circumstance in a communication to Rafalovich written during the night of April 5–6, characterizing it as revenge for Algeciras and as expressing the German fear that the loan would serve to promote a closer Russian relationship with France and a rapprochement with Britain.[95] The German decision to forego participation in the international loan was formally communicated to Witte by the German ambassador on April 6, the change of policy being explained as necessitated by internal needs for the money.

The fact that Witte found this action hasty and apparently had detected no hint of it two weeks before when Mendelssohn had visited St. Petersburg makes it plausible to assume that the failure of the hegemony which Mendelssohn was then seeking to establish for Germany among the participants in the loan had brought a decision in Berlin that German non-participation might annul the international loan agreement entirely before it had been formalized and render Russia willing to come to a separate loan arrangement with the German bankers. This would offer one more opportunity to break the Franco-Russian alliance and prevent the otherwise seemingly inevitable Anglo-Russian rapprochement.

The Russian loan thus became, with the help of the German miscalculation in strategy, a precursor and financial counterpart of a triple entente agreement. It has been suggested that "The loan question delivered the death-blow to Wilhelm's dreams of reorienting Russian foreign policy to meet German specifications."[96] While this undoubtedly attributes too

---

[94] Witte to Mendelssohn, Apr. 4, 1906, *RF*, p. 295.
[95] Girault, *Emprunts Russes et investissements*; Mendelssohn to Witte, Apr. 5, 1906, *RF*, pp. 295–296; Holstein to Bülow, Mar. 23, 1906 (draft), in Rich and Fisher, *The Holstein papers*, IV, 401.
[96] Witte to Rafalovich, Aug. 5–6, 1906, *RF*, p. 296; No. 95 Bompard to Bourgeois, Apr. 7, 1906, No. 89 Bihourd (Berlin) to Bourgeois, Apr. 7, 1906, *DDF*, IX-2, 806–807, 818–819; Boris Aleksandrovich Romanov, *Ocherki diplomaticheskoi istorii Russko-iaponskoi voiny, 1895–1907*, Moscow, 1955, p. 633; Olga Crisp, "The Russian liberals and the 1906 Anglo-French loan to Russia," *SEER*, XXXIX, no. 93 (June 1961), p. 497; Witte to Kokovtsov (Paris), Apr. 15, 1906, *RF*, p. 306; Kokovtsov, *Out of my past*, p. 115; No. 258 Spring Rice to Grey, Apr. 11, 1906, No. 275 Spring Rice to Grey, Apr. 20, 1906, FO 371/ 124 (contains report on the conclusion of the loan and of the Russian reaction thereto).

much to this blunder, it nevertheless places in its proper perspective the financial alignment which was one of the factors helping to drive Russia into the entente camp. The separate German loan agreement proposed by Fischel made it possible for Kokovtsov to be sure that, by hinting to Poincaré that he might have to turn to this if the French loan were delayed, the French loan would be completed expeditiously.[97]

This pressure seemed, in reality, wholly unnecessary since France appeared quite prepared to grant the loan not only to insure her diplomatic and strategic security but to help suppress the revolution; France herself had experienced a large number of strikes during the early months of 1906. The loan, in its final form a product of the troubled times, was signed on April 16, 1906 at the Russian embassy in Paris by British, French, and Russian bankers as well as some from Holland and Austria.[98] The loan was for two and a quarter billion francs, of which the French bankers subscribed over half.

[97] Oppel, "Russo-German relations," p. 197.
[98] Rozental', *Diplomaticheskaia istoriia*, pp. 209–210.

5   The Algeciras factor

The Morocco challenge

The rise and development of the Morocco question and the movement to bring the Russo-Japanese war to a close had by 1905 converged and together had become the focus of the negotiations which were to terminate in a new balance of power. The outcome of these intermittent negotiations had already aligned the Triple Alliance on the one hand and, on the other, the Franco-Russian alliance, the Anglo-French entente, and the Anglo-Japanese alliance against each other.

This was, however, an ill-balanced rivalry. The latter three coalitions included the now defeated Russia as well as Britain and Japan whose main strength was in their naval forces. It also comprised France, now weakened by the defeat of her alliance partner, Russia, and in any case not considered militarily a match for Germany. It was generally assumed that if Germany were successful in preventing these three coalitions from forming a combination or better still, in bringing Russia and France together under her own influence, she would be able in one way or another to control them and thus dominate Europe.

Germany used a number of tactics, all reactive to current experience and all unsuccessful, in her attempt to attain control of her rivals in Europe. The first of these was tried on the occasion of the Dogger Bank incident when ill-feeling toward Britain was still prevalent in Russia and the German Emperor sought to take advantage of the further animosity generated between Britain and Russia in the course of the episode. He used this opportunity to propose a continental alliance based on an affiliation of Germany, Russia, and France. The circumstances of the Dogger Bank incident also lent themselves to portraying Britain as acting in her role of an ally of Japan and attempting to delay or even prevent the Russian fleet from reaching its destination, the Pacific war zone. The Emperor also suggested that Russia's ally, France, had been less helpful than she might have been in assisting the eastern progress of the Russian fleet. Meanwhile, even though Germany was unsuccessful in enlisting Russian cooperation in her plan, she was able to demonstrate her own good-will by permitting the Hamburg–American Line to supply coal to the eastbound Russian fleet.

The second attempt to form a diplomatic association with Russia as the basis for a German controlled continental alliance was made in July 1905. The decisions to hold negotiations respecting both the settlement of the Russo-Japanese war and the Morocco issue had turned the German Emperor once more to thoughts of a German–Russian based continental alliance, particularly in view of the possibility that the anticipated negotiations might come soon and might inspire the creation of a supplement to the Anglo-Japanese and Franco-Russian alliances, perhaps in the form of an Anglo-Franco-Russian understanding. It was an opportune time, from the viewpoint of the German Emperor, to tighten the bonds between Russia and Germany. If this could be done by the sacrifice of the Franco-Russian alliance it might at the same time help to perpetuate the weakness of France. This fragility had been demonstrated recently by the readiness of France, under German pressure, to accept the dismissal of Delcassé, the French foreign minister, and to hold an international conference on the Morocco issue.

A timely reinforcement of the German–Russian relationship might also help to reduce the likelihood of any further strengthening of the Franco-Russian combination through a Russian loan in Paris. Furthermore, the dissolution in early June of the Norwegian–Swedish union had created an instability in the north which, it was feared, would command the attention of Britain. This provided one further reason why the isolation of Britain through the weakening of the Anglo-French entente might serve further to reduce British and Russian competition in a region in which German power might otherwise become decisive.

The meeting of the German and Russian rulers on July 23–24, 1905 at Björkö, provided an opportunity for the former to ask his imperial cousin why he thought the attempt of a few months before to bring their two countries together had failed. The Tsar attributed it to the unwillingness of France to cooperate with Germany in view of the strained relations between the two nations. The Kaiser, referring to the fact that France had agreed only two weeks before to a conference on the Moroccan issue, answered that Franco-German non-cooperation was no longer a factor.[1] In the course of their discussions the German Emperor also referred to the problem which had in his view arisen because of the very decisive Norwegian bid in early June for independence. He stated to the Tsar that he hoped to settle the Scandinavian problem to his own advantage. On the second day of the conference, July 24, aboard the Tsar's yacht *Polar Star*, the two emperors signed the Björkö agreement.

[1] Erich Brandenburg, *From Bismarck to the World War. A history of German foreign policy, 1870–1914*, trans. Annie Elizabeth Adams. London, 1927, p. 233.

The document differed in some significant ways from the one discussed the previous October.[2] Both were defensive alliances but the earlier one was intended "to localize the Russo-Japanese war as much as possible" while the latter was to remain secret and was not to come into effect until the end of the war. This last provision was intended to satisfy the German wish to avoid pulling the Russian chestnuts out of the fire. In general the new version was considered by the Kaiser to be more favorable to Germany as shown by the provision against its being applicable outside of Europe, thus avoiding any German commitment in case Russia should become involved in any further difficulty in the Far East.

The agreement, however, never became effective. Both the German and Russian governments objected to it. Bülow pointed out that by restricting it to Europe Germany "had lost the chance of bringing pressure to bear on Britain through Russia's Asiatic provinces," thus leaving the German colonial possessions exposed to British attack without using the Russian relationship as a means of preventing or warding off attack. Holstein thought that the Russian Emperor should have been urged to accept constitutional reform in order to split the ranks of the opposition and thus avoid having it appear that he was using the agreement with Germany to bolster his opposition to reform.

Russian reaction to the agreement was even more negative. Witte returned to Russia from the United States in late September and saw the first actual text of the agreement on October 4, nearly three months after its conclusion and after it had been enthusiastically described to him *en route* home by the German Emperor. He immediately realized that it was unsuitable for Russia's needs. Not only could it come into force independently of France's adherence to it but since it was intended to become effective upon the ratification of the Portsmouth treaty, the potential Franco-German conflict over Morocco could at any time find Russia at war with France as an ally of Germany.

This, however, only gave emphasis to Rouvier's clearly expressed policy of a few days before that the loan Russia so vitally needed was available only at the price of a decisive Russian commitment to support France in her current dissension with Germany over Morocco. Furthermore, even beyond this, the availability of the French money market would be tied to some degree of accommodation with Britain. Nevertheless, the interests which brought Witte and Lamsdorf, the Russian minister of foreign affairs, together in the drive to annul the Björkö agreement were mainly other than financial, as the unfolding of the Morocco crisis amply demonstrated.

The decision of the German government to open an attack on France

[2] Bompard, *Mon Ambassade en Russie*, pp. 72–76; Rich, *Friedrich von Holstein*, II, 714–719.

over the Morocco issue, the third and, for Germany, the most unfortunate effort to change the course of European diplomacy, has been explained as a reaction to the French failure to notify Germany of the Anglo-French entente of April 8, 1904. The French government did, however, notify the German ambassador in Paris, Prince Radolin, on March 23, 1904, fourteen days before its conclusion, of all the essential points in the agreement and had sent a note about this discussion to the German government through the French ambassador in Berlin, Georges Bihourd.[3] Furthermore, a few days after the completion of the entente, on April 12, 1904, Bülow told the Reichstag that Germany had "no cause to apprehend that the agreement between Great Britain and France was leveled against any individual power. It seemed to be an attempt to eliminate the points between France and Great Britain by an amiable understanding. From the point of view of German interests, they had nothing to complain of."[4]

This attitude continued to be held for some time in spite of the fact that since 1901 the Morokkanische Gesellschaft, the colonial society, and the Pan-German League had been calling for action in defense of German economic interests in Morocco.[5] These interests and demands had come to be centered in a Morocco Company which had been established in January 1903 with Pan-German support. The strong Pan-German advocacy of this cause during the coming months apparently had a considerable effect not only upon the German government but also upon the French government which feared the influence of the League in Berlin. The French saw in the situation the possibility of a strong German presence in the western Mediterranean matching that in the eastern Mediterranean brought about by the growing German role in the Ottoman Empire.

Three developments appear to have propelled the Moroccan issue into the forefront of German official thinking to the extent of giving a new direction to the foreign policy with respect to German interests in Morocco.[6] France had concluded an accord with Spain on October 3, 1904 without suggesting the opening of conversations with Germany. At the time, St. René Taillandier, the French representative in Tangier, had

[3] Otto Hammann, *Zur Vorgeschichte des Weltkrieges: Erinnerungen aus den Jahren 1897–1906*, Berlin, 1919, pp. 145–146; Jean Jules Jusserand, *What befell me. The reminiscences of J. J. Jusserand*, Boston, 1933, pp. 310–311.
[4] William Tyrell note on "German policy in Morocco," n.d. but agreeing in subject and in general point of view with an accompanying memorandum, apparently of Feb. 25, 1906, by Louis Mallet, FO 800/91.
[5] Dwight Erwin Lee, *Europe's crucial years: the diplomatic background of World War I. 1902–1914*, Hanover, NH, 1974, p. 110; Christopher Andrew, "German world policy and the reshaping of the dual alliance," *JCH*, I, no. 3 (July 1966), 150.
[6] Lee, *Europe's crucial years*, p. 111.

told Richard von Kühlmann, the German chargé d'affaires, of his projected visit to Fez to establish French predominance in Morocco. Then in November 1904 the French government had prevented Morocco from buying war materials from Germany, "thus heightening the rivalry of Krupp and Schneider-Creusot which were already in competition for Turkish business with the backing of their respective embassies."

But even with these indications of the possible attempt to "Tunisify" Morocco, Germany only warned France of possible intervention, an attitude which may be explained by the fact that German interests were protected by the Madrid Convention of 1880 and by the German agreement of 1890 with Morocco.[7] Also, even in Tunisia which Germany frequently cited as an example of an unacceptable decree of French control, German treaty rights were respected. By the end of December, however, the cumulative effect of these developments as well as the failure of a German–Russian alliance to be achieved, the incremental defeat of Russia in the Far East, and the consequent weakening of Russian and French power brought about a decision in Berlin to open a diplomatic offensive against France.[8]

It was against this backdrop that, following a blueprint fashioned by Holstein and under the single-minded management of Bülow, the German government chose Morocco as the setting for converting Europe into a more congenial arena for an expanding Germany. Under the seemingly secure shield of endeavoring to preserve the open door in Morocco while taking full advantage of the declining international position of Russia, the ally of France, the German government chose the most severe and thorough tactic for destroying its competitors in continental Europe. Germany did, in fact, have the test of nerves between themselves and the French brought out into the open. This was a conflict which at least the principals were aware was, in the immediate sense, a disagreement between the French who wanted direct negotiations and the Germans who were demanding a conference. From the French point of view the possible benefit of the first could be that it might permit them to limit the outcome to a colonial agreement between the two rivals and thus make it possible for them to by-pass the key issue of French recognition of the Treaty of Frankfurt.[9]

Sir Donald MacKenzie Wallace learned while attending the Algeciras conference that the attractions of Morocco as a colonial or commercial field of activity were developing in Germany and that the realization of

---

[7] Tyrell, "German policy in Morocco," FO 800/91.
[8] Lee, *Europe's crucial years*, pp. 111–112.
[9] Bernard Karl Dehmelt, "Bülow's Moroccan policy, 1902–1905," Ph.D. dissertation, University of Pennsylvania, 1963, p. 325.

such a prize might serve as compensation for the colonial failures and disappointments of the past and for any losses the nation "may sustain from the increase of hostile tariffs in America and elsewhere."[10] Never, he wrote, has there been a greater need for "new fields of enterprise and new markets." Germany did in fact have trade with Morocco and was believed to be a candidate for a port on the Atlantic coast of Morocco. She apparently also assumed that France intended to establish a protectorate over Morocco but elected with some reason to express her opposition to French ambitions, not on the grounds of a basic rivalry, but rather on the loftier principle of the preservation of the open door.[11]

This suggested to the German government a convocation of representatives of nations which had signed the Morocco agreement of 1880, in addition to Russia, in order to reconsider the position of Morocco in view of altered circumstances and of supposed French ambitions. The consequences would be, if this maneuver were to succeed, to deprive France of the opportunity of making any important independent decisions regarding Morocco. It could also humiliate France while casting Germany in the role of guardian of the open door and of the independence of Morocco and making Germany appear as the protector of equal commercial opportunity. These qualities and rights were highly regarded not only in Europe but throughout the entire colonial and commercial world where Germany needed every possible advantage in promoting her recently undertaken rivalry with the other imperial powers.

It was with these aspirations in mind that Bülow embarked upon his new policy on January 2, 1905, the very day of the surrender of Port Arthur, by having Richard Kühlmann let it be known in Morocco that Germany was taking a political interest in that country. Regarding this less forceful stage of the strategy, Bülow wrote: "I felt that I could prevent matters coming to a head, cause Delcassé's fall, break the continuity of aggressive French policy, knock the continental dagger out of the hands of Edward VII and the war group in England and, simultaneously, ensure peace, preserve German honour, and improve German prestige."[12] For France to proceed after this with any plan of "Tunisification," or "peaceful penetration," or of frankly instituting the protectorate which Bülow assumed she had in mind, would have been dangerous, to say the least. In mid-February when a Russian endeavor to mediate appeared likely, Bülow took a strong stand against it, saying that a recurrence of the

[10] Wallace to Knollys, Feb. 25, 1905, Wallace Papers.
[11] Ostal'tseva, "Anglo-frantsuzskoe soglashenie," 206; Carroll, *Germany and the great powers*, p. 491; No. 267 Inouye to Komura, June 13, 1905, J.F.O; Howard K. Beale, *Theodore Roosevelt and the rise of America to world power*, Baltimore, 1955, p. 356.
[12] Ian E.D. Marrow, "The foreign policy of Prince von Bülow, 1898–1909," *CHJ*, IV, no. 1 (1932), 87.

Russo-Franco-German Far Eastern Triplice of 1895 was out of the question.[13]

In fact, of course, this was the same position Bülow had taken when the Kaiser had broached the subject some months earlier. But, more importantly, such an approach to the problem would have ruined the game he had started with Delcassé which called for the French minister of foreign affairs to come to him on German terms. Instead, he chose to make his challenge to Delcassé public, thereby making the French position all the more humiliating, and to call in a new player.

It was with this in mind that on February 25 Bülow turned to President Theodore Roosevelt.[14] His appeal for American support was based on the plea that Germany wanted no territory in Morocco, asking only for an open door for commercial interests. He argued that the alternative was a French-controlled Morocco and Franco-Spanish control over the passage by which all seafaring and commercial nations enjoyed access to the route to and from the Middle and Far East. He hoped that the President would join Germany in encouraging the Sultan to demand an international conference.

The German request to President Roosevelt came, however, at a time and under circumstances which augured anything but a positive response. Only recently the United States government had had an unfortunate experience with Morocco and had emerged from it successfully with the cooperation of Britain and France.[15] The situation had arisen when, on May 18, 1904, Jon Perdicaris and his step-son, Cromwell Varley (the latter a British subject), were abducted near Tangier by Raisuli, a Rifian bandit, and held for ransom. With the help of Britain and France, Perdicaris was released on June 24, 1904. Since the acquisition of Algeria in 1830, France had been determined that no European country should be allowed to assume predominance over French interests in North Africa.

A second factor in understanding President Roosevelt's reaction to the Kaiser's invitation to join him in settling the Moroccan question was the significance of the friendship of the President with the German ambassador, Hermann Speck von Sternburg, and the closely associated view that the President was in some way a reliable accomplice or even a dupe of the

[13] Dehmelt, "Bülow's Moroccan policy," p. 229.
[14] Ibid., pp. 238–239; Adolf Hasenclever, "Theodore Roosevelt und die Marokkokrisis von 1904–1906," APG, VI, heft 3 (1928), 194–196; Beale, Theodore Roosevelt, p. 358.
[15] Dennis, Adventures in American diplomacy, pp. 443–445; Harold E. Davis, "The citizenship of Jon Perdicaris," JMH, XIII, no. 4 (Dec. 1941), pp. 517–520; St. René Taillandier (Tangier) to Delcassé, May 19, 30, Delcassé to Taillandier, May 31, Taillandier to Delcassé, June 6, 25, Jusserand to Delcassé, June 20, Gen. Horace Porter (US ambassador to France) to Delcassé, June 27, 1904, France. Ministère des Affaires Etrangères, Documents diplomatiques. Affaires du Maroc, 1901–1905, Paris, 1905, pp. 135, 137–138, 139–140, 152, 154 (hereafter DDAM).

German Emperor. But, in the first place, it should be remembered that the President was also on very close terms with Jules Jusserand, the French ambassador, who wrote that: "When grave matters were at stake, Venezuela, Morocco or the Russo-Japanese war, I was sometimes asked by the President to call on him after dinner for a serious private talk."[16] The President also enjoyed very confidential relations with the British diplomat, Sir Cecil Spring Rice, though the latter was not then stationed in Washington.

Secondly, from the time the problem of a conference over the Moroccan question arose there was apparently no doubt which position the President would take. When Jusserand first broached the question of a conference, referring at the same time to the service France had only recently performed in the Perdicaris case the President was absent in Colorado. But William Howard Taft, acting for Hay who was ill, responded that, while he could by no means answer finally, he thought that the United States could not accept a conference if France did not. Roosevelt, on his return to Washington, endorsed this view.[17] However, when Roosevelt became aware of the danger of war if the conference were not approved, he advised France to consent to the conference but with assurances of his direct support.

Regarding the British accusation that he was under the influence of the Kaiser, Roosevelt wrote to Senator Henry Cabot Lodge on May 15, 1905 that "nothing could persuade me to follow the lead of or enter into close alliance with a man who is so jumpy, so little capable of continuity of action, and, therefore, so little capable of being loyal to his friends or steadfastly hostile to an enemy."[18] Yet, in spite of this negative personal characterization, Roosevelt at times found cooperation with the Kaiser both possible and constructive, as in some aspects of their China policies.

At this time, however, Roosevelt was worried mainly about the consequences of both revolutionary activity within Russia and the international competition for control of the peace making operations. And it was precisely in this latter struggle that the President and the Kaiser were in opposing camps and that the movement supported by the President prevailed. In fact, the Kaiser ultimately became an advocate of the President as leader of the peace drive.

Meanwhile, however, the Kaiser was pursuing his competitive course and hoping to keep France isolated by preventing her from achieving the

---

[16] Jusserand, *What befell me*, p. 271.
[17] Ibid., pp. 315–317.
[18] Roosevelt to Lodge, May 15, 1905, in Henry Cabot Lodge, *Selections from the correspondence of Theodore Roosevelt and Henry Cabot Lodge, 1884–1918*, 2 vols. New York, 1925, II, 120–123; Sternburg to FO July 5, 1905, in Dugdale, *German diplomatic documents, 1871–1914*, III, 205–206.

support of Britain. Since the Emperor believed that Britain would act in accordance with the wishes of the United States, he was urging Roosevelt to encourage Britain to support the conference, thus frustrating the French hope of achieving a direct arrangement with Germany. One consequence of not halting France's course would be that she would monopolize Morocco but also that, in combination with Britain and Russia, and perhaps, after the war, with Japan as well, she would seek a partition of China and thus infringe upon American interests.[19] Another consequence would be to force Germany into a position of having to choose between war with France or accepting the offers France might make to Germany.

Another closely related factor in the German Emperor's endeavor to enlist President Roosevelt's support in the Moroccan issue was the concurrent maneuvering over the issue of peace following the Russo-Japanese war. From an early stage of the war, Germany was known to be favorable to Russia and this was a matter of considerable consequence not only to Japan but also to the United States, and tended to color President Roosevelt's attitude toward Germany during the war.[20] The President sought to mitigate the situation by a friendly stance toward the German Emperor, hoping thereby to prevent his interference in the war and the peace settlement and by cautioning Japan to avoid any hint of a threat to the German sphere in Shantung Province.

Even before the North Sea incident of October 1904 had developed, an article in the *Kölnische Zeitung* had tried to quiet rumors of a possible German intervention in the war to the advantage of Russia.[21] But the North Sea incident itself and the apparent improvement in German–Russian relations which followed simply reinforced the desire of Britain, France, and the United States to see the war ended to their satisfaction, and of the first two to draw Russia into a combination safer from German maneuvering.[22] German efforts to form an alliance with Russia from October 1904 were known in London, were a factor in sharpening British suspicions toward Germany, and had the effect of preventing a possible Japanese response to a German peace venture.

The German Emperor, like his competitors in other capitals, was influenced in his attitude toward war and peace by a number of factors. In addition to wanting to form with Russia the foundation for a continental alliance against Britain, the Kaiser also thought of avoiding the prospect

---

[19] Hasenclever, "Theodore Roosevelt," 199.
[20] Parsons, "Roosevelt's containment," 35, 37, 41; Steinberg, "Germany and the Russo-Japanese war," 1969, 1974; White, *The diplomacy*, pp. 177–178, 182–183, 196–197, 204, 213, 227.   [21] No. 414 Inouye (Berlin) to Komura, Oct. 21, 1904, JFO
[22] Aleksandr Solomonovich Dobrov, *Dal'nevostochnaia politika SShA v period Russko-Iaponskoi voiny*, Moscow, 1952, p. 295; Anderson, *First Moroccan crisis*, pp. 177–179.

of a Russian combination with Britain and France. Mediation in the war by an Anglo-French combination was seen by the Kaiser as a step toward the formation of a potentially hostile Anglo-Franco-Russian coalition which boded ill for his plans in Europe and the world. Furthermore, the Kaiser was not in favor of concluding the war at all in the early months of 1905.[23] One reason was undoubtedly the absence then of a political configuration favorable to German objectives, the Morocco question being considered a vehicle for creating such a condition.

More explicit, however, was the desire on the part of the Kaiser for greater assurance of a successful outcome for Russia, in part because this would make Russia a more valuable alliance partner for the continental alliance. But this was also in part because he wanted to turn Russia eastward as a durable participant in regional affairs in order to reduce her interest in supporting France and opposing Germany. But the Kaiser wanted above all to see the revolutionary forces in Russia mastered by a victorious imperial regime. Not until the Kaiser realized that the revolutionary forces were getting out of hand and might threaten not only the Tsar's but also the Kaiser's own throne did the German ruler counsel peace.

It was also during the early months of 1905 that President Roosevelt's cooperation with Germany in the Moroccan issue was rendered even more impossible by the fact that the United States and Britain were then elaborating a common position regarding possible Japanese peace conditions in case both belligerents should become interested in terminating the conflict.[24] President Roosevelt had, in late December 1904, taken steps to facilitate American–British thinking on the vital peace issue by inviting Sir Cecil Spring Rice, then in St. Petersburg, to come to Washington and Spring Rice apparently arrived there in late January or early February 1905.

The President wrote on February 6 to George von Lengerke Meyer, the American ambassador in Russia: "In St. Petersburg Spring Rice will call upon you. He knows just how I feel in all these matters and you can talk to him without any reserve. England's interest is exactly ours as regards this Oriental complication and is likely to remain so."[25] Secretary of State John Hay had in the meantime acted to try to help alleviate the

---

[23] Shebeko to Tsar, Jan. 22, Kaiser to Tsar, Feb. 19, 1905, in A.A. Sergeev (ed.), "Vil'gel'm II o Russko-iaponskoi voine i revoliutsii 1905 goda," *KA*, II (9) (1925), 62–65; No. 68 Hayashida (London) to Komura, Feb. 10, 1905, JFO

[24] Whitney, "British foreign policy," pp. 240–250; No. 9A Lansdowne to Durand, Jan, 14, No. 214 Hardinge to Lansdowne, Apr. 11, No. 109 Lansdowne to Durand, July 29, 1905, *BD*, IV, 69, 75–76, 155–156.

[25] Roosevelt to Meyer, Feb. 6, 1905, in Elting E. Morison (ed.), *The letters of Theodore Roosevelt*, 8 vols. Cambridge, MA, 1951, IV, pp. 1115–1116; Whitney, "British foreign policy," pp. 240–241.

concerns expressed by the German government by issuing a circular note on January 13, 1905 sounding out the powers as to their position regarding the open door and territorial integrity of China, an overture which was readily supported by the British government.[26]

German pressure was by April producing a number of significant consequences. On April 11, 1905 Britain joined France in rejecting an international conference. On April 25 the British ambassador handed a note to Delcassé assuring France that in case Germany were to request the concession of a port on the Moroccan coast, the British government would join the French government in opposing such a proposal strongly. This position must be understood in relationship to the growing Anglo-German naval rivalry and the strategic bearing of the Moroccan coast on British access to Gibraltar and the Mediterranean and the Atlantic in that region.

In spite of receiving proffered support from both the United States and Britain, the international position of France deteriorated markedly between April and June 1905. The early days of June may in fact be discerned in retrospect as marking the acceleration of a shift in European alignments which, while never able to keep pace with the continued growth of German power, nevertheless moved in the direction of endeavoring to do this and, in the process, took on the superficial semblance of a movement intended to "encircle" Germany. The French position during this period was made extremely difficult by the degree to which the Moroccan and Far Eastern questions came to focus in the person of Delcassé and made him the center of an intense German campaign to drive him from office and nullify his program of international relations which appeared to be on the verge of achieving its goal.

Unbeknown to Germany, on March 22 Delcassé had received a formal request from Russia for his good offices.[27] Russia was prepared to negotiate, if Japan would not ask for the cession of any Russian territory, a war indemnity, or the limitation of Russian military or naval forces in the Far East. The opportunity this presented is attested to by a note from Benckendorff, the Russian ambassador in London, written on March 24 stating that Rothschild had told him he was convinced that Japan was ready to negotiate and would not ask for an indemnity. It is also likely that some assurances of support were given to Delcassé by Lansdowne during March.

Maurice Paléologue was informed on March 20 by Marquis de Breteuil that King Edward had recently given Delcassé personal assurances of his approval of the French Moroccan policy. The King urged him to carry on

---

[26] Dennis, *Adventures in American diplomacy*, pp. 408–409; *USFR*, 1905, p. 1.
[27] Andrew, *Théophile Delcassé*, pp. 293–294.

with it while continuing to use all possible skill in improving relations with Germany. He added that "my government will give you every assistance in its power."[28] It should be noted that, as in the case of the army, the navy also remained alerted to the prospect of trouble. In late June, Admiral John Fisher, the first sea lord, asked the director of Naval Intelligence to prepare a statement on "the responsibility of manning the existing War Fleet in the event of sudden action against Germany." During 1905–6 the Admiralty, War Office, and the Committee of Imperial Defense organized in December 1902, considered the strategic implications of an Anglo-French war against Germany.

Delcassé had tried indirectly on April 6 to open negotiations with Germany on Morocco but without success. He later told Sir Donald MacKenzie Wallace that Germany had offered him an entente as an alternative to the entente with Britain except that the Germans were offering him inducements which provided for compensation which was vague and distant rather than realizable and present.[29] Wallace thought it very likely from what he had learned that a decision was made that Delcassé must be struck down but that the blow was delayed an entire year until Russia had been thoroughly beaten and crippled in Manchuria and Delcassé given additional rope with which to hang himself. This referred to the objectionable policies which he was considered to have continued.

The policies were those in North Africa and his practice of what Germany saw as treating her like a *quantité négligeable*. At the same time, Delcassé had failed to urge his government to prepare itself for a possible menace on the eastern frontier. Wallace was told by Johann Maria von Radowitz, the German minister, that the moment came when "the retirement of the obnoxious minister was the only means of avoiding war."

After receiving British support in refusing a conference on April 11, Delcassé tried once more on April 13 to open negotiations on Morocco, again without success. On April 25, the British ambassador in Paris, Francis Bertie, handed Delcassé a note assuring France of all possible British support in the question of a German request for a port on the Moroccan coast. Yet, on the very next day, April 26, Rouvier told the German ambassador in Paris, Prince Radolin, that he was prepared to sacrifice Delcassé, thus letting Bülow know that German pressure on France was producing disunity rather than unity in the French government. Simultaneously now, four major and discordant forces were

---

[28] Arthur J. Marder, *From the dreadnought to Scapa Flow. The Royal Navy in the Fisher era, 1904–1919*, I, London, 1961, pp. 116–119; Paléologue, *Three critical years*, p. 231.
[29] Wallace to Knollys, Feb. 21, 1906, Wallace Papers.

moving forward in unpremeditated accord: the German challenge to France in Morocco, the prospect of French mediation of the Far Eastern struggle, the mounting fear in the French government, and the effort of Britain to bolster the French position by direct support.

It is clear that to Bülow the prospect of French mediation in the Russo-Japanese war far overshadowed in importance the Moroccan issue since it was thought that successful French mediation in the Far Eastern war would lead to the creation of an Anglo-Franco-Russian alliance which both Bülow and Holstein agreed could constitute a "mutual plunder society," seeking to divide China among themselves.[30] Only after the disastrous Russian naval defeat at Tsushima on May 27–28 did the Kaiser shift to a position favorable to peace negotiations and only then, apparently, because he feared the spread of revolution within and beyond Russia. On June 3 he wrote to the Russian Emperor a very sympathetic letter advocating the opening of negotiations but recommending that Nicholas seek the good offices of President Roosevelt to bring it about.[31]

The precise issue over which Delcassé resigned on June 6 was the different evaluations which he and Rouvier, the president of the council, made of the seriousness of the German threat and of the value of the British offer of support. Delcassé held that Germany was bluffing and that the offer of British support was an effective counterpoise to such a threat. Anglo-German naval rivalry, in fact, gave Britain sufficient reason to participate actively in a possible Franco-German war by grasping the opportunity to destroy the German navy before it could develop into even more of a menace than it was, and thus confine Germany to Europe, cut off from her colonial and commercial relationships.

Lansdowne made a proposal to the French ambassador, Cambon, on May 17 that Britain and France continue to treat one another "with the most absolute confidence," keep one another "fully informed" of "everything which came to their knowledge," and "so far as possible, discuss in advance any contingencies" with which they might "find themselves confronted."[32] This suggestion, which Cambon apparently misunderstood as a British offer of a close diplomatic relationship, was seemingly not intended, as Monger has asserted, to go beyond the limited contingency of a German request for a port on the Moroccan coast and was conceived as a protection for Britain rather than France. The suggestion was, in fact, aimed at putting an end to a situation whereby "the French Government might be induced to purchase the acquiescence of Germany

[30] Andrew, *Théophile Delcassé*, pp. 290–293.
[31] Wilhelm to Nicholas, June 3, 1905, *GP*, XIX-2, 419–422.
[32] Eubank, *Paul Cambon*, pp. 101–102, 207–208; Nicolson to Morley, n.d., Nicolson Papers; Monger, *The end of isolation*, pp. 188, 197; Rozental', *Diplomaticheskaia istoriia*, pp. 130–131; No. 307 Lansdowne to Bertie, May 17, 1905, *BD*, III, 76.

by concessions of a kind which we were not likely to regard with favour in other parts of the world" and to provide a forum for a joint consideration of some common action.

Valentine Chirol of *The Times* had, in a letter of May 18, 1905, expressed in these words his own view of the approaching crisis: "It becomes more and more clear that the main object of Germany was to prove to the French that no reliance could be placed upon an understanding with England unless it was countersigned by Berlin."

Delcassé had understood Lansdowne's suggestion in the same sense as Cambon, i.e., as an offer of a very close relationship, and took the position that if the offer were not accepted Britain might turn to Germany. But Cambon thought that before going ahead with this it would be necessary to have the assurances of Rouvier as president of the council. So Delcassé brought the issue before the cabinet on June 6, 1905. Rouvier opposed Delcassé on the grounds that German opposition to this relationship was serious and that acceptance of it by France would only lead to war with Germany. This outcome may not have been unexpected in Germany since the differences between Rouvier and Delcassé were already known there.[33]

There was not then between Britain and France anything remotely resembling an offensive-defensive alliance, i.e., nothing beyond the entente concluded the year before. Consequently, unless the British government were to act on behalf of France because of Lansdowne's assurance or out of consideration for her own security, contingencies which could not be guaranteed, France would have had to bear the entire brunt of such a struggle. This was an ordeal for which she was poorly prepared. Consequently, the issue which confronted France was crucial to national security.

At the June 6 meeting the whole cabinet, excepting only Loubet, supported Rouvier and Delcassé thereupon resigned. "The incident," Lee has commented, "was an alarming proof of Germany's aggressive power and of France's defensive weakness."[34] It is also a significant commentary on the enduring continental power of Germany successfully tested one week after the naval battle at Tsushima had further depressed Russia's international prestige and raised the status of Britain and Japan as naval powers.[35] The event was, in addition, a significant enough demonstration of French weakness to cause Prime Minister Balfour to write on June 8 to King Edward that the fall of Delcassé "displayed a weakness on the part of France which indicated that she could not at present be counted on as an effective force in international politics."[36]

[33] Gooch, "Continental Agreements," 88–89.   [34] Lee, *King Edward VII*, II, 344.
[35] Monger, *The end of isolation*, pp. 199–200.   [36] Hale, *The great illusion*, p. 216.

The episode may also serve as a commentary on German lack of understanding of current French politics. For the dismissal was followed, as Radowitz had stated to Wallace, by policies very much like those of Delcassé. This outcome was never in doubt since on the very day of Delcassé's fall, Rouvier, his successor as minister of foreign affairs, called in the *Times* correspondent and stated to him that "the policy of France with regard to Anglo-French understanding would remain exactly the same." The reason for this was that Rouvier, instead of changing the government's policy, had sought other support for the existing policy. Rather than rely wholly on Britain, in which he had little or no confidence, he had attempted to find an accommodation with Germany. However, since this source of support was not realized, he had to resume the search for assurances from Britain. Germany continued her demand for a conference as a means of settling the Morocco issue.[37]

Delcassé, until his resignation, was said to have continued to pursue the plans he had already followed, i.e., those approved by the very influential Comité de l'Afrique Français, the program of which was carried into action by such persons as Paul Révoil, who was to become the principal delegate to the Algeciras conference, and Eugène Étienne who exercised great power in the French Chamber.[38] More recently the Comité had organized the Comité du Maroc which was very active in colonial affairs.

The German view of these events was based on some mistaken assumptions which were to lead to some unfortunate results. Sir Eyre Alexander Crowe later expressed the view that Germany had read into the North Sea incident the lesson that Britain would shrink from extreme measures even under severe provocation.[39] Germany presumably knew nothing of either the British suggestion of May 17 to France when Lansdowne had conveyed to Cambon the need for "absolute confidence" between Britain and France regarding the Franco-German dispute, or the warning which Lansdowne gave Metternich in June of British determination to support France either was not taken seriously or came too late to alter the course already set.[40] In fact, Metternich had advised the German government at that time that Britain would not encourage France to resist Germany and the resignation of Delcassé must have appeared as a confirmation of this assessment. This, in turn, might help to explain why, much to the surprise of both Rouvier and Bülow, the fall of Delcassé in no way modified either the German or French positions on Morocco or on the question of a conference dealing with the Moroccan issue.

[37] Monger, *The end of isolation*, pp. 194–205 ff.; Gerhard Ritter, *The sword and the sceptor*, trans. Heinz Norden, 4 vols. Coral Gables, FL, 1973, II, 64.
[38] Anderson, *First Moroccan crisis*, pp. 5–7, 132.   [39] Lee, *King Edward VII*, II, 344.
[40] Andrew, *Théophile Delcassé*, pp. 280 ff.

Germany was serious enough about the stance she had taken to prepare for a possible emergency.[41] Holstein wrote to Radolin in late June that things were not going well and that reserves had been called up for frontier areas. In a memorandum about a month later Holstein expressed his concern about what he saw as British hostility, suggesting that Britain might be ready to present Germany "with the bill for the Krüger Telegram, the Boer War episode, the naval drive and other items." He noted that the German Emperor had discussed the question of drawing Belgium and Denmark closer to Germany and Britain knew this and wanted to prevent it, perhaps by inflicting a naval defeat on Germany over the Moroccan question. On the very day of Delcassé's fall from office, however, the German Emperor had created Bülow a prince though Bülow himself maintained that this was a pure coincidence.

Apparently the ouster of Delcassé meant different things to each party. In the case of France it was clearly seen as a short range incident which had arisen over differing interpretations of the meaning of the German challenge or the value of British support. In the case of Germany there was not only a longer range objection to Delcassé's whole policy but, in the more immediate perspective, there was the desire to recoup the Moroccan venture which appeared on the verge of collapse. More particularly, for those who, like Holstein, envisioned Delcassé as a tool of British diplomacy, there was considerable anxiety as to his prospective role in the Russo-Japanese peace mediation.

Bülow moved forward with his demand for a conference while Roosevelt moved forward with his hope for Russo-Japanese peace negotiations. The Sultan of Morocco officially approved the idea of a conference on May 16 and issued an invitation to Germany on May 30 which was accepted on June 5.[42] France finally agreed to a conference on July 8 by an exchange of notes in which Germany agreed to preliminary negotiations along with a Franco-German understanding, providing that the Anglo-French and Franco-Spanish agreements would be excluded from consideration at a future conference.[43] This bargain was apparently at least in part a product of urging from St. Petersburg in an intervention to which Russia had agreed on June 25 and which took the form of a personal note from the Tsar to the Kaiser.[44]

While maneuvering France into acceptance of a conference, Bülow had, by his inept diplomacy, set the stage for a German rather than a

[41] Holstein to Radolin, June 28, 1905, Holstein Memorandum, July 31, 1905, in Rich and Fisher, *The Holstein papers*, IV, 347–348, 356.
[42] Dehmelt, "Bülow's Moroccan policy," pp. 347–357.
[43] Ibid., pp. 346–377, 413–415; Rozental', *Diplomaticheskaia istoriia*, pp. 134–136.
[44] Nos. 444, 386 Rouvier to Bompard, June 22, 25; Nos. 246, 248 Bompard to Rouvier, June 25, 27, 1905, *DDF*, VII, 110–111, 134, 139, 167.

French humiliation by playing such a large-scale game for such meager gains in a colonial territory which Germany neither needed nor wanted, while rendering it virtually impossible to reap any advantage from such an important bone of contention as the Treaty of Frankfurt. It should be noted that on June 12, a week after the resignation of Delcassé, Russia formally accepted President Roosevelt's invitation to meet the Japanese for peace negotiations, thus opening the way for a second potential block to German dominance on the European continent. Russia, while deeply disturbed by the prospect of a peace which would aim at perpetuating and even institutionalizing her defeat, humiliation, and exposed weakness, was also appalled at the prospect of further enlargement of German power and the persistent evidence of her growing ambition.

Witte had had an opportunity during his two recent visits to Paris to discover for himself how literally true his estimate of German power was and how tense the international situation was becoming. He had stopped in Paris in July on his way to the Portsmouth conference to inquire about a further loan and found both President Emile Loubet and Premier Maurice Rouvier very discouraging.[45]

There was considerable concern in Paris not only over the Morocco issue but about the word which had reached there of the meeting of the German and Russian emperors at Björkö. Loubet later told Witte that he had positive information to the effect that Japan was supporting disturbances in Russia as well as an anti-Russian movement in the European press. Loubet and Rouvier both urged Witte to be conciliatory and Rouvier advised him not to expect any further loans from Paris under present circumstances. He added that peace was absolutely necessary for the security of the Franco-Russian alliance and each of its partners. Witte was told that France would go so far as to help Russia pay an indemnity if this were required to obtain peace. The Russian minister had, however, ruled out the payment of any indemnity by Russia.

The Franco-German exchange of notes on July 8, 1905 calling for preliminary negotiations preparatory to the conference on Morocco was followed in September by the sending of Friedrich von Rosen to Paris. Rosen was the German Foreign Office specialist on Muslim countries including North Africa. He was accompanied by an expert on international law, Dr. Johannes Kriege. Rosen was sent by Chancellor Bülow in part because the German ambassador in Paris, Prince Radolin, was not considered sufficiently competent for this mission and in part because he was a spokesman for Holstein. Negotiations in Paris were conducted

[45] Witte, *Vospominaniia*, II, 404–407; Rich, *Friedrich von Holstein*, II, 525–527; Bernhard Schwertfeger (ed.), *Zur Europäischen politik 1897–1914*, vols. I, II, V. Berlin, 1919, II, 65–66.

mostly with Paul Révoil, former French minister in Tangier, governor general of Algiers, and a very effective spokesman for the powerful colonial and Moroccan interests which had supported Delcassé as well as the continuation of his policies after his dismissal. While Rosen saw Morocco as a negotiating base for improving relations, Révoil saw it also as an end in itself.

Bülow set the tone of the mission to Paris when he wrote to Rosen: "It is above all important to make clear to Prince von Radolin [the German ambassador] and to the French that the sending of Rosen is" a "last attempt to reach an understanding."[46] Nevertheless, Rosen, though he knew of the Björkö meeting but not of the outcome, thought that Germany was not in such a secure position as this implied and conjectured, for example, that faced with a choice between France and Germany, Russia would choose France.

Had Rosen known the substance of the Björkö agreement he might have realized not only how complicated such a choice could have been at that moment but also the reason the German government was then exhibiting a relatively benign attitude toward France. Furthermore, the French, as represented by Rouvier and especially Révoil, were very determined about their desires in Morocco though they were quite ready to discuss a wide range of alternatives including a general colonial settlement, possible rectifications of their African frontier with the German Cameroons, and an understanding with respect to the Bagdad railway.[47]

As for the preparation of the Morocco agenda, all the sensitive issues were apparently discussed and some, including the questions of a loan and of the construction of certain harbor facilities, were resolved and Algeciras agreed to as the meeting place of the conference. This left mainly the police and bank issues unsolved. The negotiations were concluded in two documents with a program for the coming conference signed on September 28, 1905.[48]

Following these agreements, alternative French proposals for a secret pre-conference agreement were made with the hope of reaching a quiet settlement of the remaining issues. One of these was advanced in November 1905 in an approach made unobtrusively to Richard von

[46] No. 168 Bülow to FO Sept. 19, 1905, *GP*, XX-2, 573.
[47] Mark Antony DeWolfe Howe, *George von Lengerke Meyer: his life and public services*, New York, 1919, p. 218; Friedrich Rosen, *Aus einem diplomatischen Wanderleben*, 4 vols. in 3. Berlin and Wiesbaden, 1931–59, I, 156; Hammann, *Zur Vorgeschichte des Weltkrieges*, pp. 138–139.
[48] Witte, *Vospominaniia*, II, 470 ff.; Claus Grimm, "Graf Witte und die deutsche Politik," Ph.D. dissertation, University of Freiburg, Germany, 1930, pp. 61–63; Long, "The economics," pp. 107–128; Rouvier to Bihourd (Berlin), enclosing the two documents and Rouvier to Taillandier, Sept. 30, 1905, *DDAM*, pp. 305–310.

Kühlmann, then the first secretary of the German legation in Tangier, by two French representatives. A settlement was suggested on the basis of the guarantee of a free hand for France in Morocco in exchange for a permanent guarantee of the open door in Morocco, the right of German capital to a 45 percent participation in all government undertakings in Morocco, territorial compensation for Germany in the French Congo, and the cession by France to Germany of certain rights in the Belgian Congo. The proposal was considered but not acted upon.

A defensive response

The Morocco challenge brought forcibly to the attention of the international community the significance of recent alterations in the world order. By 1905, in addition to the Japanese victory and the unpredictable ways in which it might alter the Far East and the world, there was the threat of war with Germany in case of a stalemate or German diplomatic defeat at Algeciras. Nevertheless, the latter prospect was evaluated by the members of the Anglo-French entente and the Franco-Russian alliance as being of such seriousness that each partnership took extraordinary measures to deal with it. In addition, because the Anglo-French situation was intimately related to the prospect of a German attack on and through Belgium, Anglo-Belgian military conversations were inaugurated in January 1906 at about the same time as those between Britain and France.

Even though the negotiations were conducted by these groups with discreet detachment, they shared a common set of difficulties in meeting the German challenge, such as the depletion of Russian military power in the Far Eastern war, the military weakness of France, and the absence of a British military force capable of fulfilling a significant share in a continental war. Hardinge, with his hopes firmly fixed on St. Petersburg, "saw in a revived Russia the real continental check to German threats though he knew it would take some time for the Russians to build up their resources."[49] These weaknesses were emphasized by what appeared to be an opportunity for Germany to win at Algeciras a diplomatic victory without a war. It also raised the question as to whether, if Germany were denied such a victory, the strength of these three nations would at that time be sufficient to deter a resort to war waged to assure the victory.

The situation in Europe in 1905 was the consequence of six major changes which had occurred in recent decades. One was the disturbing heritage of the awe-inspiring Prussian military victories of 1864 and after which had led to the unification of Germany. This had introduced into the European political scene a new military efficiency, directly supported by

[49] Steiner, *The Foreign Office*, p. 94.

an effective state apparatus, generally expanding economic development, and in particular, by industrial power, finding its foundations in a relatively peaceful though politically shattered European community. Europe was left thereafter to grope through the ruins of past "concert" arrangements of the old order in search of the safeguards of a new balance of power.

A second, more specific factor was the quasi-traditional British conception of Russia as the principal adversary, a notion which had more recently been actively and pointedly reinforced as a threat by the growing effectiveness of the railways being constructed in Siberia and Central Asia. These were already supplementing the existing menace to the security of China and India, and rendering more threatening the strongly anti-British feeling aroused in Russia by the accusation that Britain had encouraged the Japanese to undertake the war in the Far East. This issue and its ancillary provocations raised a demand for increased military reinforcements in the Far East and India at the very time when two other factors had also to be taken into account in planning for military needs. One of these, the third of the general phenomena, was the troublesome, concurrent, and unremitting growth of German military power along with a fourth factor, the decreasing capability of Russia, as her defeats reduced her strength and prestige, to act as a counterbalancing force on her western (i.e., the German) flank. Fifth, there was the evolution of Japan as both a maritime and a continental power, influencing not only the colonial system, particularly in the Far East, but the world balance of power. And, finally there was the United States, recently arrived at great power status but not yet at great power assertiveness, and, therefore, something of an enigma in international affairs.

These transformations in the balance of power placed the nations which were to compose the entente increasingly on the defensive, forcing them to alter considerably their defensive plans. The virtual revolution in British military thought and action which followed was characterized by a growing realization that the world in which Britain had heretofore pursued her national and imperial life was becoming increasingly dangerous. This was the message which Sir Halford John Mackinder was imparting in his contemporary article: "The Geographical Pivot of History," i.e., that a seapower pursuing commerce faced a threat from a great land-based nation with military and industrial power.[50] This was one of the lessons of the concurrent Russo-Japanese war.

---

[50] J. McDermott, "The revolution in British military thinking from the Boer War to the Moroccan crisis," in Paul M. Kennedy (ed.), *The war plans of the Great Powers, 1880–1914*, London, 1979, pp. 101–107; Mackay, *Fisher of Kilverstone*, pp. 332–349; Christopher Howard, *Splendid isolation. A study of ideas concerning Britain's international position and foreign policy during the later years of the Third Marquis of Salisbury*, London,

Accordingly, a defense plan intended to meet such a challenge was drawn up, not by the Cabinet, the Committee of Imperial Defense, or any other group acting officially, but by a few individuals associated with the British government and acting in secret. They took these measures under such conditions because they felt that in view of the changing and increasingly hostile conditions, secrecy was essential. They saw national security being threatened by an as yet only vaguely defined menace resulting from an imbalance of power on the nearby European continent and in the world.

The assumption that there was an intensifying Russian threat to India and that it was still the primary factor in the allocation of military expenditures was called into question by altered circumstances and by new groups of people prepared to challenge this assumption and to urge that greater attention be given to the threat emerging in Central Europe. These included the War Office Committee headed by Lord Esher and his protégé, Colonel Sir George Sydenham Clarke, the secretary during 1904–7 of the Committee of Imperial Defense and Major General Sir James Moncrieff Grierson, who during 1904–6 held the newly created position of director of military operations.

Those stressing the threat to Britain from Central Europe included such persons outside British military circles as Lieutenant Colonel Charles à Court Repington who had been the British military attaché in Belgium and Holland during the period 1898–1902 and who on January 1, 1905 had been appointed the military correspondent of *The Times*, Colonel Victor Jacques Huguet, the French military attaché in London since December 1904, and others. Their success depended upon convincing those in higher echelons of military or civilian administration or in more traditional functions of the soundness of the course they advocated.

This was in fact accomplished under the pressure of events and in a surprisingly short time. The General Staff had by the end of February 1905 considered a European role for the British army while the prime minister had on July 20 urged at a meeting of the Committee of Imperial Defense, an agency for strategic planning which had held its initial meeting on December 18, 1902, the need for joint naval–military operations for this purpose. A memorandum by Clarke of the following August 17 dealt with such related issues as possible German violation of Belgian territory in case of a Franco-German war, the capability of Belgium to defend herself, and the time required for two British corps to reach Belgium.[51]

1967, pp. 226–228; *The history of the Times*, III, *The twentieth century test, 1884–1912*, London, 1947, pp. 419, 462–469; Peter Viereck, "Revolution in values: roots of the European catastrophe, 1870–1952," *PSQ*, LXVII, no. 3 (Sept. 1952), 339–346.
[51] Williamson, *The politics of grand strategy*, pp. 47–48.

Since General Grierson had visited Paris in mid-March 1905 and advised the French of British support in case of a Franco-German war, Britain was in fact "on an anti-German course" before the German Emperor set foot in Morocco on March 31.[52] Colonel Huguet reported to Paris in November 1905 that in the event of such a war he estimated that Britain could mobilize as many as 150,000 men but that it would take so long for them to reach the continent that they would hardly be there in time to influence the outcome. The General Staff at this time accepted the Admiralty estimate that two army corps could be landed in Belgium on the twenty-third day after the order to mobilize.

The period from the latter part of 1905, particularly December, into the first weeks of 1906 was the most crucial with respect to the continuity and progress of this new British course. Some doubt was cast on the chances of survival of these inchoate policies and plans by the imminent prospect of a Liberal victory in the coming election. It was to provide the needed assurances on this point that the man most likely to succeed Lord Lansdowne as secretary of state for foreign affairs in the prospective new government, Sir Edward Grey, made a very clear statement of his support for a policy of giving assurances to France in his City speech of October 21, 1905.[53] It was also not accidental that three "Liberal Imperialists," Grey himself, Herbert Asquith, and Richard B. Haldane were given respectively the important posts in the new government at the Foreign Office, the Exchequer, and the War Office.

Haldane, whom the German ambassador, Metternich, described optimistically as in the "inner circle of the Cabinet," and as being very friendly to Germany, was asked to accept as a special assignment the preparation of a military force consisting of six divisions and at least one cavalry division, all of them fully equipped and ready to be transported for action on the continent in case of war with Germany. Assisting him in this project were such officers as Sir Douglas Haig, Sir William Nicholson, and Sir Wilfred Laurier.[54] Major General Sir Douglas Haig, then serving in India, was the personal choice of both Haldane and King

[52] McDermott, "The revolution in British military," 108; Williamson, *The politics of grand strategy*, p. 57; General Staff, War Office, replies to "Questions Addressed to the General Staff by the Prime Minister," Sept. 23, 1905, Cab 4/1.

[53] George Macaulay Trevelyan, *Grey of Falladon. Being the life of Sir Edward Grey afterwards Viscount Grey of Falladon*, London, 1937, pp. 89–92; General Staff memorandum to the Prime Minister, Sept. 23, 1905, Cab 4/1; Monger, *The end of isolation*, pp. 257–259.

[54] Viscount Richard Burdon Haldane, *Richard Burdon Haldane (Viscount Haldane). An autobiography*, New York, 1929, pp. 196–218; Frederick Maurice, *Haldane, 1856–1928. The life of Viscount Haldane of Cloan, K.T., O.M*, 2 vols. London, 1937–39, I, 161–203; Williamson, *The politics of grand strategy*, pp. 90–91; Lee, *King Edward VII*, II, 494–507; Ritter, *The sword and the sceptor*, II, 63–64.

Edward to be director of military training at the War Office and was appointed to that position in February 1906. The assumption was that the general plan would evolve as a joint military–naval operation though at that time Admiral John Fisher would permit no interference with his naval planning and consequently continued to work separately.

It is clear that Grey enunciated his policy in his City speech and after with considerable promise of party support. He stressed the importance of continuity in foreign policy, singling out for special emphasis the three major elements of the existing British foreign policy: the growing friendship with the United States, the Anglo-Japanese alliance which he portrayed as a defensive alliance concerned with China and India, and the Anglo-French entente. The last of these, in view of the current weakness of Russia, was in particular danger because of the possibility of the isolation of France, which had already experienced the Delcassé episode. He warned that France might be forced to make such concessions to Germany as to leave Britain isolated and exposed to a Franco-Russo-German continental coalition. This was the very kind of regrouping which the Kaiser, Count Aloys Lexa von Aehrenthal, Austrian minister of foreign affairs after October 24, 1906, and others had in mind.

The importance of having established by early December 1905 in the Foreign Office, the War Office, and the Admiralty a positive attitude toward a potential Franco-German war would be difficult to exaggerate. France was nearing the decisive encounter with Germany at Algeciras and was able on December 13 to receive assurances directly from Lord Esher who had lunch on that day with Georges Clemenceau. The latter stressed the vital importance of British military and naval action during the first week of a war with Germany. [55]

This was a more timely action than either of these governments may have realized since it was also at this time that the chief of the German General Staff, General Count Alfred von Schlieffen, wrote to the Kaiser that because of the present weakness of Russia he had reduced the number of divisions assigned to the eastern front in order to concentrate on a possible war with France.[56] Holstein agreed with this policy, adding that the most energetic steps should be taken "to break through the ring before the other nations close in completely around us."

The actual conversations from which the basic Anglo-French military arrangements emerged took place between mid-December 1905 and the end of January 1906 and were carried on by diplomatic, military and naval

---

[55] Major General Sir George Aston, "The Entente Cordiale and the military conversations," QR, CCLVIII, no. 512 (April 1932), 372 ff.; J.D. Hargreaves, "The origin of the Anglo-French military conversations in 1905," H, XXXVI, no. 128 (Oct. 1951), 248; History of the Times, III, 465; Williamson, The politics of grand strategy, p. 602.
[56] Khvostov, Istoriia diplomatii, II, 602.

persons. Major General Grierson, the director of military operations, and Captain John Ottley, who had succeeded Prince Louis of Battenberg in February 1905 as the director of Naval Intelligence, met on December 15 to discuss the military implications of a war with Germany. The two principal topics of concern were the possibility of a German violation of Belgian neutrality and the time required for Britain to land a military force on the continent for effective participation in the war.

This was followed, according to General Aston, on either December 16 or 18 by an approach to Grierson by the French military attaché, Colonel Victor Huguet, on the subject of British help in case of a German attack on France. The first of several discussions between Clarke, Esher, and Sir John French, the commander at Aldershot, was held on December 19 and dealt with coastal operations but not yet with a full commitment to a British land-based participation.

The foundation for the actual use of British forces in case of a Franco-German war, particularly one involving the violation of Belgian territory, appears to have entered the planning stage about December 20 and, according to Aston, to have been inspired by the French.[57] The conversations between Huguet and Grierson on December 20 and 21 dealt with the details of these issues such as the number of troops needed and the time required to transport them. It was also at this time that the Anglo-French military conversations reached the highest official levels: the French ambassador, Paul Cambon, had an audience on December 20 with King Edward in the course of which he recalled the secret discussions held with Lord Lansdowne until they were interrupted the previous June by the fall of Delcassé. He asked the King whether he ought to send for appropriate instructions to continue the discussions and was told: "By all means do so, it would be very useful."

Cambon reported this interview to Rouvier and was told to proceed with the discussions. He accordingly saw Sir Edward Grey on January 10, 1906. Lieutenant Colonel Charles Repington, the military correspondent of *The Times*, was drawn into these plans when he dined on December 28 with Colonel Huguet, whom he had known for some years. Repington was deeply impressed by the French military attaché with the importance of sending a British military force to cooperate with the French as soon as possible after the opening of hostilities, a view which he reported the very next day to Grey. Repington's strong advocacy of this idea appears in fact to date from this time. He began to urge the importance of British support for France not only among the appropriate officials but also in his articles in the press. (See The Military Correspondent of "The Times," *Imperial Strategy*, London, 1906.) Among the factors which appear to have

[57] Aston, "The Entente Cordiale," pp. 375–376; Williamson, *The politics of grand strategy*, p. 65; Giles St. Aubyn, *Edward VII, prince and king*, New York, 1979, pp. 335–336.

influenced his opinion strongly were the reality of the German threat to France as exemplified by the Morocco issue and the inability in the near future of Russia to mobilize in time to help.

The basic military plans were elaborated within the British government during late December 1905 and early January 1906. Grey and Haldane had agreed on January 12 that it might become necessary to implement the entente with France by preparing naval and military plans with such an eventuality in mind. Consequently, by January 16, the date of the opening of the conference at Algeciras, the first "official" meeting could be held and discussions regarding Anglo-French military cooperation carried on between General Grierson, the director of military operations, and Colonel Victor Huguet, the French military attaché in London.

The subject of military cooperation was at the same time also opened between Britain and Belgium when the British military attaché in Brussels, Lieutenant Colonel N. W. Barnardiston, wrote on this matter to the Belgian Chief of Staff, General G. E. W. Ducarne. This initiative was followed briefly by detailed discussions which were, however, soon terminated because of Belgian reluctance to risk a breach of neutrality. However, Count Schulenburg, the German military attaché in London, reported in January 1906 on British plans to rebuild the army and to develop an expeditionary force and on the proposals for landing a force in Belgium.

Since it would have been impossible to have conducted these and other conversations in such a way as to leave them officially binding on all parties, they were confined to military persons and to a limited number of cabinet level people and were never adopted as official policy since this would have necessitated exposing them to parliament and to broader public knowledge both domestically and abroad.[58]

Even though the adoption of these international military commitments never went beyond this restricted and secret state, the Kaiser let Haldane know during his visit to Berlin in September 1906 that he had heard about the talks with the French. The German government might have guessed that something like this was in the air from the fact that Grey had warned the German ambassador in early January that in case of war between Germany and France, public opinion in Britain would make it impossible for Britain to remain neutral.[59]

The British–French plans had the advantage of having concentrated on the coastal region near Belgium in the general vicinity then being suggested for a German concentration in case of war. A landing on the

[58] Grey to Bertie, Jan. 31, 1906 and notation, in Viscount Grey of Falladon, *Twenty-five years, 1892–1916*, 2 vols. New York, 1925, I, 76–79.
[59] Grey to Lascelles, Jan. 9, 1906, in Grey, *Twenty-five years*, I, 80.

Schleswig-Holstein coast, the favorite project of Admiral Fisher because it would have provided an occasion for the destruction of the German fleet, was apparently not seriously considered for military use. The British plans had started from a point where there was not a single division available for overseas duty, yet by January 1, 1907 they were ready to begin actual preparations on a budget.

A British Admiralty memorandum of early 1906 reviewed the implications of the recent war in the Far East and its consequences for the future of British naval requirements. Two pertinent recent events, the memorandum stated, the renewal of the Anglo-Japanese alliance and the annihilation of the Russian fleet, had not fundamentally altered the British situation. They had only provided a very important breathing space.[60] These events were in the long run outweighed by the fact that both great continental powers, Germany and France, had in recent years embarked on major naval construction programs. The French had newly begun their naval program, undoubtedly because of the losses of Russia but also because of the need to compensate for the continuing growth of the German navy.

These developments would have an effect on events in Morocco, Central Europe, and above all the Middle East, where armed conflict was then seen as most likely to occur. Such a prospect was reflected in the heavy concentration of British naval power in the three major fleets which were located in or near these regions: the Channel Fleet centered at Dover, the Atlantic Fleet centered at Gibraltar, and the Mediterranean Fleet centered at Alexandria. This gave emphasis to the fact that, even though the German navy was then much smaller than the British, it was aspiring to a major role mainly in Europe but to a considerable degree also beyond Europe. Furthermore, at existing rates of development the German and French naval expenditures would by 1909 have outdistanced those of Britain, thus underscoring the British need for more, better, and larger ships.

The British navy was in fact making some spectacular advances at this time. The *Dreadnought* was launched on February 10, 1906 though it was not completed until December of that year.[61] The new ship had fire power and a fire range more than double that of the pre-dreadnought battleships. The old two-power standard which had survived from the eighteenth

---

[60] Memorandum "The Building Programme of the British Navy," Feb. 15, 1906, Adm 116/866B; Peter Padfield, *The great naval race*, New York, 1974, chs. 6 and 7; Kennedy, *The rise and fall*, pp. 183–185; Mackay, *Fisher*, pp. 313, 328–330; Marder, *From the dreadnought*, I, 40–42.

[61] Marder, *From the dreadnought*, I, 43–44, 123–125; Marder, *Anatomy of British sea power*, pp. 509–510; Woodward, *Great Britain and the German Navy*, pp. 104–114; Holger H. Herwig, "The German reaction to the Dreadnought revolution," *The International History Review*, XIII, no. 2 (May 1991), 273–283.

century and had been officially accepted on March 7, 1889 by Lord George Hamilton, was now, after taking into consideration the rise of the German navy, the recent devastation of the Russian fleet, and the reliance which could now be placed on the Japanese navy, given a necessary reconsideration by a special committee headed by Prince Louis of Battenberg.

This committee recommended a two-power policy plus at least 10 percent in battleships over each of the combinations, German–Russian or French–Russian. A cruiser ratio of two to one over each of these was also recommended. It was estimated in 1906 that by the end of 1909 Britain would have six battleships of the dreadnought class and three heavy cruisers of the Invincible class whereas Germany had not in fact even decided upon the new ships until September 1905 and would probably not have more than three by 1910.

Admiral Sir John Fisher, the first sea lord, who did not see any need for French naval help, nevertheless held some discussions at this time with the French naval attaché, Captain Mercier de Lostende, though this was apparently the only time in 1905 or 1906 that Anglo-French naval conversations were held.[62] The reluctance of Admiral Fisher to discuss joint military–naval strategic plans with reference to continental operations was undoubtedly due in part to the difficult and apparently ancillary role foreseen for the navy. The dilemma was stated pointedly by General Nicholson: "Wherever we threatened to land, the Germans could concentrate superior force."

The same general circumstances which had brought the Anglo-French entente to take on many of the essential characteristics of a military alliance also led to a reconsideration of the existing military provisions of the Franco-Russian alliance. This issue was discussed in late 1905 by the French military attaché in St. Petersburg, General Louis Moulin, and the Russian chief of General Staff, General F. F. Palitsyn, and it was arranged that the latter would go to Paris in the near future for military conversations.[63] The French minister of foreign affairs, in pursuit of the planned

---

[62] Paléologue, *Three critical years*, pp. 293–294; Paul Michael Kennedy, "Mahan versus Mackinder: two interpretations of British sea power," *MM*, 2 (1974), 52; Rozental', *Diplomaticheskaia istoriia*, pp. 219–221; No. 9 Bompard to Rouvier, Jan. 26, 1906, *DDF*, IX-1, 106; Andrei Medarich Zaionchkovsky, "Franko-russkie otnosheniia do voiny 1914 goda," in Aleksandr Gavrilovich Shliapnikov, et al., *Kto dolzhnik? Sbornik dokumentirovannykh statei po voprosu ob otnosheniiakh mezhdu Rossiei, Frantsiei i drugimi derzhavami Antanty do voiny 1914 g., vo vremia voiny i v period interventsii*, Moscow, 1926, pp. 29–31; Frank Miller Laney, "The military implementation of the Franco-Russian Alliance, 1890–1914," Ph.D. dissertation, University of Virginia, 1954, pp. 220–229.

[63] No. 2523 Moulin to Étienne, Jan. 27, 1906, *DDF*, IX-1, 115–118; Beryl J. Williams, "The revolution of 1905 and Russian foreign policy," in C. Abramsky and Beryl J. Williams (eds.), *Essays in honor of E. H. Carr*, London, 1974, p. 106.

negotiations, sent instructions on February 14, 1906 to Bompard initiating the visit of General Palitsyn which was arranged for April and it was suggested that a set of topics be prepared in advance for General Palitsyn's consideration before his departure and for discussion with the French General Staff during his visit in Paris.

General Moulin also furnished the French minister of war with some of the results of a conversation he had had with General Palitsyn.[64] The Russian chief of staff had stated that in his view the German Emperor did not want war with France but would in fact prefer to achieve a rapprochement with France and a detachment of the latter from Britain and that a war between Germany on the one hand and France and Britain on the other would in reality be brought about by the maneuvers and intrigues of Britain, involved over British interests, and would evoke no interest in Russia. Judging by the lesson which had been drawn from the Russo-Japanese war, Palitsyn continued, Russia could not understand France risking her honor as a nation seriously against Germany in a colonial question like Morocco.

The most disappointing news must have been Palitsyn's assertion that the Russian government could not at that time impose another war on the Russian people. That General Palitsyn clearly saw the national defense situation as jeopardized can be seen from his assertion at that time, when so many Russian forces were still in the Far East or in transit, that the security of the western frontier could only be assured by an understanding with Germany. This does not, however, seem to have ruled out, in his view, an accommodation with Britain.

General Moulin explained that French policy was peaceful, that it was based on a strong Russia in the same way that Emperor Alexander III had declared that Russia needed a strong France, and that France had no intention of fighting a war with Germany for the benefit of Britain. On the other hand, he explained, Britain was worth more to France than Germany, particularly in preserving her colonial possessions. He warned Palitsyn of the danger of relying on the good intentions concerning France expressed by the German Emperor in his communications with Emperor Nicholas.

Moulin appreciated some of the problems Russia faced in dealing with the existing situation in Europe. He estimated that it would take about three years, i.e., until about the spring of 1909, to reestablish Russian power as a factor in Europe. This was an estimate which he may have drawn from discussions with Palitsyn who had added that even at the present time Russia was better equipped with certain weapons such as howitzers, machine-guns, and rapid-fire cannon than before the Russo-

[64] No. 2523 Moulin to Étienne, Jan. 27, 1906, *DDF*, IX-1, 115–118.

Japanese war. In a separate letter of the same date General Moulin added that the meeting in April would present an opportunity to urge Russia to channel certain military expenditures in directions of some advantage to France such as the improvement of railways, armaments, and supplies needed for mobilization.[65]

The list of desiderata for General Palitsyn and for the April meeting of the two chiefs of general staff in Paris was also sent to St. Petersburg in mid-February.[66] This stated that "the principal object ... was to assure the mutual protection of the two allies against an aggression by Germany," and suggested a reconsideration of the Franco-Russian convention of August 10, 1892 as the basic charter of the alliance and of the protocols of July 2, 1900 and February 21, 1901 as a starting point for reviewing the current situation.

It was suggested also that consideration should be given to deciding the troop strength desirable on the part of each nation in the event of war. If, as a consequence of recent events in the Far East, Russia were at present unable to master all the proportionate strength foreseen in the convention of 1892, the French General Staff would be advised as to what temporary measures the Russian government intended to take in order to observe the principles of the alliance. The French chief of staff, General Jean Brun, requested specific information such as the number of troops Russia could concentrate on the western frontier, the time required for this, at what points the troops could be concentrated, what the armament of these troops could be expected to be, and an estimate of the time required for the restoration of Russian armed strength.

The two chiefs of General Staff concluded a military protocol in Paris on April 21, 1906, the day before the publication of the Russian loan.[67] This reaffirmed the basic purpose of the 1892 accord as that of mutual protection against aggression by Germany. The German army was, accordingly, the principal object against which France and Russia would direct their struggle with all the means at their disposal.

The two General Staffs asserted that on the mobilization of the German army France and Russia would be obligated to mobilize all their forces immediately and simultaneously though it was assumed that the German attack in the initial stage would be delivered more against France. Exchange of intelligence about the German forces was given high priority. The Russians estimated that their forces would be returned from

---

[65] No. 126 Rouvier to Bompard, Feb. 14, 1906, *DDF*, IX-1, 273–274; Rozental', *Diplomaticheskaia istoriia*, pp. 222–228.

[66] No. 372 Bourgeois to Bompard, June 25, 1906, enclosing a protocol dated Apr. 21, 1906, *DDF*, X, 183–186.

[67] Kornelii Fedorovich Shatsillo, *Russkii imperializm i razvitie flota nakanune Pervoi mirovoi voiny (1906–1914 gg.)*, Moscow, 1968, pp. 56–63.

the Far East by the end of the following August and ready for some action after April 1907. General Jean Brun was able to achieve a major success by having the point eliminated from the 1900–1 protocols which called for sanctions against Britain.

The reconstruction of the Russian navy was undertaken with suitable attention to defense needs and budget deficiencies. It was decided at a meeting of the General and Naval Staffs on December 15, 1906 that for the next two decades the Baltic fleet would be limited to a defense role while the Black Sea and Pacific fleets would continue to be designated as active fleets for offensive operations.[68] The actual rebuilding of the fleet in the general sense began with a program approved on May 8, 1907 by the Council of Ministers, a program of construction which in the form it had been given by mid-July called for four battleships of the Dreadnought class, two light cruisers, eighteen destroyers, seventy-two torpedo boats, thirty-six submarines, and three transports. Actual production of the capital ships was not begun, however, until June 1909, four years after Tsushima.

The Algeciras conference

These preparations were a practical response to what the participants saw as a threat to their national integrity. It was feared that whether the Algeciras conference ended in a stalemate or in either a defeat or victory for Germany, it would place Germany in a superior position compared with her competitors. The event was, accordingly, taken very seriously in Paris and London and exercised a decisive influence on the course and outcome of the conference. Furthermore, the German government was informed by Prince Radolin, the German ambassador in Paris, even before the conference opened, of the great anxiety which prevailed in France over the possibility of war.[69] It has been argued effectively that, in spite of this widespread impression, Germany did not in fact intend to resort to armed conflict but that those actions and pronouncements which made it appear that she did so intend had been based on mistaken assumptions or were the consequence of inept handling of German's international relations.[70] Bülow seemed to be saying precisely this when he wrote to Holstein that: "The failure of the Conference would be, no matter how one looked at it, a diplomatic setback for us. Neither public opinion, Parliament, Princes, or even the army will have anything to do with a war over Morocco."[71]

[68] Shatsillo, *Russkii imperializm*, pp. 56–63.
[69] Anderson, *First Moroccan crisis*, pp. 319–320.
[70] Rich, *Friedrich von Holstein*, II, 696–713, 733–735.
[71] Bülow to Holstein, Feb. 22, 1906, in Rich and Fisher, *The Holstein papers*, IV, 396; Gordon Alexander Craig, *The politics of the Prussian army 1640–1945*, Oxford, 1955, pp.

It appears, however, that both Holstein and Schlieffen, the chief of General Staff, in fact assumed that war was intended and that only the firm stand of the Kaiser and Bülow prevented it. The object of such a war would have been the defeat of France while Russia was occupied in the Far East, thus bringing an end to the two-front war danger which Germany faced.

In fact, the consequence of not following the war strategy through was not only to humiliate Germany but to perpetuate the two-front problem. The Kaiser's opposition was not to war but to war at that time, in part because Germany was then ill-prepared as the Kaiser saw it. In his view the artillery needed renewal and the fortifications and batteries at Metz were incomplete, But in particular he was reluctant to go to war especially because he thought that the socialist menace made it unwise to move any troops outside of the country.

It seems to have been a reasonable interpretation given in Britain to the fall of Delcassé, an early increment of the campaign against France, that this event heralded German hegemony on the continent and negation of the existing balance of power. This was the challenge which virtually insured British support of France at Algeciras. The Boer war had revealed and the Russo-Japanese war had demonstrated beyond question the British mistake of relying so completely on sea power. A direct role in continental politics and strategy could no longer be postponed.

The German announcement that she wanted basically a guarantee of the open door in Morocco instead of the French intention of seeking a protectorate over the country seemed to be a reasonable way of attracting the United States, Britain, and other nations which had supported the open door in China. It also seemed a particularly attractive policy in view of the Liberal victory in Britain. Furthermore, the precaution which the German Emperor had taken to acquire Russian concurrence in the Björkö treaty, craftily and unobtrusively directed toward breaking up the Franco-Russian alliance, might, if successful, have removed Russia from the list of opponents at the future conference at Algeciras. These assumptions and plans might have succeeded in isolating France and leaving her no alternative to accepting the German demands.

None of them, however, turned out to be either accurately adjusted to the current wishes or expectations or well founded as to the inducements which they held out. The opening of the conference soon disclosed the solid support on which France was able to count.[72] These supporters were

284–285; Gordon Alexander Craig, *From Bismarck to Adenauer. Aspects of German statecraft*, Baltimore, 1958, p. 43; Peter Rassow, "Schlieffen und Holstein," *HZ*, CLXXIII, no. 2 (1952), p. 312; Bülow, *Memoirs*, II, 190–191; Ritter, *The sword and the sceptor*, II, 66–67.

[72] George Wolfgang Felix Hallgarten, *Imperialismus vor 1914*, 2 vols. Munich, 1951, 1963, I, 664.

apparently in large part held together by the fear that Germany actually intended war, a contingency which is to be sure common in many diplomatic gambles. But the members of the conference also feared that any advantage which Germany might gain at this international forum would only place her in a better position in the future to threaten again and to make further demands.

Even the assurances which the most informed persons in Paris such as President Emile Loubet, Rouvier, Paul Doumer, Clemenceau, and Radolin had given Sir Donald MacKenzie Wallace as he passed through on his way to Algeciras did not seem to have persuaded either him or them that there would be no war.[73] This remained true even though Germany had deliberately taken steps to defuse a part of the Franco-Russian opposition by agreeing that Germany would never be the aggressor and that the *casus foederis* of the Franco-Russian alliance would not be activated where she was concerned.[74]

The Algeciras conference was the arena which witnessed the transformation, under the intimidating stance of Germany, of the relatively passive Anglo-French and Franco-Russian combination into a more active, unified, and even militant triumvirate. The isolation of Germany which emerged in parallel with this process created a situation which Chancellor Bülow, in a speech of November 16, 1906 to the Reichstag, was to call "encirclement."[75]

This was not an inevitable outgrowth of the conference, it should be emphasized, in that it was not a result which was deliberately and irrevocably planned and executed by the nations which were soon to form the entente. It was rather a planned response to German pressure and maneuver, amounting in effect, as many thought, to a threat of war, toward the nations with interests sufficiently similar to induce them, under such conditions, to cooperate.

It has been suggested, referring to such German acts as the seizure and retention of Alsace-Lorraine, the strong support of Austria in the Balkans, and the naval policy, that it was in reality Germany which encircled herself. From whatever perspective one sees this issue, the fundamental elements of the concurrence which drew together the anti-German coalition were the apparent direct threat to France and Britain, their general agreement on the issues under consideration and at the conference, and the close collaboration of their representatives at the

---

[73] Wallace to Knollys, Jan. 14, 1906, Wallace Papers.
[74] No. 95 Spring Rice to Grey, Jan. 30, 1906, FO 371/171; No. 131 Spring Rice to Grey, Feb. 14, 1906, minute attached, FO 371/172.
[75] Brandenburg, *From Bismarck to the World War*, p. 260; Trevelyan, *Grey of Falladon*, p. 119.

conference, Paul Révoil and Sir Arthur Nicolson.[76] While Révoil took no important step at the conference without consulting Nicolson, the latter kept Révoil informed about the current views of the other delegates.

The conference was held between January 16 and April 7 at Algeciras in Andalusia, Spain, within full view of the Rock of Gibraltar, the symbol of British seapower and imperial authority, across the bay. The delegates were housed at the Hotel Reina Cristina, owned by a company in which the Spanish Minister President was the principal stockholder.[77] Most of the numerous reporters found accommodations at the other hotel, the Anglo-Hispano, while the sessions of the conference were held at the Ayuntamiento, the town hall.

The principal or only representatives of the major participating nations attending the conference were: Paul Révoil for France; Sir Arthur Nicolson for Britain; Count A. P. Cassini for Russia; and Johann Maria von Radowitz for Germany. The second German delegate, Count Christian von Tattenbach, played a somewhat more aggressive role through most of the conference sessions than the principal delegate. This was in large part because Tattenbach was Holstein's protégé while Radowitz had appeared as delegate because he had been replaced as ambassador at Constantinople by a Holstein protégé, Prince Hugo von Radolin. He had been sent to Spain where he still was when appointed as the senior official at Algeciras.[78] Count Rudolph von Welsersheimb represented Austria-Hungary while Marquis Emelio Visconti-Venosta represented Italy, Henry White the United States, and El Hadj Muhammad Torres, Morocco. The Spanish minister of foreign affairs, Duke Almadovar del Rio, was the president of the conference.

The objective of Germany in Morocco, while most of the time imprecisely and evasively formulated verbally, was nevertheless expressed with sufficient clarity to rally the opposition firmly behind the French counterattack.[79] Ostensibly Germany had a number of strong cards to play in the tense diplomatic game at Algeciras such as the fact that Russia could not forcefully intervene on behalf of France and if she did not do so it simply emphasized the weakness of the alliance, thus leaving

[76] Fritz Fellner, "Die Haltung Oesterreich–Ungarns während der Konferenz von Algeciras 1906," *Mitteilungen des Instituts für Oesterreichische Geschichtsforschung*, LXXI (1963), 462–463.

[77] Hallgarten, *Imperialismus vor 1914*, I, 664; S.L. Mayer, "Anglo-German rivalry at the Algeciras Conference," in Prosser Gifford and William Roger Louis (eds.), *Britain and Germany in Africa: imperial rivalry and colonial rule*, New Haven, 1967, pp. 215–244.

[78] Cecil, *German diplomatic service*, p. 265.

[79] Spring Rice to Grey, Mar. 1, 1906, FO 800/71; No. 67 Grey to Lascelles, Feb. 14, 1906, *BD*, III, 254–255; Wallace to Grenville, Mar. 21, 1906, Sir Donald Mackenzie Wallace Papers, Royal Archives, Windsor.

Germany the possibility of manipulating the situation. Meanwhile, the Russians were very conscious of their military weakness.

German sponsorship of the open door had an appeal which was both traditional and correct from the standpoint of international law and relations. It was, however, reminiscent of the "Yangtze Agreement" of 1900 by which Germany had, without offering any reciprocal advantages, sought to commit Britain to share her commercial sphere in mid-China. The German approach was also incongruous when compared with the forceful means by which the extraction of French compliance was being sought. The simplest statement of the German short-range objective was undoubtedly that expressed by the German ambassador in London, Count Paul Metternich, who stated that Germany wished to prevent France from acquiring a monopoly or a paramount interest in Morocco and that if she controlled the police she would have achieved this.

Even before the opening of the conference Nicolson had learned from the Spanish prime minister, Sigismundo Moret, that it was the German hope to allocate the police powers in the several ports of Morocco to various nations, reserving Mogador on the Atlantic coast for herself, a policy which, Nicolson commented, would lead to the partition of Morocco.[80] There is some doubt whether Germany would knowingly have invited such an outcome since there were many in the country who saw in Morocco a genuine colonial partner which had potential economic value. There was also the danger that responsibility for partition of Morocco could damage the German image among Islamic people and even endanger the goodwill necessary to sustain the Bagdad railway project.[81]

The interests among the nations represented at the conference which were opposed to Germany, while by no means identical, were nevertheless sufficiently close to sustain their unified stance. The British position at the conference, while reaffirmed a few days before the meetings began, had been clearly defined in the Anglo-French agreement of 1904.[82] This committed Britain to concede to France a special position in Morocco as a colonial neighbor, the right to carry out reforms and preserve order within the country, and the assurance that should any territory opposite Gibralter slip out of Moroccan hands it would be committed to no other country but Spain.

The British, accordingly, came to the conference committed, as Grey

---

[80] No. 9 Nicolson to Grey, Jan. 9, 1906, *BD*, III, 212.
[81] Mary Evelyn Townsend, *The rise and fall of Germany's colonial empire, 1884–1918*, New York, 1930, p. 317; Wallace to Knollys, Feb. 25, 1906, Wallace Papers.
[82] No. 12 Grey to Lascelles, Jan. 9, 1906, *BD*, III, 211–212; André Tardieu, *La Conférence d'Algésiras. Histoire diplomatique de la crise Marocaine (15 Janvier–7 Avril 1906)*, Paris, 1908, pp. 100–107, 458–460.

informed Metternich, to two major interests: the first was the maintenance of order, essential for commerce, and for this purpose considered
that the organization of the police at the port cities should, "as the most
effective way of securing this object," be entrusted to the French and
Spanish. "Our second interest," Grey continued, "was that there should
be economic guarantees for the open door." Grey, in a dispatch approved
by King Edward, affirmed that Britain had obtained this "under the
Declaration which we had exchanged [in 1904] with France."[83]

The Russian government, although professing to have no particular
interest in Morocco, in fact supported a program very similar to the
British.[84] Russia saw the need for a police force in Morocco as urgent and
considered an international force as advocated by Germany unworkable.
The officers and non-commissioned officers, the Russians held, should
know the language of the country, should have had experience in dealing
with Arabs, and should be nationals of a country enjoying some status in
Morocco. This, as Nicolson represented the Russian view, excluded
small nations while uniquely singling out France though the control
might be shared with Spain, an arrangement to which Germany objected
on the grounds that it would in effect leave France dominant.

Russia also shared the British objection to the establishment of a
German presence in such a strategic position as she would acquire if she
were to obtain control of the police in any Moroccan port either on the
Mediterranean or the Atlantic.[85] While Britain had commercial interests
more significant than Russia, her trade in Morocco being greater than any
other nation with German trade a rather small third, her primary interests
were like Russia's, strategic, and were based on access to the straits and
other Mediterranean centered approaches. Russian support of France at
the conference was reaffirmed by Cassini in conversation with Révoil
shortly before the meeting of the conference and remained constant
throughout the sessions.[86]

The support which Italy, while still a member with Germany and
Austria of the Triple Alliance, gave to the Anglo-French position was a
consequence of her Mediterranean and North African interests which

[83] No. 67 Grey to Lascelles, Feb. 14, 1906, *BD*, III, 254–255; Grey to Spring Rice, Feb. 19, 1906, FO 800/71.
[84] Nicolson to Grey, Jan. 2, 1906, Nicolson Papers; Pierre Guillen, "The Entente of 1904 as a colonial settlement," in Gifford and Louis (eds.), *France and Britain in Africa*, p. 338; Eubank, *Paul Cambon*, pp. 110, 114; Hardinge to Grey, Jan. 10, 1906, FO 371/122; Oppel, "Russo-German relations," p. 163.
[85] Mayer, "Anglo-German rivalry," 232.
[86] Paul Révoil, "Journal tenu pendant la Conférence d'Algésiras, 12 janvier–9 avril 1906," *DDF*, 2nd ser., IX-2, 858–859 (Jan. 13, 15, 1906); Rozental', *Diplomaticheskaia istoriia*, p. 186; No. 57 Lamsdorf to Cassini, Jan. 29, 1906, No. 153 Lamsdorf to Osten-Sacken, Feb. 20, 1906, in Erusalimsky, "Rossiia i Alzherirasskaia konferentsiia," 3–25; 24–25.

had already led her to a considerable accommodation with France.[87] The Franco-Italian rapprochement had begun in 1896 and by December 14, 1900 the French ambassador in Rome, Camille Barrère, had joined with the Italian minister of foreign affairs, Marquis Visconti-Venosta, in concluding an agreement which provided for the mutual recognition of the aspirations of France in Morocco and Italy in Tripoli. This agreement had been supplemented on June 30 rather than November 1, 1902, the date usually given, by a further Franco-Italian understanding which reaffirmed that of two years before, adding a mutual pledge of strict neutrality in case either was the object of aggression by a third party or was forced to declare war as a result of provocation.

Consequently, France and Italy, in spite of the latter's residuary membership in the Triple Alliance, were in effective alliance over their North African territories and one of the signers of the agreement, Marquis Emelio Visconti-Venosta, was the chief Italian delegate at Algeciras. Early in the conference, Lieutenant General F. F. Palitsyn, the Russian chief of General Staff, expressed the view that in case of war with Germany, Italy would remain neutral and that this stance would destroy the Triple Alliance.[88]

These political affinities, ranging from genuine national interests to compromises necessitated by the visible pressure and implied threat of war from Germany, provided a bond and a determination on the part of the adherents which not only survived into the conference but gathered solidarity as the meetings proceeded. Bülow at the opening of the conference apparently saw the obstacles as relatively slight.[89] He wrote to Sternburg on that day that, if it were not for the British promise of armed assistance, France would give in to the Germans and that consequently the British were "the key to the Moroccan situation." In view of this attitude, it is understandable that Germany was more inclined to blame Britain than France for maintaining the core of resistance sustained by these two nations. It should be remembered that Britain and those sympathetic with her, on the other hand, saw the key to be in German hands.[90]

The United States had essentially three reasons for attending the conference.[91] The most important was the prevention of a conflict. It was President Roosevelt's hope to achieve this by giving firm support to

---

[87] Anderson, *First Moroccan crisis*, pp. 19–33; Fay, *Origins of the World War*, I, 141–148.
[88] Paléologue, *Three critical years*, p. 147 (Jan. 22, 1906).
[89] Mayer, "Anglo-German rivalry," 226; Tweedmouth to Grey, Jan. 6, 1906, FO 800/86.
[90] Mayer, "Anglo-German rivalry."
[91] Lewis Einstein, *A diplomat looks back*, ed. Lawrence E. Gelfland, New Haven, 1968, p. 8; Allan Nevins, *Henry White: thirty years of American diplomacy*, New York, 1930, pp. 264, 267, 276–280; No. 113 Sternburg to F.O, June 8, 1905, *GP*, 421; Seward W.

Britain and France, thereby discouraging the Germans from blundering into war by making some inconvenient or impossible demand of France or by acting rashly out of overconfidence. Count Tattenbach presumably reflected this outlook when he hinted that Germany would crush the French "like cockroaches." In addition, President Roosevelt was interested in a more orderly Morocco to obviate the occurrence of another Perdicaris incident, and in preserving the territorial integrity of Morocco. The Perdicaris case, Sternburg reported, had left the President with the impression that the Moroccan government had little control over the interior of the country.

Roosevelt was also aware of German interest in a seaport on the Atlantic coast of Morocco and wanted to prevent such a town and port as Casablanca from becoming a German base of operations, perhaps against South America. In order to give the proper emphasis to these interests, the President sent the third division of the North Atlantic fleet to Gibraltar where its support of Britain and France was shown beyond a doubt. Since Germany had already been made aware of the President's readiness to use the means at his disposal, naval power in particular, to support his foreign policy, this demonstration of solidarity was undoubtedly taken seriously.

Baron Holstein had warned in February 1904, just after the inception of the Russo-Japanese war, that German aid to Russia in the war then being considered might mean a risk of war with the United States. He asked pointedly, "Are we, in fact, capable of taking on England and America?" The vigorous foreign policy of President Roosevelt and the reaction of Germany to it provide a basis for seeing in this warning, so forcefully delivered on the eve of the Algeciras conference, considerations which may not have been the least of the reasons for German willingness to make liberal concessions during the conference and to accept so obvious a defeat at its close.

There were two sets of questions before the Algeciras conference, the first, though of great significance in itself, was under current conditions far outweighed by the second. The first consisted of the major specific issues of the conference, the formation of an international bank in Morocco and the organization of police forces in the eight key Moroccan ports. Yet it was the second question which preoccupied not only the conference but all of Europe: the aims and intentions of Germany. The purely Moroccan issues were, in fact, clearly decided in relations to this

Livermore, "The American navy as a factor in world politics, 1903–1913," *AHR*, LXIII no. 4(July 1958), 871–872; Parsons, "Roosevelt's containment," 32–36; Holstein Memorandum, Feb. 22, 1904, in Rich and Fisher, *The Holstein papers*, IV, 282–283; Steinberg, "Germany and the Russo-Japanese war," 1980.

larger question and there is reason to believe that the Moroccan question might have fared quite differently in a conference unconcerned with the problem of German hegemony.

In the most realistic sense, the final stages of maneuvering among the powers began even before the conference opened and the respective roles of Britain and Russia were made clear. Grey warned Germany formally on January 9 that Britain was supporting France and in a note about this to the prime minister he explained that he had offered this information to the German ambassador as his personal opinion saying "that feeling in England and sympathy for France, if she got into trouble over the document which originated our friendship with her [i.e., the Anglo-French entente], would be so strong that it would be impossible for any government to remain neutral."[92]

On the same day, the French government, having already been assured of Russian support, asked the Tsar to make a personal appeal to the Kaiser "not to force hostilities," hoping, as Meyer, the American ambassador, interpreted the situation, for "the creation of a moral atmosphere making it impossible for the military part of Germany in extreme cases to precipitate war."[93] There was also some fear that Germany might take advantage of the present weakened condition of Russia, a thought which became of even greater concern during the first conference crisis in February.[94] Assurances were given of firm British support since, as it was expressed in the early stages of the conference, if France or Russia could be persuaded that Britain would renege on her promises it was thought that German victory could be complete and Russia and France would eventually be forced to gravitate toward the German system.[95] This appeared to be the significance of the idea expressed by Tattenbach that the key to the Algeciras conference lay in London.[96]

The German strategy appeared to be a combination of the dissemination of a divisive ambiguity regarding her objectives along with well calculated attempts to undermine the opposition. Tattenbach tried to detach Britain from France by telling Nicolson that he was going beyond the terms of the Anglo-French entente. But Nicolson was of course not impressed by this.[97] Holstein tried even before the conference had assembled to undermine British support, hinting to the British ambassador that if France were to be dissatisfied with the outcome of the

[92] Grey to Campbell-Bannerman, Jan. 9, 1906, FO 800/99.
[93] Nevins, *Henry White*, p. 265.
[94] Grey to Nicolson, Feb. 12, 1906, Nicolson Papers; Hardinge to Nicolson, Feb. 15, 1906, Nicolson Papers.
[95] No. 102 Spring Rice to Grey, Jan. 31, 1906, FO 371/171.
[96] No. 11 Cartwright (Madrid) to Grey, Jan. 15, 1906, FO 371/171.
[97] Wallace to Knollys, Feb. 13, 1906, Wallace Papers.

conference she might seek to settle the issue by invading Morocco.[98] In such a case, Holstein said, the Sultan would appeal to the German Emperor and the result would be war.

The British government, then and later, responded by reaffirming its complete support for France and the Anglo-French entente. Wallace thought that Germany was trying to obtain a position in Morocco of absolute economic and political equality with France.[99] Recently Cassini had asked his government to exercise pressure on Berlin in a conciliatory sense and "Radowitz has since avoided shaking hands with Russian colleagues."

The first test of the integrity of the divisions within the conference arose with the major crisis of early February.[100] The German representatives were then trying to draw the members away from the program whereby the French delegate, Paul Révoil, had been asking for the right to organize the police and have a predominant role in the bank and, instead, to substitute the German program of the open door. Count Tattenbach visited Nicolson on February 3 with the object of detaching Britain from France by encouraging him to make concessions, stressing that the commercial interests of both Britain and Germany were endangered by France. Instead, however, he was assured by Nicolson that he did not see British commercial interests as endangered and called Tattenbach's attention to the fact that France had been most conciliatory.

At a diplomatic reception on February 7, Rouvier asked Nelidov to telegraph to St. Petersburg a request of the French government for "an urgent intervention in Berlin" with support of the Franco-Spanish decision on the question of the police.[101] Bompard discussed this with Lamsdorf, identifying the police as the key issue of the conference and indicating that the settlement of this matter would restore safety and security in Europe, something which Russia needed very much. Since Osten-Sacken had reported that the Kaiser, even more than Bülow, would insist upon the fulfillment of all obligations, Lamsdorf and Witte adopted a cautious policy. Osten-Sacken received instructions on February 7 from Lamsdorf to try cautiously to persuade Bülow to agree to French proposals on the police question. But when he did so he received in response a threat to break up the conference, an outcome which would

[98] Anderson, First Moroccan crisis, pp. 328–332.
[99] Wallace to Knollys, Feb. 13, 1906, Wallace Papers.
[100] Harold Nicolson, Sir Arthur Nicolson, Bart. First Lord Carnock. A study in the old diplomacy, London, 1931, pp. 178–183; Rozental', Diplomaticheskaia istoriia, pp. 183–188.
[101] No. 46 Rouvier to Bompard, Feb. 8, 1906, No. 24 Bompard to Rouvier, Feb. 10, 1906, DDF, IX-1, 200, 215–218; I.I. Astaf'ev, Russko-germanskie diplomaticheskie otnosheniia 1905–1911 gg. (ot Portsmutskogo mira do Potsdamskogo soglasheniia), Moscow, 1972, pp. 35–36.

have deprived Russia of the successful outcome which, it was hoped, would open the way for a loan. Yet, the very next day Lamsdorf sent an instruction to Cassini in Algeciras which affirmed Russian support of France.

The conference had by mid-February reached a serious deadlock and Meyer wrote to Senator Lodge from St. Petersburg that Russia was becoming very concerned about the direction things were taking. Nelidov had written from Paris on February 11 that the breakup of the conference could lead to the dismissal of Rouvier and further trouble for the loan and on the following day Osten-Sacken wrote from Berlin that an article had appeared in the press denoting the German view of the police question as irreconcilable with the French.[102] Fear was expressed that after the appearance of such a statement the German government would be unable to yield further without losing prestige among the people. A minute on a dispatch from Spring Rice to Grey of February 24 was very pessimistic: "It becomes more and more clear that Germany never had any intention of giving way at all".

It was under these circumstances that Witte, at French request, addressed a letter to Prince Philipp zu Eulenburg for the Kaiser, a method of communication arranged in September 1905 during Witte's Rominten visit.[103] It stated that the situation was urgent, that at the end of April the Duma and reorganized Council would be opened and Russia would start on a new but uncharted course. Funds were needed to liquidate the expenses of the war and to accomplish this a loan was necessary but was unavailable until the Moroccan issue was resolved. Like Lamsdorf, he held out the prospect of a continental alliance; as a basis for such a coalition he urged good German–French relations and as a prerequisite for this he suggested a generous German attitude toward France. Citing the experience of the French revolution he warned that if the Russian revolution were not suppressed it could wash across the Russian frontier, making it of vital interest particularly to monarchical countries.

Lamsdorf also responded to the situation by communicating with the German government, hinting that if Germany were to concede to France, Russia would be ready to reconsider a Franco-Russo-German continental bloc.[104] He added that the German government was fully aware that the success of the conference was intimately associated with financial

[102] Beale, *Theodore Roosevelt*, pp. 374–375; Howe, *George von Lengerke Meyer*, p. 246; No. 42 Spring Rice to Grey, Feb. 24, 1906, FO 371/173.
[103] Witte to Prince Philipp zu Eulenburg, Feb. 20, 1906, *GP*, XXI-1, 195–197; Rich and Fisher, *The Holstein papers*, IV, 397.
[104] No. 153 Lamsdorf to Osten-Sacken, Feb. 20, 1906, No. 166 Lamsdorf to Osten-Sacken, Feb. 22, 1906, in Erusalimsky, "Rossiia i Alzherirasskaia konferentsiia," pp. 24–25, 30–31.

operations of the greatest importance to Russia and with the suppression of the revolution.

Lamsdorf also discussed this serious situation with the Austrian ambassador, Count von Aehrenthal, and it was apparently this along with similar acts of intercession by Britain and France which led to an intervention on the part of both the Austrian foreign minister, Count Goluchowski, and Emperor Franz Joseph.[105] The Emperor on February 23 expressed to the German ambassador, Count Carl von Wedel, the suggestion that Austria and Germany acting together would be isolated at the conference and that out of this situation there could develop a new grouping of powers separating Russia from the two other monarchies and associating her with Britain and France, concluding that it was necessary to avoid such an outcome.

Cassini reported on the same day a glimmer of hope from Algeciras which he attributed to Russia's firm stand. Tattenbach in a lengthy conference had suggested the possibility that the German government might consider concessions on the police issue if France would do likewise on the bank question, saying that this was at least a hint that Germany did not want the conference to break down. Such a result might, of course, leave the blame for the break-down wholly with Germany, and turn Russia into a more committed enemy of Germany while hastening the Anglo-Russian rapprochement.

Nevertheless, the letter which had been sent by Witte through Eulenburg brought the discouraging response that Germany was not willing to go any further in accommodating France than already indicated at the conference.[106] The message which was conveyed was that while the German government was sympathetic to the need for a solution there was a limit beyond which the Kaiser could not go. While an exceptional position could to some degree be conceded to France as a colonial neighbor of Morocco, the exclusive position which France was claiming could not be permitted since this would render the open door illusory. Lamsdorf's discussion of the issue with the German ambassador in St. Petersburg, Wilhelm von Schoen, and that of Grey with Metternich in London had elicited the very same reply.[107]

Sir Edward Grey, reflecting the position of his government during these tense and trying days, expressed in a memorandum some of the fears

---

[105] Rozental', *Diplomaticheskaia istoriia*, pp. 191–192; Anderson, *First Moroccan crisis*, p. 374.
[106] Eulenburg to Kaiser, Feb. 22, 1906, *GP*, XXI-1, 194; No. 46 Bülow Memorandum, Feb. 23, 1906, Eulenburg to Witte, Feb. 27, 1906, *GP*, XXI-1, 197–198, 202–204; Rafalovich to Nelidov, Feb. 12, 1906, in Kelin, "Novye dokumenty," 162.
[107] No. 75 Schoen to F.O, Feb. 23, 1906, *GP*, XXI-1, 211–212; Grey to Spring Rice, Feb. 23, 1906, in Erusalimsky, "Rossiia i Alzherirasskaia konferentsiia," 33.

which rendered unthinkable anything but complete support of France.[108] The French, he wrote, assume British support in case of war with Germany. If Britain were to fail in this expectation, France would never forgive Britain for leaving her in the lurch.

The United States would despise us, Russia would not think it worth while to make a friendly arrangement with us about Asia. Japan would prepare to re-insure herself elsewhere, we would be left without a friend and without the power of making a friend and Germany would take some pleasure, after what has passed, in exploiting the whole situation to our disadvantage, very likely stirring up trouble through the Sultan of Turkey in Egypt.

Grey also evolved his own view of Germany as he observed the facts of European politics during his early months in office and came to consider "German bullying" the "main threat to British security."[109] Sir Eyre Crowe, the Foreign Office expert on Germany, in a memorandum of January 1, 1907 which reviewed British relations with Germany from the Bismarck era helped to give Grey a more systematic view of this question.[110] Grey considered the memorandum "most valuable" and advocated that it "should be carefully studied."

Crowe cited the current German minister of foreign affairs, Heinrich von Tschirschky und Bögendorff, as having said to the British consul at Hamburg just a year before that, "Germany's policy always has been, and would be, to frustrate any coalition between two states which might result in damaging Germany's interests and prestige". The Algeciras test of the Anglo-French entente, Crowe stated, was made at a time when Germany did not really want a war but concluded that she could win the test because France was not ready for war and had shown in the Delcassé resignation that she would capitulate to German wishes. At the same time Britain, judging by the North Sea incident, would, in the German view, back down rather than support France. The German government had been wrong on both counts, had exposed her hand, and had only given new solidarity to the Anglo-French agreement. This interpretation of a drama in which Grey had participated only served to give the foreign minister an even more assured grasp of German policy than when he had promised more than a year before to support France.

Grey maintained this position in spite of the horror with which he contemplated the prospect of war. He saw the present as a most difficult and unfavorable time while the opportunity to find a more secure future, he thought, lay in checking Germany by a rapprochement with Russia.

<hr>

[108] Grey memorandum, Feb. 20, 1906, FO 800/91.
[109] Keith Robbins, *Sir Edward Grey. A biography of Lord Grey of Falladon*, London, 1971, p. 158.
[110] Crowe, "Memorandum on the Present State of British Relations with France and Germany," Jan. 1, 1907, Cab 1/7.

Some days before, Grey had written to this effect to Nicolson, adding the optimistic thought that the recovery of Russia would change the situation in Europe.[111] This would create a more favorable situation for France and would ultimately decide the relative positions of France and Germany in Morocco.

Sir Charles Hardinge touched on a similar theme when he wrote to Nicolson that such a favorable change might be achieved in about two years.[112] Wallace enlarged further upon this thought in a letter to Sir Francis Knollys, private secretary to King Edward, in which he faced squarely the prospect that the conference might fail and France might consequently find it necessary to turn to Britain for military assistance.[113] Military specialists, he commented, saw no danger of war during the current year since the reorganization of the German artillery had not yet been completed. By next year, however, the military situation would be greatly changed.

The optimistic outlook of these dispatches was apparent also in a minute which Sir Charles Hardinge appended to Grey's memorandum of February 20. He noted not only that in a war with Germany France would have the support of Russia but also that Britain was "absolutely 'solidaire'" with France on the Morocco question. This, he thought, would deter Germany from a war in which she would lose her entire merchant marine and almost all her foreign trade. Also, if France were left in the lurch, an alliance between France, Germany, and Russia would soon develop. This arrangement had twice been proposed during the past six years and was a plan which the Kaiser fancied since it would mean that France and Russia would become satellites within the German system. Furthermore, Hardinge continued, there were a number of politicians in Russia who favored the French alliance purely for economic reasons while their preference for a German entente was based on fear of her hostility.

There were contradictory and confusing reports from Germany which, at so crucial a time, provided little guidance. A report of March 1 related that Holstein, in an interview with General L. V. Swaine, had given assurances that while the Emperor intended to hold out on the police question, Germany would not attack France even if the German view were not accepted.[114] A comment on this dispatch stated simply that it was becoming clear "that Germany never had any intention of giving way at all."

The crucial point in the conference was reached on Saturday, March 3,

---

[111] Grey to Nicolson, Feb. 12, 1906, Nicolson Papers.
[112] Hardinge to Nicolson, Feb. 15, 1906, Nicolson Papers.
[113] Wallace to Knollys, Jan. 28, 1906, Wallace Papers.
[114] No. 68 Lascelles to Grey, Mar. 1906, FO 371/173.

when a decision became necessary on a question of procedure which was in fact of great substantive importance with respect to the major issues.[115] France and Britain saw the advantage of ultimately having a vote on the police question, regarding which there was an absolute deadlock between Révoil and Radowitz and on which the Germans had lost so much sympathy, rather than turning attention to the bank question on which the conference was less divided.

Not only had Germany taken up a seemingly immovable position on this issue but France would have found it difficult to concede since Révoil, according to Wallace's observation, would have considered it impossible to do so "in face of the increasing excitement of public opinion in France." Révoil on his part was determined to face a rupture rather than make any concessions on the police question. It had been announced from Paris that "Rouvier will make no further concession, fears he has already gone too far."[116] Thus, the intransigence of the German delegation matched by that of the French appeared to threaten the survival of the conference. It is also questionable what position Austria would have taken in case of a show-down since the Austrian and German perspectives on the basic issues were different.

The vote of March 3 was consequently taken and favored leaving the bank issue for further study and later consideration and turning to the police question.[117] This meant that the German delegates had been outmaneuvered in their effort to prevent this. The vote was ten to three, leaving Germany supported only by Austria and Morocco, even Italy voting on the side of the majority with France, Britain, Russia, and the others. Bülow was so incensed about this humiliating development that he took full charge of the handling of the conference questions. This change was reflected at Algeciras in the assumption of control there by Radowitz, replacing Tattenbach in this role when the latter lost the support of Holstein. The days which followed were eventful with respect to the issues at stake. A source of potential weakness arose when the Rouvier government fell on March 7, followed a week later by a new government with Jean-Marie Ferdinand Sarrien as prime minister and Léon Bourgeois as minister of foreign affairs.

These difficult times were also full of promise because of a visit of a few days to Paris of King Edward on his way to Athens.[118] During his brief

[115] Nicolson, *Sir Arthur Nicolson*, pp. 189–191; Albertini, *Origins of the war*, I, 171; Wallace to Knollys, Feb. 23, 25, 1906, Wallace Papers; Paul Révoil, "Journal tenu pendant," 921–924; Tardieu, *La Conférence d'Algésiras*, pp. 233 ff.

[116] Wallace to Grenville, Mar. 12, 1906, Wallace Papers; Fellner, "Die Haltung Oesterreich–Ungarns," 462–469.

[117] No. 61 Nicolson to Grey, Mar. 3, 1906, *BD*, III, 283–284.

[118] Lee, *King Edward VII*, II, 510, 520–521; Bertie to Grey, Mar. 5, 1906, *BD*, III, 284; Schwertfeger, *Zur Europäischen politik*, II, 105, 113–114 (reports from Paris of Mar. 6, 7, 1906).

visit in early March he saw the outgoing president of France, Emile François Loubet, the new president, Clement Armand Fallières, as well as Rouvier, Baron de Courcel who had just returned from Berlin, and others. Even though the King was traveling incognito his presence was known and was understood in the light of a serious effort to bring about an Anglo-Russian rapprochement. This was fortified by the renewed Anglo-Japanese alliance and by the unity shown by Italy toward both France and Britain. These had important implications for European peace, an impression which was merely confirmed by the German view of these maneuvers as an attempt to isolate her.

Anglo-Franco-Russian solidarity, demonstrated in the vote of March 3, survived the governmental change in France and retained its integrity throughout the conference. Lamsdorf signalled this firm stance when he published an article on March 2 in the semi-official *L'Etat Russe* denouncing German policy at the conference and upholding the French.[119] The German ambassador in St. Petersburg, Schoen, interpreted Lamsdorf's views in the same way, writing that the Russian foreign minister appeared willing to give up the traditions and values of German friendship in exchange for French gold while Witte was more friendly toward Germany but was above all an opportunist who saw French or German support according to Russian needs. Nevertheless, the solidarity announced by Lamsdorf was reinforced by the other nations allied at the conference. The new minister of foreign affairs, Bourgeois, continued the firm French policy of his predecessor by renewing Révoil's instructions and was supported in this by Georges Clemenceau and by Sir Edward Grey.

Reassurance of Russian support was given at a crucial point in the conference when the German government considered that its success was nearly assured. This was done by the publication in the French journal, *Le Temps*, on March 21, of the official instructions of the Russian delegate at the conference, Cassini, along with an assertion that Russia held the German plan for the internationalization of the Moroccan police to be unacceptable.[120] This Russian position was viewed in Berlin as a gratuitous insult and as an effort on Witte's part to break up the prospect of a convergence of Germany, Russia, and France.

The wide-spread German resentment over this matter helps to explain

---

[119] Anderson, *First Moroccan crisis*, pp. 368–369; No. 85 Schoen to FO Mar. 3, 1906, No. 87 Mar. 4, 1906, *GP*, XXI-1, 234–235, 251–254.

[120] Benckendorff to Grey, Mar. 21, Grey to Benckendorff, Mar. 23, 1901, FO 800/71; Rich, *Friedrich von Holstein*, II, 741–742; No. 65 Bülow to Schoen, Mar. 22, No. 101 Schoen to F.O, Mar. 23, 1906, *GP*, XXI-1, 312–313, 313–314; Schwertfeger, *Zur Europäischen politik*, II, 110 (extract of report from Berlin, Apr. 11, 1906); No. 89 Bihourd (Berlin) to Bourgeois, Apr. 7, 1906, *DDF*, IX-2, 818–819; No. 258 Spring Rice to Grey, Apr. 11, 1906, FO 371/124; Holstein to Bülow, Mar. 23 (draft), Holstein to Bülow, Mar. 25, 1906, in Rich and Fisher, *The Holstein papers*, IV, 401–402.

why it became a Russo-German incident of great importance, even to the extent of seeking to use it to get rid of Lamsdorf as minister of foreign affairs and of denying Russia access to the German money market. This latter act on the part of the German government was, in turn, seen by Witte "as an unwarranted insult" which made him deeply embittered and is said to have been instrumental in changing him from a supporter of a continental league directed against the maritime power of Britain to a supporter of a closer relationship with the latter.[121] The prohibition against German participation in a Russian loan was issued in the last days of March, too late to expect Russia to change her position at Algeciras but in time to leave an unfortunate rift in Russo-German relations by encouraging an Anglo-Russian rapprochement.

The Algeciras conference was forced to devote its energies and talents so largely to current diplomatic issues and machinations that it was unable either to resolve the problems confronting Morocco, to satisfy the purely Moroccan interests or ambitions of any of the participants, or in the remotest way to resolve the larger European issues. The formal German demand which had provided a rationale for the conference had been at least verbally satisfied since the open door as well as the independence and integrity of Morocco and its ruler had been recognized.[122]

This is the reason that Prince Bülow was able to write optimistically that even though the conference did not give Germany

> all we wished, it did represent the essentials of what we had striven to attain ...
> France did not obtain the Protectorate at which she aimed, not, above all, that command of all armed forces in Morocco she had demanded in the spring of 1905.
> We had made a victorious stand for commercial freedom in Morocco ... The attempt to exclude us from a great international decision had been successfully thwarted.[123]

It was clear, however, that the principal German expectations were left unrealized and, instead of achieving the isolation of France, Germany herself was isolated. France on the other hand was reinforced by the strengthening of the Anglo-French entente and the Franco-Russian alliance and by the growing determination of Britain and of some elements in Russia to seek an understanding and thus complete the Triple Entente. Friedrich von Holstein, whose policies and practices had accounted for most of the aggressive conduct of Germany during the conference and whose role had been assumed by Bülow after the set-back

---

[121] Long, "The economics," pp. 173–174; Barbara Vogel, *Deutsche Russlandpolitik: das Scheitern der deutschen Weltpolitik unter Bülow, 1900–1906,* Dusseldorf, 1973, pp. 227–231; Spring Rice to Grey, Apr. 12, 1906, in Gwynn, *Letters and friendships,* II, 75; Rozental', *Diplomaticheskaia istoriia,* pp. 198–199.
[122] Anderson, *First Moroccan crisis,* pp. 192–195.
[123] Bülow, *Memoirs,* II, 203.

in March, submitted his resignation on April 2 although it was not
accepted until after Bülow had fainted on April 5 on the floor of the
Reichstag during some critical remarks by August Bebel, the socialist
member.[124]

France and those nations supporting her were clearly on the winning
side at Algeciras, a fact which was apparent by the predominance which
France retained in Morocco and by the sympathetic approval this
achievement was given by her allies. Police power in the cities had to be
shared with Spain while an inspector general of the police was to be a
Swiss citizen resident in Tangier with the duty of reporting his findings to
the diplomatic corps.[125] A State Bank of Morocco was organized at
Tangier under French law. Its board was to be made up of representatives
of all participating countries who also participated in the capital of the
bank and it was empowered to issue paper money and act as a royal mint
and as a treasury for Morocco.

The real consequences of the conference lay in other arenas of political
activity. André Tardieu who attended the conference as a journalist,
wrote with reference to the Anglo-French understanding that a consequence of the meetings was that "the Entente passed from a static to a
dynamic state."[126] This was not too different from the observation of
Henry White, the American delegate, who wrote to his German colleague
in Rome that the real victor was Britain, to which the Kaiser wrote the
marginal note "Correct." The Kaiser, in fact, was said to have been
extremely bitter over the outcome which had dashed any hope of an
alliance with either Britain or Russia and thus of neutralizing the
traditional hostility of France.[127] Count Cassini, the Russian representative at the conference who had helped to achieve the victory, was
immediately rewarded for his services with promotion to the rank of
actual privy counselor, the highest grade in the official hierarchy except
for the chancellor of the empire.[128]

---

[124] Cecil, *German diplomatic service*, p. 299.
[125] Nicolson, *Sir Arthur Nicolson*, pp. 443–447 (summary of the Final Act of the Algeciras
Conference, Apr. 7, 1906). Same in Tardieu, *La Conférence d'Algésiras*, pp. 504–506.
[126] Nicolson, *Sir Arthur Nicolson*, p. 199.
[127] Osten-Sacken to Izvolsky, June 1, 1906, in Hélène Iswolsky (ed.), *Au service de la Russie,
Alexandre Iswolsky. Correspondance diplomatique, 1906–1911*, 2 vols. Paris, 1937–39, I,
44–45.
[128] No. 269 Spring Rice to Grey, Apr. 14, 1906, citing *Journal de Sainte-Petersbourg*, Mar.
30, 1906, FO 371/175.

6   After Portsmouth and Algeciras

Russia's new course

The conferences at Portsmouth and Algeciras had twice in seven months provided a forum in which to consider the changing relationships of the major powers. The conferences, however, were quite different in their effect on the balance of power and in their outcome. The Portsmouth conference weighed the consequences of the Russo-Japanese war and awarded Japan a generous share of the claims for which she had gone to war. It was clear that both parties had been weakened by the war, a conclusion which was confirmed in the conference negotiations. Even Russia's rivalry with Germany, however, left her able to maintain her Far Eastern balance with the diplomatic support of France and Britain.

The Algeciras conference, by contrast with that at Portsmouth, met to consider a threat rather than a military victory. It did so in an atmosphere of great international tension and considerable fear of its outcome which could have been a major war or an alteration in the power structure of Europe, a change which would have been unwanted by a large majority of the nations there. The results of the conference were also different from those reached at Portsmouth. While Germany was denied her demands, it was understood that she still wanted to achieve them and this factor remained a latent threat up to 1914. Instead of becoming a fully cooperative member of the community of nations as Japan did, Germany remained a separate and potentially hostile element in the international community.

The discussion and settlement of the Far Eastern as well as the European issues which had been raised after these conferences were carried on by a new group of officials, persons other than those associated politically and directly with the outbreak and conduct of the war. In Russia, where the revolution had already broken out, Petr Arkad'evich Stolypin became the chairman of the Council of Ministers on July 10, 1906, a position roughly equivalent to prime minister. Vladimir Nikolaevich Izvolsky had become minister of foreign affairs on the previous May 12 and became the spokesman for a policy which sought to achieve the strengthening of Russia, along with an accommodation with Japan and Germany.

Izvolsky was fortunate in the emergence at that time in Japan of a moderate government ready to compromise, bringing together elements led by General Katsura Taro, the war-time prime minister, and by Prince Saionji Kimmochi with the latter as prime minister. Saionji was associated with the Seiyukai party and with Prince Ito; he replaced Katsura as prime minister on January 6, 1906. Baron Hayashi Tadasu, who had been minister to Britain during the war, became the minister of foreign affairs, replacing Baron Komura Jutaro who had been the principal Japanese negotiator at both the Portsmouth and Peking conferences. The corresponding administrative changes in Britain and France have been noted above.

The appointment of Aleksandr Petrovich Izvolsky on May 12, 1906 to succeed Vladimir Nikolaevich Lamsdorf as the Russian minister of foreign affairs did not in itself signify the adoption thereby of a wholly new foreign policy. The "new course" in Russian foreign policy correctly associated with his name was one which took into consideration the new international conditions, the emergence of Germany and Japan, and the victory of Japan, which gave her a dominant position in the Far East. It was also one which his predecessor either had already begun or might have been ready and able to implement further if his tenure of office had not been cut short

Lamsdorf was most likely replaced because he was made to share with Witte the condemnation of Germany for his role in maintaining the independent Russian stance on the Björkö issue and the pro-French position at the Algeciras conference. He also shared with Witte and others the blame for the Russo-Japanese war. Yet, ironically, it was these very events which at once helped to rule out Lamsdorf's continuance in office and to furnish two of the major elements of his successor's foreign policy.

Izvolsky's qualifications for the position of minister of foreign affairs were in some respects rather standard and in others very appropriate, even timely. His gentry family was of Polish origin and had served the Russian sovereigns since the reign of Alexander I. He had been a student at the Imperial Lyceum, located at Tsarskoe Selo in a wing of the palace, close to the imperial family when it was in residence there. The students were drawn from the ranks of the gentry and included such persons as Prince Gorchakov in whose Chancellery Izvolsky served as an attaché upon his graduation. It was the beginning of a varied career during which he served in diplomatic posts in Washington and at the Vatican, in Bavaria, in Japan, and finally in Copenhagen.

His appointment in Copenhagen was from the standpoint of his advancement to the office of minister of foreign affairs, his most important position. It was in Copenhagen that he was able to become associated in a close and advantageous way with the Russian imperial family. This was a factor which had helped to advance the official careers of three of his predecessors in Copenhagen: Baron Artur Pavlovich Morenheim who became ambassador in Paris, Count Mikhail Nikolaevich Murav'ev who became minister of foreign affairs, and Count Aleksandr Konstantinovich Benckendorff who became ambassador in London.[1] Still another predecessor as minister was Count Karl Karlovich Toll, Izvolsky's father-in-law.

In Copenhagen Izvolsky had met and held many conversations with the Russian Empress Dowager Maria Fedorovna (Dagmar), daughter of King Christian IX of Denmark, sister of King Frederick VIII and of Queen Alexandra of England, widow of Emperor Alexander III, and mother of the reigning emperor, Nicholas II. This opened the way for Izvolsky to transmit indirectly to the Emperor through the Empress Dowager, who was always consulted before a minister to Copenhagen was named, and even directly to the Emperor his views on a variety of subjects including the plans then under consideration for constitutional reform.

It was during one of his audiences that the Emperor told him that Count Lamsdorf would retire before the opening of the Duma and that he had him in mind as his successor. According to Count Witte, upon his return from the Portsmouth conference he heard of the plan to appoint Izvolsky in place of Lamsdorf and advised the latter to resign so that it would not appear that he had been dismissed.[2] It was also in Copenhagen on April 14, 1904, that Izvolsky had the opportunity of discussing Anglo-Russian relations with King Edward during the latter's visit there.

Since the growing influence of Germany was so important to the emerging coalition, Izvolsky's attitude with respect to that country was a crucial factor. Even though he was frequently identified as pro-British, it is significant that so keen a judge of people and events as Sir Charles Hardinge, the British ambassador in St. Petersburg, was not eager to have Izvolsky replace Count Lamsdorf.[3] He wrote to Lord Lansdowne that he was not optimistic about the consequences of the disappearance of Lamsdorf from the official scene even though he considered him weak and unwilling to commit himself to anything without consulting the Emperor. Still, he wrote "he is one element of law and order and is, I really believe, well disposed toward us."

The candidate to succeed him, Hardinge continued, was the Russian

[1] Seeger, *Recollections of a foreign minister*, pp. 3–22.
[2] Witte, *The memoirs of Count Witte*, pp. 648–649.
[3] Hardinge to Lansdowne, Dec. 6, 1904, FO 800/140.

minister in Copenhagen, Izvolsky, a "pupil of Lobanoff, and I must say I should regard his appointment with considerable misgiving." Sir Cecil Spring Rice, also a perceptive observer, reflected even greater pessimism with respect to Izvolsky.[4] He wrote to Sir Edward Grey that: "he can hardly be said to have any fixed policy except perhaps a sort of sentimental interest in the Slavs. The danger is that whereas Lamsdorf had a very great knowledge of the European situation and a clear and impartial judgment, Izvolsky has little knowledge and his judgment may easily be affected by personal considerations which never touched Lamsdorf at all." Spring Rice also stressed what he considered to be Izvolsky's pro-German sympathies. Balfour and some others, on the contrary, apparently believed that Lamsdorf had become the victim of a German intrigue.

Sir Arthur Nicolson, the British ambassador who worked more closely with Izvolsky than either of his two predecessors and elaborated with him the Anglo-Russian agreement of 1907, was more optimistic in his appraisal of the new Russian foreign minister.[5] He described him as "very liberal in his views, and is probably the most advanced in the Cabinet in his political opinions." Izvolsky had been in diplomatic life for thirty years and was seen by his colleagues "as a Western European with very little knowledge of Russia." Nicolson warned, however, that even though Izvolsky was "loyally and sincerely anxious for an understanding with Great Britain," he would do nothing that would be "unfavorably viewed in Berlin" and would consider carefully opinions that prevailed at court, warnings that might well have applied in the case of any, but particularly a new and inexperienced foreign minister.

The fact that these British views of Izvolsky were shared by some German diplomatic colleagues who knew him such as Baron Wilhelm von Schoen, the ambassador in St. Petersburg with whom Izvolsky was on very close terms and who supported him as Lamsdorf's successor, raises the possibility that his appointment had a significance other than his alleged preference for or against Germany. There were some in Berlin, including the influential Friedrich von Holstein, whose view of the change placed the emphasis on their dissatisfaction with his predecessor, Count Lamsdorf, who had become associated in their minds with the failure of the Björkö policy, and with the pro-French attitude of Russia during the Algeciras conference, and who was, therefore, considered to be anti-German.[6]

[4] Spring Rice to Grey, May 24, 1906, in Gwynn, Letters and friendships, II, 73.
[5] No. 4 Annual Report for Russia for 1906, Jan. 2, 1907, FO 371/318; Oppel, "Russo-German relations," pp. 204–208.
[6] No. 64 A Johnstone (Copenhagen) to Grey, May 27, 1906, BD, IV, 235–236; Efremov, Vneshniaia politika Rossii, p. 49.

In London, some saw Lamsdorf's departure from office as a victory for the pro-German party and Balfour went so far as to compare his fate to that of the French foreign minister, Delcassé, who had been sacrificed in June 1905 because of German displeasure with his policies and his effectiveness. But there is, apparently, no available evidence that German dislike for Lamsdorf had any comparably direct bearing on his replacement.

Another and perhaps more likely explanation for the ministerial change may be found in some combination of internal factors. Like Witte, Lamsdorf was associated with the Far Eastern disaster and had been denounced and made a scapegoat for this in spite of the fact that he was not one of those most responsible for it. Like Witte he was a firm believer in the imperial regime he served though he feared public appearances which might cast him in the role of defender of Russian foreign policy. Lamsdorf, in fact, was said to have feared that such an occasion might arise in the new Duma since this new legislative body might be expected to inquire into the causes of the war. This would have placed him in the impossible position of being unable to defend his role in it without implicating if not inculpating the Emperor, in which case he would have felt compelled to accept the blame himself and resign.[7] It is likely, therefore, that the departure of Lamsdorf, while chronologically related to the appointment of Izvolsky and to the crystallization of the policy associated with his name, was not causally related to the inception or realization of that policy.

The manner in which Izvolsky was selected and the program with which he immediately associated himself make it clear that he was the spokesman for a policy which enjoyed considerable support not only on the part of the Emperor but also of other influential persons in the government, including the diplomatic service. In his memoirs he noted not only his discussions with the Emperor but also his submission to him of a policy statement for his approval and to the senior members of the Russian diplomatic establishment for their consideration.[8] Just before his appointment on May 12 he discussed these plans with Count Benckendorff in London, A. I. Nelidov, the Russian ambassador in Paris, and N. V. Murav'ev, the Russian ambassador in Rome, referring to his statement as a plan for a "Triple Entente."

Izvolsky's plan stressed the fact that Russia's most immediate and important need was peace. He portrayed this as a prerequisite for the

---

[7] No. 119 Spring Rice to Grey, Feb. 12, 1906, *BD*, IV, 224–225.
[8] Igor Vasil'evich Bestuzhev, *Bor'ba v Rossii po voprosam vneshnei politiki, 1906–1910*, Moscow, 1961, p. 7; Eduard Markovich Rozental', "Frantsuzskaia diplomatiia i Anglo-russkoe sblizhenie v 1906–1907 gg. (k voprosu o vkliuchenii Rossii v Antantu)," *ISSR*, no. 5 (1958), 129.

internal reconstruction which was necessary in itself as well as for obtaining foreign loans. Among the aspects of reconstruction to which he gave very high priority was restoration of the badly shaken national self-confidence. The establishment of new directions and of a new emphasis in foreign policy which would make it possible to inspire abroad a sufficient degree of confidence and general public support for Russian securities was, in his view, only the inverse of this internal challenge.

Izvolsky hoped to achieve this objective through the diplomatic resolution of specific problems which, by avoiding a large-scale, partisan commitment to a single nation or group in international affairs, would give Russia the more neutral stance she badly needed at that moment. In particular, a solution to problems reached with Britain dealing with Asia would not as he saw it be in conflict with an agreement with Germany regarding European problems. His plan was in general one of which Lamsdorf would almost certainly have approved and which was supported by the liberal and some of the conservative press including the Constitutional Democrats' *Rech* as well as *Novoe Vremia*.

In his initial policy statement as well as in other places, Izvolsky stressed a second major aspect of his foreign policy, i.e., that, in the main, it would be essentially a revised version of the one that had guided his predecessor, both characterized as being focused on maintaining a balance of forces in the west. The outcome of the war required, in addition, that Izvolsky add a factor which had not heretofore had the same significance in Russian foreign policy, viz., a prudent attention to Japan as a component in the balance of power.

The diplomacy which Izvolsky administered was designed to restore and preserve, under conditions of diminished Russian prestige and power, the badly damaged national security. The specific aims of his policy were the security of Russia against Germany and Japan and the improvement of the straits regime for Russia. These may be summarized briefly, as noted by Baron Taube, under three major diplomatic courses of action.[9] The first sought the maintenance and consolidation of the Franco-Russian alliance, which had become, since the last years of the reign of Emperor Alexander III, the basis of Russian foreign policy and which had recently been strengthened under the hammer blows of Björkö and Algeciras.

The second course of action was expressed in the plan for the liquidation, by diplomatic and economic arrangements with Britain and Japan, of the tensions still threatening relations with these countries. This would hopefully provide Russia with an improved regime at the Turkish straits, greater security in her distant Pacific regions, and a more secure

---

[9] Taube, *La politique russe*, pp. 115–116.

base from which to confront the German challenge.[10] Izvolsky wrote in his memoirs: "If Russia turned her back on France and England and engaged in a contest for preponderance in Asia, she would be obliged to renounce not only her historic role in Europe but also her economic and moral independence *vis-a-vis* Germany." Russia would, he asserted, become "for all intents and purposes a vassal of the German Empire." This could come about, he continued, if Russia were to become engaged in another struggle with Japan, leaving Germany to deal at will with Britain and France as appeared to have been the intention during the Moroccan crisis.

Thirdly, according to Taube, it was Izvolsky's aim to seek and maintain the best possible relations with Germany as the essential factor in Russia's external security and internal well being. This assumed a sufficient external balance of power to avoid a reversion to the insecurities and imbalance inherent in the Björkö alignment, i.e., it assumed the realization of the first two objectives noted above. Izvolsky carried out this aspect of his policy effectively and dutifully, endeavoring to allow no real deterioration to occur in Russian relations with Germany. It was in view of this that while pursuing the British relationship he was careful to exchange periodic assurances with Germany that their relationship was not deteriorating.[11] This aim was pursued in conversations with the German ambassador in St. Petersburg and in more formal direct conferences in Berlin with the German minister of foreign affairs.

In discussing the European aspect of the issue with his confidential adviser, the distinguished authority on international law, Baron M. A. Taube, Izvolsky commented specifically on the point often encountered and attributed particularly to King Edward VII, i.e., that he was generally expected to follow an anti-German policy.[12] He emphasized that the contrary was the case and that he wanted only broadly based agreements capable of guaranteeing Europe from surprises on the part of Germany. He hoped that such understandings would be able to provide a foundation for going beyond generalities, seeking more effectively to solve specific problems.

While Izvolsky was not opposed to the spirit of the Björkö treaty, he found it too sentimental and must have experienced some uneasiness from the fact that he subscribed on practical grounds to the Franco-Russian alliance which the Björkö treaty in effect ruled out. It was, however, the opinion of the French minister in Copenhagen that his colleague, Izvolsky, was not a strong partisan of the Franco-Russian

---

[10] Rozental', *Diplomaticheskaia istoriia*, pp. 230–231; Bestuzhev, *Bor'ba v Rossii*, pp. 129–131; Seeger, *Recollections of a foreign minister*, p. 83.

[11] Bestuzhev, *Bor'ba v Rossii*, p. 51; Astaf'ev, *Russko-germanskie diplomaticheskie otnosheniia*, p. 61.

[12] Taube, *La politique russe*, pp. 135–136; Lee, *King Edward VII*, II, 284–285, 289.

alliance. By way of defining the nature of such specific settlements, Izvolsky noted that the Emperor had ordered him to negotiate with Germany on the subject of the northern, i.e., the Baltic-Scandinavian, question and that an agreement with Britain dealing with common Asian problems would in no way interfere with the successful settlement of such a question with Germany.

At the same time, Izvolsky continued, an accommodation with Britain could make a very important contribution to the European balance. Not only was there the prospect of gaining access to the money market in London but there were also particular benefits to be anticipated from association with a stable and conservative Britain.[13] These considerations were comprehensible if one compared the national needs of Russia from an international position. The Three Emperors' Alliance had in the past provided Russia with ideological affinities and support which was minimized in the case of the new, powerful Germany and absent in the case of the closest Russian ally, France, a product of revolution and considered a center of radicalism. A tie with Britain could provide such a political mooring. This was in fact an increasingly practical necessity for Russia as she hove into the present unfriendly international seas, unprepared to match the ambition and defensive-offensive outward thrust of her geographically and ideologically closest neighbor, Germany.

This circumstance suggested not only to Izvolsky but also to his supporters, as it had to Izvolsky's predecessor in office, that the issue was not merely, as had sometimes been suggested, one of choosing between Britain and Germany. It was rather a question of weighing adherence exclusively or largely to a nation such as Germany, the real advantages of which might be marginal and the disadvantages of which might be fatal. This latter could mean subjection to Germany, alienation from France, and possible conflict with Britain. This had to be compared with the advantages of adherence to a group which might provide a safeguard against these prospects and, at the same time, offer some positive benefits.

The latter might include providing Russia with a stronger base of support for negotiation with Germany and a continuing partnership with France. The advantages might also give Russia easier access to French financial resources. Furthermore, it might provide the opportunity to work toward the resolution of problems in Asia, including that concerned with Japan as well as some long suspended because of the prevailing Anglo-Russian rivalry. Such a balance would permit Russia not only to limit her liabilities in the Far East but to adjust the balance in the Balkans where Izvolsky saw the equality with Austria based on the treaty of 1897 as in need of correction in Russia's favor. The great importance of the French and especially the British ties in maintaining the traditional

[13] Newton, *Lord Lansdowne*, p. 308.

balance was a consequence of the fact that in the post-war period Russia was militarily, politically, and financially weaker than formerly and more in need of dependable sources of support while Germany and Japan were correspondingly stronger.

One of these problems concerned the Far East where defeat indicated beyond a doubt that the previous policy had been in error either in conception, operation, or both. By early 1907 even Witte, who had tended to see the nation's security in drawing close to Germany, expressed agreement with Izvolsky that what was needed was a "durable understanding with Japan on a broad basis," enabling Russia "to live in amicable and undisturbed relations with Great Britain and Japan."[14] Witte had come, especially after the Björkö affair, to see the foreign policy of Germany as being "so erratic, and so impulsive, and so eminently selfish," that this factor was itself an additional reason for seeking to come to terms with Britain.

Izvolsky viewed Russia's role in the Far East as secondary to that of Europe and Siberia as a reserve where population overflow from European Russia could be accommodated.[15] At the same time he did not see Siberia in a light comparable to the way Cecil Rhodes had viewed Africa, as a necessary outlet for British surplus population, capital, and energies. By contrast, Izvolsky characterized Witte's railway project in Siberia as "of a purely artificial character, satisfactory only to the unbounded ambitions of that statesman and anything but helpful to the true welfare of Russia, underpopulated as it was and undeveloped technically and economically."

Izvolsky expressed a further and very practical consideration when, in the course of the quest for security through links with Japan which the current negotiations promised to provide, he assured the French ambassador, Maurice Bompard, that Russia had abandoned completely the projects for expansion in the Far East which had moved some in the past, and was ready to accept all the economic and political consequences of the treaty of Portsmouth without any spirit of revenge.[16] An accommodation with Britain would lay the Far Eastern problem to rest while Russia concentrated on more immediately meaningful matters.

Japan and the balance of power

The Russo-Japanese treaty concluded at Portsmouth on September 5, 1905 signalled the climax of an era in which Imperial Russia reached its

[14] No. 96 Nicolson to Grey, Feb. 15, 1907, FO 371/321.
[15] Seeger, *Recollections of a Foreign Minister*, pp. 118 ff.
[16] Ibid., p. 121; No. 1 Bompard to Pichon, Jan. 17, 1907, *DDF*, X, 620–623.

greatest expansion and which had been characterized by intense Russo-Japanese maneuvering for strategic leverage on the eastern rim of Asia. It was also a preliminary assessment of the victory and defeat respectively of the two rivals as well as a preview of the altered pattern of behavior which their relations would assume in the course of the following years. The reordering of the balance of power in northeastern Asia which was to characterize the succeeding era was based on the decisions formulated at the Portsmouth conference and at consultations held over the ensuing years.

At the Portsmouth conference the principal Japanese plenipotentiary, Baron Komura Jutaro, demanded the transfer to Japan of the rights to the railway which China had granted to Russia in 1898, i.e., the railway from Harbin to Port Arthur, including in addition the Kuantung leased territory.[17] Instead, the railway was in fact transferred to Japan not southward from Harbin but from Changchun, a point 150 miles south of Harbin.[18] However, during the Russo-Japanese discussion held in 1906, the Japanese had also demanded the freedom of navigation on the Amur and Sungari rivers, advantageous rights of transporting commodities into Siberia itself, and unlimited rights of navigation along the coast of the Russian Far East.[19] The Russian press referred to these demands as an attempt at the economic conquest not only of Manchuria but of the entire Russian Far East and they were in fact held unacceptable by the Russian government.

Even before the Portsmouth settlement had been reached Japan had taken steps to absorb areas which the course of the war had made accessible to her. She had begun the process of acquiring control of Korea both by railway construction and by administrative governance, the latter a process which five years later led to outright annexation of the country.[20] Also, having swept the Russian navy from the Far Eastern seas, she had by August 7, 1905, before the Portsmouth conference had assembled, occupied Sakhalin island. The *Jiji* commented that with Tsushima in the south and Sakhalin in the north, Japan now held the gateways to the Sea of Japan. The writer also noted the importance of holding in addition the entire continental region opposite Sakhalin island, i.e., the southern coast of the Russian Far East along with the mouth of the Amur river. Not only had the destruction of the Russian fleet at Tsushima given Japan

[17] White, *The diplomacy*, p. 277.
[18] Japan. Dept. of Railways, *An official guide to Eastern Asia*, I. *Chosen & Manchuria, Siberia*, Tokyo, 1920, pp. 274.
[19] Peter Alexander Berton, "The secret Russo-Japanese alliance of 1916," Ph.D. dissertation, Columbia University, 1956, p. 3; Igor Vasil'evich Bestuzhev, "Bor'ba klassov i partii Rossii po voprosam vneshnei politiki nakanune Bosniiskogo krizisa (1906–1908 gg.)," *IZ*, LXIV (1959), 170–179.   [20] *Japan Times*, July 11, 1905.

sufficient naval supremacy to support these expectations but at the Portsmouth conference Baron Komura strongly urged that possession of this strategic region was necessary for the security of Japan.[21]

There was early and disturbing evidence that as a consequence of her strategically advantageous gains Japan would seek to monopolize her new possessions and that she might be willing to bend the rules in order to achieve this.[22] The British ambassador, Sir Claude MacDonald, was informed in January 1906 by the Japanese minister of foreign affairs, Kato Takaaki, that during the negotiations with China in December Baron Komura had had a stipulation made in article XII of the treaty giving Japan most-favored-nation privileges. The specific purpose of this was to serve as a means of extending her tenure in the Kuantung peninsula.

At the expiration of the remaining eighteen of the twenty-five-year lease originally granted to Russia, Japan would be able, on the grounds of the most-favored-nation treaty rights, to cite the example of the ninety-nine-year lease granted by China to Germany in Kiaochow as evidence of her claim to an extension of her rights in Kuantung. This established more than a suspicion that Japan had no intention of vacating the leased territory at the expiration of the treaty term. A notation on the dispatch to the effect that this was a slender thread on which to hang so important a claim was answered by another notation which stated that "Technically this may be so, but as an arrangement it serves."

The Japanese tendency toward monopoly was further exemplified by the way she regulated the conduct of commercial and industrial enterprise in Manchuria. While Japanese goods entered through the low customs towns of Antung and Dairen, those of Britain and France were imported through Newchuang where higher customs had to be paid.[23] Furthermore, railway rates were 5 sen per ton mile at Newchuang while they were 2 sen per ton mile from the other two towns.

Also, such towns as Shaho, Antung, Tatungkou, and Mukden were not at first open to any but Japanese merchants. A general survey of the situation in Manchuria during late February and early March 1906 was

[21] Japan Foreign Office, "Protocols of the Peace Conference between Japan and Russia," pp. 14, 23–27; Japan. Foreign Office, "Manshu ni Kansuru Nisshin Dampan Hikki," Nov. 17–Dec. 18, 1905.

[22] No. 16 MacDonald to Grey, Jan. 18, 1906, FO 371/84; Iriye, *Pacific estrangement*, pp. 93 ff.

[23] Helen Dodson Kahn, "The great game of empire: Willard D. Straight and American Far Eastern policy," Ph.D. dissertation, Cornell University, 1968, pp. 119–120; No. 117 Satow to Grey, Mar. 17, 1906, enclosing Hosie to Satow, Mar. 14, 1906, No. 8 Fulford to Satow, Feb. 28, 1906, No. 125 Satow to Grey, Mar. 19. 1906, enclosing Nos. 10, 11, 12, Fulford to Satow, Mar. 8, 10, 11, 1906, No. 144 Satow to Grey, Apr. 3, 1906 enclosing "The Japanese in Manchuria," by Chao Erh-hsun, an extract from the Peking *Jih Pao*, Mar. 23, 1906, all in FO 405/166.

made by Alexander Hosie as acting commercial agent, by the British consul at Newchuang, H. E. Fulford, from that town, and by others.

The findings of these and other British observers were comparable to the American conclusions as well as to those reached by a Chinese delegation sent to investigate under Hsü Shih-ch'ang, soon to be the viceroy of Manchuria, and led to the conclusion that Japan was in the process of absorbing southern Manchuria. It was often difficult to distinguish events in the confusion of post-war circumstances. There was also clearly a lack of coordination on the part of the various arms of the Japanese government operating in Manchuria, simple delays to be anticipated in all but ideal conditions, as well as intentional acts of discrimination against foreign merchants and residents. However, on balance, there was no doubt on the part of either the British or American officials that their rights and interests would be preserved with considerable difficulty.

The intervention of several persons of authority was asked in behalf of a modification of the Japanese course in south Manchuria. Sir Claude MacDonald, the British ambassador, appealed to the minister of war, General Terauchi Masatake, and the minister of foreign affairs, Marquis Saionji Kimmochi.[24] MacDonald was on terms of close friendship with the former who, in response to his complaint, explained that his department did not want "to open the door until the house was a fit place for occupation." MacDonald answered that though he did not quarrel with this, he found that while the front door was shut, "the back door was open to Japanese merchants, who were taking all the best rooms." Terauchi replied that these were only supplying the troops. MacDonald took up the question with Marquis Saionji with somewhat better immediate results. The foreign minister personally visited Manchuria and gave assurances that Antung and Tatungkou would be opened for trade on May 1 and Mukden on June 1. Dairen, he stated, would be opened as soon as possible.

Prince Ito Hirobumi also added his influence to the effort to slacken the pace of Japanese monopolization of southern Manchuria. Having been appointed the resident general in Korea in December 1905, he spoke at a joint meeting of cabinet and genro on May 22, 1906 about Japanese interests and rights in Korea and Manchuria.[25]

Japan's interests in Korea, he stated, were a matter of life and death and were therefore of a primary nature. Her only interests in Manchuria, on

---

[24] No. 74A MacDonald to Grey, Aug. 13, 1906, enclosing Saionji to Macdonald, Apr. 11, 1906, FO 405/166.
[25] Han Woo-Kuen, *The history of Korea*, Honolulu, 1971, pp. 449–450; Hamada Kengi, *Prince Ito*, Tokyo 1936, pp. 213 ff.

the other hand, consisted in the need to create there a military and commercial hegemony with Port Arthur and the South Manchurian railway as the bases of operations. The other powers with commercial interest there would not look favorably on any Japanese military intervention which might seek to nullify the policy of the open door and the principle of equal opportunity for business enterprise. Severe notes of protest were in fact received from the United States and Britain within six months of the Portsmouth settlement.

Such a sharp diplomatic reaction, Ito stated, could be reflected in Korea by denunciations in the foreign press and discontent among the Koreans themselves. Ito pointed out that, in addition to reports that Japan intended to monopolize southern Manchuria, there were also some to the effect that Russia was preparing for a war with Japan and that China was concerned about both of these. He advocated the abolition of the Japanese military government in Manchuria in favor of a civil government and urged that the government not prolong the existing regime. He was supported in these recommendations by Count Inouye Kaoru and Baron Hayashi Tadasu but opposed by such generals as Yamagata Aritomo, Kodama Gentaro, Katsura Taro, and Terauchi Masatake, and Admiral Yamamoto Gonnohyoei. The military government was nevertheless abolished in October 1906 and the Japanese troops withdrawn in April 1907.

The proponents of a firm policy had by the end of the year evolved a plan intended to take advantage of the weakness of Russia, the effective support of Britain, and the extensive foothold Japan had gained on the continent.[26] The Japanese post-war plans were suggested in December 1906 by Lieutenant Colonel Tanaka Giichi of the Japanese General Staff in a confidential conversation with the Russian military attaché, Colonel Vladimir Konstantinovich Samoilov. Colonel Tanaka had already elaborated a plan entitled the "Plan of National Defense for the Empire" which was revised by Marshal Yamagata and presented to the Emperor on October 16, 1906.

The plan included the following: the cooperation of the army and navy in case of war; the conception of Russia as the enemy; the recommendation that military action should be directed against Manchuria with Harbin as the target, the accompanying naval action to be directed against Vladivostok; in fulfillment of the Anglo-Japanese alliance, the suggestion that an attack should be directed at Russia in case of an Anglo-Russian

[26] Stanislav Seliverstovich Grigortsevich, *Dal'nevostochnaia politika imperialisticheskikh derzhav v 1906–1917 gg.*, Tomsk, 1965, pp. 50 ff; Roger F. Hackett, *Yamagata Aritomo in the rise of modern Japan, 1838–1922*, Cambridge, MA, 1971, pp. 234–235; Oyama Azusa, *Nihon Gaikoshi Kenkyu*, Tokyo, 1963, pp. 170–177 (contains Japanese plan); Iriye, *Pacific estrangement*, pp. 172–173.

clash in Central Asia; the proposed goal that Japan's "efforts to expand our national sovereignty and enhance our interests in China must excel others"; if action in China were necessary, the hope was that the army would conquer south China and the navy would control the Formosa straits and harass the southern coastal cities.

It is of particular interest that Tanaka's first draft included military plans to be used in case of hostilities with the United States. These called for an attack on the Philippine Islands and the occupation of Manila. Also, in case of war with Germany or France, the plans called correspondingly for attacks on Kiaochow or Indochina. But these provisions were eliminated by Yamagata, leaving only the measures intended to deal with Russia and China. The plan was accompanied by corresponding requests for increases in the armed forces. It was sent on to the Supreme Military Council and in May 1907 the prime minister, Prince Saionji, declared the plan appropriate; it had been adopted as imperial policy in April 1907.

The sudden and uncomfortable closeness of the special spheres of interest of Russia and Japan on the Asian mainland gave rise to a high degree of competition and a sense of urgency in developing these spheres, spurred on by the rising tide of Chinese nationalism, and supported in turn by American interest in investment possibilities. An American commercial role in Manchuria was promoted in these years through W. W. Rockhill, F. M. Huntington Wilson, Willard Straight and others.

The disclosure by the outcome of the Sino-Japanese war of the weakness of China and the prospect that a Far Eastern competitor might monopolize China had inspired anxiety among the western powers over the balance of power and the monopolization of commerce. These projects on behalf of the open door for business enterprise and Chinese survival were supplemented in 1907 when the Chinese government appointed General Hsü Shih-ch'ang as the new viceroy in Manchuria with T'ang Shao-yi as governor of Fengtien, the province in which Mukden was located, two officials who played significant political roles in the years to come.

These preparations were aimed directly at Japan which was already in the process of solidifying her hold on south Manchuria. Japan had hastily constructed the Antung–Mukden railway during the war and with the completion in April 1906 of the Seoul–Uiju railway the Manchurian and Korean railway networks were united through Antung and Uiju, located respectively on the Manchurian and Korean banks of the Yalu river.[27]

Japan followed this up when she organized the South Manchurian Railway Company on June 7, 1906, and established the government general of the Kuantung Territory on August 1, 1906, with a governor

[27] White, *The diplomacy*, p. 337.

general at first chosen exclusively from among the senior army generals
with the rank of lieutenant general or general. The position was later
opened up for the appointment of civilians. This official exercised both
civil and military jurisdiction, including the supervision of the South
Manchurian Railway Company and the conduct of diplomatic relations
with China.[28]

The new Japanese administration soon began to carry out improve-
ments in railway service. Both freight and passenger capacity were
increased and new cars and locomotives were introduced. Plans were
effectuated to span the 80 miles between the northern terminus of the
Japanese railway at Kuanchengtze and Kirin and the 40 miles between
Hsinmintun on the imperial Chinese line and Fakumen, the latter a
Chinese line with half the capital acquired from the South Manchurian
railway. In relation to the Chinese line a new port was planned for
Hulutao, ice free and 60 miles nearer Mukden than Dairen.

The Chinese and American programs were also aimed at Russia in
north Manchuria where she extended her control throughout the zone of
the remaining parts of the Chinese Eastern Railway. Specifically, Russia
continued in the post-war period a trend already set from the beginning of
her experience with this concession. This was a trend toward increasing
Russian civil control in Harbin, the "Moscow of Asia," and throughout
the rest of the railway zone, an ambition for which China asserted that
Russia had no claim.

In the aftermath of the war there was a renewed continuation of this
Sino-Russian struggle but with an intensification of the effort on both
sides and with an increasing degree of Russian success. On December 29,
1906 the Board of Directors of the Chinese Eastern Railway Company
issued the General Regulations of Civil Administration which introduced
civil administration in Harbin and several other towns in the railway zone.
Under this new regulation the Department of Civil Administration was
established in July 1907 under General Dmitrii Leonidovich Horvath,
already the general manager of the Chinese Eastern Railway.

One of the purposes served by the establishment of firmer Russian
controls in the railway zone, it was asserted by a contemporary publicist,
Dmitrii Grigorevich Ianchevetsky, was the defense of the Russian stake
in northern Manchuria.[29] The foundation of an adequate defense of the
region was the Chinese Eastern railway which traversed it. Even though
an advocate of good relations with China, he felt that under conditions as

[28] No. 165 MacDonald to Grey, Aug. 8, 1906, Imperial Ordinance No. 196 "Regulations
for the Organization of the Governor-General of Kuantung," FO 371/87; Hosie,
Manchuria, pp. 153–156.
[29] Dmitrii Grigorevich Ianchevetsky, *Groza s Vostoka. Zadachi Rossii i zadachi Iaponii na
Dal'nem Vostoke: ocherki*, Revel, 1907, pp. 48–58, 74–86.

they were then, handing the railway back to China was tantamount to handing it over to Russia's enemy, Japan. If this were to be permitted, it would place Japan in a position to carry out rapid troop movements to three key points in the Russian Far East – Transbaikal in the west, Priamur in the north, and the Vladivostok region of the Maritime Province in the east. It was clear, he asserted, that this would place Russia in a hazardous position and that the railway must be retained in Russian hands and operated with American efficiency in order to preserve North Manchuria as a buffer between Japan in the south and the Russian Far Eastern region.

While urging the strategic significance for Russia of northern Manchuria, Ianchevetsky saw also its importance as a center to which commerce would be attracted away from the Japanese sphere of influence in South Manchuria. Harbin, he thought, should be a center for foreign trade, settlement, and enterprise with foreign concessions as in Shanghai or T'ientsin. With this kind of an open door policy Harbin could attract foreign capital and enterprise while Chinese capital could be encouraged to build collateral lines to the Chinese Eastern railway, opening up such towns and centers as Kirin, Tsitsihar, and Ninguta and connecting the Russian town on the Amur, Blagoveshchensk, and the proposed Amur line with the Manchurian mainline.

This proposal was an astute response to the Japanese plans for southern Manchuria since it would provide a railway network to match the projected Japanese railway expansion in South Manchuria on terms which would offer greater opportunity for Chinese participation than Japan had contemplated in her zone. Ianchevetsky expressed a prevailing view when he opposed a trans-Mongolian railway which, while it might give Russia easier access to Mongolia, it might also be competitive with the Chinese Eastern railway and, at the same time, deflect interest from the proposed Amur railway line. In the long run, the commercial aspects of Russia's policy in North Manchuria were so successful that in 1913 more than 80 percent of all goods leaving northern Manchuria went to Vladivostok rather than Dairen.

The passage by stages of Korea under the control of Japan in the aftermath of the Russo-Japanese war evolved in time a new source of irritation along the frontier of these two nations. The establishment of a protectorate by the Japanese–Korean agreement of November 17, 1905 was followed in December by the appointment of Ito Hirobumi as resident general and his assumption of that office in February 1906. The attempt of the Korean government to seek outside help received no response either in Russia which was then struggling with a domestic revolution or at the Second Hague Conference to which the Koreans sent a delegation.[30] It seems rather to have encouraged the Japanese to bring about the abdication of Emperor Kojong on July 19, 1907 and to follow this by concluding a further treaty with Korea on July 24 by which the entire central and local administration of the country was brought directly under Japanese control.

One of the consequences of these events was the increased emigration of Koreans into the neighboring Kando (Ch'ientao) region of Manchuria and into the Russian Far East, particularly the Maritime province where the Korean population apparently increased from just over 34,000 in 1906 to about 100,000 in 1910.[31] A liberation movement began among the Koreans and the Uiyonggun or Righteous Army, inspired by a similar movement organized at the time of the Japanese incursions in 1592 and 1598, was formed at Pos'et in the Maritime province in 1906 and commanded by Tsoi Dia Khen [Ch'oe Chae-hyong], who had lived in this region since childhood, attended Russian schools, and been influenced by the Russian revolution.

The rising among the troops which broke out in Seoul in August 1907 led to the final dissolution of the Korean army and to many of the soldiers joining the partisan military units. These carried out attacks into Japanese-ruled Korea, amounting reportedly to about 1,400 of such attacks carried out in 1908 by some 70,000 partisans.[32] These activities had their negative effect on Russo-Japanese relations even though there was some attempt on the part of the Russians to discourage these incursions from Russian territory.

The post-war contention for control of Outer Mongolia became an unequal tripartite struggle in which China found it difficult to match the determination and drive of Russia and Japan, assisted by an anti-Chinese movement among the Mongols. The resurgence after the Russo-Japanese war of Chinese interest in recapturing her lost primacy in the border regions in fact provided the incentive for Russia to frustrate this effort and to make good her own claims.

In Mongolia Russia met with a more heartening response than formerly because of the growing dissatisfaction of the princes and lamas with the revival of China's efforts to assert her traditional rights and the desire on the part of the Mongols for some leverage to prevent it. Consequently, Russian efforts in her own behalf met with approval and

---

[30] Han, *History of Korea*, p. 451; Stanislav Seliverstovich Grigortsevich, "Uchastie koreitsev russkogo Dal'nego Vostoka v antiiaponskoi natsional'no-osvoboditel'noi bor'be (1906–1916 gg.)," *VI*, no. 10 (1958), pp. 139–151.

[31] John J. Stephan, "The Korean minority in the Soviet Union," *M*, XIII, no. 3 (Dec. 1971), 139; Kim Syn-Khva [Kim Sung-Hwa], *Ocherki po istorii sovetskikh koreitsev*, Alma Ata, 1965, p. 40.

[32] Kim, *Ocherki po istorii*, pp. 68–69; Grigortsevich, "Uchastie koreitsev," 139–142.

encouragement. Russian concern about Mongolia had developed long before the Russo-Japanese war and in 1900 Witte had demanded that China recognize Russia's special interest in railway construction in Manchuria, Mongolia, and Sinkiang even as against China's own freedom of action. The effort failed but it served formal notice of Russia's long-range intentions and gave warning that she would be likely to seek ways and means of supporting her claims when the opportunity arose.

Russian consular reports from Urga in 1905 provided warnings of Chinese plans to introduce administrative reforms. Simultaneously, there emerged the growth of displeasure among the Mongols as well as the alienation of the people from the local Chinese elements and with it the first steps of the princes and lamas towards separation from China. These events signaled an unusual opportunity for Russia to lay the foundation for her own power in Mongolia.

In spite of the weakness of China, her recent plans in Mongolia were calculated to strengthen her claims through vigorous and determined action and to thwart the Russian expansion plans. Earlier Chinese settlement in Mongolia had been carried out in support of the Ch'ing dynasty's administrative control there in its more vigorous years when the Chinese presence in Mongolia became large enough to call for an effort to supply food for the Chinese. But in 1902 Mongolia was thrown open for Chinese settlement and a further step was taken in this direction in 1906, aimed specifically at settling Chinese farmers along the route to Urga where a colonization bureau was opened in 1911.

Along with this went plans which called for permanent garrisons in Mongolia and for a Mongol army under Chinese direction. Even more far reaching designs were forecast by plans looking to the development of mining enterprises, the establishment of a Chinese bank, and the construction of a railway from Kalgan in Inner Mongolia to Urga. Clearly the outcome of such developments would be a change in the balance of power which could redound to the detriment of Russia. It could become a direct contraposition with China along a very exposed Russian frontier. It raised also the possibility of the creation there of an opponent in Japan who might be induced by the Mongols to support them against the Chinese if Russia did not.

The Russian response was to seek to keep Mongolia from further engulfment by China by encouraging the Mongol desire to oppose the Chinese through enhancing the Russian presence there. The Russo-Chinese Bank, especially since 1900, had been used by Russia to stimulate various economic projects in Mongolia such as Mongolor, a mining company which faced bankruptcy a year after its establishment but was rescued by the Russians because of its political usefulness.

In 1905 a Russian consulate was opened at Uliassutai and another at Kobdo in 1911, both in western Mongolia. But progress was disappointing and in 1908 Russo-Mongol trade turnover was only 8 million rubles compared with 50 million for Sino-Mongol trade. This led in 1910 to the establishment of a committee at Irkutsk to promote Russian trade in Mongolia.

It was with the hope of inclining this precarious balance somewhat more in her own favor that Russia conceived the idea of seeking an accommodation with Japan through her ally, Britain. The British government in the hands of the new Liberal government, though as firmly committed as its predecessor to an understanding with Russia, faced the alliance with Japan with far less enthusiasm.[33] Sir Edward Grey, in a comment on a dispatch of late November, indicated that his readiness to respond to a Russian request for assistance with her negotiations with Japan would depend on Russian response to Britain's desire for an acceptable Anglo-Russian understanding. While Britain was left with a growing naval threat from Germany and France, it was estimated by the Admiralty that at the moment Japan could defy the eastern fleets of Britain, the United States, Germany, and France.

It was also considered possible that Japan might threaten the United States in the Philippine Islands and even the American Pacific coast before the estimated date for the completion of the Panama Canal in 1915. These conditions raised a question as to whether under these circumstances the Anglo-Japanese alliance might require of Britain some inconvenient cooperation in China or elsewhere. In such a case there was some concern that the United States might call upon Britain when the alliance was reaching its termination to choose between her friendship and that of Japan. "Faced by such a dilemma," the memorandum states, "the British people would certainly throw the alliance overboard," an interesting statement in light of the British decision after the first world war to take this very step. Yet the alliance still had some advantages such as preventing a Russo-Japanese combination against Britain in India, avoiding the threat of the Japanese fleet, and the naval security which Britain enjoyed in the Far East under the alliance with Japan.

The post-war proceedings and apparent objectives of Japan and China demanded greater attention than heretofore because of the problems of the insecurity of this remote and inadequately accessible Pacific borderland. The Russian Pacific region had been severely damaged, economi-

---

[33] CID 84th meeting, Feb. 15, 1906, FO 371/85; Monger, *The end of isolation*, p. 286; Memorandum "The Building Programme of the British Navy," Feb. 15, 1906, Adm 116/866B Naval Staff Memoranda 1889–1912; G. S. Clarke, memorandum, Dec. 15, 1906, Cab 17/67; No. 791 Nicolson to Grey, Nov. 28, 1906, FO 371/87.

cally, socially, strategically, and diplomatically during the recent encounter with Japan and only partially rehabilitated by the diplomatic arrangements at Portsmouth. War-time disruption had inspired the wish and the sense of urgency not only to make good the losses but to improve more generally the regional economic and strategic self-sufficiency.

Some of the pre-war patterns of economic and strategic development of the Russian Far East had been planned in part as a means of strengthening the defenses of the region and had to some extent been carried out before the Russo-Japanese war. These had continued to be advocated by some members of the Russian government during the war, particularly as defeat appeared increasingly to be an almost certain outcome. Such projects were seen then as a means of strengthening the country against Japan. Baron Roman Romanovich Rosen, in the United States as a delegate to the Portsmouth conference, spoke to a group of businessmen in Philadelphia, urging them to help in this endeavor by considering investments and other business ventures in Russia.[34]

One of these enterprises, known as the Northeastern Siberian Company, was a mining concession which had formerly been part of a concession acquired before the Russo-Japanese war by two former military officers, Aleksandr Mikhailovich Vonliarliarsky and Aleksandr Mikhailovich Bezobrazov.[35] The company was organized by John Rosene of Seattle and it was suggested that, in addition to mining, it would perform a broader role such as supplying many of the needs of a railway planned to run through the Chukotka peninsula region and of the Russian army in the Russian Far East. Grand Duke Nikolai Nikolaevich was a shareholder and supporter of this project and it was seen by Loicq de Lobel, the promoter of a geographically related railway scheme, as a very useful endeavor.

Loicq de Lobel, a French promoter acting as spokesman for an American group including Edward H. Harriman, James J. Hill, and others, on November 25, 1905 presented for the consideration of the Russian Council of Ministers a revised draft of a project for a railway to serve northeastern Siberia and to be connected with North America.[36] The proposed railway would extend about 5,000 versts from Kansk on the Transsiberian Railway, north of Lake Baikal by way of Kirensk, Iakutsk,

[34] Viacheslav Vladimirovich Lebedev, *Russko-amerikanskie ekonomicheskie otnosheniia, 1900–1917 gg.*, Moscow, 1964, pp. 89–90.

[35] George Sherman Queen, "The United States and the material advance in Russia 1881–1906," Ph.D. dissertation, University of Illinois, Urbana, 1941, p. 105; White, *The diplomacy*, pp. 35, 40.

[36] Grigortsevich, *Dal'nevostochnaia politika*, pp. 85–88; S. V. Slavin, "Avantiura Loik de Lobelia [Loicq de Lobel] i Tsarskii dvor," *LS*, no. 1, 1949, pp. 227–237; V. Adoratsky, V. Maksakov, M.N. Pokrovsky (eds.), "N. N. Romanov i amerikanskaia kontsessiia na zheleznuiu dorogu Sibir'-Aliaska v 1905," *KA*, VI (43) (1930), 173–175.

and Verkhne-Kolymsk to Cape Dezhnev and could be extended eastward by tunnel to Alaska. It should be noted that a railway traversing this region had already been suggested in 1890 by the American proponent of a railway bridging the old and new worlds, William Gilpin.[37]

The promoters of the more recent venture were asking for a zone twelve miles wide on each side of the tracks with the right to colonize it, an aspect of regional reinforcement which the Russian government itself undertook after 1905 with notable results.[38] While the grant was requested for ninety years, it was provided that it could be repurchased in thirty years. The potentiality of attracting American capital and of contributing to the strategic security of the region were both understood to be considerations of importance in evaluating the proposal. The renewal of the Anglo-Japanese alliance, the planning then being done with respect to an Amur railway, and the outbreak of revolution were also factors in thinking about the railway. The project was submitted on December 1, 1905 for the consideration of a special committee presided over by Count Witte and attended by the Grand Duke Nikolai Nikolaevich, the president of the Council of State Defense.[39] A negative decision was finally rendered in April 1906.

The conception of strategic and economic policy in the Russian Far East which came to prevail after 1905 called for the building of an Amur railway line to supplement the Chinese Eastern line through Manchuria as a route to Vladivostok. The idea of such a line was at least as old as the planning for the Transsiberian line in the early 1890s. By the middle of the decade the Sino-Japanese war inspired the idea of avoiding the difficult terrain of the Amur valley region and shortening the distance to Vladivostok by projecting the railway across Manchuria, ostensibly in the interest of providing a more effective means of common defense for Russia and China against a further occurrence of Japanese aggression.

But more recently the Russo-Japanese war had called into question even Russia's capability of defending herself against the Japanese, consequently serving to revive the notion of a railway line traversing the Amur valley. This time it came to be considered in the context of a Russian self-strengthening program and of a general improvement of railway services. Attention had been drawn to this need not only by the defeat in the recent war but also by the revolution that followed it and paralyzed the railway in early 1906 when it was needed for the transpor-

---

[37] William Gilpin, *The cosmopolitan railway. Compacting and fusing together all the world's continents*, San Francisco, 1890, pp. 1–30.

[38] Lewis H. Siegelbaum, "Another 'Yellow Peril': Chinese migrants in the Russian Far East and the Russian reaction before 1917," *MAS*, no. 2 (1978), 319–321.

[39] Lebedev, *Russko-amerikanskie ekonomicheskie*, pp. 106–107.

tation of troops, especially those scheduled for return to European Russia for demobilization.

The proposal to build the Amur line was approved by the State Duma on April 14, 1908 by a vote of 212 to 101, strongly supported by members of the Right and Octobrists and the construction of the 1,200 mile line began in the same year at Kuenga, a junction 30 miles west of Stretensk where the Transbaikal line ended.[40] Construction took eight years with all the difficulties caused by engineering and labor problems as well as the annoyance of swarming mosquitoes. With the building of the bridge nearly a mile and a half long across the Amur at Khabarovsk, the line was fully opened for traffic in 1916 in the midst of another war in which Japan was to figure both as ally and adversary. It was built in an arc through the forbidding and sparsely populated wilderness and swamps lying northward and paralleling the Amur River, well beyond the range of artillery fire directed from the right bank of the river.

The porto franco at Vladivostok which had been in effect only since 1904 was, with the exception of some items such as machinery, abolished as part of the same effort to strengthen this distant frontier.[41] G. A. Krestovnikov, the president of the Moscow Stock Exchange Committee and member of the State Council, saw the issue as related to the continuing relations of this Pacific region with the rest of Russia. Spiridon Dionisievich Merkulov, a conservative who during the civil war was to serve briefly as head of the anti-Soviet Provisional Government, wrote a pamphlet opposing the porto franco on the grounds that it constituted just one more obstacle to attracting population to the Russian Far East. This view was also strongly supported and advocated in 1907 by many members of the business community of European Russia and was adopted on January 28, 1909 by the vote of a large majority in the Duma.

Arc of tension

The Algeciras conference was a defeat for Germany and a victory for France and her supporters only in the most restricted sense. It was unquestionably a humiliation for Germany and it unmistakably reasserted instead of negating the objectives of the Anglo-French and Franco-Russian compacts. Nevertheless, the existing political realities were only

[40] No. 195 Nicolson to Grey, Apr. 15, 1908, FO 418/40; Bestuzhev, *Bor'ba v Rossii*, pp. 169–170; Harmon Tupper, *To the great ocean, Siberia and the Trans-Siberian railway*, London, 1965, pp. 169 ff.
[41] No. 92 Nicolson to Grey, Feb. 8, 1909, FO 371/727; Bestuzhev, *Bor'ba v Rossii*, pp. 175–176; Spiridon Dionisevich Merkulov, *Porto-franko i kolonizatsiia Priamurskago kraia russkim naseleniem*, St. Petersburg, 1908, pp. i–ii, 22–25.

underscored by the event. Fear of Germany was increased by the experience and existing measures of defense were disclosed to be inadequate and in need of improvement. For Britain the naval race with Germany, recently given renewed stimulation by the destruction of the Russian fleet, was the central issue. Furthermore, both in Britain and on the continent the very fact of determined German endeavors to destroy the competing diplomatic combinations, even though unsuccessful, had left a legacy of apprehension concerning the endurance of the European balance of power. Some foresaw a final Franco-German struggle ending with the acceptance of a dominant Germany; others feared that the same outcome might be achieved gradually by the strategic and timely application of pressure.

Meanwhile, increasing German pressure on Russia produced at the same time a diversion of the latter's already diminished power and a golden opportunity for Japanese aggrandizement. The Japanese government prepared a threefold program to take advantage of this. This projected: the monopolization of as much of Manchuria as circumstances permitted; a reassertion of the demands on Russia unrealized at the Portsmouth conference; and the realization of new demands which would expand her continental beachhead against Russia and China.

The new German Empire, while remaining basically continental, had also a maritime component. Like the British Empire, with which it was highly competitive, Germany was endeavoring in these years to secure access to commercial and naval ports beyond Europe and to straits and other suitable means of reaching them. Since the German home ports were in northern Europe, the way to the Atlantic and to the Middle and Far East was a circular route leading through or near the home waters of the major maritime nations of Europe. It was, therefore, a natural focus of rivalry if not potential conflict.

The problems characteristic of the northern segment of this route had been touched upon in July 1905 during the interview of the Russian and German emperors at Björkö. The Baltic problem had, according to a report of the German Emperor, been discussed by the two emperors at this meeting, thus correctly placing it with the Björkö treaty in the context of Anglo-Russian relations.[42] The Kaiser had already expressed his agreement with a memorandum of Holstein in which he had warned against a German–Danish alliance as a means of drawing Denmark into

[42] Troels Fink, *Ustabil balance, Dansk Udenrigs-og Forsvarspolitik 1894–1905*, Aarhus, 1961, p. 239; Wilhelm to Bülow, July 25, 1905, *GP*, XIX-2, 458–465; Wilhelm to Nicholas, Aug. 2, 1905 in Bernstein, *The Willy–Nicky correspondence*, pp. 119–120; Seeger, *Recollections of a foreign minister*, p. 75.

the German orbit.[43] Holstein wrote that such an act would be regarded as a Danish renunciation of her independence and would leave the Danes to turn for help to the two nations which he thought wanted to maintain the status quo in the Baltic so they could concentrate their efforts elsewhere, Britain and Russia. Consequently, continued Holstein, to draw Denmark into the German orbit would require either that the British fleet be otherwise engaged or that the German fleet, by itself or in conjunction with an ally, would need to be more or less equal in strength to its potential opposition.

Since the Holstein memorandum had been written, the Baltic problem had been further complicated by the declaration on June 7, 1905 by the Norwegian Storting of the dissolution of the union with Sweden. This was the situation when the emperors met at Björkö though the process set in motion by the June declaration was continued after the meeting. The dissolution was approved by a popular plebiscite and was followed in turn by the acquiescence of the Swedish Rikstag on September 24. Finally, by the Convention of Karlstadt concluded on October 26, 1905 Norway and Sweden gave official and formal sanction to the dissolution. Conclusive treaties guaranteeing the status quo in the North Sea and the Baltic were signed on April 23, 1908, the former in Berlin, the latter in St. Petersburg with the result that the limitations imposed on Russia by the treaties of 1855 and 1856 were nullified.

The issue of Scandinavian neutrality had been brought to public attention by an article written on March 26, 1902 by the Norwegian poet, novelist, and dramatist, Bjørnstjerne Bjørnson, in which he referred to a memorandum of 1889 by the noted Russian international legal scholar, Fedor Fedorovich Martens, suggesting the neutralization of Denmark, Norway, and Sweden.[44] Martens had followed this in November 1903 by an article in the *Revue des Deux Mondes* entitled "La neutralisation du Danemark" suggesting that Denmark, because of its geographical position on the Sound and the Belts, might be neutralized by its own declaration or under an international guarantee.

The Danish prime minister, Johan Henrik Deuntzer, had sounded out British views as to the efficacy of a Danish "declaration of perpetual neutrality," assuming that sufficient naval and military forces would be maintained to make it possible that her neutrality would be respected. The British government gave the question considerable thought and

---

[43] Holstein memorandum, Feb. 5, 1905, Schoen (Copenhagen) to Holstein, Feb. 11, 1905, in Rich and Fisher, *The Holstein papers*, IV, 324–325.

[44] Fink, *Ustabil balance*, pp. 110–112; Goschen to Lansdowne, Feb. 6, 1904, enclosing notes from Admiralty and War Office, Cab 4/1.

reached the conclusion that since they could not in time of emergency safely send ships into the Baltic Sea or land troops on its shores, neutralization was an acceptable solution provided it was observed by other nations. The most realistic challenge to Danish neutrality at this time came, in fact, with the passage through Danish waters of the Russian Baltic fleet during October 17–19, 1904.[45] Japan protested this, particularly since the Danish government agreed to send pilots to Libau instead of having them board the Russian ships as they entered Danish waters.

The most recent aspect of the Scandinavian question, of course, had been raised by the drift of Norway and Sweden toward a separate and independent status. Britain and France had guaranteed the integrity of the United Kingdom of Norway and Sweden against Russian retaliation by the Canrobert Convention. This was concluded at Stockholm on November 21, 1855 on the initiative of Emperor Napoleon III who had sought to strike at Russia in the Baltic by enlisting the Kingdom of Norway and Sweden as an ally against Russia in the Crimean war. Napoleon had sent General François Canrobert, a former commander in the Crimean peninsula, to negotiate directly with King Oscar. The war ended before the plans had been completed. But the allies, Britain and France, had reaffirmed this guarantee in a convention concluded on March 30, 1856 and annexed to the Treaty of Paris settling the Crimean war. The treaty included an engagement by Russia not to fortify the Aaland Islands.[46]

With the occurrence of the separation, the question was whether a further guarantee of each of the two separate kingdoms might not be useful in averting future dangers.[47] There was, for instance, the possibility of a Russian seizure of the Norwegian province of Finmark, which lay between Russian Finland and the Atlantic Ocean. This would give Russia an excellent and practically ice-free naval base at Tromsoe, only 20 miles from Russian territory. It was feared that the possession of such a commanding position might tempt Russia to take over the entire Scandinavian peninsula, shaking the European balance of power to its foundations. It would also provide Germany with a reason for taking over Denmark and, with it, the control of the Baltic.

The whole Baltic situation appeared thus to have become fluid at the very same time that the Björkö meeting had sought to readjust the European balance of power. Consequently, it seemed fitting that the German Emperor should have gone soon after his meeting with the Tsar

---

[45] Fink, *Ustabil balance*, pp. 198–199.

[46] E. A. Adamov (ed.), *Sbornik dogovorov Rossii s drugimi gosudarstv 1856–1917*, Moscow, 1952, pp. 40–41; John Shelton Curtiss, *Russia's Crimean War*, Durham, NC, 1979, pp. 478–479.   [47] Memorandum, June 8, 1905, Cab 4/1.

for a visit to Copenhagen. From there he wrote the Tsar that he had learned that the Danish foreign minister, Count Frederick Raben-Levetzau, and others seemed already to have accepted the idea that in case of war and of an attack in the Baltic region by some outside power, Russia and Germany would immediately take steps to safeguard their interests by occupying Denmark and holding it during a war but would guarantee the territory and future existence of the country and the dynasty.[48]

Izvolsky, then the Russian minister in Copenhagen, learned of the German Emperor's thoughts when he interviewed him during his visit and was told by the Emperor that the peace of Europe could be kept only by a union of Russia, Germany and France directed specifically against Britain. Izvolsky agreed but noted that France would not join such a grouping because of Alsace-Lorraine.[49] The Kaiser became very angry and remarked that he had thrown down the gauntlet to France and that since she had declined to accept the challenge, he concluded that she had renounced "for good and all" her claims to the provinces.

Izvolsky gathered from the interview that the two emperors had also discussed the Baltic, particularly the Danish, issue at Björkö though he had no way of knowing just what had passed between them. One option that seemed open to both countries was to join with Russia in neutralizing the Danish straits. However, this was seen by some as a dangerous tactic and the German ambassador in London, Count Metternich, and in Washington, Speck von Sternburg, warned against it.[50] It would, some thought, mean pulling the Russian chestnuts out of the fire, arousing Britain against Germany, and calling for an agreement with Russia over the price of the maneuver.

The Danish government viewed the changed situation as, in part, a consequence of the deflection of Russian military and naval power to the Far East and the ultimate defeat there at the hands of Japan of both these means of Russian defense and, in part also, as an outgrowth of Anglo-German rivalry.[51] The latter had flared up in November 1904 in the pages of *Vanity Fair* and the *Army and Navy Gazette* as a war scare and had raised the prospect that Britain might launch a strike against the German fleet before it grew beyond control. This prospect was aggravated by an article in the French journal *Le Gaulois* of July 12, 1905, attributed to Delcassé and later by articles in *Le Matin* during October 6–13, 1905 concerning a British offer to France. According to this, in case of war with

---

[48] Troels Fink, *Spillet om Dansk Neutralitet 1905–09 L.C.F. Lütken og Dansk Udenrigs- og Forsvarspolitik*, Aarhus, 1959, pp. 22 ff; Wilhelm to Nicholas, Aug. 2, 1905 in Bernstein, *The Willy–Nicky correspondence*, pp. 119–120; Seeger, *Recollections of a foreign minister*, pp. 75–78.   [49] Seeger, *Recollections of a foreign minister*, pp. 67–68.
[50] Konrad Bornhak, *Die Kriegsschuld: Deutschlands Weltpolitik, 1890–1914*, Berlin, 1929, p. 283.   [51] Fink, *Spillet om Dansk Neutralitet*, pp. 22 ff.

Germany Britain would blockade the Elbe mouth and seize Schleswig-Holstein with 100,000 men.

Though Britain officially disavowed having made such an offer, Delcassé stated in 1922 that he had received such a British offer on June 4, 1905 and that he reported to this effect at the cabinet meeting on June 6, at which he was ousted. It has been suggested that King Edward might have done this on his own to support Delcassé and certainly it was the King's conviction that Britain must support France in the Moroccan issue. Whatever the source, the article made a strong impression in Germany, and the Kaiser's visit to Copenhagen in July 1905 after the meeting with the Tsar at Björkö was seen as evidence of this interest.

It is also known that the British government was vitally concerned about what the outlook for Denmark and particularly Schleswig-Holstein in relation to the Jutland peninsula would be in case of a war with Germany.[52] In a private communication Sir Charles Ottley, director of Naval Intelligence, disclosed his apprehension over the main problem which he perceived to be the indecision of the Danish government in choosing between reliance on Britain or Germany. He had no doubt that Britain could make short work of the German navy, cut Germany off from overseas and have the grass "springing between the cobblestones in Hamburg and Bremen". Furthermore, he wrote, Britain could not make peace with Germany until Schleswig-Holstein had been returned to Denmark.

The Moroccan and Björkö incidents also turned attention to the possible reflection in the Baltic of Russo-German interests. Should the Moroccan situation give rise to a war, the tension between Russia and Germany along with the general complications in Europe could also lead directly to trouble for the Scandinavian countries. It was in anticipation of such a possibility that the Danish government had gone to considerable trouble to strengthen its defenses and the Kaiser had shown an ominous interest in these measures by sending a Lieutenant Colonel R. von Bieberstein to inspect them.[53] The outcome of such possible developments held the prospect of bringing about a change in the balance of power in northern Europe comparable to that which would be produced in the Mediterranean by a change at the Turkish strait. The preference of the Scandinavian countries as well as that of Britain was for a general guarantee for the Scandinavian region which would hopefully have the same enduring outcome as the successful general guarantee given to Switzerland at the Congress of Vienna. An Anglo-Scandinavian alliance

---

[52] C. Ottley to V. Baddeley, Nov. 16, 1906, FO 800/91.
[53] Julius Moritzen, "Denmark the buffer state of the north," *AMRR*, XXXII, no. 3 (Sept. 1905), 305; Astaf'ev, *Russko-germanskie diplomaticheskie otnosheniia*, pp. 82–85.

to effectuate this common interest or an official commitment of the Aaland issue to Britain, France, Germany, and Russia, the signatories of the mid-nineteenth-century agreement on the subject, would, however, be objectionable. It would be seen as leaving open the possibility for Britain to dominate the Baltic and the Gulf of Finland and make easier a naval strike at the German coast or at the heart of the Russian Empire, St. Petersburg.

The Baltic question was one of the first with which Izvolsky had to deal as foreign minister though a great amount of the work it required was actually handled by Baron Taube in his role as counselor in the Foreign Office.[54] One of the major Russian interests at the time was in the question of the use and prospective fortification of the Aaland Islands, an issue which had arisen with the dissolution of the Swedish–Norwegian union.

Baron Taube saw the dissolution of this Union as raising a number of issues for Russia which he placed in logical and chronological order as follows: the future relationship between Sweden and Norway; the territorial integrity and permanent neutrality of the newly independent state of Norway; the inevitable abrogation of the Canrobert Convention guaranteeing the former union against Russian aggression; the preservation of the status quo of the Swedish possessions and other territories in the Baltic; the continuation, in response to Russian interest, of the suppression of the "servitude" of, i.e., the prohibition against the fortification of, the Aaland Islands as established by the convention of 1856; and, finally, the question raised by Germany of the status quo in the region of the North Sea.

The Russian government saw ways in which the Baltic situation could be altered to her own advantage though some saw little hope of achieving any of these because of the need to take account of British and German interests, conflicts, and expectations. P. A. Stolypin, the prime minister, was eager to have some means of suppressing revolutionary activities such as the smuggling of arms into Russia from the Baltic through the indented Finnish coastline. The Grand Duke Aleksandr Mikhailovich proposed to alleviate this and other security problems by the construction of a naval station on the Aaland Islands to guard the access to the gulfs of Bothnia, Finland, and Riga. But the proposal stimulated a press campaign in Europe and the project was defeated. The fortification of the islands was of course of direct concern to Sweden, which, along with other powers, favored the continuation of the prohibition against fortifying them.

[54] Phelps, "Izvolskii and Russian foreign policy," pp. 154–171; Taube, *La politique russe*, pp. 123–145; Raymond E. Lindgren, *Norway–Sweden: union, disunion, and Scandinavian integration*, Princeton, 1959, pp. 228–232; Intelligence Dept., War Office memorandum, Mar. 2, 1904, memorandum on "Naval Aspects of the Question of the Swedish-Norwegian Union," n.d. but perhaps June, 1905, Cab 4/1; Adamov, *Sbornik dogovorov Rossii*, pp. 40–41.

The question of fortifying the Aaland Islands was seen by Baron Taube in its relationship to three eventualities: a war with Sweden which was an unreal possibility; a war against the Crimean war allies, i.e., Britain and France, a hypothesis which was unlikely but one which posed a situation in which the question of Russian "servitude" obligations to these powers regarding the islands would not be a prominent issue but would nevertheless be one in which they would have reason to oppose Russia; war against Germany, an eventuality which seemed improbable without British and French participation with Russia and in which these powers would hardly deny Russia the use of the Aaland Islands against Germany.[55] Although Taube opposed raising so difficult a question, Izvolsky wanted to pursue it and Taube concluded that Izvolsky wanted a success and was determined to achieve this by completing the job of nullifying the Crimean humiliation begun during the time of Prince Gorchakov, who had, nevertheless, been able in 1870 to invalidate the Black Sea clauses of the Paris treaty; in parallel, Izvolsky would seek to eliminate the Baltic restraints.

The negotiations to guarantee the independence and integrity of Norway were begun in the fall of 1906 and the final outcome of this was the treaty signed at Christiania [Oslo] on November 2, 1907 by Norway, Russia, Germany, France, and Britain. Meanwhile, the German and Russian emperors had met at Swinemünde on the German Baltic coast at the mouth of the Oder River during August 3–6, 1907 and had discussed without final or formal agreement the problems of whether or not the Björkö treaty was still in force and of the status quo in the Baltic.[56] Izvolsky had also held discussions with Eric Trolle, the Swedish minister and must have learned at first hand of the fears many Swedes had of what they saw as a threat from Russia, the "danger in the north." The agreement at Swinemünde on the question of the Björkö treaty was, as already noted, that it was inoperative and that Russia would not insist on the adherence of France to any Russo-German agreement but would give Germany a guarantee not to conclude any agreements with Britain regarding the Turkish straits. This was clearly an effort to combine a close Russo-German relationship with an Anglo-Russian rapprochement.

This relationship was brought into being by a secret Russo-German protocol of October 29, 1907 dealing with Baltic issues guaranteeing the territorial status quo and preserving the inviolability of both powers in the Baltic.[57] It was assumed that the two riparian nations, Denmark and

---

[55] Taube, *La politique russe*, pp. 128–129.
[56] Torsten Burgman, *Svensk opinion och diplomati under Rysk-Japanska kriget 1904–1905*, Uppsala, 1965, pp. 152 ff; Bestuzhev, *Bor'ba v Rossii*, pp. 150–152.
[57] Adamov, *Sbornik dogovorov Rossii*, pp. 395–396.

Sweden, would conclude corresponding agreements with the two empires guaranteeing the inviolability of their territories and the status quo in the Baltic, that Germany considered the convention of 1856 contradictory to the desired objectives, and that the protocol would be kept secret for the time being.

The most significant and challenging location for Germany along this strategic maritime route was the British Isles, the operational head-quarters of the navy. In June 1897, when he was planning the next phase of the German naval development, Admiral Alfred von Tirpitz, the state secretary of the Imperial Naval Ministry [Kriegsmarinampt], wrote to the German Emperor: "For Germany the most dangerous naval enemy at the present time is England . . . Our fleet must be so constructed that it can unfold its greatest military potential between Heligoland and the Thames."[58] Its major strength, accordingly, must be in battleships rather than cruisers and its purpose would be to neutralize or destroy British sea power.

The concept of a naval role in German foreign relations had begun to develop during a period when the concurrent evolution of the Franco-Russian alliance and the need to prevent the French Atlantic fleet and the Russian Baltic fleet from joining forces to effect a blockade of the German coast and maritime approaches had made the French rather than the British navy appear to be the most immediate antagonist.[59]

It was also a time when the early writings of Admiral Alfred Thayer Mahan were making a strong impact on naval thinking. While the evolution of the new naval role in German foreign policy proceeded from the growing basically commercial interests which had long characterized the German continental and overseas expansion, these were the very same needs which Admiral Mahan had identified as requiring naval protection. In these basic ways, accordingly, the strategic needs of Germany drew considerable encouragement, justification, and guidance from the strategic thinking of Mahan.[60]

The core of the German naval problem was the solution of a twofold predicament, in both cases involving a challenge to the international stature and aspirations of both Britain and Germany. One of these was the realization that the seas beyond Europe were largely controlled by the British navy. This brought many of the leaders of both political and academic life in Germany to the conclusion that a truly independent

---

[58] Tirpitz, *My memoirs*, I, 69–79; Kennedy, "German world policy," 608–609; Steinberg, *Yesterday's deterrent*, pp. 125–148, 209; Steinberg, "The Copenhagen complex," 29; Langer, *Diplomacy of imperialism*, II, 430–442.

[59] Tirpitz, *My memoirs*, I, 67–68; Steinberg, *Yesterday's deterrent*, p. 68.

[60] William Edmund Livezey, *Mahan on sea power*, Norman, OK, 1947, pp. 64–69; Kennedy, *The rise and fall*, pp. 223–224.

exercise of commercial freedom and of access to overseas colonial regions and commercial centers would ultimately demand the destruction of the universal power of Britain.[61] Meanwhile, however, it would seem that the "risk" which Germany was preparing in case Britain would consider attacking the German navy when completed could hardly have been greater than the "risk" Germany would herself experience throughout the twenty-year period of the so-called "danger zone" during which this instrument of destruction would be less than complete and would constitute a challenge, itself inviting destruction by the intended victim. In addition, Tirpitz argued that naval strength of such a magnitude would enhance the alliance value of Germany in a potential coalition with France and Russia.

The German navy, by contrast with the army which had regional and class roots, became the symbol of national unity and of aspirations for national power. National support for the naval program was impressive, particularly if it is realized that the best organized and most articulate parts of this support were directed specifically at Britain.[62] The General German League, which four years later became the Pan-German League, was organized in 1890 as a protest against the Anglo-German agreement of July 1, 1890 by which Germany had recognized a British protectorate over Zanzibar, Pemba, and the dominions of the Sultan of Witu in exchange for the cession of Heligoland to Germany.

Another influential organization, the Navy League, was organized on April 30, 1898, apparently under the direction of Victor Scheinburg of the *Berliner Politische Nachrichten*, financed by the Krupps and other steel producers, and within a year had about 100,000 members. Its journal *Die Flotte* stressed the importance of the navy as "an instrument of world policy." Finally, it is significant that the intellectual leaders who gave their support to this new expression of nationalism included such influential men as Gustav Schmoller, Hans Delbrück, Otto Hintze, and Friedrich Rätzel.

The storm of ill-will toward Britain which was gathering force in Berlin in these years and particularly the fact that it was increasingly furnishing the rationale for large-scale, active naval preparations is often held not to have been widely understood in Britain until 1900. However, the earlier warning signals were quite clear, particularly to those who had the

---

[61] Ludwig Dehio, *Germany and world politics in the twentieth century*, New York, 1960, pp. 78–90; Fritz Fischer, *Germany's aims in the First World War*, London, 1967, pp. 7–18.
[62] Mildred S. Wertheimer, *The Pan-German League 1890–1914*, New York, 1924, pp. 24–26; Langer, *Diplomacy of imperialism*, II, 651–655; Eckart Kehr, *Battleship building and party politics in Germany, 1894–1901; a cross section of the political, social, and ideological preconditions of German imperialism*, trans and ed. Pauline R. Anderson and Eugene N. Anderson, Chicago, 1973, pp. 178–179.

opportunity to observe in the German press and the public forum the views of the numerous advocates of a firmer policy. This was notably true after the publication of the Krüger Telegram on January 3, 1896. Within the next few weeks the British journals, the *Army and Navy Gazette* on January 18, and the *Morning Post* on January 21, followed by others, began to warn of the threat from Berlin.

The impact of the new German naval policy on the British thinking and planning was gradual and cumulative, becoming highly significant after the turn of the century. By this time two other factors had been added: by 1897 Britain had lost the naval lead she had enjoyed a decade earlier and in October 1899 the Boer war had broken out with its revelation of British military backwardness, both emphasizing the obsolescence of isolation. These factors helped to accentuate the significance of the adoption by the German Reichstag on June 28, 1900 of the second naval law, doubling the number of battleships to thirty-eight.[63] This was followed during 1900–1 by the adoption of plans for an 11,600 ton battleship of the Wittlesbach class.

These developments helped to encourage a number of significant changes in Britain's defense and diplomatic comportment. One was the proposal that a new naval base be established at Rosyth on the Firth of Forth directly across the North Sea from a German naval base. This proposal was still unfulfilled, however, at the outbreak of the first world war. Another plan was for the redistribution of British naval forces. In the proposal of November 1904 France still figured as the principal naval adversary. But in the course of the next months the anti-German element had begun to be effective and the further course of the Russo-Japanese war and the direction followed by the Moroccan issue altered the perspective with the recognition of the German naval menace to the exclusion of the French preoccupation.

The new British naval arrangements included three major fleets: the Channel Fleet with its strategic center at Dover, the Atlantic Fleet with its base at Gibraltar, and the Mediterranean Fleet based at Malta. The diplomatic restructuring provided Britain with additional ships for the new defense concentrations. Ships were moved to home waters from the western hemisphere after working out a near alliance with the United States, from the Pacific after the alliance settlements with Japan, and from the Mediterranean after France became a friendly power.

German interests, as the Algeciras conference had disclosed, were active in another significant location along this strategic arc, the region of the passage between the Atlantic and the Mediterranean, not only in

---

[63] Marder, *Anatomy of British sea power*, ch. 24; Kennedy, *The rise and fall*, p. 209; Mackay, "The Admiralty, the German navy," pp. 341–346.

Morocco but also in Spain and its associated islands. In January 1903 a German Morocco Company was founded, supported by the Pan-German League in its demand for a foothold in Morocco.[64] Demands were also made on Spain, which included a cable concession in the Canary Islands to be used, it was assumed, to land a cable on the Moroccan coast as a means of securing a base there for further claims. There was also a proposal for the construction of warships for Spain in return for German control of the arsenal at Ferol. This proposal, however, was quickly neutralized by the French government which gave notice to the Spanish government that France would expect a similar facility at Cartagena.

The reaction of the British, French, and Spanish governments was to take measures to protect their interests against what appeared to be a German effort to extend to the western Mediterranean their influence, which was already a significant factor in the eastern Mediterranean. Britain took action hoping to guarantee her interests in Gibraltar, France to protect her stake in Morocco, and Spain to safeguard her own territorial interests, all acting, however, in such a way as to be least offensive to Germany. The arrangement took the form of an exchange of notes on May 15, 1907 by Britain and France with Spain declaring their wish to preserve the status quo "in the western Mediterranean, on the coast of Morocco, and in that part of the Atlantic Ocean which washes the shores of Europe and Africa." It was agreed also that, should the necessity arise for consultation, it would be tripartite.

German interests and influence had penetrated much more widely and intensively in the eastern than in the western Mediterranean region and were expected to become there a factor of still greater significance. One of these interests was the Bagdad railway which Baron Marschall von Bieberstein identified as the "foundation of German policy in Turkey." Since British and French financial support for this enterprise had in effect been withdrawn in 1903, though the company was left with a considerable surplus, the next section of the railway would cross the Taurus and Amanus ranges and was the most costly part of the operation[65]. It was at this point that Germany had herself to face the task of financing the undertaking and of bringing into focus the enterprises of the Deutsche Bank and the more general Near Eastern activities sponsored directly or indirectly by the German Foreign Office. The section of the railway was completed to Eregli in 1904 but the construction was not resumed until 1910 when the difficult Taurus mountain section as attempted.

[64] Mackay, "The Admiralty, the German navy," pp. 341–346; Monger, *The end of isolation*, pp. 318–322; Busch, *Hardinge of Penshurst*, pp. 119–121.
[65] H. Charles Woods, "The Bagdad railway and its tributaries," *GJ*, L, no. 1 (July 1917), 40; John B. Wolf, *The diplomatic history of the Bagdad railroad*, Columbia, MS, 1936, p. 48.

Another change in German policy was the one delineated in Prince von Bülow's note of February 17, 1906 to the General Staff. This directed a de-emphasis on colonization since settlers might have to be sacrificed in case of war. Instead, the focus would be placed increasingly on the economic development of regions such as the Ottoman Empire which were accessible by overland communications and therefore even in war less vulnerable to the British navy. The history of the railway from 1906 to 1911 was essentially the history of the effort to implement this policy in the face of difficulties which confronted the builders and which, in the perspective of the pre-war period, prevented its completion.

The man chosen for this momentous assignment was Karl Helfferich who as a professor at the University of Berlin and as a writer on the gold monetary standard and on the promotion of foreign trade had gained wide recognition as an economist.[66] He had also become known to Chancellor Bülow and to the Kaiser and was perhaps their chief adviser on matters pertaining to the Near East. In 1901 he became assistant secretary in the Colonial Department of the Ministry of Foreign Affairs. In 1906 he was appointed assistant general manager of the Anatolian railway and a year later, at the age of 34, he became assistant general director of the Deutsche Bank with general supervision over all the enterprises of the bank in the Near East. The choice of so distinguished and promising a person for this position at a time when the railway venture was facing difficulties was as encouraging to Germany as it was disappointing in some foreign circles.

The German venture in the Middle East, in fact, did make some progress. By 1907 the Anatolian railway had, by contract with the Ottoman government, undertaken a land reclamation project, the irrigation of 132,000 acres of arid land lying southeast of Konia, a commitment of considerable significance in this desert region.[67] German banks were also established in the Ottoman Empire, including the Deutsche Bank, the Deutsche Orientbank, and others, functioning as promoters of German and more general enterprise. Even by 1907 the results were evident. Both imports and exports to and from Germany had by then shown progress. Ottoman exports to Germany had grown from 30,400,000 marks in 1900 to 55,100,000 in 1907 while German imports to the Ottoman Empire had grown from 34,400,000 to 81,500,000 marks in the same years.

A further issue of major concern in this region for France and for Europe in general grew out of an unsuccessful attempt of Count Kasimir Badeni, the prime minister of Austria-Hungry, to solve a Czech–German

---

[66] John G. Williamson, *Karl Helfferich, 1872–1924. Economist, financier, politician*, Princeton, 1971, pp. 78–83; Earle, *Turkey, the Great Powers*, pp. 97 ff.

[67] Woods, "The Bagdad railway," 40–41.

language problem by two laws of 1897. The outcome was the stimulation of a major national cause which stirred up the already discordant nationalities of the Habsburg Empire and threatened its stability if not its existence.[68] Groups such as the Pan-German League welcomed such an opportunity to fan the flames of discontent and encourage the dissolution of the Habsburg regime.

Some of those who held this view hoped that should a dissolution of the empire occur it could be expected that the German portion of Austria–Hungry might be incorporated into the German Empire. This might create a much enlarged German Empire reaching across Europe from the North and Baltic Seas to the Mediterranean. In addition, by 1899 Germany had been seeking a port at Trieste, the location of the Austrian naval base on the Adriatic Sea. To some in Paris this suggested a German Empire with naval bases at Trieste, Constantinople, and in Morocco in addition to the existing ones in the Baltic and North Seas.[69]

The incident in Czechoslovakia had occurred at a time when France was experiencing a series of political misfortunes. In August 1898, when France was caught in a humiliating position at Fashoda and needed support, Russia issued a rescript to the diplomatic corps proposing what was to become the First Hague Peace Conference. Whether the Russian desire was to promote disarmament in order to avoid the need to provide her armed forces with the new rapid fire field guns was not certain. It was suspected, however, that the disarmament proposal might have been inspired by the concurrent German and Austrian plans to equip their armies with such new firearms. The disturbing fact remained that Russia was proposing a disarmament conference at the very moment when her ally, France, was facing a show-down with Britain at Fashoda. In October 1899 the outbreak of the Boer war was a blow to France's immediate enemy, Britain, but in the longer run a blow to a prospective ally against Germany.

Two major diplomatic innovations followed from the apprehension aroused by the fear of the augmentation of the German Empire. The first of these was the principal objective of Delcassé's journey to St. Petersburg in August 1899. The disappearance from the family of nations of Austria–Hungary would mean the elimination of the Triple Alliance which had been the rationale for the Franco-Russian alliance. It was Delcassé's wish to base the Franco-Russian alliance henceforth on the

---

[68] Robert A. Kann, *A History of the Habsburg Empire, 1626–1918*, Berkeley, 1980, pp. 428–429.

[69] Irwin Abrams, "The Austrian question at the turn of the twentieth century," *JCEA* IV, no. 2 (July 1944), 186–201; Eurof Walters, "Franco-Russian discussions on the partition of Austria-Hungary," *SEER*, XXVIII, no. 70 (Nov. 1949), 184–192; Ritter, *The sword and the sceptor*, II, pp. 107–228.

balance of power in Europe. Also, while not able to prevent Germany from absorbing the German portions or even all of Austria, nevertheless he wanted to prevent Germany from acquiring any part of the Adriatic coastline.

The details of a new accord were accordingly elaborated by an exchange of letters on August 8–9, 1899 leaving the chiefs of staff of France and Russia to work out the military details in conferences during 1900 and 1901. The second major diplomatic change, the development of the Anglo-French entente and of an Anglo-Franco-Russian understanding, was accomplished by 1907.

7   Imperial truce

Formation of the Entente

The Anglo-Russian negotiations, suspended at the outbreak of the Russo-Japanese war, were resumed at the earliest possible moment after the conclusion of the Portsmouth agreement. Sir Charles Hardinge, the British ambassador to Russia since May 16, 1904, in early September 1905 sent a note of congratulations on the signing of the peace to Count Lamsdorf, the minister of foreign affairs. In response, Lamsdorf sent a message which included an invitation to resume the negotiations.[1] Behind this cordial exchange was the goodwill built up in the course of the amicable settlement earlier that year of the North Sea incident, in part also by Hardinge's persistent efforts to overcome Russian ill-will toward Britain generated during the war. Behind the cordial exchange was also the weakened condition of the Russian Empire and the restraint on her freedom of action by the emergence on her eastern and western flanks of Japan and Germany.

It was also in September that Hardinge had a significant interview with Nikolai Genrikhovich Hartwig, the immediate assistant of Lamsdorf, who gave more specific encouragement to the resumption of the Anglo-Russian negotiations. Hartwig stated that Anglo-Russian cooperation in Macedonia and Crete showed that there was no need for conflict between these nations in the Near East and hoped for a situation in which Russia could be left "a free hand for the impending struggle with Germany on the shores of the Bosphorus."[2] Hartwig concluded by saying that Russia had no real ambition to invade India, that the existing Afghan–Russian frontier was ideal, and that he was sure that a satisfactory settlement could be reached with respect to Persia.

Those in the British government who shared Hardinge's sense of urgency about the importance of a close link with Russia, his suspicion of German motives and ambitions, and his concern lest these two nations form a diplomatic affiliation, included some influential persons. The

---

[1] Busch, *Hardinge of Penshurst*, pp. 91–93; Steiner, *The Foreign Office*, pp. 92–96.
[2] No. 573 Hardinge to Lansdowne, Sept. 26, 1905, FO 65/1702.

minister of foreign affairs, Sir Edward Grey, was from the start of his tenure of office committed to the ententes especially with France but also with Russia, but only gradually came to share Hardinge's distrustful attitude toward Germany. When Hardinge left his ambassadorial position in St. Petersburg to become permanent undersecretary of foreign affairs on February 1, 1906, he was replaced by Sir Arthur Nicolson. Nicolson had had long experience in the foreign service, most recently as the British representative at the Algeciras conference and his views on the current situation were very similar to those of Hardinge. In addition, both had an invaluable advantage, close association with King Edward. The King had little sympathy for and sometimes little rapport with his imperial German relative, Emperor Wilhelm.

The preliminary discussions which took place during the last months of 1905 are significant because they were the outcome of a fundamental reconsideration of Russian foreign policy in the perspective of the nation's new international position. The humiliating defeat, the enervating revolution, and the pervading weakness and disorientation were unavoidable conditions which influenced all possible courses of action. In this setting the Björkö treaty was an invitation to pursue a course in close relationship with Germany or, perhaps alternatively, with Germany, Austria, and France. This was the route to security, as some saw it, but which would, as others saw it, have been a way of showing defiance or even of seeking revenge toward Britain and Japan.

A fundamental problem with which both the British and French had to contend in accomplishing an Anglo-Russian accommodation was the attraction Germany held for Russia. This encompassed the fact that, however unpopular Germany may have been to some in Russia, German relations with both the court and the government were close and friendly. There was also an awareness of and respect for the German support of the monarchical principle, the need to remain on good terms with a country which had such military strength, and the economic and politically dominant position of Germany in Europe.

Fear of Germany increased during the Algeciras conference in both London and St. Petersburg. In the latter capital, however, this tended at first to bring to the fore some of those who saw the danger as being so great that only an alliance directly with Germany would provide adequate security, Three major factors, nevertheless, continued to point to Britain as the nation which had a particularly significant role to play in Russia's future: the sheer ineptness of German diplomacy which during the Algeciras conference and loan negotiations appeared to be leading Europe toward war and almost literally driving Russia into the arms of Britain; the readiness of both France and Britain to provide an attractive diplomatic plan for an Anglo-Russian accommodation; and the particular capability of Britain to provide assistance in Russia's Near Eastern difficulties with Germany, especially at the Turkish straits, and in the Far East where Russia needed assistance in making a rapprochement with Britain's ally, Japan.

One of the most difficult questions which confronted Russia was how to achieve the anticipated benefits of an understanding with Britain without risking an adverse response from Germany. Failure to resolve this problem could mean the exertion of greater pressure on Russia to accept the Björkö agreement or a demand for a voice in the settlement of the Persian problem. The latter could put Russia in a position similar to that of France in the Morocco situation. During the negotiations Izvolsky was left in no doubt as to the intense interest of Germany in their subject matter and proceedings. In May 1906 when negotiations were ready to begin, word was passed on from Berlin to Schoen, the German ambassador in St. Petersburg, for the benefit of the Russian government and particularly of Izvolsky, that should any subject be discussed by Britain and Russia which concerned Germany, such as the Bagdad railway, Berlin must be consulted.[3]

In October 1906 when the exchanges had reached a serious point Izvolsky went in person to Berlin for more direct discussion. The visit was somewhat camouflaged to appear as part of a purely private journey in the course of which he left St. Petersburg on October 1, avoiding Berlin by going first to Tegernsee in Bavaria for a family visit.[4] He then proceeded to Paris where he met with President Fallières and with the minister of foreign affairs, Léon Bourgeois, and explained to the British ambassador in Paris, Sir Francis Bertie, his reasons for turning down the invitation to be received by King Edward in London.[5] He explained that he had already made commitments with the French government and that going to London would encourage the suspicion that the discussions with Britain had advanced further than in fact they had. This was a clear warning that, as Sir Arthur Nicolson appraised the situation, during the negotiations Izvolsky would be keeping "one eye on Berlin."[6]

His stay in Berlin took place during October 28–30 and was occupied by discussions with the Kaiser, the chancellor, Prince von Bülow, and Heinrich von Tschirschky und Bögendorff, the minister of foreign affairs who had succeeded Richthofen earlier that year and whose assumption of

[3] No. 102 Bülow to Schoen, May 19, 1906, *GP*, XXV-1, 11–12.
[4] Izvolsky to Nelidov, Sept. 14, Nov. 8, 1906, in Iswolsky, *Au service de la Russie*, I, 209, 215–217; Seeger, *Recollections of a foreign minister*, p. 251.
[5] Bertie to Grey, Oct. 22 (2 dispatches on the same day), 1906, *BD*, IV, 243–244.
[6] Nicolson, *Sir Arthur Nicolson*, p. 215.

office soon helped to bring about the resignation of Friedrich von Holstein.[7]

Izvolsky went to Berlin for at least two important reasons. One was the need to convince some of his hesitant colleagues that Germany would not really object to an agreement with Britain.[8] The other reason, important in the immediate sense but especially in the longer range, was hinted at by Izvolsky's omission of a visit to London during his tour in western Europe. Fundamentally, as Benckendorff explained, this amounted to the sober reality that in her present circumstances Russia could not afford to be on bad terms with Germany.[9]

Remembering that Germany had professed to have only commercial interests in Morocco, it was only prudent, as Izvolsky had stated to Stephen Pichon, the French minister of foreign affairs, to learn what Germany meant by a similar assertion with respect to Persia lest Russia find herself in the same unenviable position as France had been regarding Morocco. This was particularly true since it would be precisely in that very region of Persia which would probably fall to Russia in case of a regional apportionment that Germany might also have competitive banking, railway, or commercial interests.

Izvolsky had discovered that the discord dating from the period of the Algeciras conference was still strong in Berlin and was careful to make it clear to Bülow that the Anglo-Russian negotiations were not aimed at Germany. Their purpose, he emphasized, was to eliminate points of Anglo-Russian discord and to give his assurance that if anything were discussed touching on German interests Germany would be consulted. He also called attention to what he saw as the aggressive intentions of Japan and emphasized that Russia was in no condition to face another war with Japan.[10] This meant that Russia was forced to conclude an agreement with Britain dealing with Tibet, Afghanistan, and Persia in order to pacify that southern frontier. Until the Far East was also stabilized, however, Russia would be unable to play an active role in European politics.

Bülow told Izvolsky that it was in the German interest that the Bagdad railway be considered a German, i.e., not an international, undertaking and that she be consulted on any question related to it. Izvolsky assured Bülow on this matter and stated that Russia was ready in the meantime to enter into an agreement with Germany on any matters of common concern, especially Baltic affairs, and to mollify the German impression of

---

[7] Cecil, *German diplomatic service*, pp. 298–300.   [8] Robbins, *Sir Edward Grey*, p. 161.
[9] Bertie to Grey, Oct. 22 (second dispatch) 1906, *BD*, IV, 243–244.
[10] No. 333 Lascelles to Grey, Oct. 29, 1906, *BD*, IV, 246–249; Grigortsevich, *Dal'nevostochnaia politika*, pp. 121–123.

the future Anglo-Russian agreement.[11] It was clearly a relief to Izvolsky to have met apparent acceptance of these assurances and to have found no determined German opposition to the Anglo-Russian negotiations.

Another issue, that concerning the Turkish straits, loomed very large in Russo-German relations because it was important to Germany and because an influential group in Russia was concerned about it both for its own sake and because of its importance to Germany. The growing German stake in the railways and economy of the Ottoman Empire was transforming the balance of power not only at the straits but also in the Balkans. At the same time, the Russian diplomatic program in this region, as it emerged under the leadership of Izvolsky, called for free egress through the Turkish straits into the Mediterranean and a more favorable regime for Russia in the Balkans. Russian emphasis on her desire for the free use of the straits was, as the British government readily acknowledged, in the most immediate sense a consequence of her experience during the Russo-Japanese war when Britain had kept a number of Russian warships bottled up in the Black Sea that would have been useful in the Pacific.

The situation at the straits had already changed to such an extent by 1903 that a meeting of the Committee of Imperial Defense on February 11 of that year concluded that even if Russia had possession of Constantinople and completely free use of the straits "it would not fundamentally alter [i.e., for Britain] the present strategic position in the Mediterranean."[12] This was at a time, however, when Britain was considering the possibility of agreements with both France and Russia and was ready to offer Russia a settlement regarding the straits which she would be likely to welcome. The outbreak of the Russo-Japanese war, however, halted the venture.

The meeting of February 11 had considered two significant questions. The first concerned the difference it would make to the balance of power in the Mediterranean if Russia were to obtain, by the possession of Constantinople, free access to the Mediterranean Sea through the Dardanelles, the latter being, as was still the case in 1906, closed against other powers. The unanimous response was that while this would provide certain naval advantage for Russia it would not fundamentally alter the existing strategic position in the Mediterranean.

Secondly, it was held that Russian access to Constantinople and the

---

[11] Rozental', *Diplomaticheskaia istoriia*, p. 132.
[12] Balfour Memorandum, Feb. 14, 1903, Cab 4/1–1B; Hardinge, "Memorandum respecting the Passage of Russian War Vessels through the Dardanelles and Bosphorus," Nov. 16, 1906, FO 800/91; Marian Kent, "Constantinople and Asiatic Turkey, 1905–1914," in F.H. Hinsley (ed.), *British foreign policy under Sir Edward Grey*, Cambridge, 1977, pp. 156–157.

Dardanelles and the use of them would not make any marked difference in British strategic dispositions as compared with existing conditions. Consequently, it would be possible to make important concessions to Russia in relation to the Dardanelles without altering fundamentally the existing British strategic position in the Mediterranean.

With the end of the Russo-Japanese war and of the Algeciras conference, the Russian government raised the subject of the straits. The suggestion of the Russian chargé d'affaires in London, Stanislav Al'fonsovich Poklevsky-Koz'ell, in late November 1906, that Russia would welcome British support in bringing about some modification of the straits regime was repeated with some modification in March 1907 by the Russian ambassador, Count Benckendorff.[13] He stated that Russia would like to have the straits opened to permit exit from the Black Sea if this privilege could be limited only to herself. If this were not possible, she would prefer that, in view of her present insufficiency of naval power, the question should not even be raised. In the interview with Benckendorff, Grey took a very positive position, saying that it would be regrettable to settle the current issues regarding Asian frontiers while leaving unresolved the question of the straits which "had been the root of the difficulties between the two countries for two generations."

Valentine Chirol, the prominent *Times* reporter, joined in this positive attitude toward resolving, in cooperation with Russia, the straits problem along lines congenial to Russia.[14] The principal opponent, he maintained, would be Germany and such a joint effort could well serve to "cement" the Anglo-Russian entente as the Algeciras experience had cemented the Anglo-French entente. The straits issue of course entailed more than just the German railway passing through this contested region, important as this and all its economic and strategic implications were. It included also the close and special relationship evolving between Germany and Turkey, an influence ultimately cordial neither to Britain nor Russia.

By this time the negotiations were under way and Britain was already considering this option. A memorandum of November 16, 1906 reviewed the situation and in effect reaffirmed the conclusion of three years before. It added that Britain was prepared to make a concession to Russia by approving her desire for an alteration in her favor of the straits regime. It

[13] No. 532 Grey to Nicolson, Nov. 30, 1906, IO 2718–1907; Grey memorandum, Mar. 15, 1907, FO 418/38; Oswald Hauser, "Die Englisch–Russische Konvention von 1907 und die Meerengenfrage," in M. Göhring and A. Scharff, *Geschichtliche Krafte und Entscheidungen: Festschrift zum fünfundsechzigsten Geburtstage von Otto Becker*, Wiesbaden, 1954, pp. 238–240; No. 120 Grey to Nicolson, Mar. 19, 1907, *BD*, IV, 280–281.

[14] Chirol to Nicolson, Mar. 19, 1907, Nicolson Papers; Evgenii Viktorovich Tarlé, "Evropa v epokhu imperializma, 1871–1919," in his *Sochineniia*, vol. 5, Moscow, 1958, pp. 146–148; Nicolson to Grey, Mar. 27, 1907, FO 800/71.

emphasized, however, that this could not be the subject of a bilateral agreement since other nations had an interest in the straits.

A General Staff memorandum worked out at this time was in effect a reappraisal of a situation which had been examined several times before, each time with about the same disappointing conclusion for Britain.[15] The Committee of Imperial Defense had asked the General Staff and the Naval Intelligence department the very basic question as to the practicability of forcing the Dardanelles either with or without a cooperating force as the most expeditious way to bring a war with Turkey to a prompt and satisfactory conclusion.

In the first place, the General Staff memorandum recommended against unaided action by the fleet. A combined naval-military expedition, it suggested, might succeed by aiming at the Gallipoli Peninsula destroying the forts at the entrance, and expecting that such a blow would topple the Sultan from power. But, an operation aimed at the head of Islam must be expected to affect other Muslims, including those under British rule. A general uprising of Muslims against the British could drive them from the straits and render their positions in India difficult. The General Staff recommended against even such a joint expedition on the grounds that the risk was too high. This, accordingly, was the message Britain was prepared to give to Russia.

The British response to the Russian proposal was in fact to make a counter-proposal dependent for its fulfillment on the Russian performance in the current negotiations.[16] The thought was emphasized that if the straits question should arise it would be a significant aid in giving it proper consideration if British public opinion had been favorably impressed or if some tangible benefit had been given such as Russian support of the status quo in the Persian Gulf. Meanwhile, Russia accepted the original British statement, expressing pleasure at British willingness to discuss the issue and "that closing of Straits is no longer a cardinal point of British policy."[17]

Anglo-Russian negotiations had opened with the Tibetan question on the grounds that it was considered relatively easy to settle. However, the recurrence of the Persian financial problem and the involvement in it of Germany gave Persia a priority in the Anglo-Russian discussions which it was to retain. The reduced financial condition of the Russian government which made it impossible for Russia to supply the required funds opened

---

[15] "General Staff Memorandum upon the Possibility of a Joint Naval and Military Attack upon the Dardanelles," Dec. 19, 1906, Cab 4/2.

[16] Hardinge to Nicolson, Mar. 29, 1907, Nicolson Papers; Bovykin, *Ocherki istorii vneshnei politiki*, p. 67.

[17] Nicolson to Grey, Mar. 27, 1907, FO 800/71; Hardinge note, Apr. 2, 1907, No. 65 Nicolson to Grey, Apr. 14, 1907, *BD*, IV, 286.

the opportunity for Persia to seek alternate help and for Britain and Germany to furnish it. In particular, the insolvency of the Russian Discount and Loan Bank, the instrument of Russia's aggressive policy in Persia, was disclosed in the spring of 1906.[18] This situation became known at a time when Russia had for some months been unsuccessfully endeavoring to conclude with Persia an agreement which would have given more formal recognition of her privileged position in the country; instead, the lack of funds promised a curtailment of the Russian advance in Persia.

The desperate situation was discussed at a special session of the Committee of Finance on June 12, 1906. It was decided to transform the bank into an institution receptive to private capital both Russian and foreign and thus no longer the instrument of Russian policy that it had been. Persia was to be urged to look to both Russia and Britain for a major loan. Under these circumstances and with both German and Belgian capital apparently awaiting the opportunity to break through the financial barrier, the Persian government in August sought from Britain a loan of 500,000 tomans through the Indo-European Telegraph Company on condition that the concession of the company, granted for fourteen years, be extended for twenty years.

A special ministerial conference of August 29, 1906 dealing with financial policy in Persia reflected the new course in Anglo-Russian relations. The conference held unanimously that further financial conflict with Britain was impossible, that the best policy was one of agreement with Britain, and voted to accept British proposals for satisfying Persian needs. The new regulations for the Discount and Loan Bank, proposed by the minister of finance and inviting the use of both French and Belgian capital, were approved by the Council of Ministers and, on June 22, 1907, sanctioned by the Emperor.

The conversion of this new Persian policy into specific negotiable components capable of being reconciled with British interests before the intrusion of the more competitive German influences was the subject of a special ministerial conference held on September 20, 1906.[19] The conference dealt with Persia in relation to the negotiations for an agreement with Britain, and Izvolsky and Kokovtsov were determined and effective advocates of an understanding with Britain. The presiding officer,

---

[18] Anan'ich, "Uchetno-ssudnyi bank Persii," pp. 306–314; Anan'ich, *Rossiiskoe samoderzhavie*, pp. 125–131; Anan'ich, "Krizis ekonomicheskoi politika tsarizma," pp. 270–271; Alevtina Fedorovna Ostal'tseva, "K voprosu ob imperialisticheskikh protivorechiiakh mezhdu Angliei i Rossiei vo vremia zakliucheniia soglasheniia 1907 g.", *Nauchnye doklady vysshei shkoly, istoricheskie nauki*, no. 4 (1958), 147–148.

[19] Popov, "Anglo-russkoe sopernichestvo," 54–61 (Journal of the conference of September 20, 1906); Hauser, "Die Englisch-Russische Konvention," 233–236.

Izvolsky, pointed out the necessity of harmonizing the various Russian views on the subject as well as trying to understand the views of Britain, the nation whose interests ran so close geographically to those of Russia itself on a continent-wide scale. The moment had come, Izvolsky indicated, when Russia must decide between two alternatives, neither wholly satisfactory. One would serve her interests in part. The other would present a situation in which one could be assured that Russia's well-being could be guaranteed or, given the conditions of rivalry, whether she would be in a position to make her voice heard in future international councils. The immediate issue of a loan to Persia, since it must now be decided in concurrence with Britain, raised the question of a more general agreement and, consequently, of recognition of the spheres of interest desired by Britain.

Kokovtsov, as minister of finance, addressed the question of the loan but stated that it was difficult to separate financial and economic questions, and went on to point out that these in turn were inseparable from major political developments. This brought him to the observation that the political significance of Russia had recently been considerably diminished and, consequently, this meant that, as compared with the former policy of seeking an outlet on the Persian Gulf with a railway leading to it, Russia must come to grips with the reality that such a plan was viewed as hostile by Britain. Finally, Russia had to recognize the fact that Britain remained in firm control of southern Persia and that attacking her in order to achieve an outlet on the Gulf would at present be impossible.

Kokovtsov advocated that, on the contrary, Russia should seek a firm agreement with Britain which would control loans and establish the legality of the Russian sphere of interest in the region bordering Russia and lying north of a line drawn through Kasri-Shirin-Hamadan-Teheran-Mashkhad-Ashkhabad. This line would close off on its western extremity the most likely point of entrance of the Bagdad railway into Persia by the route open to the German railway company according to the concession of 1903. This agreement permitted the construction of a branch of the Bagdad railway from Sadiye on the main line up to Khaneqin on the Persian frontier. Locating this frontier crossing at a point where it would enter Persia in the Russian zone would prevent German railway access without Russian approval to the Transcaspian railway, to the capital of Persia, and to a region in which Russia had already established a firm footing through the acquisition of concessions and by other means.

Both Kokovtsov and Izvolsky were concerned about the security of the section of the Russian frontier which was conterminous with that of

Persia, and of the large Russian expenditure in Persia of over 70 million rubles in loans and enterprises in addition to the debt of over 30 million rubles owed to Russia by the Shah and his family. Kokovtsov could see no possibility in the near future of subjecting the country to Russia. On the contrary, the construction of the Bagdad railway meant the approach of German influence to Persia and, he emphasized particularly, to a region near Russia. Russia must not permit either Germany or Britain to penetrate the region of Persia bordering on Russia.

In later correspondence with opponents of an Anglo-Russian agreement, Izvolsky stressed that Russia could be excluded from Persia not only by the growth of the Persian revolutionary movement but also by the growing influence of Germany.[20] Russia in her present state of military and political weakness would be unable to continue the struggle in the east with Britain. Instead, Russia and Britain must consider mutual concessions.

Sir Arthur Nicolson received a draft of the British proposal for a settlement regarding Persia in mid-November, 1906, just after Izvolsky's return from Berlin.[21] Since some of the issues had already been discussed in a preliminary way in September when the loan was under consideration, Nicolson was able to start with considerable knowledge of the positions already taken by each of the parties. The issues which had emerged were the fundamental ones concerning the delineation of Persia into spheres of influence or interests, the struggles for Seistan, and the influential presence of Germany.

The proposal included the following features: respect for the integrity and independence of Persia and along with this the maintenance of good order and pacific development within the country and the establishment for all countries of equal opportunity for commerce and industry; the observance of a special interest in the recognition of peace and order within the Persian provinces contiguous to the Russian frontier on the one hand and the frontiers of Afghanistan and Baluchistan on the other; an engagement on the part of Britain not to seek any concessions of a political or commercial nature between a demarcation line yet to be drawn and the Russian frontier on the one hand, and on the part of Russia to observe similar restrictions in the area between a line drawn from the Afghan frontier through Gazik, Birjand, Kerman, and Bandar Abbas and the frontiers of Afghanistan and Baluchistan on the other.

[20] Bestuzhev, "Bor'ba klassov i partii," p. 138; Ostal'tseva, "K voprosu," 148.
[21] No. 735 Nicolson to Grey, Nov, 4, 1906, enclosing Napier to Nicolson, Nov. 3, 1906, *BD*, IV, 408–411; Nicolson to Grey, Nov. 5, 1906, Nicolson Papers; Nicolson to Grey, Nov. 7, 1906, *BD*, IV, 250–251; No. 16 Staal to Giers, Feb. 19, 1888, in Aleksandr Feliskovich Meyendorff, *Correspondence diplomatique de M. de Staal [Egor Egorovich Staal], 1884–1900*, 2 vols. 1929, I, 392–393, II, 136–137; Ostal'tseva, "K voprosu," 148–154.

When Izvolsky became minister of foreign affairs in May 1906 he had disseminated a series of articles in *Novoe Vremia* while a sympathetic publicist, D. G. Ianchevetsky, had developed similar ideas in *Rossia* and *Sankt Peterburgskie Vedomosti*. Both advocated a policy of accommodation with Japan, hoping to reach the opponents of such a course. Ianchevetsky, in addition, urged the strengthening of the Russian Far East by the settlement of population, the promotion of agricultural self-sufficiency, the construction of an Amur railway, the augmentation of the regular military forces to replace the out-moded cossacks, representation of the people of this region in the Duma, eventual return of southern Sakhalin to Russia, retention of the porto franco in that area, and other measures.

The Japanese government responded to the Russian proposal in June, a policy for this action having been established at a joint meeting of cabinet and genro on May 22 at the home of the prime minister, Saionji Kimmochi.[22] A resolution was adopted defining a fundamental policy consisting of two complementary directives: that measures should be taken immediately in Manchuria to prepare against a Russian war of revenge; and that steps should also be taken to win over Russia and to encourage her to forget the past. Japan was thus prepared to talk peace while pursuing a vigorous defense policy and by July 1906 the first discussions were held at St. Petersburg between the Russian plenipotentiary, Senator Nikolai Andreevich Malevsky-Malevich, later the Russian ambassador to Japan, and the Japanese minister, Baron Motono.

The main Russian objective for seeking to confirm the status quo was complicated internally by the demand for the abolition of the porto franco in the Russian Far East, vigorously expressed at a special conference on September 24 by representatives of the Moscow stock market. It was also complicated by Japanese reiteration of her demands for the free navigation of the Amur and Sungari rivers, advantageous rights of transporting her wares into Siberia, and unlimited fishing rights along the coast of the Russian Far East, demands which the Russian press referred to as the economic conquest by Japan of Manchuria and the entire Russian Far East. Russia on her part was also trying to enhance her Far Eastern position, demanding that China "recognize the validity of conventions and agreements signed by Russian agents and Chinese local officials in 1901–1902." These included concessions for the operation of gold, iron, and coal mines in the Manchurian regions of Heilungkiang and Kirin.[23]

Russo-Japanese negotiations had by November 1906 reached a stalemate, a point at which S. A. Kotliarevsky, a Constitutional Democrat,

---

[22] Berton, "The secret Russo-Japanese alliance," p. 3; Bestuzhev, *Bor'ba v Rossii*, pp. 170–171.   [23] Edwards, "The Japanese Alliance," 342.

professor of law at Moscow University, and a commentator on foreign policy for *Russkaia Mysl*, suggested in that journal that negotiations be broken off. At the same time, the governor general of the Amur, General Pavel Fedorovich Unterberger, forewarned that another war with Japan was inevitable.[24] Grigorii Antonovich Planson, the Russian consul general in Seoul, visited Japan in the fall of 1906 and reported the disappointment over the Portsmouth treaty among the people of Japan who had dreamed of an indemnity and of the acquisition of a vast territory up to Lake Baikal.

These aspirations, Planson stated, were part of a surge of nationalist feeling.[25] He also reported the extent of Japanese military preparations and the awareness in Tokyo of Russian unpreparedness to defend the Russian Far East, particularly Vladivostok. He predicted that when the present Japanese armament program was completed the state of preparedness would be as good as it had been in 1903, and that if negotiations were to fail there would be an ultimatum and an attack on Vladivostok by land and sea. These appraisals were supported by the reports of the Russian military attaché in Japan, V. K. Samoilov, and of the Russian minister, I. P. Bakhmetev.

A special conference met on December 3, 1906 to discuss whether to make further concessions to Japan or to prepare for war.[26] Izvolsky's defense of making concessions on the grounds of necessity was accepted in spite of the military opposition. The Council of State Defense which met on December 10, to consider measures for the defense of the Far East confronted a situation in which, as they saw it, Japan was planning a war. It was also feared that the size of Japan's land forces concentrated in Korea and Manchuria was sufficient to undertake the occupation of all Manchuria and to lay siege to Vladivostok and the lower Amur. The General Staff was directed to draw up plans for defense against a backdrop of demands from General Unterberger for the immediate dispatch to the Far East of a large military force. The tension was, however, abated sufficiently to permit the negotiations to proceed when Izvolsky arranged for the early withdrawal of the Russian forces from northern Manchuria instead of waiting until April 15, 1907, the time stipulated in the Portsmouth treaty.

The Russian chargé d'affaires in London, Poklevsky-Koz'ell, visited Grey on November 28, before Russo-Japanese differences had been

---

[24] Otto Becker, *Der Ferne Osten und das Schicksal Europas 1907–1918*, Leipzig, 1940, p. 10; Bestuzhev, *Bor'ba v Rossii*, p. 163.

[25] Leonid Nikolaevich Kutakov, *Portsmutskii mirnyi dogovor (iz istorii otnoshenii Iaponii s Rossiei i SSSR, 1905–1945 gg.)*, Moscow, 1961, p. 88.

[26] Bestuzhev, *Bor'ba v Rossii*, pp. 163–164; Grigortsevich, *Dal'nevostochnaia politika*, pp. 110–111.

moderated, to discuss Japanese activities in the Far East and to suggest that it would be highly desirable if Russia could obtain from Britain a guarantee of the status quo in that region.[27] This, he stated, might have "a certain moral effect upon the Japanese and need not clash with the conditions of our Japanese alliance."

This call for British intervention in the suspended Russo-Japanese negotiations received at first a cool reception from the British government, particularly since the Anglo-Russian negotiations had also come to a halt. Hardinge expressed this view in a communication to Nicolson, saying that Britain had not intervened in the Portsmouth negotiations and saw no reason for intervention in this case.[28] He added, taking note of the stalemated Persian negotiations, that Russia had thus far done nothing to entitle her to make claims on Britain and added: "If Izvolsky raises the question, say you are without instructions." There was also some concern that British intervention might lead to estrangement with Japan.[29]

Accordingly the message was transmitted to Poklevsky-Koz'ell by Hardinge that a British representation to Japan was out of the question. Nicolson at this point suggested that Izvolsky might hesitate to conclude an Anglo-Russian agreement unless Russo-Japanese accommodation had been reached since he might fear that concluding a treaty with Britain and accepting the restrictions this might entail in the Middle East would leave him committed and without leverage in dealing with Japan with respect to the Far East where restrictions might also be encountered.[30]

The next effort to obtain British support was a suggestion from Poklevsky-Koz'ell of a reciprocal Russo-Japanese declaration of their recognition of the status quo and territorial rights of the two countries along the lines of the Anglo-Japanese treaty which only raised Hardinge's suspicions that Izvolsky was trying to enlarge the Anglo-Russian agreement to include the entire Far East.[31]

The British attitude, however, finally changed because, as Grey wrote, Russo-Japanese negotiations had gone beyond the original objective of dealing only with items left from the Portsmouth negotiations and had reached the point where there was "a distinct connection between" the Anglo-Russian and Russo-Japanese negotiations "and the two sets of negotiations ought to proceed pari passu."[32] The Japanese ambassador agreed to this and mutual promises were exchanged to keep each other informed of the progress of the negotiations. Later, the British hoped that

[27] No. 532 Grey to Nicolson, Nov. 30, 1906. *BD*, IV, 254–255.
[28] Hardinge to Nicolson, Dec. 12, 1906, Nicolson Papers.
[29] Ibid.   [30] No. 41 Nicolson to Grey, Jan. 19, 1907, FO 371/269.
[31] Hardinge to Nicolson, Jan. 23, 1907, Nicolson Papers.
[32] Hardinge to Nicolson, Mar. 19, 1907, Nicolson Papers; No. 51 Grey to Lowther, Mar. 7, 1907, FO 371/269; Nicolson to Grey, Mar. 27, 1907, FO 800/71.

1. Manchuria

these two agreements might be concluded "as simultaneously as possible" and that each might contain a similar article guaranteeing "the integrity and independence of China." The coincidence of the signing came, in fact, to be viewed as a way of assuring that they would in fact both be concluded.

Japan and entente

The commanding strategic-diplomatic position of Japan after her victorious emergence from the war forced a reversal of the priority order agreed upon by Britain and Russia for the negotiation of their proposed agreement. In June 1906 the negotiation of the Anglo-Russian compact, then considered diplomatically unrelated to a Russo-Japanese accord, had started with the Tibetan question because it was thought to be easier to resolve. Within six months both Anglo-Russian and Russo-Japanese negotiations were stalemated and it was soon apparent that a clue to the resumption of the diplomatic process was the involvement of Japan. It was decided that an Anglo-Russian understanding would be related to and even dependent upon the achievement by Russia of a satisfactory settlement with Japan. Finally, it became clear that the clue to the further activation of this chain of events would be a Franco-Japanese understanding and that the clue to such an agreement was a loan to Japan.

The diplomatic deadlock in the case of the Russo-Japanese negotiations was, accordingly, broken by the timely and successful intervention of the French minister of foreign affairs, Stephen Pichon. France, in fact, had her own reasons for wanting a settlement with Japan. The Japanese victory in a war in which France had assisted Russia even to the extent of permitting the Russian fleet to use the port facilities at Cam Ranh Bay in Indochina had raised considerable apprehension in the Comité de l'Asie Française and in the French government itself. Most immediately, there was the question of the security of these Far Eastern possessions in addition to the French interests in Yünnan, such as railway rights which were strategically somewhat comparable to those of Russia in Manchuria in that they were located in the vicinity of the victorious, growing Japanese Empire.

The Japanese ambassador to France, Kurino Shinichiro, supported this assessment when he stated in his report of the negotiations that in his view the principal reason the French government wanted an entente with Japan was their concern about the security of Indochina. That this was generally known was evident from information contained in *Le Temps* of August 16, 1904 stating "that the plan of invasion into Indo-China already lies ready in the Japanese general staff."[33] There had in fact been several such scares regarding Japanese intentions. The most serious immediate problem, however, was the impact of Japanese victory on the intellectuals of Indochina, already imbued with French concepts of individual rights and now confronted with a prospect of realizing them, a circumstance which had by December 1905 caused the French to turn to a modified colonial policy of "association."

Fortunately for the security concerns of France as well as Russia and other western powers, Japan had at this time been trying unsuccessfully to recoup her wartime financial losses by applying for loans in London and Berlin. Takahashi Korekiyo, who had successfully arranged foreign loans for Japan during the war, then turned to France where Kurino, the Japanese ambassador, took up the loan question in November 1906 with

[33] No. 389 Inouye (Berlin) to Komura, Sept. 24, J.F.O; No. 3 Kurino to Hayashi, Sept. 5, 1907, *NGB*, vol. 58, p. 89.

the foreign minister, Stephen Pichon.[34] The French government, for its part, had of course a strong desire for the success of both the Anglo-Russian and Russo-Japanese negotiations, an objective which Pichon saw might be realized with Japanese help. It was therefore fortuitous in the most timely and advantageous sense that the Tsar himself in mid-December transmitted directly to Bompard during an audience a request for French help in the Russo-Japanese negotiations which had come to a halt on December 13, 1906.

The plan which the French government adopted was to have the Paris money market serve the strategic needs of Russia and France as it had French needs in marshalling Russian support at the Algeciras conference and the Japanese as well as the Russian governments were informed accordingly.[35] An agreement with Japan in exchange for the approval of a loan could be used as a means of retarding or even curbing the spread of Japanese influence or control in the Yangtze valley and south China and might open the way for cooperation between Anglo-French and Japanese financiers in relation to the Szechuan and Hankow–Canton railways.[36]

The French were determined to make a loan to Japan depend upon Japanese willingness to make concessions both to herself and Russia. At the same time, however, France had to be mindful of the fact that Europe was the main and decisive political arena of her alliance with Russia. Consequently, if France appeared so favorably disposed toward Japan that Russian Far Eastern interests might suffer, the attraction of a tie with Germany or even the rumored plans of Aehrenthal for a Three Emperors' Alliance might prove too great for Russia to resist. Furthermore, strengthening Japan too much could of course make the Far East a more difficult place for all western nations. The major risk, as Hardinge pointed out in a minute on Bertie's note to Grey of November 12, would be that just such a difficult position might arise for France over a Franco-Japanese treaty or might be brought about if Russia were to decide on a war of revenge against Japan. Such a treaty might in these circumstances serve to deter Russia to the advantage of Japan.

The insecurity which pervaded the Far East in the aftermath of the Russo-Japanese war was, in addition to the rivalry which beclouded the

---

[34] Rozental', *Diplomaticheskaia istoriia*, pp. 133–134; Edwards, "The Japanese Alliance," 345–349; Bompard, *Mon ambassade en Russie*, pp. 250–254; Bertie (Paris) to Grey, Nov. 12, 1906, FO 371/87; No. 168 Bompard to Pichon, Dec. 15, 1906, No. 1 Jan. 17, 1907, *DDF*, X, 561–565, 620–623.

[35] Herbert Feis, *Europe, the world's banker, 1870–1914*, New Haven, 1930, pp. 134–135; No. 2 Pichon to Bompard, Jan. 10, No. 1 Bompard to Pichon, Jan. 17, 1907, *DDF*, X, 613, 620–623; No. 96 Nicolson to Grey, Feb. 16, 1907, FO 371/321.

[36] No. 677 Grey to Bertie, Nov. 29, 1906, FO 371/87.

Persian situation, one of the determining factors responsible for generating and shaping the three agreements which were to bind Britain, France, Russia, and Japan into the entente.

The Far Eastern phase of this affiliation was evoked by a Japanese request for a loan, formally broached in an interview on November 14, 1906 between the Japanese ambassador, Kurino Shinichiro, and Takahashi on one side and the French minister of foreign affairs, Stephen Pichon, on the other. Izvolsky was also in Paris at this time and is known to have had several conferences with M. A. Gerard, the French ambassador in Tokyo, and may also have had a share in these discussions.

Pichon, at this and future discussions, let it be known that the French government was willing to approve such a loan on condition that Japan guarantee the security of French rights and interests in the Far East as well as those of Russia in that region. The French minister of foreign affairs in fact made it clear in the early stages of the discussions with the Japanese ambassador that the issuance of a loan would be conditioned on the satisfactory guarantee in treaty form of the strategic and economic requirements not only of France but of Britain and particularly Russia as well.[37] Writing later of the loan to Japan, Ambassador Gerard stated: "It was clear that France could only offer this assistance to Japan if the latter should resolve to inaugurate with Russia an era, not only of peace, but of confidence, and that is exactly what Japan desired."

Some thought had been given in the early stages of the negotiations to the possibility of bringing together Britain, France, Russia, and Japan in a quadruple arrangement. Even though this idea was soon abandoned, apparently at the suggestion of Paul Cambon, the experienced French ambassador in London, the three treaties which ultimately emerged instead were coordinated in ways which suggested not only in the case of the three western nations but also of Japan the original unitary concept.[38] Motono, the Japanese minister in St. Petersburg, remarked, in a conversation with Nicolson, about the probable displeasure of Germany in case of an obvious development of friendly relations between Britain, Russia, and Japan. It seemed to be a clear harbinger of a more peaceful future for the Far East that Motono went even further and expressed himself optimistically about the possibility of an "entente quadruple" consisting

---

[37] No. 3 Kurino to Hayashi, Sept. 5, 1907, *NGB*, vol. 58, pp. 88–96; No. 41 Nicolson to Grey, Jan. 19, 1907, FO 371/269; No. 652 Pichon to Bompard, Nov. 17, 1906 (personal) Pichon to Cambon, Nov. 22, 1906, No. 9, 106 Pichon to French envoys in Tokyo, London, Feb. 2, 1907, *DDF*, X, 446–447, 471–472, 641–642; Phelps, "Izvolskii and Russian foreign policy," pp. 20–22.

[38] No. 149 Grey to Bertie, Mar. 12, 1907, FO 371/269; No. 172 Nicolson to Grey, Apr. 1, 1907, FO 371/272; Edwards, "The Japanese Alliance," 354; Nicolson to Grey, Feb. 22, 1907, Nicolson Papers; No. 120 Nicolson to Grey, Mar. 6, 1907, FO 371/269.

of Britain, Japan, Russia, and France, i.e., a combination of the Anglo-Japanese and Franco-Russian alliances which Germany had anticipated and feared.

The suggestion of a quadruple alliance apparently had first been advanced seriously by the French government as a means of stabilizing and perpetuating the situation which ensued upon the conclusion of the Russo-Japanese war with the release of Russia from the debilitating influence of the war and hopefully also from the threat of an imminent resumption of the war.[39] It was hoped that Russia might, if provided with a congenial international environment, resume what the French government saw as a normal role in Europe. Such a development could bring about a restoration of the temporarily distorted balance of power in Europe. Even though a quadruple alliance in the formal sense did not materialize, there had emerged an attempt to bring about at least in substance if not in form the merger of the Anglo-Japanese and Franco-Russian alliances.

There was an important factor which appeared to some, particularly in Paris and London and potentially in St. Petersburg should the scheme be broached there, to render this a cure worse than the ailment. This was the fear of giving offense to Germany as a consequence of excluding the latter from the group. Even though Grey saw the potential benefits of such a quadruple arrangement, he disapproved of it in practice because he considered it impossible of achievement without creating the impression that it was directed against Germany which also had interests in both the Near and Far East.[40] He held that three separate ententes could achieve essentially the same objective of solidarity without the same risks.

Negotiations concerning the French loan to Japan were to be completed before the making of a Franco-Japanese agreement could seriously begin, a circumstance which delayed the agreement until March 1907. One of the principal obstacles to the progress of the loan was the strong opposition of Izvolsky who expressed great concern over the aggressive posture of Japan and wanted to delay the issuance of the loan until after the completion of the Russo-Japanese negotiations. The Russian government had in fact intimated accordingly to the French government their desire "that no Japanese loan should be entertained until the negotiations with Japan had been satisfactorily concluded."[41] Izvolsky, while establishing these desiderata which would satisfy Russia's actual Far Eastern requirements as he saw them, had also been concerned about setting a

[39] No. 411 Pichon to Panafieu, Sept. 7, 1907, *DDF*, XI, 271–272; Nicolson to Grey, Feb. 22, 1907, Nicolson Papers.
[40] No. 81 Cambon to Pichon, Mar. 13, 1907, *DDF*, X, 690–692.
[41] No. 41 Nicolson to Grey, Jan. 19, 1907, FO 371/269.

standard of security which would convince his internal opponents of the adequacy of his program. Kurino, at the same time, was endeavoring in Paris to overcome this objection by minimizing the Japanese threat and facilitating the work of Takahashi who was trying to acquire the loan as soon as possible.

One further consideration must have been prominent in Izvolsky's thinking as it was in the minds of all the principal participants – the German reaction to these plans. The German ambassador in St. Petersburg, Schoen, was instructed to warn Russia that Germany would understand that Britain, France, Russia and Japan would want to remove points of difference between them.[42] But he added: "We cannot understand and do not find that necessity for security justified that Russia should conclude a coalition with the three above mentioned states, which even if it seems to have defensive aims, yet by the nature of things is directed against us and must threaten our world position." Schoen was to add that such a combination would not be "compatible with the continuation of her previous relationship with us; Russia would then inscribe herself on the role of our enemies." Izvolsky tried, with perhaps some difficulty, to explain that it was not a coalition and was not directed against Germany.

The French government thus became an intermediary between the Japanese who insisted upon an immediate loan while continuing their military preparations for an allegedly expected showdown with Russia. The latter expressed the fear that the Japanese loan would impair their own opportunities in the French money market and that the Japanese military posture would increase the insecurity of their Far Eastern territory and interests. The first phase of the complex and protracted struggle ended March 4, 1907 when, Izvolsky having been sufficiently reassured to withdraw his objection, Takahashi signed with the British and French financiers a temporary contract for the issuance of the loan.[43]

The Franco-Japanese agreement, which by assent of the two principals followed the completion of the loan and barely alluded to the loan, was the first of the three principal arrangements which, added to the already completed Anglo-French entente, composed the Quadruple Entente. The discussions relating to the treaty had started before the financial details were completed but after that date began to assume a more definite and permanent form.[44]

The loan and the agreement of which it was a part were actually

[42] Phelps, "Izvolskii and Russian foreign policy," p. 26.
[43] Nicolson to Grey, Mar. 6, 1907, FO 371/269.
[44] No. 28 Kurino to Hayashi, Mar. 8, 1907, No. 30 Kurino to Hayashi, Mar 13, 1907, *NGB*, vol. 58, p. 47.

beneficial to both signatories. As Hayashi wrote to Komura, the loan provided "a significant benefit for what Japan offered France."[45] This was expressed in the principle of mutuality or reciprocity which formally characterized the entire treaty and was introduced in the first French proposal which was handed to Kurino on March 27. It called for a mutual guarantee of the integrity and independence of China in order to maintain peace and security.[46] This was instrumental in alleviating for both France and Japan their concern about a resumption of the war. It also led to the conclusion of a series of Russo-Japanese understandings affecting both France and Russia and the balance of power in Europe and the Far East; it continued to be renewed as late as 1916 in the midst of the war. Furthermore, in case of a general conflict it practically assured both France and Russia of either Japanese support or neutrality.

However, the loan remained for Japan unquestionably the principal consideration in the compact. The loan introduced Japan to the French loan market from which she had been excluded during the Russo-Japanese war. Also, the relationship had by 1912 led to the establishment of a Japanese–French Bank and by 1913 France had loaned or invested in Japan nearly a 1.5 billion francs.

A somewhat contradictory guarantee was next extended, on behalf of the signatory nations, to those parts of China which were contiguous to their existing possessions, i.e., those provinces of China which bordered Indochina in the case of France and Taiwan and Korea in the case of Japan, regions in which each was conceded a sphere of special interest. Since Fukien was a province in which Japan claimed special interest, the fact that it lay across a strait from rather than abutting on its neighboring province was dealt with by defining its special status in a separate secret article which asserted its propinquity to Taiwan.

This was done at the suggestion of Pichon who found the concept of special interest, particularly when carried as far as the case of Taiwan, contradictory to the independence and integrity of China.[47] In view of this objection, language was avoided in the remainder of the treaty which might suggest spheres of interest. In spite of the seemingly contradictory positions with respect to China, solicitude about the integrity of China was clearly intended to have some significance since the principle of equality for commercial and industrial enterprise was closely associated with it.

The fundamental benefits were supplemented by others such as those

[45] No. 28 Hayashi to Komura, Apr. 24, 1907, *NGB*, vol. 58, pp. 56–57; Feis, *Europe, the world's banker*, pp. 425–429.
[46] No. 35 Kurino to Hayashi, Mar. 27, 1907, *NGB*, vol. 58, p. 48.
[47] No. 37 Kurino to Hayashi, Mar. 28, Komura to Hayashi, Apr. 4, 1907, *NGB*, vol. 58, p. 49.

acquired by the most-favored-nation policy which each of the two nations wanted applied on behalf of the interests of their subjects or citizens, commerce, and industries in the territory of the other.[48] Japanese interests in the Kuantung leased territory in Manchuria were protected under the word "occupation" in the part of the final treaty which dealt with those parts of the Chinese Empire "where they (i.e., France and Japan) have the rights of sovereignty, protection or occupation," the other two words having reference to the regions mentioned above.

There were further important considerations such as the strengthening of economic ties between France and Japan, an oblique reference to the Japanese desire for access to the French money market, and the resolution of conflicts between the two nations. The latter, from the Japanese side, referred to a hope for greater freedom of access to Indochina and the avoidance of conflicts in the province of Fukien, the latter being a factor in generating a desire for the special secret article dealing with the province. The strengthening of the Japanese position may have been a factor helping to tranquilize the American-Japanese war scare by late summer 1907.

Pichon, the French minister of foreign affairs, indicated by March 28 that he wanted to conclude the agreement as soon as possible.[49] The reason for this, the British ambassador in Paris explained, was that Germany was trying to divide Britain and France. The question of the relationship of Germany to the treaty negotiations became a matter of some importance in early May when the existence of the negotiations was revealed to the press, particularly when a press report appeared to the effect that a quadruple alliance had been advocated to bring together the Anglo-Japanese and Franco-Russian alliances.[50]

This underscored the isolation of Germany and raised the question of her relationship to the emerging treaty arrangements. Kurino expressed the view in response that "Germany had no territory in the Far East like ... England, America or Russia." Kiaochow, he continued, was not a colony, "[I]t is a territory ceded or leased by China." Consequently, a treaty to guarantee "the preservation of mutual possessions" as in the case of France or Russia would be unnecessary. Nevertheless, a check of the German language newspapers showed that some Austrian papers did consider that the proposed Franco-Japanese treaty would have the effect

[48] No. 34 Hayashi to Ito (resident general, Korea) Apr. 11, 1907, *NGB*, vol. 58, pp. 51–52.
[49] No. 37 Kurino to Hayashi, Mar. 28, No. 38 Kurino to Hayashi, Mar. 31, 1907, *NGB*, vol. 58, p. 49.
[50] No. 55 Kurino to Hayashi, May 6, No. 51 Komura to Hayashi, May 10, 1907, *NGB*, vol. 58, pp. 60, 60–63.

of isolating Germany while one German paper saw the treaty aimed at driving Germany out of Kiaochow.[51] The Munich *Neueste Nachrichten* saw Japan as preparing the ground for seizing all territories of western nations in the Far East at some propitious moment.

The Franco-Japanese agreement was concluded at Paris on June 10, 1907 and signed by Kurino Shinichiro, the Japanese ambassador, and Stephen Pichon, the French minister of foreign affairs. It consisted of three parts: the first dealt with the integrity and independence of the Chinese Empire and the special rights of the two signatory nations in that country; the second was a declaration which assured most-favored-nation treatment for both; and the third was the secret explanatory note dealing with the relationship of Taiwan and Fukien.[52]

The agreement was the product not only of the discussions between the two principals but also of advice and suggestions solicited at times from the governments of Britain and Russia. Formulas for expressing the basic concepts in the treaty were developed after consulting comparable existing agreements, particularly that defining the terms of the Anglo-Japanese alliance although care was taken to avoid raising in Izvolsky's mind the suspicion that Britain, France, and Japan had collectively concerted their views apart from him.[53]

A further outstanding feature of the treaty was the general approval with which it was received both in France and Japan.[54] The press in both countries was positive in its approval and Kurino reported from France that "eminent men in this country . . . continue to express great satisfaction to me." The president of France commented that the treaty would "help prolong the life of the present cabinet." The possibility of a Japanese–German agreement appears to have troubled Britain only if it were to disturb the Anglo-Japanese relationship.

The negotiations which were to eventuate in a Russo-Japanese agreement grew out of the same discussions for a French loan to Japan which gave rise also to a Franco-Japanese agreement. Pichon expressed this relationship clearly to the Japanese ambassador, Kurino, when he stated that the British and French foreign ministers had informed Izvolsky that the conclusion of a Japanese loan would be dependent upon the conclu-

[51] No. 27 Nishi (Vienna) to Hayashi, May 10, 1907, *NGB*, vol. 58, p. 63; No. 211 Lascelles to Grey, May 13, No. 52 Cartwright (Munich) to Grey, May 16, 1907, FO 371/272.

[52] No. 76 Kurino to Hayashi, June 4, No. 66 Hayashi to Kurino, June 8, No. 70 Hayashi to Aoki, June 8, 1907, *NGB*, vol. 58, pp. 77–79, 80–82, 82–83.

[53] No. 172 Nicolson to Grey, Apr. 1, 1907, No. 192 Nicolson to Grey Apr. 10, 1907, FO 371/272; No. 38 Komura to Hayashi, Apr. 27, 1907, *NGB*, vol. 58, p. 57.

[54] No. 70 Kurino to Hayashi, May 23, 1907, *NGB*, vol. 58, p. 70; No. 70 Lowther (Tokyo) to Grey, May 10, 1907, enclosing excerpts from Japanese newspapers, FO 371/272; No. 122 Grey to Lowther, June 7, 1907, FO 371/273.

sion of an accord between Russia and Japan resolving those outstanding issues which had a bearing on the execution of the treaty of Portsmouth.[55] Bompard conveyed this message to Izvolsky, giving particular emphasis to the desire of the French government for Franco-Russian solidarity.[56] This condition was essential both to the balance of power in Europe and to mitigating the concerns of both parties in the Far East.

The next step was taken when Motono visited Izvolsky on January 18, 1907 and learned of the latter's readiness to discuss an accommodation.[57] Izvolsky immediately touched on the relationship of the entente groups when he stated that "an entente with Great Britain would be of no avail unless a satisfactory treaty is concluded with a pacific object in view of the future relations between Japan and Russia." The Russian foreign minister demonstrated the degree of his commitment to a peaceful settlement by offering to make concessions in order to achieve a guarantee that Russo-Japanese relations would be maintained in a peaceful condition.

These sentiments appeared to match the desires of Japan as expressed by Motono in his report of the conversation and by Hayashi in his reaction to this news.[58] The former expressed the opinion that Japan urgently needed to preserve the peace in the Far East during the recovery of her national strength while Hayashi essentially concurred stating that Japan had no intention of carrying out any aggressive action against Russia but, on the contrary, wanted only cordial relations. He directed Motono to request a specific Russian proposal for achieving these objectives.

The need for a Russo-Japanese agreement at this point was supposedly to achieve a lasting peace and security in the Far East by fulfilling the objectives intended by one or other of the parties to have been resolved in the incomplete aspects of the treaty of Portsmouth. And, even though the final document contained evidence of more far-reaching expectations, the unpreparedness of both parties to risk at that time a recurrence of a war equal in scope to the recent conflict leaves one with an unescapable conviction that this unfinished business constituted a first priority. The conference between Motono and Izvolsky on February 4 dealt with this basic factor as well as such other issues as Russian suspicions of Japan's motives, the status quo in the Far East, the withdrawal of forces from Manchuria, and others.[59]

Izvolsky gave a dramatic characterization of the Russian objectives by

[55] No. 2 Pichon to Bompard, Jan. 10, 1907, *DDF*, X, 613.
[56] No. 1 Bompard to Pichon, Jan. 17, 1907, *DDF*, X, 620–623.
[57] No. 5 Motono to Hayashi, Jan. 19, 1907, *NGB*, vol. 58, pp. 97–98; Masato Matsui, "The Russo-Japanese agreement of 1907: its causes and the progress of negotiations," *MAS*, VI, no. 1 (1972), 38 ff.
[58] No. 9 Hayashi to Motono, Feb. 2, 1907, *NGB*, vol. 58, p. 98.
[59] Nos. 18 Motono to Hayashi, Feb. 6, 1907, *NGB*, vol. 58, pp. 98–100.

citing an article from the *Contemporary Review* of February 1907 by the British journalist, E. J. Dillon, entitled "Russia and Japan." This began with the thought that "The only solid peace basis is friendship between Russia and Japan." It continued by advocating that Russia renounce her dream of dominance on the Pacific along with thoughts of revenge and accept the status quo as defined in the treaty of Portsmouth and that Japan abandon the temptation to prepare for a future war. Izvolsky stated that if Japan were ready to accept this position, he was ready to sign a treaty with pleasure.

Motono's report of his interview of February 5 indicates that he considered Izvolsky sincere in his desire to promote friendly relations with Japan, that he saw the foreign minister as truthfully portraying such friendship as a pressing need for Russia, and that he was aware that it was Izvolsky who had prevailed upon the Russian government to consider giving up its aggressive policy.[60]

Hayashi appeared to accept this appraisal but Komura, then the Japanese ambassador in London, emphasized that necessity as Motono had noted, was the factor which had motivated Izvolsky.[61] Russia, he stated, was clearly unable at this time to pursue the further expansion of her influence or possessions in the Far East and had therefore no alternative to abandoning her aggressive policy, a situation which, he thought, might prevail for some decades. He also foresaw the continuation of the existing internal turmoil and with it a tendency for Russia to turn to more appealing and immediate interests in the Ottoman Empire, a change which would require a secure boundary in the Far East.

It is notable that at this very time the secretary of the Chinese Ministry of Colonies, according to an article of March 16, 1907 in the *Nan Fang Pao*, wrote to the President that: "As Mongolia touches Russian territory, the defense of its frontier is more important than that of Manchuria," and recommended a change in the administration in order to check possible encroachment; a plan was included for the division of Mongolia into four provinces with more local authority to take action.[62]

Under these circumstances, Komura saw an entente with Russia as a distinct advantage for Japan since the preoccupation of Russia with internal difficulties and western diplomatic distractions during the next few years would leave Japan ample time and occasion to develop her interests in northern Manchuria and the Amur region. Also, by turning

[60] No. 20 Motono to Hayashi, Feb. 6, 1907, *NGB*, vol. 58, pp. 100–101.
[61] No. 15 Hayashi to Motono, Feb. 8, No. 12 Komura to Hayashi, Feb. 15, 1907, *NGB*, vol. 58, pp. 101–102, 102–103.
[62] No. 170 Jordan to Grey, Apr. 4, 1907, enclosing an extract of Mar. 16, 1907 from *Nan Fang Pao* dealing with the proposed division of Mongolia.

her attention to areas in the west, Russia would help to absorb the attention of Germany and other European countries, in turn drawing their attention away from the Far East.

Ito Hirobumi, the resident general in Korea, saw the opportunity in a different perspective.[63] He held that at the time there was nothing more important than clearing up the questions of Korea and Manchuria, especially Korea which was clearly marked for Japanese annexation. The Korean people were becoming increasingly anti-Japanese and were looking to other nations for sympathy and support. The Korean question, he emphasized, had to be dealt with as promptly as possible.

Motono discussed the Russian proposals with Izvolsky on February 18 and received a copy of the draft proposal on February 20.[64] The draft was expressed in very general terms, providing for such conditions as good neighborly relations and mutual guarantees of territorial integrity, a style of which Komura approved, suggesting only the addition of a precise guarantee of the territorial integrity.[65] Motono also agreed with the substance of the proposals and recommended the advisability of acceding to them but suggested that there were circumstances which were not covered in them. It would be necessary, he held, that the two parties share similar views about the necessity of establishing a lasting peace in the Far East.

One of the means of achieving this would be to avoid on the part of both parties any intention of endangering the territorial integrity of China or of applying pressure on China from the direction of Mongolia. This would mean, first of all, that Russia's intentions concerning Mongolia must be ascertained and Russia's guarantee obtained to respect the territorial integrity of China, particularly with regard to Mongolia.

The next issue raised by Motono was of much more immediate importance to Japan; it concerned Korea. He suggested pointedly that Russia must agree to its annexation and that Japan would annex it at the first opportunity. To insure that this option should not be subjected to Russian intervention, Russia should be apprised of this intention without delay.

A third item of great importance, in Motono's view, concerned Manchuria. There were some unclear matters in this region surviving from the Portsmouth agreement which needed attention. He recommended that both parties agree to respect the open door and "China's titular sovereignty in Manchuria" and that they retain freedom of action in their respective "spheres of influence," the latter being explicitly

---

[63] No. 7 Ito to Hayashi, Mar. 30, 1907, *NGB*, vol. 58, p. 118.
[64] No. 41 Motono to Hayashi, Feb. 21, 1907, *NGB*, vol. 58, pp. 103–107.
[65] No. 14 Komura to Hayashi, Feb. 28, 1907, *NGB*, vol. 58, p. 108.

partitioned. He held that constant conflict would ensue if Japan, under the cover of the open door and equal opportunity, attempted to penetrate northern Manchuria to curb Russian influence or if Russia were to do the same in the south. Another question in this region concerned the Sungari River which flowed out of southern Manchuria northeastward into the Amur beyond the Russian frontier; he stressed that this issue must be settled during the current negotiations.

The Japanese counter-proposal emphasized precisely these national concerns.[66] Its four articles dealt respectively with: the engagement of each party to respect the territorial integrity of the other, an undertaking similar to a clause in the Franco-Japanese understanding; the recognition of the independence and territorial integrity of China; the demarcation of discrete spheres of influence in Manchuria; and the position of Korea. Izvolsky accepted articles I and II of this counter-proposal as well as articles III and IV in their original form but wanted them constituted as articles I and II of a secret treaty of which it was suggested as a third article a proposal which would in effect have created a sphere of Russian interest in all of Mongolia and "the bordering territories of China outside of Manchuria," presumably meaning Sinkiang.[67]

These exchanges completed the disclosure of the issues with which the negotiations would have to deal: the determination of the Japanese government to annex Korea; the intention of the Russian government to make Japan pay dearly for this by surrendering as much as possible of the strategically important regions of Sinkiang and Mongolia; and the demarcation of northern and southern Manchuria into spheres of influence, leaving the Sungari River open to Japanese navigation and to Japanese entry into the northern Russian zone. These issues had to be discussed against the backdrop of Russian fear of a Japanese renewal of the war to complete what were seen as the unfulfilled objectives of 1905, of Japanese fear that a Russian war of revenge could not be expected to be held indefinitely in abeyance, and of Chinese fear that the Japanese negotiations with France and Russia were only preliminary to the partition of China.[68] This, in addition to the urgency which he saw of settling the Korean question, furnishes a clue as to the attitude of Prince Ito who in June wrote that the Russo-Japanese war was the result of both parties insisting on their demands and being unwilling to give an inch; he hoped that the current negotiations would meet with greater flexibility.

Izvolsky touched on the essence of the Korean issue when he inquired

[66] Report on the Conference of Genro (elder statesmen), Mar. 3, No. 32, Hayashi to Motono, Mar. 5, 1907, *NGB*, vol. 58, pp. 108–109, 109–112.

[67] No. 92, Motono to Hayashi, Apr. 3, 1907, *NGB*, vol. 58, pp. 120–121.

[68] No. 14 Hayashi to Komura, Mar. 5, No. 46 Consul Shimakawa (Kirin) to Hayashi, July 18, 1907, *NGB*, vol. 58, pp. 112, 168.

as to the meaning of the words "further development."[69] This was an expression used in article IV of the Japanese counter-proposal which asked Russia to recognize the conditions existing between Japan and Korea, including those brought about by the Japanese–Korean agreements of 1904–5, and to engage not to interfere with the further development of those relations. The term was, as Izvolsky clearly understood, a euphemism for the ultimate annexation of Korea and signified a goal with which all Japanese officials participating in the negotiations were in agreement.

There were, however, three important questions to be resolved. The first arose from the disagreement inherent in the position assumed by the Japanese minister of foreign affairs, Hayashi, who held that the control granted to Japan in Korea by the Portsmouth treaty was sufficient to include annexation and that of the Russian minister of foreign affairs, Izvolsky, who denied this and wanted compensation for what he saw as a demand for further concessions beyond the scope of the Portsmouth agreement.[70] The second question on which there was a considerable difference of opinion was the amount of compensation Japan was warranted in granting to satisfy Izvolsky's demands, while the third question was whether, if Izvolsky's terms appeared out of proportion, Japan could afford to drop the issue from the present negotiations. The relative merits of incorporating the Korean issue in the public as compared with the secret treaty were examined with reference to the Japanese need for Russian concurrence and to the dimensions of the Russian demand for compensation. The Japanese government was ready to make some concessions in exchange for Russian approval though official views ranged from Hayashi's readiness to forego it entirely to the strongly expressed opinions of Ito who considered Russian approbation to be vital.[71] Ito cited in support of his contention the rising tide of anti-Japanese sentiment in Korea and the likelihood of the Koreans appealing for foreign support as well as the difficulty, as shown by the example of Egypt, of eliminating extraterritoriality.

There remained the question of whether to state openly in a public treaty the Japanese objective along with Russian approval and thus have both nations frankly committed to annexation or to conceal these commitments in a secret treaty. The Japanese government preferred the former,

---

[69] No. 63 Motono to Hayashi, Mar. 12, No. 109 Hayashi to Ito, June 18, 1907, *NGB*, vol. 58, pp. 114–115, 156.

[70] No. 114 Motono to Hayashi, May 1, 1907, *NGB*, vol. 58, pp. 134–135.

[71] No. 65 Hayashi to Ito, May 4, 1907, Ito to Saionji, June 11, 1907, *NGB*, vol. 58, pp. 136–137, 153–154.

thus achieving Russian support against Korean and other foreign opposition. The difference was apparently immaterial to Russia though Izvolsky showed some preference for a secret article.

Russian strategy for acquiring compensation for concessions in exchange for Korea was entirely centered in Mongolia. Japan had tried to avoid this by associating this region with China at large under the general rubric of respect for her independence and territorial integrity.[72] Komura, who seems to have wanted to avoid at all cost recognizing any Russian demands in Mongolia, sought to accomplish this by making the cost to Russia very high and suggested that the Russian claims in Mongolia be considered in parallel with those of Japan in all of Manchuria.[73]

Hayashi tried to avoid the issue altogether by asserting that the question of Mongolia lay beyond the scope of the current negotiations.[74] Ito, however, supported the credibility of the Russian position by pointing out that if the Russian claims regarding Mongolia were in conflict with the integrity of China and thus with the Anglo-Japanese alliance the same could be said of the Japanese position with respect to Fukien province under the Franco-Japanese entente.[75]

Izvolsky began, as these counter-thrusts imply, by seeking successfully to associate Mongolia with Korea in the negotiating process and, while apparently ready to go as far as to oppose Japanese annexation of Korea, was also ready to approve annexation in exchange for Japanese concessions to Russian acquisitions along her frontier with China.[76] This was followed by a Russian proposal which, having in view perhaps the critics of Izvolsky in St. Petersburg, asked that Japan recognize "the preponderance of Russian interests in Mongolia and in the bordering territories of China outside of Manchuria," presumably referring to Mongolia and Sinkiang.[77]

The negotiations were, however, soon reduced to the subject of Mongolia and later to the question as to whether this should include both Inner and Outer Mongolia.[78] Russian access to Inner Mongolia would mean the direct availability of the Chinese frontier and of a railway route

[72] No. 32 Hayashi to Motono, Mar. 5, 1907, *NGB*, vol. 58, pp. 109–112.
[73] No. 29 Komura to Hayashi, Apr. 8, 1907, *NGB*, vol. 58, p. 122.
[74] No. 36 Hayashi to Ito, Apr. 12, No. 68 Cabinet decisions, Apr. 16, 1907, *NGB*, vol. 58, pp. 122–124, 124–126.
[75] No. 28 Ito to Hayashi, May 5, 1907, *NGB*, vol. 58, pp. 137–138.
[76] No. 63 Motono to Hayashi, Mar. 12, No. 15 Ito to Hayashi, Apr. 13, 1907, *NGB*, vol. 58, pp. 114–115, 124.
[77] No. 92 Motono to Hayashi, Apr. 3, 1907, *NGB* vol. 58, pp. 120–121.
[78] Nos. 114, 115, 116, Motono to Hayashi, May 1, No, 105 Hayashi to Ito, June 14, 1907, *NGB*, vol. 58, pp. 134–136, 154–155.

to Kalgan in Inner Mongolia.[79] Since a Russian presence in Inner Mongolia would clearly have been a greater danger to the security of China proper and to the balance of power in the Far East than would be the case in Outer Mongolia, the latter was seen as the lesser evil and was ultimately conceded in exchange for Korea.

Since this was a time when China was planning an administrative redivision of Inner and Outer Mongolia into four new provinces presided over by two viceroys, and thus presumably drawing this region closer to the Chinese administrative center, and when there was already some Japanese influence in this area, there was clearly reason for Russian concern. It was believed that the Chinese movement to establish firmer control in Mongolia, presumably Outer Mongolia, was being encouraged by the Japanese; meanwhile the Japanese were active on their own behalf in Inner Mongolia and the Russians were actively promoting their interests in Outer Mongolia.

The settlement of the Manchurian problem comprised four separate issues. One was the demarcation of the railway by the Protocol of June 13, 1907.[80] This invested Russia with actual and legal possession of Kuan-chengtze and left the town of Changchun, two miles to the south, to Japan. Each of these places was to serve as the respective railway terminal for the two countries. A second issue, the demarcation of discrete spheres of influence in Manchuria, was resolved in the final treaty of July 30, 1907 by drawing a line across Manchuria dividing northern Russian from southern Japanese spheres of interest.[81]

The other two issues were different in both kind and purpose. The third concerned the Japanese demand to be allowed the right to share in the navigation of the Sungari River, a privilege then enjoyed only by Russia and China. Russia could only have seen the granting of such a demand as an opening wedge to a Japanese attempt not only to enter the

[79] No. 147 Motono to Hayashi, June 1, 1907, *NGB*, vol. 58, pp. 146–150; MacDonald to Lansdowne, July 5, 1902, FO 46/554; E.J. Harrison, *Peace or war east of Baikal?*, Yokohama, 1910, pp. 358–359; Satow to Lansdowne, Mar. 2, 1904, FO 17/1764; memorandum, "The Correspondence relating to the Proposed Agreement between Great Britain and Russia on the Subject of Thibet," Apr. 18, 1907, *BD*, IV, 341–342 (part on Mongolia); Grey to Nicolson, June 27, 1906, Nicolson Papers; A.L. Popov, "Tsarskaia Rossiia i Mongoliia," *KA*, XXXVII, no. 6 (1929), 45, 47–48; Ivan Mikhailovich Maisky, *Sovremennaia Mongoliia (otchet Mongol'skoi ekspeditsii snariazhennoi Irkutskoi kontoroi Vserossiiskogo tsentral'nogo soiuza potrebitel'nykh obshchestv "Tsentrosoiuz"*, Irkutsk, 1921, p. 253.

[80] *USFR*, 1907, pp. 780–783; Japan. Dept. of Railways, *An Official Guide to East Asia*, I, 261–267, 274; Mikhail Lazarovich Pavlovich, "Vneshniaia politika i Russko-iaponskaia voina," in L. Martov, et al. (eds.), *Obshchestvennoe dvizhenie v Rossii v nachale XX-go veka*, St. Petersburg, 1910, II, pt. 1, pp. 13–14.

[81] No. 239 Motono to Hayashi, July 30, No. 184 Motono to Hayashi, July 4, 1907, *NGB*, vol. 58, pp. 173–175, 160–161.

Russian sphere of influence in northern Manchuria but also to penetrate
the Russian Amur valley region itself. The forceful opposition shown by
Russia caused Japan to retreat on this issue and to reserve her alleged
rights.[82] Finally, the prohibition of the transportation of troops across the
Chinese Eastern Railway by the Portsmouth treaty was partially adjusted
to permit the movement of troops and their equipment when these were
intended for use in the Amur or maritime provinces.[83]

The Russo-Japanese agreement was concluded on July 30, 1907.[84]
Copies of the public convention were distributed before its announcement to Germany, Austria, France, the United States, Britain, Italy,
Spain, the Ottoman Empire, and China while copies of the secret articles
were given to France and Britain which had already been apprised of
many phases of the treaty-making process.[85] The treaty consisted of a
convention of two articles to be published, a secret agreement of four
articles, and an additional article.

The published convention was a mutual engagement to respect the
territorial integrity of the respective spheres of the two signatories along
with the principle of equal opportunity therein and the independence and
territorial integrity of China. The secret articles were an engagement to
respect each other's spheres of interest in Manchuria, the existing rights
of Japan in Korea as well as the "further development" of Japanese–
Korean relations, the special interests of Russia in Outer Mongolia, and
the confidentiality of the agreement itself. The additional article specified
a division of Manchuria into spheres of interest by a line drawn between
the northern Russian and the southern Japanese zones.

Germany and the entente

The Anglo-Russian agreement, the idea for which had in the first place
drawn the two nations together, remained in effect the capstone of the
quadruple entente. When he finally launched it, Izvolsky in effect made it
interdependent with the Russo-Japanese entente.[86] While he had
explained to Motono that "an entente with Great Britain would be of no
avail unless a satisfactory treaty is concluded with pacific object in view of
the future relations between Japan and Russia," his thoughts as conveyed

[82] No. 123 Hayashi to Motono, June 20, No. 180 Motono to Hayashi, June 29, 1907, *NGB*,
   vol. 58, pp. 158, 159–160.
[83] No. 111 Hayashi to Motono, May 27, 1907, *NGB*, vol. 58, pp. 144–146.
[84] No. 239 Motono to Hayashi, July 30, 1907, *NGB*, vol. 58, pp. 173–175.
[85] No. 227 Motono to Hayashi, July 24, No. 160 Hayashi to Motono, July 27, 1907, *NGB*,
   vol. 58, pp. 170, 173.
[86] No. 5 Motono to Hayashi, Jan. 19, 1907, *NGB*, vol. 58, pp. 97–98; No. 11 Nicolson to
   Grey, Jan. 19, 1907, FO 371/269; No. 41 Nicolson to Grey, Jan. 19, 1907, *BD*, IV,
   268–269.

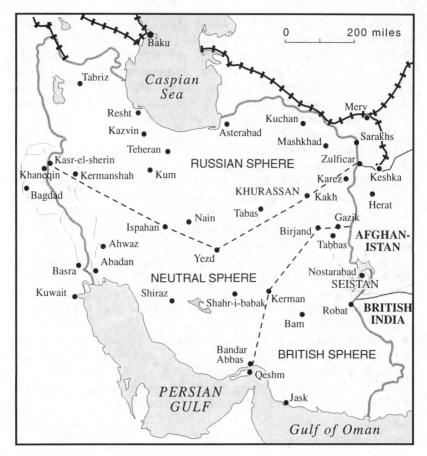

2. Persia

to Nicolson through Motono had a somewhat different emphasis. According to this indirect version, Izvolsky expressed the fear that Russia might have to conclude unsatisfactory commercial and fisheries conventions with Japan and could not at the same time afford to conclude with Britain, the ally of Japan, an agreement "which would in the eyes of many place a distinct check on Russian policy in the Middle East." This would invite criticism of a policy which would be disadvantageous for Russia in both the Far and Middle East.

One further Russian objective in associating these two sets of negotiations was suggested by the fact that Russia had already unsuccessfully requested British help in moving the Russo-Japanese negotiations forward. It is possible that, having achieved a more pre-eminent role in the negotiations because of the significance of the French money market, Izvolsky may have been seeking to apply some pressure to Britain. In any case, just before the actual resumption of the Anglo-Russian negotiations, Benckendorff, then in St. Petersburg, passed along the hint that Russia wanted British help in the negotiations with Japan.[87]

The delay which had in effect halted Anglo-Russian negotiations since the presentation of the British proposals regarding Persia on November 17, 1906, was ended by two decisions reached or formalized at a special ministerial conference held at Tsarskoe Selo on February 14, 1907 under the chairmanship of the foreign minister, Izvolsky.[88]

The first of the decisions made at the conference was that concerning the division of Persia into spheres of interest as advocated in the British proposal of the previous November 17. Izvolsky had opened the meeting by restating the issue of an agreement with Britain, encompassing both the problem of financial aid to Persia and of the demarcation of the country into spheres. He noted the traditional Russian conception that all of Persia must fall under Russian influence and that this should include a railway across the country to an accessible point on the Persian Gulf which could be fortified.

But recent events had shown, Izvolsky noted, that such a plan would now be unworkable and had raised the question as to the need to remove the grounds for conflict with Britain. The most suitable means of achieving this would be to join Britain in a demarcation of Persia into spheres of influence. The idea was adopted in principle by the conference on his recommendation.

The second decision was that, having struck a bargain with Britain which conceded her major demand, Russia must seek to derive some advantage from a related bargain with Germany which would also concede her major objective, the further projection of the Bagdad railway. There was ample evidence at this time of a continued vigorous development of German economic and potentially political power and prestige in Persia.

German commerce in Persia, small in 1901–2, had tripled in value by 1906–7 and the first ship of the Hamburg–American Line, the *Canadia*, had reached the Persian Gulf in 1906, while the following year the Deutsche Orientbank had received the right to begin operations in

[87] No. 78 Nicolson to Grey, Feb. 10, 1907, *BD*, IV, 272–273.
[88] S.A. Pashukanis (ed.), "K istorii Anglo-russkogo soglasheniia 1907 g.", *KA*, no. 2–3 (LXIX–LXX) 1935, 19–24; Benno Aleksandrovich Siebert [Zibert] (ed.), *Graf Benckendorffs diplomatischer schriftwechsel*, 3 vols. Berlin, 1928, I, 1–9; Phelps, "Izvolskii and Russian foreign policy," pp. 108–134; Kazemzadeh, *Russia and Britain*, pp. 488–490; "Protocol of the conference," *BD*, IV, 270–271; Astaf'ev, *Russko-germanskie diplomaticheskie otnosheniia*, pp. 74–77.

Teheran.[89] The Persian hope of drawing Germany into the sphere of her foreign relations as a lever against both Russia and Britain and the German vision of a projection of the Bagdad railway into and even beyond Persia were other factors which helped to create for Russia a very real image of a competitor in Persia potentially more formidable than Britain.

The Russian plan was to offer Germany, in exchange for certain specified benefits, Russian abstinence from further opposition to the German railway plans. The railway promised to compete with Russia's future development in the Persian region not only because it would furnish a connecting link between Europe and India through Persia but also because of the German plan to project a spur of the Bagdad railway up to or even beyond Khaneqin on the Persian frontier and thus threaten even the well established Russian grip on northern Persia.

Consequently, the conditions Russia planned to ask of Germany were: that Germany should guarantee that no branch of the railway should be built in the direction of the Persian frontier as, for instance, up to Khaneqin; that Britain and Germany should support Russia in extending the prohibition on railway construction, now fixed at 1900, to 1910 and in prohibiting the construction, without Russian consent, of any railways in the Russian sphere of influence in northern Persia; and the extension in favor of Russia of the Russo-Turkish treaty of 1900 relating to railway construction in Asia Minor. The military members of the conference consented to this arrangement reluctantly and only after issuing a warning that Russian strategic interests could not be reconciled with the Bagdad railway. The advantages to Turkey, they noted, could only be equalized by corresponding development of the Russian Caucasian railway system along with corresponding reinforcement of Russian troops on the frontier.

Each of these decisions gave rise to an appropriate and timely proposal under the same date of February 20, 1907, one going to Britain and the other to Germany. The proposal to Britain showed, as Nicolson commented, a remarkable degree of convergence of Anglo-Russian thinking on the sensitive Persian issue.[90] Negotiations carried on even before the formal presentation of this counter-proposal had disclosed to the British government the following qualifying Russian viewpoints: the readiness of

---

[89] Ross J. S. Hoffman, *Great Britain and the German trade rivalry, 1875–1914*, Philadelphia, 1933, pp. 159–162; Martin, *German–Persian diplomatic*, pp. 107–108, 120.

[90] Erskine memorandum, pp. 42–44; also No. 101 Nicolson to Grey, Feb. 20, 1907, enclosing a Russian counter-draft, *BD*, IV, 431–432; Angus Hamilton, *Problems of the Middle East*, London, 1909, pp. 192–194, 200; No. 86 Nicolson to Grey, Feb. 13, 1907, enclosing No. 6 Lt. Col. Napier to Nicolson, Feb. 9, 1907, FO 418/38; No. 88 Nicolson to Grey, Feb. 19, 1907, FO 418/40; No. 25 Nicolson to Grey, Feb. 19, 1907, FO 371/320; No. 96 Nicolson to Grey, Feb. 16, 1907, No. 98 Nicolson to Grey, Feb. 19, 1907, *BD*, IV, 275–276, 428–431.

Izvolsky to accept at least the general concept of the British demand for the demarcation of spheres of influence in Persia; the continuing reluctance of the Russian military leaders to allow Seistan to be included in the British sphere, a concession which appeared to the British as the "irreducible minimum" necessary for the defense of India; the Russian intention of seeking some settlement with Germany regarding the penetration of the Bagdad railway into Persia; the need to agree on a policy with respect to existing and possible future concessions to be observed by each of the signatories in the sphere of influence of the other; and the Russian suggestion, anticipated in London even before the Russian decision of February 14, that some compensation would be expected for the concession regarding spheres of interest, such as a willingness to discuss a change in the regime of the Turkish straits.

The parallel proposal addressed to the German government under the same date of February 20 was handed to von Schoen in St. Petersburg. The proposal was a further step in a series of discussions which Izvolsky had held with Schoen in St. Petersburg and with Prince Bülow, the German chancellor, in Berlin during Izvolsky's visit there the previous October.[91]

These discussions had dealt with Russo-German relations with reference to Asia Minor and Persia. It was, the proposal continued.

mutually understood that Russia, conscious of the interests of Germany in the question of the Bagdad railway, will make no decision touching this question without previous mutual amicable agreements with the Berlin cabinet. Furthermore, it was proposed that the latter is ready to take into consideration the interests of Russia and to approve every arrangement between the cabinets of St. Petersburg and London likely to aid the general peace and to eliminate subjects of litigation between the two parties.

The German reception of these Russian proposals of February 20 was not encouraging.[92] The German ambassador, Schoen, forwarded to Berlin some of his own observations with the draft; viz., he objected to the clause making the conditions under which foreign capital might participate in the Bagdad railway subject to the approval of Russia, to making prior agreement with Russia necessary before a connecting line could be built joining the Bagdad railway with lines to be built in Persia, and with requiring Germany to renounce her rights in northern Persia except in the case of railways, highway, and telegraph lines.

Heinrich von Tschirschky, the German minister of foreign affairs,

---

[91] Phelps, "Izvolskii and Russian foreign policy," pp. 116–123; No. 60 Schoen to Bülow, Feb. 20, 1907, enclosing Izvolsky's proposal, GP, XXV-1, 122–124.

[92] Bestuzhev, Bor'ba v Rossii, pp. 143–144; Phelps, "Izvolskii and Russian foreign policy," pp. 119–134; Jaeckel, Die Nordwestgrenze, p. 208.

agreed in general with these objections and held that Germany should have some better arrangement such as the right to connect the Bagdad railway with any railways built in Persia by Russia and better commercial access to northern Persia such as the use of the Transcaucasian railways. He suggested waiting to see the outcome of the Anglo-Russian negotiations. In fact, the German counter-proposal was not submitted until July 3, 1907; in it the prospect was mentioned of Russia soon building a line to the Turko-Persian frontier where it could connect with a Sadiye–Khaneqin branch of the Bagdad line. The right to build the latter branch had already been granted to Germany by the Turkish Bagdad railway concession of 1903.[93]

Russian readiness to consider the demarcation of spheres in Persia was a concession which advanced Anglo-Russian negotiations past their most serious remaining obstacle. Most of the salient features of this new relationship had already been elaborated by the two nations.[94] There were factors of the greatest importance which demanded, for instance, that there should be a third or neutral zone between the British and Russian spheres.

The most evident of these was the need to obviate the dangers which might arise from their spheres being either contiguous or too close together. Another danger might develop if the demarcation were seen as a complete partition of the country between the two principals. The response to this was to avoid all possible appearances of a partition, including the use publicly of such terms as "spheres of interest" or "spheres of influence." Instead it was to be emphasized that the two nations were merely claiming areas of special interest near the frontiers of their Asian territories and that the remainder of the country would be untouched by the Anglo-Russian agreement. It was hoped that this would avert the possibility of demands by other nations including Germany, for a share in the "division."

The prospect remained, however, that Russia might sometime construct a railway in the neutral zone, perhaps through it to a port on the Persian Gulf, a danger which the provision for equal access to the neutral zone did not dispel. This meant that one of the two essential conditions for an agreement with Russia, as suggested by Sir Charles Hardinge, that Russia should not have an outlet in the Indian Ocean and that Britain should obtain an unrivalled position in the Seistan triangle, had not been

[93] No. 231 Schoen to Bülow, July 3, 1907, enclosing a revised proposal, *GP*, XXV-1, 137–140.
[94] Nos. 225, 647, 662, 735, Nicolson to Grey, Sept. 17, 24, 19, Nov. 4, 1906 (enclosing Napier to Nicolson, Nov. 3, 1906), Grey to King Edward, Sept. 24, 1906, *BD*, IV, 392–393, 393–394, 396–399, 408–411, 395; O'Beirne to Nicolson, May 2, 1907, Nicolson Papers.

realized. The question of a railway in fact arose within a year of the conclusion of the Anglo-Russian convention. In an *aide-memoire* of August 15, 1908 Russia proposed agreement in principle to a line from Julfa on the Russo-Persian border to Mohammerah on the Gulf. The British government was unprepared to approve this and consequently responded on October 9, 1908 with the suggestion that Persian finances be put in order before any railways were constructed.

There were three other important issues, all advanced by Britain, which were brought into focus by the Russian agreement on demarcation. One concerned the Russian frontier with Afghanistan.[95] The Russian counter-proposal had drawn a line along the southern edge of the Russian zone which was made to curve north-eastward from Kakh toward the Afghan frontier to a point on that frontier near Kuhsan. Since Britain had a vital interest in the territorial integrity of Afghanistan and, moreover, was responsible for its foreign policy, it was regarded in London as urgent that no part of the Perso-Afghan frontier should be within the Russian sphere.

Consequently, Britain was prepared to insist not only that the curved line be straightened in order to remove that part of the Russian zone from its proximity to Afghanistan but that the terminal point of the Russian zone be moved northward to a location near Zulficar where the Russian, Persian, and Afghan frontiers converged. In addition to leaving no frontier between the Russian zone and Afghanistan, this also had the advantage of removing the Russian zone some miles further from the British, This alteration was approved by Izvolsky.

A second vital issue in addition to the demarcation into spheres of interest was the acquisition of British control over the "Seistan triangle," the southeastern corner of Persia lying east of a line drawn from Bandar Abbas on the Gulf, through Kerman and Birjand to a point on the Afghan border near Gazik.[96] This included not only Persian Seistan up to the Helmand River beyond which lay Afghan Seistan but all of the southwestern Persian frontier south of the neutral zone and facing southern Afghanistan and Baluchistan. This strategic region constituted not only the vital link in the shortest railway route from the Transcaspian line in

---

[95] Erskine memorandum; also Nos. 125, 342 Nicolson to Grey, Mar 10, June 24, 1907, *BD*, IV, 437–440, 477–481; Minute signed by Hardinge, Feb. 26, 1907 and approved by Grey, attached to an enclosed draft convention by Izvolsky, to be sent to Nicolson, No. 30 Grey to Nicolson, Mar. 8, 1907, *BD*, IV, 433, 435–436; Hardinge to Nicolson, May 15, 1907, Nicolson Papers; memorandum on "Persian Railways," June 20, 1911, IG Political and Secret Memoranda, C 122.

[96] Erskine memorandum; also No. 521 Grey to Nicolson, Nov. 17, 1906, enclosing a British draft proposal, *BD*, IV, 415–416; Fraser, *India under Curzon*, pp. 116–117; Hamilton, *Problems of the Middle East*, pp. 198–199; Kazemzadeh, *Russia and Britain*, pp. 407–423.

Central Asia in the north and the Gulf of Oman in the south but also the best point of departure for a Russian attack on India as well as the best position from which the British could prevent such an attack.

The terminal point of the demarcation line at Bandar Abbas conveniently gave the British a commanding position at the entrance to the Persian Gulf although some had thought that Linge, a coastal town some miles to the west, would have been better for this purpose than Bandar Abbas and that Britain should control the nearby islands of Qeshm, Hengam, and Larak. Nevertheless, both Nicolson and Hardinge saw the acquisition of the Seistan triangle as the principal achievement of the treaty and, Hardinge added, as one of the greatest accomplishments to be hoped for along with apparent Russian renunciation of her plans for an outlet on the Indian Ocean.[97]

A third issue which Britain tried, in this case vainly, to resolve through the regular processes of the treaty settlement was her desire for a joint agreement establishing the status quo in the Persian Gulf region. This question was raised at the insistence of the viceroy and the Government of India. The viceroy had, along with the King, objected strongly to Grey's idea that allowing Russia access to the Gulf would be harmless as well as necessary to achieve a settlement with Russia. This view of allowing Russia a position on the Gulf was shared, it should be noted, by the commander in chief in India, Lord Kitchener, though it was strongly opposed by Lord Curzon.

The Russian government, however, was equally adamant in refusing this proposal, arguing quite reasonably that only part of the Persian Gulf was contiguous to Persia and that other nations and interests were concerned with the Gulf.[98] One of the interested parties to which Izvolsky alluded was Germany, having particularly in mind the Bagdad railway and its anticipated terminus at Kuwait on the Gulf. Izvolsky's attitude toward the Gulf question was seen by Nicolson, moreover, as further evidence of concern for maintaining good relations with Germany. While the arena in which these events were centered was the Persian Gulf, the events themselves had no direct bearing on Anglo-Russian relations or even on Persia. Nevertheless, Russia conceded British interest in the status quo in the Gulf and a declaration to that effect was published with the treaty.

[97] O'Beirne to Nicolson, May 2, Hardinge to Nicolson, May 2, Nicolson to Hardinge, May 8, Hardinge to Nicolson, May 15, 1907, Nicolson Papers; Robbins, *Sir Edward Grey*, p. 161.

[98] Erskine memorandum; also No. 225, Grey to Nicolson, June 6, No. 342 Nicolson to Grey, June 24, 1907, *BD*, IV, 465–468, 477–481; Mary M. McCarthy, *Anglo-Russian rivalry in Persia*, Buffalo, 1925, p. 51; Beryl J. Williams, "Great Britain and Russia, 1905 to the 1907 convention," in F.H. Hinsley (ed.), *British foreign policy under Sir Edward Grey*, Cambridge, 1977, pp. 145–146.

The location of Teheran, the Persian capital, in the Russian zone gave rise to a problem which the British government had originally planned to solve by making this city a separate enclave.[99] But the decision was made to forgo such an arrangement with the understanding that Russia would not oppose, without previous agreement with Britain, any grant of concessions in the neutral zone to British subjects or to those of a third power. The special influence which might accrue to Russia as a consequence of her inclusion of Teheran within her zone could be useful in preventing any nation, particularly Germany, from acquiring concessions in the neutral zone of the country.

It was also necessary to provide that existing concessions in the respective zones of Russia and Britain should be maintained.[100] Specifically it was proposed that there should be a transfer to Russia and Britain respectively of the Teheran–Mashkhad and Mashkhad–Nasratabad telegraph lines, the latter terminating in the principal city of Seistan province. The exchange of telegraph lines was accepted by Russia on August 24 and was brought into effect through notes accompanying the treaty. British forfeiture of access to the Trebizond–Tabriz commercial route over which there passed annually goods worth a quarter of a million pounds and to Isfahan, the terminus of the Bushire–Shiraz and Mohammerah–Ahwaz routes meant a significant curtailment of British commerce in the neutral zone.

The negotiations reached their formal completion with the conclusion, on August 31, 1907, collaterally with the treaties concerned with Afghanistan and Tibet, of the Anglo-Russian agreement dealing with Persia. It gave assurance of the preservation of the integrity and independence of Persia and of the public peace in order to promote national development and make possible the equal opportunity for other nations to engage in commerce and industry. It further specified that the two signatory nations had special interests in certain regions, in the region of Persia adjoining her frontier in the case of Russia and in the regions adjoining Afghanistan and Baluchistan in the case of Britain. Each of these nations was precluded from seeking or supporting any concessions in the zone of the other. The rules pertaining to access to the neutral zone, as already noted, were specified as were those pertaining to the use of customs revenues.

The Anglo-Russian agreement also included the settlement of the two

[99] Erskine memorandum; also No. 125 Nicolson to Grey, Mar. 10, 1907, *BD*, IV, 437–440.
[100] Erskine memorandum; also Nos. 57, 220, 277 Nicolson to Grey, Apr. 2, 22 (enclosing an *aide-mémoire* of the same date), May 23, 1907, *BD*, IV, 454–457, 459; O'Beirne to Nicolson, May 2, 1907, Nicolson Papers; Frank Hall Gafford, "The Anglo-Russian condominium in Persia, 1907–1912," Ph.D. dissertation, University of Texas, 1940, p. 103.

nations with Afghanistan and Tibet. The negotiations concerning Afghanistan, while apparently without any obstacles as difficult to surmount as the demarcation of spheres in Persia, did nevertheless disclose issues capable of endangering the fragile Anglo-Russian relations. The early weeks of the British effort to encourage Russia to disclose her wishes in regard to Afghanistan coincided with the period of the Afghan Amir's visit to India between early January and early March 1907 as well as with the period during which Britain was anxiously awaiting the first Russian response to her Persian proposals.[101] Consequently, even the favorable Russian response of February 20 on the Persian demarcation issue could have brought exorbitant demands for an Afghan settlement. While continuing to prod Russia to state her Afghan terms, Britain, after the basic decision on demarcation, tried to limit Russian freedom of action by laying down her own requirements.

These specified: that the Russian government should recognize Afghanistan as outside her own sphere of influence and under British guidance in matters of external policy; that Russian and Afghan officials might arrange to have direct communications on purely local and non-political matters; that Russia might send no agents into Afghanistan; that Russia discontinue giving bounties in subsidies to Russian trade with Afghanistan; and that Russia might enjoy the same facilities in Afghan trade as were available to British and British–Indian merchants.[102]

None of these, it was hoped, would rule out an agreement which the Russian military group might approve. Izvolsky had conveyed to Nicolson on February 19 their reluctance to accept any severe strategic limitations and had stated that an arrangement regarding Afghanistan must precede a settlement of the Persian question. He added that the military party was anxious that Afghanistan should not be changed from a buffer state into a state entirely under British control nor should Britain either build railways within the country or organize the Amir's troops.

The special ministerial conference held under the chairmanship of Izvolsky on April 27 to deal with the major Afghan problems was the forum for basic decisions which made possible an Anglo-Russian agreement on this subject.[103] Both Izvolsky and Poklevsky-Koz'ell had met in

---

[101] J.E.S. memorandum, "Question of direct relations between Russia and Afghanistan," June 10, 1907, IO Political Dept. 371/324.

[102] No. 104, Nicolson to Grey, Feb. 23, 1907, enclosing a document communicated by Nicolson to Izvolsky, *BD*, IV, 525–526; No. 25 Nicolson to Grey, Feb. 19, 1907, FO 371/320.

[103] Pashukanis, "K istorii Anglo-russkogo soglasheniia," 25–29 (Journal of the Special Conference, Apr. 27, 1907); Igor Mikhailovich Reisner (ed.), "Anglo-russkaia konventsiia 1907 goda i razdel Afganistana (po materialam sekretnogo arkhiva byvshego M.I.D.)," *KA*, no. 3 (10) (1925), 55–58.

advance with Nicolson and discussed some of the key issues of the negotiations.[104] Izvolsky inquired about the prospects of Britain sending commercial agents into Afghanistan, of Anglo-Indian officers training Afghan troops, and of the construction of strategic railways in Afghanistan. He expressed concern about Afghanistan becoming an outpost of the Indian Empire. Grasping fully the significance of these inquiries, Nicolson, in conversations with Izvolsky and Poklevsky-Koz'ell, explained as fully as possible the British position on each.

The discussions at the conference of April 27, on the same day between the British military attache, Lieutenant Colonel H. D. Napier, and the Russian chief of General Staff, Palitsyn, at the second special conference on August 24, and at other times through diplomatic channels, reflected mutual readiness to understand and to consider compromises shown in the preliminary conversations. Izvolsky, who led the discussions at both conferences, pointed out at the first the importance to Russia of Afghanistan.[105] General Palitsyn pointed out that whereas Britain, in case of hostilities with Russia, had a number of access routes such as the Baltic, the Black Sea, and others, Russia, with the cession of Seistan to the British sphere, had only Afghanistan and wanted to be assured that it would not be used for purposes inimical to Russia.

At the same time, Russian military leaders in particular were aware of the current unsatisfactory military situation in Russian Central Asia and knew that improving it would be costly and, under present conditions, difficult. Furthermore, the emergence of the national and revolutionary movement had raised Russian apprehension that their Muslim subjects might be more fanatical and less loyal than those of Britain and that this might somehow make it easier for Britain to turn the Afghans against Russia. Lord Kitchener's defense preparations in India were seen as having a potentially aggressive intent and as adding one further reason for seeking assurances of Britain's peaceful motives.

The seriousness of Russian apprehension over the vulnerability of her southern flank is exemplified in a number of ways. The pamphlet dealing with *The Afghan Question* had been written by Captain P. A. Rittikh who had earlier traveled in India and Persia and had written on railway prospects in Persia. His pamphlet, written in 1906, advocated that Russia

[104] Nos. 147, 175 Nicolson to Grey, Mar. 20, Apr. 2, 1907, *BD*, IV, 526–527, 528–529; Rader, "Decline of the Afghan problem," pp. 292–320.
[105] No. 16 Napier to Nicolson, Apr. 27, 1907, *BD*, IV, 530–532; Pashukanis, "K istorii Anglo-russkogo soglasheniia," 32–39 (Journal of the Special Conference, Aug. 24, 1907); No. 557 Nicolson to Grey, Aug. 27, 1906, enclosing a report of Lt. Col. Napier to Nicolson, Aug, 20, 1906, FO 371/128; the military correspondent of *The Times*, *Imperial Strategy*, London, 1906.

look to Persia to compensate herself for losses in the Far East. He had made a study of Afghanistan as a possible theater of Anglo-Russian war which he held would have taken place even if the Russo-Japanese war had not. The pamphlet expressed thanks for assistance to Lieutenant Colonel Snesarev, an officer of the General Staff and of the intelligence division who was also a specialist in Afghanistan and whom Lieutenant Colonel Napier had met while visiting the General Staff. It was also known that the Russian General Staff had supplemented its knowledge of Central Asia by translating into Russian the *Times'* correspondent's book on *Imperial Strategy*. Colonel Napier, in his report of these matters, used the word "fantastic" to describe Russian "apprehension of the harm that we could do her in Central Asia."

It is significant that the Russians weighed the Afghan question in a broad international perspective. Izvolsky suggested that the Russian threat in 1900 to seek direct relations with Afghanistan had been followed two years later by the conclusion of an Anglo-Japanese alliance which he saw as both contrary to British policy and aimed at Russia and, he might have added, as having important implications for the Indian frontier issue. Since the Afghan question was closely associated with the broadest questions of world politics, Izvolsky advocated the view that the agreement with Japan would be incomplete if Russia did not have guarantees from Britain.

The same urgent message was received from the Russian ambassador in Constantinople, I. A. Zinov'ev, who stressed the importance of achieving the release of the Black Sea fleet from its present enforced inactivity by acquiring access to the Mediterranean. This was possible, he wrote, only if Russia could enlist the sincere cooperation of Britain. He urged that, compared with this, all plans for the invasion of India must be considered fantasy and if Britain were willing to consider a solution to the straits question, Russia should make concessions in the Central Asian, i.e., the Afghan, question.

Even though Izvolsky bargained far more shrewdly with Nicolson than these sentiments, expressed for the most part candidly among Russian officials, would imply, the actual settlements reflected more accurately the thoughts exchanged at official Russian gatherings.[106] Stolypin had stated that internal conditions did not allow the country to pursue an aggressive foreign policy; rather there must be concentration on internal reconstruction.

This was consistent with Izvolsky's warning that the Russo-Japanese war and internal conditions had placed Russia in a very difficult position

[106] No. 358 Nicolson to Grey, July 3, 1907, *BD*, IV, 547–549.

and that Russia had to be concerned about the prospect of a two front war, not only being concerned about Austria and the Balkans on one side but Japan on the other, the latter being at the moment he spoke not a completely tranquil front. Russia should recognize, Izvolsky emphasized, that she had no interests of any real value in either Afghanistan or India and that they were useful only strategically for goading Britain. On the other hand, these places had real value for Britain, in particular India, the center of her Asian possessions and interests. Russia should, he concluded, recognize the fact that Afghanistan, so strategically important for Britain, was outside her own sphere of interest and within that of Britain.

The convention concerning Afghanistan constituted the second part of the Anglo-Russian treaty settlement reached on August 31, 1907. It disavowed any intention of changing the political status of the country, the British government engaging to exercise its influence only in a peaceful way and to avoid taking or encouraging any measures threatening Russia. Russia, on the other hand, recognized Afghanistan as outside of her sphere of influence and declared herself ready to conduct all political relations with Afghanistan through Britain and to send no agents into that country.

Britain on her part gave assurances that she would neither annex nor occupy any part of Afghanistan nor interfere in the internal administration of the country provided the Amir fulfilled his treaty engagements toward her. Britain and Russia were to observe equality of opportunity in Afghanistan for commerce. The convention concerning Afghanistan would come into force, it was provided, when the British government had notified the Russian government of the Amir's consent to its terms.

The agreement dealing with Tibet, the third and final part of the Anglo-Russian settlements, was the earliest actually completed. This was because there were in this instance fewer and less complicated issues in conflict than in the case of Persia or Afghanistan. Four of the five points of the proposal which Britain submitted for discussion were accepted forthwith. These were: the recognition of the suzerainty of China in Tibet, the engagement of Britain and Russia not to send representatives to Lhasa, not to procure any concessions for railways, roads, telegraphs, mining, or other rights in Tibet, and the engagement of Russia not to send any officials into Tibet.[107]

It was the second British proposal which aroused Russian objections, the suggestion that her geographical position in India gave Britain a special interest in seeing that the external relations of Tibet were not

---

[107] Nos. 352, 114 Nicolson to Grey, June 8, 13, 1906, Foreign Office memorandum on Thibet, Apr. 18, 1907, *BD*, IV, 332–339.

"disturbed" by any other power. It soon became clear that Russia was particularly apprehensive with respect to the future of the Dalai Lama, the accessibility of Lhasa to her Buddhist subjects, and the availability of Tibet for scientific expeditions.

There were also certain features upon which Britain was ready to insist. She was not, for example, prepared initially to accept a role precisely equal to that of Russia but wanted rather a position of special interest in the foreign relations of Tibet.[108] There was special access to Tibet acquired through the treaties of September 7, 1904 and the adhesion treaty of April 27, 1906 with China. British occupation of the Chumbi valley depended upon the Tibetan performance of the first of these. Furthermore, Britain was not prepared to admit that Tibet was an ordinary province of China, holding rather that it was a "feudatory state under Chinese suzerainty with large autonomous powers," including the power to conclude treaties with conterminous states regulating mutual commerce, frontiers, and other matters. While Britain had no objection to permitting access by bona fide Buddhist pilgrims to Lhasa and to their religious leader, the Dalai Lama, she was determined that neither this nor any other channel should become a means of conveying political ideas between Russia and Tibet and thus a means of enhancing the Russian position there. In fact, Russia appeared more immediately concerned with using her influence with the Dalai Lama to improve her position in Mongolia.

The arrangement concerning Tibet, concluded like the other two on August 31, 1907, consisted of five articles and an annex. It recognized the suzerainty of China in Tibet and obligated Britain and Russia to negotiate with Tibet through the Chinese government except as provided in the British treaties of September 7, 1904 with Tibet and of April 27, 1906 with China. This did not prevent Buddhist subjects of either Britain or Russia from entering into direct relations with the Dalai Lama on purely religious matters. Both the British and Russian governments engaged neither to send representatives to Tibet nor to acquire for themselves or their subjects any concessions for railways, roads, telegraphs, mines, or other rights, nor to have any Tibetan revenues in any form assigned to themselves or their subjects.

An annex affirmed that the occupation of the Chumbi valley by British forces would be terminated on the payment of the annual installment of the indemnity, provided that the trade marts mentioned in the convention

---

[108] Memorandum, on Thibet, *BD*, IV, pp. 346 ff; Alastair Lamb, *The McMahon line. A study in the relations between India, China and Tibet, 1904–1914*, 2 vols. London, 1966, I, 85–86, 93, 102; Nicolson to Grey, June 20, 21, July 5, 1906, Nicolson Papers; Nicolson to Grey, June 26, 1906, FO 800/71.

of September 7, 1904 had been effectively opened for three years and that the Tibetans had complied in all respects with the terms of the convention. The longer-range result was, therefore, to place Britain and Russia on the same footing in Tibet. Grey was apparently not interested in consolidating the prospective gains from the occupation of the Chumbi valley but rather in making Tibet a buffer against a Russian advance. The final installment of an indemnity was paid on January 29, 1908 and British troops were ordered withdrawn from Tibetan territory.

The formal signing of the three parts of the Anglo-Russian agreement was preceded by a further Russo-German diplomatic meeting.[109] The initiative was apparently that of Izvolsky who had visited Berlin in October 1906, drawn up some desiderata for an accommodation with Germany in February 1907, and discussed more concrete plans with Baron Taube of the Russian Foreign Office in mid-July. A special ministerial conference was held on July 27, 1907 in preparation for the negotiations which were held during August 3–6 at Swinemünde on the Baltic coast at one of the mouths of the Oder River. The meeting was held without the knowledge of either Britain or France. It was attended by the emperors of Russia and Germany, the prime minister of Russia, Stolypin, and the chancellor of Germany, Bülow, the foreign ministers of the two countries Izvolsky and Tschirschky as well as other staff members.

The meeting at Swinemünde was the outcome of influences reaching well beyond the scope of Izvolsky's plans or projections even though it was clear that it might well serve his purposes. In fact, he was able to a considerable extent to control its deliberations.[110] The conclusion of the defensive Spanish agreements with Britain and France had stimulated a defensive reaction in Berlin to the point of expressing some thoughts about the advantages of a return to the Three Emperors' Alliance. A version of this, the old alliance with the addition of France, was even then being advocated by the Austrian minister of foreign affairs, Aehrenthal.

It was Bülow who decided to bring the German and Russian sovereigns together and to provide an agenda while Izvolsky who had been planning a conference with Germany well before the conclusion of the Anglo-

[109] Taube, *La politique russe*, pp. 133–145; Bestuzhev, *Bor'ba v Rossii*, pp. 142–144; Mühlberg to Bülow, July 22, Tschirschky Note, Aug. 7, Schoen to Bülow, Aug. 10, 1907, *GP*, XXII, 57–60, 67–68, 68–72; Williams, "Great Britain and Russia," 139–140; Astaf'ev, *Russko-germanskie diplomaticheskie otnosheniia*, p. 82.
[110] Osten-Sacken to Izvolsky, June 28, July 6, 12, 14, 26, Aug. 9, 17, Urussov to Izvolsky, May 12, July 11, 1907, in Iswolsky, *Au service de la Russie*, I, 90–100, 157, 164; Henry Wickham Steed, *Through thirty years, 1892–1922. A personal narrative*, 2 vols. New York, 1924, I, 248–252; No. 472 Aehrenthal to Khevenhuller, Apr. 25, 1907, in Eurof Walters, "Aehrenthal's attempt in 1907 to re-group the European powers," *SEER*, XXX, no. 74 (Dec. 1951), p. 214–216; Astaf'ev, *Russko-germanskie diplomaticheskie otnosheniia*, pp. 82–94.

Franco-Spanish agreements saw his opportunity and decided to prepare to press his own agenda. He explained to Baron Taube of the Russian Foreign Office that he wished to balance the Anglo-Russian agreement which dealt with Asia with a Russo-German agreement which would be concerned with Europe, specifically the Baltic. At his request and specifications, Taube drew up a protocol by which Russia and Germany could guarantee the status quo in the Baltic.

Izvolsky's actual proposal to Bülow was that in return for making the Baltic a closed sea to all but the riverine countries, Germany would cooperate in trying to induce Sweden "to accept the abrogation of Aland [island] servitudes," thus making it possible for Russia to fortify them, a proposition to which Bülow did not react.[111] It should be noted that one of the factors attracting Russia to the British combination was her fear of German designs on her Baltic coast.

The agenda drafted under Bülow's direction for the Swinemünde meeting consisted of six points, the first of which called for a recognition of the perpetuation of the Björkö treaty. This was not as impractical a gesture even at this point as it might seem if it is remembered that this treaty was concluded ten months before Izvolsky assumed office as foreign minister. Nor would it seem illusory if one takes into consideration that at least in the view of Schoen, the German ambassador in St. Petersburg, Izvolsky was not only not considered pro-British but also was not thought of as the originator of the Anglo-Russian negotiations. In fact he was seen as rather friendly to Germany.

The second item of the agenda, in this case of special interest to Austria, was concerned with disarmament and the Second Hague Conference (June 15–October 18, 1907), while the third dealt with the Bagdad railway and Persia as discussed above. The fourth of Bülow's proposals noted the Balkan problem of special concern to Russia and Austria while the fifth concerned the neutralization of the Baltic as Izvolsky had contemplated, and the sixth and final points were concerned with Russian finances and the prospect of German loans.

The principal immediate achievement of Izvolsky at Swinemünde was the preservation of at least a formal balance in Russian foreign policy through the pursuit of German good will which he and his predecessor had considered essential for national security.

More tangible evidence of this was realized with the conclusion on October 29, 1907 of the Protocol preserving the status quo in the Baltic.[112]

---

[111] Nicolson, *Sir Arthur Nicolson*, pp. 262–263; Fischer, *Germany's aims*, p. 22.
[112] Taube, *La politique russe*, pp. 147–171; Grey, *Twenty-five years*, I, 138–146; Fink, *Spillet om Dansk neutralitet*, pp. 104–106; Adamov, *Sbornik dogovorov Rossii*, pp. 150–152.

Because the details of this transaction were secret and because the contents of the agreement were not known, this protocol gave rise to considerable international uneasiness.

Since the Russian response to the German proposal regarding the Bagdad railway in relation to Persia was forthcoming only in March 1908, this significant question was not resolved at the Swinemünde conference. Nor was it settled at the Russo-German discussions held at Potsdam during November 4–5, 1910.[113] However, with the German attitude somewhat moderated by the Agadir crisis, a Russo-German agreement dealing with the Persian Bagdad railway question was finally concluded on August 19, 1911. Germany agreed at that time to forego such economic concessions in the Russian sphere of Persia as roads, railways, and telegraphs while Russia agreed that she would eventually construct a railway from Teheran to Khaneqin on the Turkish frontier where Germany would connect it with the Bagdad railway by a branch from Sadiye.

The Anglo-Russian convention was finally signed on August 31, 1907 at the Russian Foreign Office by Sir Arthur Nicolson and Aleksandr Petrovich Izvolsky. Those who had been immediately engaged in fashioning it were satisfied and relieved rather than enthusiastic over their handiwork. Izvolsky had lived in fear of failure and had gone to the Swinemünde meeting in the hope of achieving a satisfactory resolution of the Bagdad railway–Persian issue. A week before the agreement was to be formally concluded, he had sought once more for a broad administrative support for his Afghan policy by submitting it again to a special ministerial conference on August 24. There he went systematically through the Afghan agreement and was able to obtain the vital support of the Council of Ministers, particularly Stolypin and the chief of General Staff, on the significant grounds that the internal conditions of Russia did not then permit her to pursue an aggressive foreign policy.[114] Once more he was able to win approval, on clearly reasonable but unpopular grounds, of this blueprint for a departure in Russian foreign policy.

International alert

The regional impact of the decades long Anglo–Russian encounter had, by the turn of the twentieth century, been profound. It had to a considerable extent transformed the balance of power in the Central

[113] Fay, *Origins of the World War*, I, 271–275; Kazemzadeh, *Russia and Britain*, pp. 593–596; Adamov, *Sbornik dogovorov Rossii*, pp. 405–407; Astaf'ev, *Russko-germanskie diplomaticheskie otnosheniia*, pp. 265–283.
[114] Pashukanis, "K istorii Anglo-russkogo soglasheniia," 36–37.

Asia–India frontier political-strategic arena. In the first place, Russian power and influence had been greatly enhanced by her territorial acquisitions in Central Asia and by the consequent direct access this permitted to the frontiers of Afghanistan and Persia, the countries which constituted so important a part of the protective rampart of British India. At the same time, Russian power and opportunity for further acquisitions had been considerably augmented, to the detriment of Britain, by better access to the Turkish straits.

These successes had brought into being for Russia a new set of relationships with the regions to the south. She was now a more imminent menace not only to the Indian frontier but, by virtue of her better strategic position at the straits, to the Mediterranean and the route to India. She promptly aspired to use this route to improve her role in the commercial and strategic opportunities to the south.

Incidental to her new territorial gains, Russia had also, as a consequence of having incorporated large numbers of people in Central Asia and of her closer relations with Persia, obtained greater potential leverage in the Near and Middle East. The historical and cultural affinity of the newly annexed people and their geographical juxtaposition with the Muslim countries to the south opened the door for new political and strategic opportunities.

These Russian achievements had, however, been considerably attenuated by other parallel developments. One of these was the emergence of Japan as a new power both on a Far Eastern and a world scale. Japan was, especially in the latter perspective, closely associated with the outcome and consequences of her victory in the Russo-Japanese war. This had deprived Russia of important territorial gains and had severely limited her prospective acquisitions, and had cast a shadow on her prestige both at home and abroad. An even more direct and menacing challenge to Russian power and prestige, particularly unwelcome since it affected very fundamentally her position in the Near and Middle East where Britain and Russia had heretofore been the sole major rivals, was the rise and rapid acceleration of German power.

Germany was a challenge to an almost equal degree to both Britain and Russia. Her ambitions with respect to the expansion of her seapower and commerce were of particular concern to Britain. Russia, in addition to having Germany as a European neighbor, was especially apprehensive about the German Bagdad railway as a barrier to her freedom of action at the straits and in Persia. In addition, German territorial acquisitions in the Far East had their implications for the future course of the rivalry there.

The German challenge was on balance more significant to Russia than the Japanese not only because it was better understood but also because it was considered inherently more dangerous. Germany was also a greater obstacle to harmony not only because of the German presence directly on the western frontier of Russia and at the vital straits passage to the world but also because Germany proved less amenable than Japan to a lasting harmonious settlement.

Another aspect of change in the balance of power which evolved in the course of the Anglo-Russian rivalry or as a consequence of it was the impact it had already had on the people of the region. At the time the Anglo-Russian accommodation was reached Russia had brought the people of Central Asia firmly under her control. On the other hand, the people of western Asia whose independence Britain had successfully defended from Russian encroachment remained at least formally independent. The awakening and evolution among the people of the region of a sense of ethnic and even national identity at which Sir Henry Rawlinson had hinted some decades before was showing signs of becoming a reality.

The support which the national awakening was able to lend to the British endeavor to sustain the independence and territorial integrity of the border states against the Russian advance was real but still largely ineffective. Religious and cultural response to the Christian incursion and monarchical efforts to protect and preserve the royal prerogatives and domain were insufficient against the better armed and organized opposition. The conflict exposed the internal weaknesses, the many aspects of technological and organizational backwardness, or disadvantages of location which had yet to be dealt with. But the experience left in those regions not absorbed or retained by Russia or China a will to carry on the quest for independence and national identity. This provided a justification for the British effort which was only indirectly associated with imperial security.

The Anglo-Russian agreement addressed three fundamental and related problems. The traditional and more easily and widely understood one was the Russian threat to the security of India. This was best known because of the protracted Anglo-Russian frontier conflict recently centered in Tibet, Afghanistan, and Persia. A lesser known aspect of Anglo-Russian rivalry, however, was the contention within Russian official circles as to the precise emphasis to be given, in the diplomatic balance, between Britain and Germany, a theme which remained even after the conclusion of the Anglo-Russian agreement the determinative factor in observing and applying it.

The persistence of the second of these problems is shown by the difficulty Izvolsky found in trying to sustain Russian support for the agreement. He had, as noted above, deemed it wise to test the support on which he could count for the Anglo-Russian treaty a week before he ventured to sign it. Soon after its conclusion there again arose threatening demands in the rightist press for its termination.[115] Once more, therefore, in a special ministerial conference of December 13, 1907, Izvolsky found it necessary to defend his policy against demands that the limiting partnership with Britain be scrapped and that Russia establish a protectorate in Persia. It was decided, however, to abstain from any open intervention. Action was to be limited to strengthening the Russian consular guards in Persia and to concentrating Russian forces on the Persian frontier. It was clear that in St. Petersburg at least the Anglo-Russian agreement rested on insecure foundations.

The other major problem addressed by the Anglo-Russian agreement, more recent in origin and far more challenging to the prevailing world order than the frontier struggle itself, was the German challenge not only in Europe but particularly in the Middle and even the Far East. This had by 1907 given rise in a disguised but by no means secret form to a widespread coalition against Germany. While this had by no means eliminated the pre-existing Anglo-Russian rivalry, it tended by overshadowing it in current importance and by keeping it sufficiently in abeyance to leave the impression that it had in fact ended it. Izvolsky, however, made the more accurate view very clear only a few days after the signing of the agreement when he told King Edward at Marienbad with amazing frankness that he saw trouble ahead with Germany over Persia.[116] He must have implied that the traditional problem had, in his view, merely been overlaid by a new problem which, at the very least, was no improvement.

The German chargé d'affaires in St. Petersburg, Hans von Miquel, wrote only three weeks later a remarkably unemotional appraisal of the new agreement, commenting that it was a coalition of the powers which he found was aimed at Germany and with which Germany would have to reckon.[117] "This necessity for a close unit," he concluded, "is a compliment, though a troublesome one, for the German army, the German navy, our merchants, and the general capacity of the German people for development."

Captain Philip Dumas, the British naval attaché in Berlin, put his finger on an important facet of this state of affairs when he expressed the view that the German people had an army which had given them the

---

[115] Bestuzhev, "Bor'ba klassov i partii," p. 153.
[116] Goschen to Grey, Sept. 5, 1907, Nicolson Papers; William Kerr Fraser-Tytler, *Afghanistan. A study of political developments in Central Asia*, London, 1950, p. 177.
[117] No. 326 Miquel to Bülow, Sept. 27, 1907, *GP*, XXV-1, 45–47.

status of a great power but that in sea power they had failed to achieve this status.[118] He saw their need for naval strength as attributable to the German view of themselves as having passed through, "on account of the Algeciras Conference, a period of humiliation in 1906."

The new coalition came into being as a check on the growing dominance of Germany in Europe and beyond at a time when the growing British fleet was about to be supplemented by the French fleet and in time by a rebuilt and perhaps more effective Russian fleet.[119] Preparations for a continental struggle had been simplified and perhaps delayed by the advent of the Russo-Japanese war. General Count Alfred von Schlieffen, the German chief of General Staff, reported to the Kaiser in December 1906 that because of the present weakened condition of Russia the number of divisions assigned to the eastern front had been reduced to ten, making the present a very suitable time for a war with France. This was a judgment in which Holstein concurred.[120]

The changes contemplated by the British navy, however, were far more of a challenge to German maritime ambitions and a new program of ship building was launched under strong pressure from the German Navy League, the membership of which had by then grown to some 900,000. There was interest shown in the new dreadnought type of battleship by October 1905 though an order was not actually placed for the first of these, the *Nassau*, until about a year later and the first of the German dreadnoughts was not actually laid down until July 22, 1907 and these were completed only in the fall of 1909.[121]

An amendment to the naval law of 1900 had been introduced in the Reichstag on November 27, 1905 but it experienced many delays due to economic and political changes as well as other factors and was not finally passed until March 27, 1908. It was expected as a consequence of this building program that by 1917 Germany would be able to add seventeen battleships and six large or battle cruisers to the fleet. This would give Germany by the latter date a total of fifty-eight of these two classes of large ships.

The impact of this German naval expansion on the British outlook has recently been appraised in this way by a German historian: "That the

[118] Captain Dumas to Lascelles (Berlin), Feb. 12, 1908, *BD*, VI, 118.
[119] Woodward, *Great Britain and the German Navy*, pp. 151–152.
[120] Khvostov, *Istoriia diplomatii*, II, 602.
[121] Marder, *Anatomy of British sea power*, p. 540; Marder, *From the dreadnought*, I, 135–136; Hajo Holborn, *A history of modern Germany, 1840–1945*, New York, 1969, p. 336; No. 511 Count de Salis (Berlin) to Grey, Nov. 19, 1907, *BD*, VI, 68–70; Jonathan Steinberg, "The German background to Anglo-German relations, 1905–1914," in F.H. Hinsley (ed.), *British foreign policy under Sir Edward Grey*, Cambridge, 1977, pp. 199–210; Hauser, "Die Englisch-Russische Konvention," 233.

political need for this step [i.e., the British self-strengthening movement, here especially the conclusion of the Anglo-Russian agreement], so unnatural for Britain, arose because of the pursuit of security against the apparent German aspirations for hegemony exemplified in the massive build-up of the fleet. This is painful for the German observer to recognize but is unquestionable."

The Anglo-Russian agreement, like the Franco-Japanese and Russo-Japanese treaties, was conceived and concluded in response to the apprehensiveness of the partners over Germany and, particularly in the case of France and Russia, also over Japan. Such a purpose might have been expected to form a closer bond between the partners than the territorial settlement, which completely satisfied neither and which was patently imperfect. The agreement was seen by both the British and Russian governments as a factor in the balance of power, in particular by Britain as a means of acquiring another ally in the struggle with Germany at sea, including the Persian Gulf, and of detaching Russia from Germany. From this point of view it was a relatively successful venture even though the parties differed widely as to their expectations from the settlement itself. Britain generally favored it and Russia maintained a reluctant attitude toward the limitations inherent for her in all three parts of the settlement.

The same paramount objective made the Franco-Japanese and Russo-Japanese agreements possible, both having been brought into being by French loans and encouragement as well as the need for security. The latter objective was sought not only because Japan was competitive with Russia and France in the Far East but also because, particularly in the case of Russia, Japan was also a competitor in the large sense and was therefore in a position to influence the international balance of power by reducing the effectiveness of Russia as a partner of France and thus of France itself in forming a counterpoise to Germany. The possibility of the emergence in Europe of a continental alliance, which had intermittently threatened Britain and France for so long, appeared to have been rendered somewhat less likely as a threat and with it the closely related prospect of the rise of German hegemony in Europe.[122] However, the fact remained that whereas Japan had reached a settlement of the outstanding issues with her immediate rivals and had become a member of the entente, in the case of Germany vital and challenging problems remained unresolved.

The question as to which party received the better bargain, while secondary to the main issue of security, remained nevertheless important. The essential regional factors were that Britain had secured, or thought she had come as close as she was able to come to securing, "the

[122] Hauser, *Deutschland und der Englisch-Russische*, p. 5.

safeguarding of the strategical position on the Indian frontier.''[123] Russia, already under pressure on her flanks from Germany and Japan, had received a respite from German pressure on her southern approaches. It was in many ways of tertiary importance that Russia had surrendered her long-held ambition of reaching the Persian Gulf coast and of acquiring Seistan while she gained an ally in dealing with Germany and Japan. It was in the same perspective that Britain surrendered free access to northern Persia and exclusive access to Afghanistan in order to gain at least a temporary cessation of the Anglo-Russian territorial rivalry as well as greater assurance of having an ally in the conflict with Germany.

Both bargained with some handicaps though it was clear, at least in retrospect, that Britain took less advantage of her assets than Russia. There were two principal long-range factors which constituted the essence of the embroilment. One was the territorial demarcation of established, potential, or expected regions; the other was the anticipated impact of the agreement on the Persian people and on Muslims everywhere. Since it is known that Grey and Morley entered upon the negotiations ready and willing to concede to Russia access to the Persian Gulf and were only dissuaded from this under pressure from the King and the viceroy, it is possible that in other instances less easy to detect Grey might with greater determination and firmness have been able to achieve a better bargain. Since it was Grey who insisted upon the demarcation of spheres of influence in Persia, the undertaking which the people interpreted as partition, it is also possible that popular reaction was insufficiently taken into account.

The covert nature of so many essential aspects of this "diplomatic revolution," as it has been called, meant that for most people many of the quintessential portions of the picture were missing.[124] Only a very limited number of persons could have known of the desperate search for national security then in progress in Anglo-French conversations and in the incompletely realized conception of a coordinated network of diplomatic combinations extending from Japan to Spain and Britain intended as a shield against Germany. This was also true of the hazardous game Russia was playing directly with Germany over the straits and the Bagdad railway–Persian issues.

The absence of these and other vital factors from the field of knowledge of most of those who commented on the Anglo-Russian or other entente agreements in the daily and periodical press, almost the only means of

[123] Memorandum, "The Anglo-Russian Convention," Jan. 29, 1908, IG Political and Secret Memoranda, C 140; Grey, *Twenty-five years*, I, 154.
[124] Hale, *The great illusion*, pp. 226–253; Boris Emmanuilovich Nol'de, *Dalekoe i blizkoe: istoricheskie ocherki*, Paris, 1930, pp. 44–58.

reaching the public at that time, meant that there was little means of achieving anything but an incomplete interpretation and understanding of these crucial events.

One of the critics closest to the events being considered in the negotiations was Cecil Spring Rice, the British minister in Teheran and recently the chargé d'affaires in St. Petersburg. Spring Rice was not one of the principal participants in forming the agreement. In fact he complained at one point to Grey that his views during the negotiations were "neither invited nor desired."[125] He had urged during the negotiations that the treaty neglected the vital interests of Britain in northern Persia while leaving the Russian bank to monopolize this region to the detriment of the British Imperial Bank and British business.

Even worse, Spring Rice maintained that the treaty would not prevent the Russian advance southward any more than the Russo-Japanese treaties of 1896 and 1898 dealing with Korea had prevented Russia from continuing her pressure on that country. Only the resistance of Persia herself could do this and such resistance, he pointed out, could become general and not necessarily to the interest of Britain. The Persian government had heretofore relied on British resistance to Russia to maintain its independence and the treaty would signal the withdrawal of Britain from this role and turn both the government and people against Britain.

Spring Rice also perceived that the demarcation into spheres of influence would be interpreted as in fact partition of the country. Morley had, in fact, compared it with the eighteenth century partitions of Poland, views which Grey and Nicolson did not accept. Any attempt to regulate the disposal of the neutral zone would of course confirm all suspicions of a partition and lead to a comparison with Morocco. Meanwhile, an anti-popular and anti-Muslim perception of the treaty would appeal to Muslim solidarity in Persia and in the British Empire and tend to enhance the power and prestige of Germany.

The formal announcement of the agreement to the new Parliament by King Edward on January 29, 1908 touched off a debate which began first in the House of Lords. Lord Curzon, after assuring Lord Lansdowne the Conservative leader in the Lords, that he would not attack the agreement in principle but would discuss only "the nature of the bargain made," launched an attack on February 6 which lasted two hours.[126] "It gives

---

[125] No. 69 Spring Rice to Grey, Apr. 11, 26, 1907, *BD*, IV, 450–453, 457–458; Williams, "Great Britain and Russia," 144.

[126] Murray, "British policy and opinion," pp. 128–132; Robbins, *Sir Edward Grey*, p. 162; Ronaldshay, *The life of Lord Curzon*, II, 38; Gafford, "The Anglo-Russian condominium," pp. 102–104; Jaeckel, *Die Nordwestgrenze*, p. 206; Henry Mortimer Durand, "Sir Alfred Lyall and the understanding with Russia," *JRCAS*, I, pt. 3 (1914), 38–39, 45.

up," he stated, "all that we have been fighting for for years ... the efforts of a century sacrificed and nothing or next to nothing in return." He pointed out, as Spring Rice also noted, the commercial, political, and economic interests Britain had lost in Persia including free access to twelve of the largest cities. He called attention to the small worthless nature of the British share in the parcelling out of the country and asked how Muslims elsewhere in the British Empire would be reassured when "they could see for themselves how carelessly their Persian brethren had been treated." Curzon saw the Tibet treaty as "an absolute surrender" and, regarding Afghanistan, he held that Britain had obtained "nothing in return for very substantial concessions."

The Earl of Ronaldshay, who was very close to Curzon and was his biographer, also disapproved of the partition of Persia and regretted the impact of this on the people of Persia. In addition, he was not convinced that the agreement would keep the Russians out of Seistan.

Sir Henry Mortimer Durand, drawing upon his long experience in the region dealt with in the treaty, including a period of duty as the British minister in Persia, also disagreed with some significant aspects of the division of spheres in Persia. He noted, as Curzon had, that the line separating the Russian from the neutral zone had been drawn in such a way as to leave in the Russian zone some cities in which British trade and influence were strong if not actually paramount, such as Kermanshah, Hamadan, Isfahan, and Yezd.

Furthermore, since this line had been referred to as the Durand line, he pointed out that in reality his proposed line had been drawn further north and had not excluded these cities from a zone readily available to British subjects. He added also that the southern zone had been both politically and commercially much more in British hands than the northern zone was in Russian hands.

The views of Lord Curzon and those who saw the Persian situation as he did were more optimistic than many of their colleagues with respect to the durability of the British position in Persia. Consequently, they were opposed to making the kinds of concessions the proponents of the Anglo-Russian agreement saw as necessary. The latter reflected the more pessimistic views expressed at the conference of November 1902 which had attempted to find a safe policy regarding the conditions under which British tenure in Persia and on the Persian Gulf would be possible.[127] The differences between the two opinions arose principally over differing estimates of Russia's capability of forcing her way to the Gulf.

The British press reflected both positive and negative views of the

---

[127] Jaeckel, *Die Nordwestgrenze*, p. 205; *History of the Times*, III, 501–502; Murray, "British policy and opinion," pp. 97, 99–101; Valentine Chirol, "Indian borderlands. The Russian and German pressure before the war," *Asia* (April 1919), 366.

treaty, the political center of the press being generally favorable while the socialists were opposed on the grounds that no treaty at all should have been made with the tsarist regime.[128] *The Manchester Guardian* of September 2, 1907 pointed out that the Foreign Office, in negotiating for the nation's good and for world peace, must take foreign countries as it found them. The same newspaper of September 26 saw the treaty as legalizing the existing trends in Persia, Afghanistan, and Tibet and quashing the fear of an invasion of India and generally accepting the treaty "so long as we don't become allies."

Valentine Chirol, foreign affairs editor of *The Times*, saw as alternatives to the treaty: a rupture with Russia under most unfavorable military conditions or a final partition of Persia into spheres, not of influence but of permanent domination. On the other hand, a letter to *The Times* in mid-May 1907 signed by George Bernard Shaw, John Galsworthy, and Robert B. Cunninghame Graham, the latter also expressing socialist views and a writer interested in travel and travelers, expressed alarm that Britain was negotiating with Russia and thus taking sides against the people of the countries affected. Henry W. Massingham, writing in *The Nation* of September 7, 1907, warned that the treaty would force Persia to turn to Germany since Britain, her traditional friend, had deserted her and Russia was the traditional enemy.

The Russian reaction to the treaty, as shown by the press, was generally favorable among the liberals and some conservatives, dissent being largely on the far right and left.[129] Izvolsky presented the treaty to the Duma on his first appearance before that body on March 11, 1908; in his speech he stressed its contribution to the maintenance of the general peace. Paul Miliukov followed the next day in a speech which supported Izvolsky, asking for the approval of the agreement in the Duma with some reserve since he was concerned about Japanese expansion and did not think that the partition of Manchuria into spheres of influence was favorable to Russian interests; consequently he wanted an agreement with Britain and the United States. The liberal *Rech*, in an article of September 26, 1907 on "The General Meaning of the Anglo-Russian Agreement," followed on September 28 by an article on "The Anglo-Russian Agreement in the European Press," also accepted the agreement although it added that Britain had fared better than Russia. But with her superior political structure and diplomacy, this was to be expected.

---

[128] Efremov, *Vneshniaia politika Rossii*, pp. 65–66; Bestuzhev, *Bor'ba v Rossii*, pp. 170–171; No. 145 Nicolson to Grey, Mar. 18, 1907, FO 418/38; Rogers Platt Churchill, *The Anglo-Russian convention of 1907*, Cedar Rapids, IA, 1939, pp. 332–333.

[129] Browne, *The Persian revolution*, pp. 172–195; Kazemzadeh, *Russia and Britain*, pp. 501–502; Ramazani, *The foreign policy of Iran*, pp. 94, 127–128; Percy Molesworth Sykes, *A history of Persia*, 2 vols. London, 1969, II, 412–417.

5. Dairen, the Japanese "capital" in Manchuria

The conservative, government-related *Novoe Vremia* wrote in March 1907 that the Franco-Russian and Anglo-Japanese alliances and the Anglo-French entente had placed Germany in a position of "splendid isolation," that the Portsmouth treaty had brought Russia to the realization that her former Asian policy would endanger her remaining Far Eastern possessions, and that this had shown her need to seek an agreement with Britain, an arrangement which gave Britain greater freedom to concentrate on her home naval problem. This in turn was uncongenial to Germany which might be expected to try to prevent the realization of the aims of the Anglo-Russian treaty. Lenin at one extreme stated that the two parties had apportioned Persia, Afghanistan, and Tibet and laid the groundwork for a war with Germany while the right organ *Golos Moskvy* of September 26, 1907 held that the agreement was unfavorable to Russia, particularly noting her exclusion from Afghanistan and Tibet.

Repercussions in Persia were violent, in large measure because the people there saw the British concurrence in the treaty as betrayal.[130] The agreement had been made without Persian consent and, in their view, amounted to a partition of the country. A popular view was expressed in a series of articles which appeared in the influential nationalist newspaper,

---

[130] Percy Molesworth Sykes, *A history of Afghanistan*, 2 vols. London, 1940, II, 236; memorandum, "The Anglo-Russian Convention," Jan. 29, 1908, IG Political and Secret Memoranda, C 140.

6. South Manchurian Railway station, Mukden

Habl ol-Matin, on September 9, 10, 11, 14 and after, the fourth including the text of an explanatory note from the British minister to the Persian minister of foreign affairs. The author of the articles drew a tempting but incorrect and invidious comparison between the alleged British objective in the treaty and in some previous international transactions but was puzzled by the reports in the British and Russian newspapers which tended to show that there was far greater satisfaction with the treaty in London than in St. Petersburg. This seemed to the writer to indicate that Britain had received the better of the bargain.

The diplomatic note handed to the Persian minister of foreign affairs had tried to correct the impression of the British motive set forth in the early articles and to emphasize that the British desire, far from wanting to create a situation which could lead to partition, had in fact desired to secure the independence and integrity of Persia. From this point of view the satisfaction with the treaty expressed in the London papers might have arisen from a conviction that the Indian frontier had been rendered more secure. To what extent this influenced the negative impression of Britain which had been created by the treaty would be difficult to know.

Nevertheless, while the articles which followed were somewhat less violent in tone, it seems clear that British influence and popularity, which had been at their height before the treaty, were among the first conspicuous casualties of it and were replaced by an image of perfidy. This change helped to open the door for the emergence of German popularity which came later. Meanwhile, another outcome of the treaty was the tragic end of the constitutional regime. This was brought about by measures against it taken by the Shah on June 23, 1908 with the help of the Cossack brigade commanded by the Russian, Colonel Vladimir Platonovich Liakhov, operating now in an "officially" Russian zone.

The impact of the convention in Afghanistan, while less dramatic than in Persia, was nevertheless potentially of considerable importance.[131] Lord Minto, viceroy of India, in a letter of September 10, 1907, informed the Amir, Habibullah, of the treaty as it pertained to Afghanistan. He stressed its purpose in reaffirming the sovereign rights of the ruler and the principle of non-interference in the internal affairs of the country. It stated formally for the first time, he pointed out, the principle that Afghanistan was to be considered to lie outside the sphere of Russian interest and that all political relations with Afghanistan were to be conducted through the British government.

Finally, Minto explained, the treaty affirmed the right of Russian and Afghan frontier officials to deal with purely local questions and of equal treatment for British and Russian commerce in Afghanistan. The Amir replied in a letter of September 29, 1907 written while on tour saying that he could not deal with so important a subject until his return to Kabul. Though the Amir returned to the capital on November 25, this was in effect the end of the correspondence with the ruler on the subject of the treaty.

The apparent reason for this was explained by the British agent in Kabul, Fakir Syed Iftikhar-ud-Din, who wrote on January 25, 1908 that while the Amir was inclined to approve the agreement, Sardar Nasrulla Khan, an influential spokesman for the anti-British faction, had said of the British: "Allow them to open only a pinhole; they will make it wider by their skill, so that in a short time they will pass through it on elephants."[132] The treaty was seen by some as a prelude to British control or to partition. There were apparently others in the Afghan Council of State who saw the treaty as an opening for Russian intrigues.

Meanwhile, the Amir's continuing silence caused increasing concern in

---

[131] British agent at Kabul to IG, Jan. 25, 1908, FO 371/514; Vartan Gregorian, *The emergence of modern Afghanistan. Politics of reform and modernization, 1880–1946*, Stanford, 1969, pp. 227, 394–395; Reisner, "Anglo-russkaia konventsiia 1907," 61–63; Nos. 225, 243, O'Beirne to Grey, May 19, 21, 1908, FO 371/516; Minto to Morley, June 23, 1908, Nicolson Papers; No. 6 Tyrrell to Lowther, June 10, 1910, FO 371/978; Ira Klein, "The Anglo-Russian convention and the problem of Central Asia, 1907–1914," *JBS*, XI, no. 1 (Nov. 1971), 129.

[132] IO to FO July 31, 1908, enclosing IG to Morley, Sept. 28, 1908, FO 371/514; Hardinge to Nicolson, Oct. 13, 1908, Nicolson Papers; No. 50 Nicolson to Grey, Nov. 3, 1908, IO 3082 PI 1907; viceroy to Amir of Afghanistan, Dec. 8, 1908, FO 800/97; Gregorian, *Emergence of modern Afghanistan*, pp. 211–212.

London, particularly as the possibility remained that Russia might in some way use this opportunity to further her own ends. While the Russian press disclosed no hint of anything but complete loyalty to the joint official commitments, it did indicate some Russian concern that Germany might seek to advance her own aims or that the Anglo-Afghan differences might give rise to open hostilities. Furthermore, the fact that the Young Turk Committee of Union and Progress in the Ottoman Empire, in the process of seeking support for their program and for their candidate for sultan and khalif, Muhammad V, the brother of the reigning sovereign, sent representatives to Kabul, only added to the complications there.

Lord Minto was one of those who viewed these conditions as fertile ground for Russian intrigues which could be fatal to British interests in Afghanistan. He found it impossible to believe that the conclusion of the treaty could have changed the traditional Russian frontier policy and he went beyond this to suspect that Russia had accepted the treaty in the first place on the assumption that the Amir would refuse to endorse it.

This would open the door to the Russian intrigues so familiar in the past and which could easily be initiated by suggesting to the Amir that the British intended not only to build railways and telegraphs in Afghanistan, a prospect which alone was anathema to the Amir and his supporters, but to bring the country under their control. To prevent such an eventuality from arising, Minto suggested that either a letter or an emissary be sent to the Amir to urge his acceptance of the convention.

Lord Minto, acting under instructions from Viscount Morley, the secretary of state for India, wrote a letter to the Amir dated July 25, 1908 tactfully calling his attention to the fact that his own letter of September 10, 1907 remained unanswered, assuring him of British goodwill, and asking for an answer.[133] He also warned Morley, whose suggestions in writing the letter he sought, of the likelihood that the Amir would not agree and urged that the government consider what action to take in such a difficult position. Morley responded recognizing the impact of this situation on British prestige, particularly in India, and suggesting that the situation be frankly discussed with the Russian government.

The Amir's reply of August 14, 1908 conveyed to the viceroy the views of his Council opposing the convention but did not respond to the main issue. Nasrulla Khan, who had drafted the Amir's letter, appeared to be asserting strongly his opposition to the treaty. The issue was discussed with Izvolsky in October and, much to the relief of the British govern-

---

[133] Klein, "The Anglo-Russian convention," 126–147; Viktor Petrovich Leont'ev, *Inostrannaia ekspansiia v Tibete v 1888–1919 gg.*, Moscow, 1956, pp. 107–117; Precis of Arminius Vambery, "Die Englisch-Russische Vereinbarung," *Deutsche Revue* (Stuttgart), May 1907, FO 371/321.

ment, the Russian foreign minister agreed that the convention would be considered in force even without the Amir's approval.

The British government continued patiently to try to convince the Amir of the advantages he stood to gain by accepting the convention as in force, in spite of the fact that Afghanistan had been disregarded when it was being negotiated. Yet these very efforts were seen by the mistrustful nationalists in Kabul as further evidence of foreign malevolence.

The Tibetan settlement seemed at first the most secure and dependable of the three. There were the British treaty with Tibet, approved by an accommodation with China, and an agreement with Russia recognizing both and acknowledging the suzerain rights of China. There were, however, two potential flaws in the arrangement. One was the internal weakness of China and her inability to make good adequately her influence in Tibet. The other was the alertness of Russia for opportunities to resume her own quest for influence in Tibet and to seek every opportunity to strike a bargain with Britain over Tibet in order to increase the security of her own tenure in Outer Mongolia.

The collapse of China's authority in the revolution of 1911 left a power vacuum in the borderlands including Mongolia and Tibet. Responding to this and to the Russian endeavor to secure primacy in Outer Mongolia and to resume her pursuit of an influential role in Tibet, the British government shifted to a policy of securing political influence of its own in Tibet.

Reflecting on this long-delayed and hard-fought entente, Nicolson wrote with restraint to his wife: "I am sure that the best has been done in the circumstances and the only alternative was no agreement at all."[134] He was more explicit and reassuring in a note to Grey, writing that the agreement might provide 15–20 years of "peace and breathing time and in political affairs we cannot with safety look further ahead." Grey, choosing his words carefully stated with limited correctness rather than enthusiasm in his autobiography: "In its primary and cardinal object, the security of the Indian frontier, the Agreement was completely successful."[135] If these seemingly modest expectations were in fact low in comparison with the stakes Britain had held at the start of the struggle, they were higher than those held before the entrance of Germany into the fray. However, in retrospect at least three potent influences appear to have been underestimated by not being noted in these exchanges – the latent hopes of the Russians, the Germans, and the Indian nationalists.

[134] Nicolson, *Sir Arthur Nicolson*, p. 256; Nicolson to Grey, May 8, 1907, *BD*, IV, 292–293.
[135] Grey, *Twenty-five years*, I, 160.

Appendix 1
British Proposal to Russia*
January 1, 1904

Afghanistan   Russia to recognize Afghanistan as entirely within the British sphere of influence, and as under British guidance in all matters of external policy.

Direct communication to be allowed between Russian officials and officials designated by the Ameer as to matters of purely local character and of non-political complexion. Such communications to pass only between specially designated officials connected with the local administration of affairs adjoining the frontier. Russia not to send agents into Afghanistan.

It will be necessary that His Majesty's Government should obtain the approval of the Ameer of Afghanistan before any arrangement dealing with this question is concluded.

Thibet   Russia to recognize that Thibet, by reason of geographical position, is entirely within the British sphere, and to undertake not to send agents into that country.

Persia   Great Britain to recognize that Russia, as the 'Limitrophe' Power, has special interests in the north of Persia, and to engage not to seek for her own account, or on behalf of British subjects or others, any concession in the north of Persia, and not to obstruct, directly or indirectly, applications for concessions in that region supported by the Russian Government.

Russia, on her part, to recognize the special interests of Great Britain in the south of Persia, and to engage not to seek for her own account, or on behalf of Russian subjects or others, any concessions in the south of Persia, and not to obstruct, directly or indirectly, applications for con-

---

* Lansdowne Memorandum, Jan. 1, 1904, No. 1 Proposed Agreement with Russia, CAB 37/68, 1904 No. 1.

cessions in that region supported by the British Government.

With a view to preserving the integrity and independence of Persia which both Powers have agreed to maintain, Great Britain and Russia engage that, in the event of Persia applying for assistance, whether financial or administrative, they will endeavour to act in concert, and that, failing co-operation, neither Power will render such assistance without the knowledge of the other, or on conditions which prejudice the liberty of either to lend similar assistance in the future.

The Treaty rights of Great Britain in all parts of Persia to be respected, and British trade to receive equal treatment with that of all other Powers.

In the event of the embargo on railway construction in Persia being removed, Great Britain and Russia to consult together with a view to arriving at an amicable arrangement respecting the control and construction of the lines projected in their respective spheres of influence.

Great Britain to undertake not to erect fortifications on the southern littoral of Persia and in the Gulf so long as Persia retains her independence, it being clearly understood that no other Power should have a right to erect them.

Seistan

The Russian Government to recognize the Province of Seistan and the provinces coterminous with the British frontier in Baluchistan as entirely under British influence, and to abstain from interfering in northern Persia with the trade routes leading through them.

Manchuria

Great Britain to recognize the special interests of Russia, as the 'limitrophe' Power in Manchuria, to abstain from interference with the Russian control of the Manchurian Railway, and not to take exception to any reasonable measures of precaution which the Russian Government might adopt for insuring the safety of the line.

The Treaty rights of Great Britain in all parts of the Chinese Empire to be respected, and British trade to receive equal treatment with that of all other Powers.

The Russian Government to fix a date for the evacuation of Manchuria, and more particularly for that of Newchwang.

Appendix 2
Franco-Japanese Agreement*
Concluded at Paris – June 10, 1907

Agreement

The Government of His Majesty the Emperor of Japan and the Government of the French Republic, animated by the desire to strengthen the amicable relations existing between them, and to remove from those relations all cause of misunderstanding for the future, have decided to conclude the following Arrangement:

"The Governments of Japan and France, being agreed to respect the independence and integrity of China, as well as the principle of equal treatment in that country for the commerce and subjects or citizens of all nations, and having a special interest to have the order and pacific state of things preserved especially in the regions of the Chinese Empire adjacent to the territories where they have the rights of sovereignty, protection or occupation, engage to support each other for assuring the peace and security in those regions, with a view to maintain the respective situation and the territorial rights of the High Contracting Parties in the Continent of Asia."

In witness whereof, the undersigned: His Excellency Monsieur Kurino, Ambassador Extraordinary and Plenipotentiary of His Majesty the Emperor of Japan to the President of the French Republic, and His Excellency Monsieur Stephen Pichon, Senator, Minister of Foreign Affairs, authorized by their respective Governments, have signed this Agreement and have affixed thereto their seals.

Done at Paris, the 10th of June 1907.

> (*LS*)   S. [Shinichiro] Kurino
> (*LS*)   S. [Stephen] Pichon

Declaration

The two Governments of Japan and France, while reserving the negotiations for the conclusion of a Convention of Commerce in regard to the relations between Japan and French Indo-China, agree as follows:

* *NGB*, vol. 58, pp. 81–82.

The treatment of the most favored nation shall be accorded to the officers and subjects of Japan in French Indo-China in all that concerns their persons and the protection of their property, and the same treatment shall be applied to the subjects and protégés of French Indo-China in the Empire of Japan, until the expiration of the Treaty of Commerce and Navigation signed between Japan and France on the 4th of August, 1896.

Secret Explanatory Note

In order to avoid all misunderstanding in the interpretation of the Agreement this day concluded, the Governments of Japan and France declare that Fukien is, by reason of propinquity to Formosa, comprised in the regions of the Empire of China where the two High Contracting Parties are particularly desirous to have the order and peace maintained.

Appendix 3
Russo-Japanese Agreement*
Concluded at St. Petersburg – July 30, 1907

Russo-Japanese Convention

The Government of His Majesty the Emperor of Japan and the Government of His Majesty the Emperor of all the Russias desiring to consolidate relations of peace and good neighborhood which have happily been restored between Japan and Russia, and wishing to remove for the future all causes of misunderstanding in the relations of the two empires, have agreed upon the following provisions:

Article I

Each of the High Contracting parties engages to respect the existing territorial integrity of the other, as well as all rights not in conflict with the principle of equal opportunity, accruing to each of the parties from the treaties, conventions and contracts now in force between them and China, copies of which have been reciprocally exchanged between the Contracting Parties, from the treaty signed at Portsmouth on August 23/September 5, 1905, and from the special conventions concluded between Japan and Russia.

Article II

The two High Contracting Parties recognize the independence and territorial integrity of the Chinese Empire and the principle of equal opportunity for the commerce and industry of all nations therein and engage to uphold and support the maintenance of the status quo and respect for this principle by all pacific means at their disposal.

In witness whereof, the undersigned duly authorized by their respective Governments, have signed this Convention and have affixed their seals,

Done at St. Petersburg, the 30th day of the 7th month of the 40th year of Meiji, corresponding to the 30th (17th) of July, 1907.

* *NGB*, vol. 58, pp. 173–175.

(signed) Ichiro Motono
(signed) Izvolsky

Secret Agreement

The Government of His Majesty the Emperor of Japan and the Government of His Majesty the Emperor of all the Russias desiring to remove for the future all causes of friction or misunderstanding concerning certain questions relating to Manchuria, Korea and Mongolia have agreed upon the following provisions:

Article I

Having in view the natural gravitation of political and economic interests and activities in Manchuria, and desiring to avert the complications likely to arise from competition, Japan engages not to seek, for her own account or on behalf of Japanese subjects or others, any railway or telegraph concessions in Manchuria to the north of the line of demarcation specified in the Additional Article of this Convention and not to obstruct, directly or indirectly, applications for such concessions in that region supported by the Russian Government. Russia, on her part, inspired by the same pacific motives, engages not to seek, for her own account or on behalf of Russian subjects or others, any railway or telegraph concessions in Manchuria to the south of the line of demarcation above noted and not to obstruct, directly or indirectly, applications for such concessions in that region supported by the Japanese Government.

It is well understood that all rights and privileges belonging to the Chinese Eastern Railway Company by virtue of the contracts for construction of this railway on date of August 16/28, 1896 and June 13/25, 1898 shall remain in force upon the branch of that railway lying to the south of the line of demarcation specified in the Additional Article.

Article II

Russia, recognizing the relations of political solidarity existing between Japan and Korea in consequence of the Japanese–Korean conventions and agreements, copies of which have been communicated to the Russian Government by the Japanese Government, engages not to obstruct or interfere with the further development of those relations, and Japan, on her part, engages to extend to the Government, consular officers, subjects, commerce, industry and navigation of Russia in Korea, pending the conclusion of a definitive treaty, the treatment in all respects of the most favored nation.

Article III

The Imperial Government of Japan, recognizing the special interests of Russia in Outer Mongolia, engages to abstain from all interference which may prejudice these interests.

Article IV

The present Convention shall be strictly confidential between the two High Contracting Parties.

In faith whereof the undersigned, duly authorized by their respective Governments, have signed and sealed this agreement.

Done at St. Petersburg, July 17/30, 1907.

(signed) Ichiro Motono
(signed) Izvolsky

Additional Article

The line of demarcation between northern Manchuria and southern Manchuria mentioned in Article I of this Convention is established as follows:

Starting at the northwest point of the Russo-Korean frontier and describing a succession of straight lines, the line runs, after passing by Hunchun and the northernmost point of Lake of Pirteng to Hsiushuichan, thence it follows the Sungari River to the mouth of the Nunchiang to ascend thereafter the course of this river to the mouth of the Tola Ho. From this point the line follows the course of this river to its intersection with 122 degrees of easter meridian Greenwich.

Ichiro Motono
Izvolsky

Letters Exchanged

A letter from the Envoy Extraordinary and Minister Plenipotentiary of Japan stationed in Russia to the Russian Minister for Foreign Affairs with respect to the maintenance of the status quo and territorial integrity of China in Outer Monogolia.

Your Excellency have expressed to me the desire of the Imperial Russian Government to have a reservation relating to principles of status quo and equal opportunity suppressed in the secret article concerning Mongolia as these principles are categorically stated in Articles I and II of the open convention and that it was entirely unnecessary to repeat this once more in the article touching especially on Monoglia. I have the honor to inform Your Excellency that the Imperial Government has no objection to suppress in the article in question the above mentioned reservation as it is well understood between the two Governments that the provisions of Article II of the secret convention relating to Mongolia do in no way constitute a derogation to the principles of status quo and equal opportunity laid down in Articles I and II of the open convention.

I have the honor to submit this letter to Your Excellency and to request your acknowledgement of the receipt of it and your reply to it.

A reply from the Russian Minister for Foreign Affairs to the Envoy Extraordinary and Minister Plenipotentiary of Japan stationed in Russia with respect to the maintenance of the status quo and territorial integrity of China in Outer Mongolia.

Your Excellency in a letter of today's date informed me that the Japanese Government has no objection to suppress in the article of the secret convention above mentioned the provisions relating to the said principles as it is well understood between the Russian Government and the Japanese Government that the provisions of the secret convention relating to Mongolia in no way constitute a derogation to the principles of status quo and equal opportunity laid down in Articles I and II of the ostensible convention.

Acknowledging the receipt of your letter, I take this occasion to submit my esteem and courtesy to Your Excellency.

Appendix 4
Anglo-Russian Convention*
Concluded at St. Petersburg – August 31, 1907

Convention

His majesty the King of the United Kingdom of Great Britain and Ireland and of the British Dominions beyond the Seas, Emperor of India, and His Majesty the Emperor of All the Russias, animated by the sincere desire to settle by mutual different questions concerning the interests of their States on the Continent of Asia, have determined to conclude Agreements destined to prevent all cause of misunderstanding between Great Britain and Russia in regard to the questions referred to, and have nominated for this purpose their respective Plenipotentiaries, to wit:

His Majesty the King of the United Kingdom of Great Britain and Ireland and of the British Dominions beyond the Seas, Emperor of India, the Right Honourable Sir Arthur Nicolson, His Majesty's Ambassador Extraordinary and Plenipotentiary to his Majesty the Emperor of All the Russias;

His Majesty the Emperor of All the Russias, the Master of the Court Alexander Isvolsky, Minister for Foreign Affairs;

Who, having communicated to each other their full powers, found in good and due form, have agreed on the following:

Agreement concerning Persia

His Britannic Majesty's Government and the Russian Government, having mutually engaged to respect the integrity and independence of Persia, and being animated by a sincere desire for the preservation of order throughout that country and for its peaceful development, as well as for the permanent establishment of equal advantages for the trade and industry of all other nations;

Considering that each of them has, for geographical and economic reasons, a special interest in the maintenance of peace and order in certain provinces of Persia adjoining, or in the neighbourhood of, the Russian frontier on the one hand, and the frontiers of Afghanistan and Baluchistan

* William Erskine Memorandum, Dec. 31, 1907, IO Political & Secret Memoranda C 121.

on the other hand, and being desirous of avoiding all cause of conflict between their respective interests in the above-mentioned provinces of Persia;

Have agreed on the following terms:

I.

Great Britain engages not to seek for herself, and not to support in favour of British subjects or in favour of the subjects of third Powers, any Concessions of a political or commercial nature – such as Concessions for railways, banks, telegraphs, roads, transport, insurance, &c. – beyond a line starting from Kasr-i-Shirin, crossing Ispahan, Yezd, and Kakhk and ending at a point on the Persian frontier at the intersection of the Russian and Afghan frontiers, and not to oppose, directly or indirectly, demands for similar Concessions in this region which are supported by the Russian Government. It is understood that the above-mentioned places are included in the region where Great Britain undertakes not to seek the Concessions referred to.

II.

Russia, on her part, engages not to seek for herself and not to support in favour of Russian subjects, or in favour of the subjects of third Powers, any Concessions of a political or commercial nature – such as Concessions for railways, banks, telegraphs, roads, transport, insurace &c. – beyond a line going from the Afghan frontier by way of Gazik, Birjand, Kerman, and ending at Bunder Abbas, and not to oppose, directly or indirectly, demands for similar Concessions in their region which are supported by His Britaniic Majesty. It is understood that the above-mentioned places are included in the region where Russia undertakes not to seek the Concessions referred to.

III.

Russia, on her part, engages not to oppose, without previous arrangement with Great Britain, the grant of any Concessions whatever to British subjects in the regions of Persia within the lines mentioned in Articles I and II.

Great Britain undertakes a similar engagement as regards the grant of Concessions to subjects of His Imperial Majesty in the same regions of Persia.

All existing Concessions within the lines mentioned in Articles I and II are maintained.

IV.

It is understood that the revenues of all the Persian customs, with the exception of those of Farsistan and of the Persian Gulf, revenues guaranteeing the amortization and the interest of the loans concluded by the Government of the Shah with the "Banque d'Escompte et des Prets de Perse" up to date of the signature of the present Arrangement, shall be devoted to the same purpose as in the past.

It is equally understood that the revenues of the Persian customs of Farsistan and of the Persian Gulf, as well as those of the fisheries on the Persian shore of the Caspian Sea and those of the posts and telegraphs, shall be devoted, as in the past, to the service of loans concluded by the Government of the Shah with the Imperial Bank of Persia up to the date of the signature of the present Agreement.

V.

In the event of irregularities occurring in the amortization or the payment of the interest of the Persian loans concluded with the "Banque d'Escompte et des Prets de Perse" and with the Imperial Bank of Persia up to the date of the signature of the present Convention, and in the event of the necessity arising, for Russia to establish control over the sources of revenue guaranteeing the regular service of the loans concluded with the first-named bank, and which are situated in the regions mentioned in Article II of the present Agreement, or for His Britannic Majesty to establish control over the sources of revenue guaranteeing the regular service of the loans concluded with the second-named bank, and which are situated in the regions mentioned in Article I of the present Agreement, the British and Russian Governments undertake to enter beforehand into a friendly exchange of ideas with a view to determine, in agreement with each other, the measures of control in question, and to avoid all interference which would not be in conformity with the principles governing the present Agreement.

Convention respecting Afghanistan

The High Contracting Parties, in order to assure the perfect security of their respective frontiers in Central Asia and to maintain in these regions a solid and lasting peace, have concluded the following Convention:

Article I

His Britannic Majesty's Government declare that they have no intention of changing the political status of Afghanistan.

His Britannic Majesty's Government further engage to exercise their influence in Afghanistan only in a pacific sense, and they will not themselves take, or encourage Afghanistan to take, any measures threatening Russia.

The Russian Government on their part declare that they recognize Afghanistan as outside the sphere of Russian influence, and they engage that all their political relations with Afghanistan shall be conducted through the intermediary of His Britannic Majesty's Government; they further undertake not to send any Agents into Afghanistan.

Article II

The Government of His Britannic Majesty having declared in the Treaty signed at Kabul on the 21st March, 1905, that they recognize the Agreement and the engagements concluded with the late Ameer Abdur Rahman, and that they have no intention of interfering in the internal government of Afghan territory, Great Britain engages not to annex or to occupy in contravention of that Treaty any portion of Afghanistan or to interfere in the internal administration of the country, provided that the Ameer fulfils the engagements already contracted towards His Majesty's Government under the above-mentioned Treaty.

Article III

The Russian and Afghan authorities, specially designated for the purpose on the frontier or in the frontier provinces, may establish direct relations with each other for the settlement of local questions of a non-political character.

Article IV

His Britannic Majesty's Government and the Russian Government affirm their adherence to the principle of equality of commercial opportunity in Afghanistan, and they agree that any facilities which may have been, or shall be hereafter obtained for British and British-Indian commerce and traders, shall be equally enjoyed by Russian commerce and traders. Should the progress of commerce establish the necessity for Commercial Agents, the two Governments will agree as to what measures shall be taken, due regard, of course, being had to the Ameer's sovereign powers.

Article V

The present Arrangements will only come into force when His Britannic Majesty's Government has notified to the Russian Government the consent of the Ameer to the terms stipulated above.

Agreement concerning Thibet

The Governments of Great Britain and Russia recognizing the suzerain rights of China in Thibet, and in view of the fact that Great Britain, by reason of her geographical position, has a special interest in the maintenance of the status quo in the external relations of Thibet, have made the following Agreement:

Article I

The two High Contracting Parties engage to respect the territorial integrity of Thibet and to abstain from all interference in its internal administration.

Article II

In conformity with that admitted principle of the suzerainty of China over Thibet, Great Britain and Russia engage not to enter into negotiations with Thibet except through the intermediary of the Chinese Government. This engagement does not exclude the direct relations between British Commercial Agents and the Thibetan authorities as provided for in Article V of the Convention between Great Britain and Thibet of the 7th September, 1904, and confirmed by the Convention between Great Britain and China of the 27th April, 1906; nor does it modify the engagements entered into by Great Britain and China in Article I of the said Convention of 1906.

It is clearly understood the Buddhists, subjects of Great Britain or of Russia, may enter into direct relations on strictly religious matters with the Dalai Lama and the other representatives of Buddhism in Thibet; the Governments of Great Britain and Russia engage, as far as they are concerned, not to allow those relations to infringe the stipulations of the present Agreement.

Article III

The British and Russian Governments repectively engage not to send Representatives to Lhassa.

Article IV

The two High Contracting Parties engage not to seek or obtain, whether for themselves or their subjects, any Concessions for railways, roads, telegraphs, and mines, or other rights in Thibet.

Article V

The two Governments agree that no part of the revenues of Thibet, whether in kind or in cash, shall be pledged or assigned to Great Britain or Russia or to any of their subjects.

Annex to the Agreement between Great Britain and Russia regarding Thibet

Great Britain reaffirms the Declaration, signed by his Excellency the Viceroy and Governor-General of India and appended to the ratified Convention of the 7th September, 1904, to the effect that the occupation of the Chumbi Valley by British forces shall cease after the payment of three annual instalments of the indemnity of 2,500,000 rupees, provided that the trade marts mentioned in Article II of that Convention have been effectively opened for three years, and that in the meantime the Thibetan authorities faithfully comply with the terms of the said Convention of 1904 in all respects. It is clearly understood that if the occupation of the Chumbi Valley by the British forces has not for any reason been terminated at the time anticipated in the above Declaration, the British and Russian Governments will enter upon a friendly exchange of views on this subject.

The present Convention shall be ratified, and the ratifications exchanged at St. Petersburgh as soon as possible.

In witness whereof the respective Plenipotentiaries have signed the present Convention and affixed thereto their seals.

Done in duplicate at St. Petersburgh, the 18th (31st) August, 1907.

(*LS*)   A. Nicolson
(*LS*)   Isvolsky

Bibliography

MANUSCRIPT SOURCES

Public Record Office Documents
Foreign Office

A General Correspondence
Central Asia FO 106
China (including Tibet) FO 17
Japan FO 46
Morocco FO 99 (Algeciras Conference): 434 April–June 1905; 435 July–Sept.
  1905; 436 Oct.–Dec. 1905; (FO 371 Political, after 1906); 171, 172, 173, 174,
  175 (1906); 374 (1907)
Persia FO 60
Russia FO 65
Turkey (including Baghdad Railway) FO 78

B Confidential Prints
Central Asia FO 539
China FO 405
Japan FO 410
Persia FO 416
Russia FO 418
Tibet and Mongolia FO 535

C Other
Protocols of Treaties FO 93
Ministers and Officials FO 800
II Other Government Departments Series

Admiralty
Adm 1 Admiralty Secretariat, Papers
Adm 12 Indexes and Compilations, Series III
Adm 116 Indexes and Compilations, Cases
Adm 121 Mediterranean Correspondence

Cabinet
Cab 1
Cab 4 Committee of Imperial Defence Memoranda: miscellaneous (Series B)
Cab 5 Committee of Imperial Defence Memoranda: colonial defence series
  (Series C)

314

Cab 6 Committee of Imperial Defence Memoranda: defence of India (Series D)
Cab 7 Committee of Imperial Defence Memoranda:
Cab 16 Committee of Imperial Defence ad hoc sub-committees of enquiry
Cab 17

War Office
WO 106 Directorate of Military Operations and Intelligence, Papers

Commonwealth Relations Office – India Office Library
Political and Secret Department
Dispatches from India
External Files
Home Correspondence
Letters from India
Memoranda C 120, C 121, C 122, C 125, C 126, C 140
Political Files

Private Papers
Lord Ampthill Correspondence, IOL, MSS Eur. E233
Sir Francis Bertie Papers, PRO FO 800 (159–191)
Lord Curzon Papers, IOL, MSS Eur. F111
Sir Edward Grey Papers, PRO FO 800 (35–113)
Lord George Hamilton Papers, IOL, MSS Eur. C125, C126, D508, D510
Sir Charles Hardinge Papers, Cambridge University Library
Sir John Jordan Papers, PRO FO 350
Lord Lansdowne Papers, PRO FO 800 (115–146)
Sir Frank Lascelles Papers, PRO FO 800 (6–20)
Sir Arthur Nicolson (Lord Carnock) Papers, PRO FO 800 (336–381)
Lord Salisbury Papers, Christ Church, Oxford University
Sir Ernest Mason Satow Papers, PRO, PRO 30/33
Sir Donald Mackenzie Wallace Papers, Royal Archives, Windsor
Japan. Foreign Office
"Diplomatic Correspondence", letters, telegrams, misc. items
"Manshu ni Kansuru Nisshin Dampan Hikki," Nov. 17–Dec. 18, 1905
"Nichiro Kosho Shi," 2 vols., Foreign Office circulation
"Nichiro Kowa Dampan Hikki, tsuki Ryokaku Zenken Hiseishiki Kaiken Yoroku (Aug. 9–Sept. 5, 1905)", Foreign Office circulation
"Protocols of the Peace Conference between Japan and Russia", Foreign Office circulation

PRINTED SOURCES

Abrams, Irwin. "The Austrian question at the turn of the twentieth century." *JCEA*, IV, no. 2 (July 1944), 186–201.
Adamov, E. A. (ed.) *Sbornik dogovorov Rossii s drugimi gosudarstv 1856–1917.* Moscow, 1952.
Adler, Cyrus. *Jacob H. Schiff*, 2 vols. New York, 1928.
Adoratsky, V., Maksakov, V., Pokrovsky, M. N. (eds.) "N. N. Romanov i amerikanskaia kontsessiia na zheleznuiu dorogu Sibir'-Aliaska v 1905." *KA*, VI (43) (1930), 173–176.

Albertini, Luigi. *The origins of the war of 1914.* Trans. and ed. Isabella M. Massey, 3 vols. London, 1952.

Alzona, Encarnacion. *Some French contemporary opinions of the Russian revolution of 1905.* New York, 1921.

Amfiteatrov, Aleksandr Valentinovich. *Franko-russki soiuz i 9-oe ianvaria: pis'mo k Zhanu Zoresu.* Geneva, 1905.

Anan'ich, Boris Vasil'evich. "Iz istorii Anglo-russkogo sopernichestva v Persii nakanune Russko-iaponskoi voiny (Persidskii zaliv)." *Uchenye zapiski* Leningradskogo gosudarstvennogo pedagogicheskogo universiteta im. A. I. Gertsena, vol. 194 (1958), 229–264.

"Krizis ekonomicheskoi politika tsarizma v Persii v 1904–6 gg." *IZ*, LXXIV (1963), 245–275.

"Rossiia i kontsessiia d'Arsi." *IZ*, LXVI (1960), 278–290.

Rossiia i mezhdunarodnyi kapital, 1897–1914. Leningrad, 1970.

Rossiiskoe samoderzhavie i vyvoz kapitalov 1895–1914 gg. (po materialam uchetno-ssudnogo banka Persii). Leningrad, 1975.

"Uchetno-ssudnyi bank Persii v 1894–1907 gg." In Akademiia nauk SSSR. *Monopolii i inostrannyi kapital v Rossii.* Moscow, 1962, pp. 274–314.

Anderson, Eugene Newton. *The first Moroccan crisis, 1904–1906.* Chicago, 1930.

Andrew, Christopher. "German world policy and the reshaping of the dual alliance." *JCH*, I, no. 3 (July 1966), 137–151.

Théophile Delcassé and the making of the Entente Cordiale. New York, 1968.

Arktur (pseud.) [Ivan Ivanovich Dusinskii]. *Osnovnye voprosy vneshnei politiki v sviazi s programmoi nashei voenno-morskoi politiki.* Odessa, 1908.

Astaf'ev, I. I. *Russko-germanskie diplomaticheskie otnosheniia 1905–1911 gg. (ot Portsmutskogo mira do Potsdamskogo soglasheniia).* Moscow, 1972.

Aston, George [Aston, Major General Sir George]. "The Entente Cordiale and the military conversations." *QR*, CCLVIII, no. 512 (April 1932), 363–383.

Asylbekov, Malik Khantemiruly. *Zheleznodorozhniki Kazakhstana v pervoi russkoi revoliutsii 1905–1907 gg.* Alma Ata, 1965.

"The Baghdad railway convention 5 March 1903." In Hurewitz, J. C. *Diplomacy in the Near and Middle East,* 2 vols. New York, 1956, I, 252–263.

Baransky, Nikolai Nikolaevich. *V riadakh sibirskogo sotsial-demokraticheskogo soiuza. Vospominaniia o podpol'noi rabote v 1897–1907 godakh,* 2-e izd. Tomsk, 1961.

Barclay, Thomas. *Thirty years. Anglo-French reminiscences (1876–1906).* London, 1914.

Barker, J. Ellis. "The Triple Entente and Triple Alliance." *NC*, LXIV, no. 37 (July 1908), 1–17.

Beale, Howard K. *Theodore Roosevelt and the rise of America to world power.* Baltimore, 1955.

Becker, Otto. *Der Ferne Osten und das Schicksal Europas 1907–1918.* Leipzig, 1940.

Becker, Seymour. *Russia's protectorates in Central Asia. Bukhara and Khiva, 1865–1924.* Cambridge, 1968.

Bee, Minge C. "The Peterhof agreement." *CSPSR*, XX, no. 2 (July 1936), 231–250.

Bennigsen, Alexandre and Lemercier-Quelquejay, Chantal. *Islam in the Soviet*

Union. Foreword by Geoffrey E. Wheeler. London, 1967.

Beresford, Charles. *The break-up of China: with an account of its present commerce, currency, waterways, armies, railways, politics, and future prospects*. New York, 1900.

Beresford, Col. C. E. de la Poer. "Russian railways towards India." *PCAS* (1906), 3–24.

Bernstein, Herman. *The Willy-Nicky correspondence. Being the secret and intimate telegrams exchanged between the Kaiser and the Tsar*. New York, 1918.

Berton, Peter Alexander. "The secret Russo-Japanese alliance of 1916." Ph.D. dissertation, Columbia University, 1956.

Bestuzhev, Igor Vasil'evich. "Bor'ba klassov i partii Rossii po voprosam vneshnei politiki nakanune Bosniiskogo krizisa (1906–1908 gg.)." *IZ*, LXIV (1959), 136–185.

Bor'ba v Rossii po voprosam vneshnei politiki, 1906–1910. Moscow, 1961.

Bickford, J. D. and Johnson, E. N. "The contemplated Anglo-German alliance, 1890–1901." *PSQ*, XIII, no. 1 (Mar. 1927), 1–57.

Bing, Edward J. (ed.) *The secret letters of the last Tsar, being the confidential correspondence between Nicholas II and his mother, Dowager Empress Maria Feodorovna*. New York, 1938.

Bolsover, G. H. "Aspects of Russian foreign policy, 1815–1914." In Pares, B. and Taylor, A. J. P. (eds.) *Essays presented to Sir Lewis Namier*. London, 1956, pp. 320–356.

Bompard, Maurice. *Mon ambassade en Russie (1903–1908)*. Paris, 1937.

Bondarevsky, Grigorii L'vovich. *Bagdadskaia doroga i proniknovenie germanskogo imperializma na Blizhnii Vostok (1888–1903)*. Tashkent, 1955.

Bornhak, Konrad. *Die Kriegsschuld: Deutschlands Weltpolitik, 1890–1914*. Berlin, 1929.

Bourne, Kenneth. *Britain and the balance of power in North America, 1815–1908*. Berkeley, 1976.

Foreign policy of Victorian England 1830–1902. Oxford, 1970.

Bovykin, Valerii Ivanovich. *Ocherki istorii vneshnei politiki Rossii konets XIX veka-1917 goda*. Moscow, 1960.

Brandenburg, Erich. *From Bismarck to the World War. A history of German foreign policy, 1870–1914*. Trans. Annie Elizabeth Adams. London, 1927.

Brandt, Maximilian August von. *China und seine Handelsbeziehungen zum Auslande*. Berlin, 1899.

Browne, Edward G. *The Persian revolution of 1905–1909*. London, 1966.

Bülow, Bernhard Heinrich Martin Karl von. *Memoirs of Prince Bülow*, 4 vols. Boston, 1931.

Burgman, Torsten. *Svensk opinion och diplomati under Rysk-Japanska kriget 1904–1905*. Uppsala, 1965.

Busch, Briton Cooper. *Britain and the Persian Gulf, 1894–1914*. Berkeley, 1967.

Hardinge of Penshurst: a study in the old diplomacy. Hamden, CT, 1980.

Buxhoeveden, Baroness Sophie. *Before the storm*. London, 1939.

Calchas [Garvin, James Louis]. "The Anglo-Russian agreement." *LA*, CCLV (1907), 323–334.

Cambon, Paul. *Correspondence 1870–1924*, 3 vols. Paris, 1940.

Cameron, Meribeth. "Chang Chih-tung." In Hummel, Arthur W. (ed.) *Eminent*

Chinese of the Ch'ing period (1644–1912), 2 vols. Washington, 1943, I, 27–32.

Carlgren, W. M. *Die Renaissance des Dreikaiserbundes. Ein Grosspolitischer plan Aehrenthals im. Jahre 1906.* Stockholm, 1954.

Carrère d'Encausse, Hélène. *Islam and the Russian Empire: reform and revolution in Central Asia.* Berkeley, 1988.

"Organization and colonization of the conquered territories." In Allworth, Edward (ed.) *Central Asia: a century of Russian rule.* New York, 1967, pp. 151–171.

"Social and political reform." In Allworth, Edward (ed.) *Central Asia: a century of Russian rule.* New York, 1967, pp. 189–206.

"The stirring of national feeling." In Allworth, Edward (ed.) *Central Asia: a century of Russian rule.* New York, 1967, pp. 172–188.

Carroll, E. Malcolm. *Germany and the great powers 1866–1914. A study in public opinion and foreign policy.* Hamden, CT, 1966.

Cecil, Lamar J. "Coal for the fleet that had to die." *AHR*, LXIX, no. 4 (July 1964), 990–1005.

The German diplomatic service, 1871–1914. Princeton, 1976.

Chamberlain, Gordon Blanding. "Japan, France, and the Russian Baltic Fleet: a diplomatic sidelight on the War of 1904–1905." Ph.D. dissertation, University of California, Berkeley, 1972.

Chapman, Maybelle Rebecca (Kennedy). *Great Britain and the Bagdad railway 1888–1914.* North Hampton, MA, 1948.

Chirol, Valentine. "Indian borderlands. The Russian and German pressure before the war." *Asia* (April 1919), 361–367.

Churchill, Rogers Platt. *The Anglo-Russian convention of 1907.* Cedar Rapids, IA, 1939.

Colquhoun, Archibald R. *Russia against India. The struggle for Asia.* New York, 1900.

Craig, Gordon Alexander. *From Bismarck to Adenauer. Aspects of German statecraft.* Baltimore, 1958.

The politics of the Prussian army 1640–1945. Oxford, 1955.

Crisp, Olga. "The Russian liberals and the 1906 Anglo-French loan to Russia." *SEER*, XXXIX, no. 93 (June 1961), 497–511.

Curtiss, John Shelton. *Russia's Crimean War.* Durham, NC, 1979.

Curzon, George N. "The fluctuating frontier of Russia in Asia." *NC*, XXV (Feb. 1889), 267–283.

"The Transcaspian railway." *PRGS*, XI (May 1889), 273–295.

Davies, Godfrey. "The pattern of British foreign policy: 1815–1914." In Schuyler, Robert L. and Ausubel, Herman. *The making of English history.* New York, 1952, pp. 600–605.

Davis, Harold E. "The citizenship of Jon Perdicaris." *JMH*, XIII, no. 4 (Dec. 1941), 517–526.

Dehio, Ludwig. *Germany and world politics in the twentieth century.* New York, 1960.

Dehmelt, Bernard Karl. "Bülow's Moroccan policy, 1902–1905." Ph.D. dissertation, University of Pennsylvania, 1963.

Dennett, Tyler. *John Hay from poetry to politics.* New York, 1933.

"President Roosevelt's secret pact with Japan." *CH*, XXI (Oct. 1924), 15–21.

Roosevelt and the Russo-Japanese War. New York, 1925.

Dennis, A. L. P. *Adventures in American diplomacy 1896–1906.* New York, 1928.

Dilks, David. *Curzon in India,* 2 vols. London, 1969–70.

Dillon, Emile Joseph. "The Anglo-Russian agreement and Germany." *CR,* XCII (1907), 690–700.

"Was the North Sea incident made in Germany?" *CR,* LXXXVI (Dec. 1904), 883–901.

Dobrov, Aleksandr Solomonovich. *Dal'nevostochnaia politika SShA v period Russko-iaponskoi voiny.* Moscow, 1952.

Drage, Geoffrey. *Russian affairs.* London, 1904.

Dua, Ramparkash A. *The impact of the Russo-Japanese War on Indian politics.* Delhi, 1966.

Dugdale, E. T. S. *German diplomatic documents, 1871–1914,* 4 vols. New York, 1928–31.

Durand, Henry Mortimer. "Sir Alfred Lyall and the understanding with Russia." *JRCAS,* I, pt. 3 (1914), 20–45.

Earle, Edward Mead. *Turkey, the Great Powers and the Bagdad Railway. A study in imperialism.* New York, 1923.

Edwardes, Michael. *British India, 1772–1947. A survey of the nature and effects of alien rule.* New York, 1967.

High noon of empire, India under Curzon. London, 1965.

Edwards, E. W. "The Far Eastern agreements of 1907." *JMH,* XXVI, no. 4 (Dec. 1954), 340–355.

"The Japanese Alliance and the Anglo-French Agreement of 1904." *H,* XLII, no. 144 (Feb. 1957), 19–27.

Efremov, Pavel Nikolaevich. *Vneshniaia politika Rossii (1907–1914 gg.).* Moscow, 1961.

Einstein, Lewis. *A diplomat looks back,* ed. Lawrence E. Gelfland. New Haven, 1968.

Enteen, George M. "Writing party history in the USSR: the case of E. M. Iaroslavskii." *JCH,* XXI, no. 2 (Apr. 1986), 321–339.

Entner, Marvin L. *Russo-Persian commercial relations, 1828–1914.* Gainesville, 1965.

Erusalimsky, A. S. "Rossiia i Alzherirasskaia konferentsiia." *KA,* XLI–XLII (4–5) (1930), 3–61.

Eubank, Keith. *Paul Cambon, master diplomatist.* Norman, OK, 1960.

Eyre, James, K. Jr. "Russia and the American acquisition of the Philippines." *MVHR,* XXVIII (1942), 539–562.

Fay, Sidney Bradshaw. "The Kaiser's secret negotiations with the Tsar, 1904–1905." *AHR,* XXIV, no. 1 (Oct. 1918), 48–72.

The origins of the World War. 2 vols. New York, 1966.

Fedorov, Mikhail Pavlovich. *Real'nyia osnovy sovremennoi mezhdunarodnoi politiki; doklad v Obshchestve Vostokovedeniia.* St. Petersburg, 1909.

Feis, Herbert. *Europe, the world's banker, 1870–1914.* New Haven, 1930.

Fellner, Fritz. "Die Haltung Oesterreich–Ungarns während der Konferenz von Algeciras 1906." *Mitteilungen des Instituts für Oesterreichische Geschichtsforschung,* LXXI (1963), 642–477.

Fink, Troels. *Spillet om Dansk Neutralitet 1905–09 L.C.F. Lütken og Dansk*

Udenrigs-og Forsvarpolitik. Aarhus, 1959.

Ustabil balance, Dansk Udenrigs-og Forsvarspolitik 1894–1905. Aarhus, 1961.

Fischer, Fritz. *Germany's aims in the First World War.* London, 1967.

Ford, Thomas K. "The genesis of the first Hague Conference." *PSQ*, LI, no. 3 (Sept. 1936), 354–382.

France. Ministère des Affaires Etrangères. *Documents diplomatiques français (1871–1914).* 2nd series (1901–1911), 41 vols. Paris, 1930.

Documents diplomatiques. Affaires du Maroc, 1901–1905. Paris, 1905.

Francis, Richard M. "The British withdrawal from the Baghdad railway project in 1903." *HJ*, XVI, no. 1 (Mar. 1973), 168–178.

Fraser, Lovat. *India under Curzon and after.* London, 1911.

Fraser-Tytler, William Kerr. *Afghanistan. A study of political developments in Central Asia.* London, 1950.

Friedberg, Aaron L. *The weary titan. Britain and the experience of relative decline, 1895–1905.* Princeton, 1988.

Futrell, Michael. *Northern underground. Episodes of Russian revolutionary transport and communications through Scandinavia and Finland 1863–1917.* London, 1963.

Gafford, Frank Hall. "The Anglo-Russian condominium in Persia, 1907–1912." Ph.D. dissertation, University of Texas, 1940.

Galperin, A. *Anglo-iaponskii soiuz, 1902–1921.* Moscow, 1947.

Gates, Rosalie Prince. "The Tibetan policy of George Nathaniel Curzon, Viceroy of India. Jan. 1899–Apr. 1904, Dec. 1904–Nov. 1905." Ph.D. dissertation, Duke University, 1965.

Gerard, Auguste. *Ma mission au Japon, 1907–1914.* Paris, 1919.

Ma mission en Chine (1893–1897). Paris, 1918.

Germany. Auswärtiges Amt. *Die grosse Politik der europäischen Kabinette 1871–1914. Sammlung der diplomatischen Akten der Auswärtigen Amptes,* 40 vols. Berlin, 1922–7.

Geyer, Dietrich. *Russian imperialism: the interaction of domestic and foreign policy, 1860–1914.* New Haven, 1987.

Gilpin, William. *The cosmopolitan railway. Compacting and fusing together all the world's continents.* San Francisco, 1890.

Girault, René. *Emprunts Russes et investissements français en Russie 1887–1914.* Paris, 1973.

Goerlitz, Walter. *History of the German General Staff.* New York, 1954.

Golionko, V. P. "Vooruzhennoe vosstanie matrosov Tikhookeanskogo Flota v 1905–1907 gg." In Naida, S. F. *Voennye moriaki v period pervoi russkoi revoliutsii 1905–1907 gg.* Moscow, 1955, pp. 276–320.

Golovachev, Petr Mikhailovich. *Rossiia na Dal'nem Vostoke.* St. Petersburg, 1904.

Gooch, George Peabody. *Studies in modern history.* New York, 1931.

Gooch, George Peabody and Ward, A. W. (eds.) *The Cambridge history of British foreign policy: 1783–1919,* 3 vols. New York, 1923.

Gopal, Surendra. *British policy in India, 1858–1905.* Cambridge, 1965.

Goudswaard, Johan Marius. *Some aspects of the end of Britain's "splendid isolation." 1898–1904.* Rotterdam, 1952.

Great Britain. Foreign Office. *British documents on the origins of the war, 1898–*

1914, 11 vols. London, 1926–38.

Greaves, Rose Louise. "British policy in Persia, 1892–1903," *BSOAS*, XXVIII (1965), pt. 1, 34–60; pt. 2, 284–307.

Persia and the defense of India 1884–1892. A study in the foreign policy of the Third Marquis of Salisbury. London, 1959.

Gregorian, Vartan. *The emergence of modern Afghanistan. Politics of reform and modernization, 1880–1946*. Stanford, 1969.

Grenville, John A. S. "Great Britain and the Isthmian Canal, 1848–1901," *AHR*, LXI (Oct. 1955), 48–69.

Lord Salisbury and foreign policy: the close of the nineteenth century. London, 1964.

Grey of Falladon, Viscount. *Twenty-five years, 1892–1916*, 2 vols. New York, 1925.

Grigortsevich, Stanislav Seliverstovich. *Dal'nevostochnaia politika imperialisti-cheskikh derzhav v 1906–1917 gg*. Tomsk, 1965.

"Uchastie koreitsev russkogo Dal'nego Vostoka v antiiaponskoi natsional'no-osvoboditel'noi borbe (1906–1916 gg.)." *VI*, no. 10 (1958), 139–151.

Grimm, Claus. "Graf Witte und die deutsche Politik." Ph.D. dissertation, University of Freiburg, Germany, 1930.

Grothe, Hugo. *Die Bagdadbahn und das Schwäbische Beuernelement in Transkauk-asien und Palästina. Gedanken zur kolonisation Mesopotamiens*. Munich, 1902.

Grulev, Mikhail Vladimirovich. *Sopernichestvo Rossii i Anglii v Srednei Azii*. St. Petersburg, 1909.

Guillen, Pierre. "The Entente of 1904 as a colonial settlement." In Gifford, Prosser and Louis, William Roger (eds.) *France and Britain in Africa. Imperial rivalry and colonial rule*. New Haven, 1971, pp. 333–368.

Gurko, Vladimir Iosifovich. *Features and figures of the past: government and opinion in the reign of Nicholas II*. Stanford, 1939.

Gwinner, Arthur von. "The Bagdad railway and the question of British coope-ration." *NC*, CCCLXXXVIII, no. 65 (June 1909), 1083–1094.

Gwynn, Stephen L. (ed.) *The letters and friendships of Sir Cecil Spring Rice. A record*, 2 vols. Boston, 1929.

Hackett, Roger F. *Yamagata Aritomo in the rise of modern Japan, 1838–1922*. Cambridge, MA, 1971.

Haldane, Richard Burdon, Viscount. *Richard Burdon Haldane (Viscount Hal-dane). An autobiography*. New York, 1929.

Hale, Oron James. *Germany and the diplomatic revolution: a study in the diplomacy of the press, 1904–1906*. Philadelphia, 1931.

The great illusion 1900–1914. New York, 1971.

Hallett, Holt S. "France and Russia in China." *NC*, XLI (Mar. 1897), 487–502.

Hallgarten, George Wolfgang Felix. *Imperialismus vor 1914*, 2 vols. Munich, 1951, 1963.

Hamada, Kengi. *Prince Ito*. Tokyo 1936.

Hamilton, Angus. *Problems of the Middle East*. London, 1909.

Hammann, Otto. *Bilder aus der letzten Kaiserzeit*. Berlin, 1922.

Zur Vorgeschichte des Weltkrieges: Erinnerungen aus den Jahren 1897–1906. Berlin, 1919.

Han Woo-keun. *The history of Korea*. Honolulu, 1971.

Hardinge, Arthur H. *A diplomatist in the East*. London, 1928.

Hardinge of Penshurst, Lord. *Old diplomacy: the reminiscences of Lord Hardinge of Penshurst*. London, 1947.

Hargreaves, J. D. "The origin of the Anglo-French military conversations in 1905." *H*, XXXVI, no. 128 (Oct. 1951), 244–248.

Harrison, E. J. *Peace or war east of Baikal?* Yokohama, 1910.

Harrison, W. "Mackenzie Wallace's view of the Russian revolution of 1905–1907." *OSP*, new series, IV (1971), 73–82.

Hasenclever, Adolf. "Theodore Roosevelt und die Marokkokrisis von 1904–1906," *APG*, VI, pt. 3 (1928), 184–245.

Hauser, Oswald. *Deutschland und der Englisch-Russische Gegensatz, 1900–1914*. Berlin, 1958.

   "Die Englisch-Russische Konvention von 1907 und die Meerengenfrage." In M. Göhring and A. Scharff, *Geschichtliche Kräfte und Entscheidungen: Festschrift zum fünfundsechzigsten Geburtstage von Otto Becker*. Wiesbaden, 1954, pp. 233–265.

Helfferich, Karl Theodor. *Die deutsche Türkenpolitik*. Berlin, 1921.

Henderson, W. O. "German economic penetration in the Middle East, 1870–1914." *EHR*, XVIII, nos. 1 & 2 (1948), 54–64.

Herwig, Holger H. "The German reaction to the *Dreadnought* revolution." *The International History Review*, XIII, no. 2 (May 1991), 273–283.

The history of the Times. III. *The twentieth century test, 1884–1912*. London, 1947.

Hoffman, Ross J. S. *Great Britain and the German trade rivalry, 1875–1914*. Philadelphia, 1933.

Holborn, Hajo. *A history of modern Germany, 1840–1945*. New York, 1969.

Holstrem, Vladimir. "Ex Oriente Lux: a plea for Russo-American understanding," *NAR*, CLXIX, no. 512 (July 1899), 6–32.

Hone, J. M. and Dickinson, Page L. *Persia in revolution. With notes of travel in the Caucasus*. London, 1910.

Hosie, Alexander. *Manchuria. Its people, resources and recent history*. Boston, 1910.

Hosking, Geoffrey A. *The Russian constitutional experiment; government and Duma, 1907–1914*. Cambridge, 1973.

Howard, Christopher. *Splendid isolation. A study of ideas concerning Britain's international position and foreign policy during the later years of the Third Marquis of Salisbury*. London, 1967.

Howe, Mark Antony DeWolfe. *George von Lengerke Meyer: his life and public services*. New York, 1919.

Hunt, Michael H. *Frontier defense and the Open Door. Manchuria in Chinese–American relations, 1895–1911*. New Haven, 1973.

Hurewitz, J. C. *Diplomacy in the Near and Middle East*, 2 vols. New York, 1956.

Iakunin, A. F. "Revoliutsiia 1905–1907 gg. v Kazakhstane." In Ivanov, L. M., Pankratova, A. M., and Sidorov, A. L. (eds.) *Revoliutsiia 1905–1907 gg. v natsional'nykh raionakh Rossii: sbornik statei*. Moscow, 1955.

Ianchevetsky, Dmitrii Grigorevich. *Groza s Vostoka. Zadachi Rossii i zadachi Iaponii na Dal'nem Vostoke: ocherki*. Revel, 1907.

Iaroslavskii, Emelian [Minei Izraelevich Gubelman]. *Russko-iaponskaia voina i otnoshenie k nei bol'shevikov.* Moscow, 1939.

Ignat'ev, Anatolii Venediktovich. *Russko-angliiskie otnosheniia nakanune pervoi mirovoi voiny (1908–1914 gg.)* Moscow, 1962.

Vneshniaia politika Rossii v 1905–1907 gg. Moscow, 1986.

Iklé, Frank W. "The triple intervention: Japan's lesson in the diplomacy of imperialism." *MN*, XXII, nos. 1–2 (1967), 122–130.

Imbert, Paul. "Le chemin de fer de Bagdad." *RDM*, 5th period (vols. 1–60, 1901–10), XXXVIII (1907), 655–682.

Iriye, Akira. *Pacific estrangement. Japanese and American expansion, 1897–1911.* Cambridge, MA, 1972.

Iswolsky, Hélène (ed.) *Au service de la Russie, Alexandre Iswolsky. Correspondence diplomatique, 1906–1911,* 2 vols. Paris, 1937–39.

Itakura, Takuzo. *Kokusai funso shiko.* Tokyo, 1935.

Ivanov, L. M., Pankratova, A. M., and Sidorov, A. L. (eds.) *Revoliutsiia 1905–1907 gg. v natsional'nykh raionakh Rossii: sbornik statei.* Moscow, 1955.

"Iz dnevnika Konstantina Romanova, 1905 god." *KA*, I (44), (1931), 126–151; II (45), (1931), 112–129.

Jaeckel, Horst. *Die Nordwestgrenze in der Verteidigung Indiens 1900–1908 und der Weg Englands zum Russisch-Britischen Abkommen von 1907.* Cologne, 1968.

Japan. Foreign Office. *Komura Gaikoshi.* 2 vols. Tokyo, 1953.

Nihon Gaiko Bunsho, vols. XLVII, LVIII. Tokyo, 1953.

Department of Railways. *An official guide to Eastern Asia, I. Chosen & Manchuria, Siberia.* Tokyo, 1920.

Jelavich, Barbara. "British means of offense against Russia in the 19th century." *RH*, I (1974), 119–135.

Johnson, Franklyn Arthur. *Defense by committee. The British Committee of Imperial Defense, 1885–1959.* London, 1960.

Jones, R. B. "Anglo-French negotiations, 1907: a memorandum by Sir Arthur Milner." *BIHR*, XXXI (Nov. 1958), 224–227.

Judge, Edward H. *Plehve: repression and reform in Imperial Russia 1902–1904.* Syracuse, 1983.

Jusserand, Jean Jules. *What me befell. The reminiscences of J. J. Jusserand.* Boston, 1933.

Kahn, Helen Dodson. "The great game of empire: Willard D. Straight and American Far Eastern policy." Ph.D. dissertation, Cornell University, 1968.

Kalmykov, Andrew D. *Memoirs of a Russian diplomat. Outposts of the empire, 1893–1917.* New Haven, 1971.

Kaneko Kentaro. "Beikoku daitoryo kaiken shimatsu." Japan. Foreign Office Circulation, July 9, 1907.

Kann, Robert A. *A history of the Habsburg Empire, 1626–1918.* Berkeley, 1980.

Kantorovich, Anatolii. *Amerika v borbe za Kitai.* Moscow, 1935.

Kantorowicz, Hermann. *The spirit of British policy and myth of the encirclement of Germany.* Trans. W. H. Johnston, preface by Gilbert Murray. New York, 1932.

Kawai, Kazuo. "Anglo-German rivalry in the Yangtse region 1895–1902." *PHR*, VIII, no. 4 (Dec. 1939), 413–433.

Kazemzadeh, Firuz. *Russia and Britain in Persia, 1864–1914. A study in imperialism.* New Haven, 1968.

"Russian imperialism and Persian railways." In McLean, Hugh, et al. (eds.) *Russian thought and politics*. Karpovich memorial volume. *Harvard Slavic Studies*, IV (1957), 355–373.

Keddie, Nikki R. "Iranian politics 1900–1905: background to revolution." *MES*, V, no. 1 (Jan. 1969), 3–31.

"The origins of the religious-radical alliance in Iran." *PP*, no. 34 (July 1966), 170–180.

Sayyid Jamal ad-Din "al-Afgani": a political biography. Berkeley, 1972.

Keep, John L. H. *The rise of social democracy in Russia*. Oxford, 1963.

Kehr, Eckart. *Battleship building and party politics in Germany, 1894–1901: a cross section of the political, social, and ideological preconditions of German imperialism*, trans and ed. Pauline R. Anderson and Eugene N. Anderson. Chicago, 1973.

Kelin, F. V. (ed.) "Novye dokumenty ob Alzhezirasskoi konferentsii i zaime 1906 g." *KA*, I (44) (1931), 161–165.

Kennedy, Paul Michael. "German world policy and the Alliance negotiations with England, 1897–1900." *JMH*, XL, no. 4 (Dec. 1973), 605–625.

"Mahan versus Mackinder: two interpretations of British sea power." *MM*, 2 (1974), 39–66.

The rise and fall of British naval mastery. New York, 1976.

"Tirpitz, England and the second navy law of 1900: a strategical critique." *MM*, 2 (1970), 33–57.

Kent, Marian. "Constantinople and Asiatic Turkey, 1905–1914." In Hinsley, F. H. (ed.) *British foreign policy under Sir Edward Grey*. Cambridge, 1977, pp. 148–164.

Khaptaev, P. T. *Istoriia Buriat-Mongol'skoi ASSR*, vol. 1. Ulan-Ude, 1954.

Khvostov, Vladimir Mikhailovich (ed.) *Istoriia diplomatii*. II. *Diplomatiia v novoe vremia, 1871–1914*. Moscow, 1963.

Kim, C. I. Eugene and Kim, Han-Kyo. *Korea and politics of imperialism, 1876–1910*. Berkeley, 1967.

Kim, Syn-Khva [Kim Sung-Hwa]. *Ocherki po istorii sovetskikh koreitsev*. Alma Ata, 1965.

Klein, Ira. "The Anglo-Russian convention and the problem of Central Asia, 1907–1914." *JBS*, XI, no. 1 (Nov. 1971), 133–147.

Kokovtsov, Vladimir Nikolaevich. *Out of my past: the memoirs of Count Kokovtsov, Russian minister of finance, 1904–1914, chairman of the council of ministers, 1911–1914*, ed. H. H. Fisher. Stanford, 1935.

Korff, Sergei Aleksandrovich. *Russia's foreign relations during the last half century*. New York, 1922.

Korostovets, Ivan Iakovlevich [Korostowetz, J. J.] *Prewar diplomacy: the Russo-Japanese problem: treaty signed at Portsmouth, U.S.A.* London, 1920.

Krushanov, A. I. (ed.) *Vladivostok (sbornik istoricheskikh dokumentov, 1860–1907 gg.)* Vladivostok, 1960.

Kumar, Ravinder. *India and the Persian Gulf region, 1858–1907. A study in British imperial policy*. Bombay, 1965.

Kuropatkin, Aleksei Nikolaevich. *The Russian army and the Japanese war*, 2 vols. New York, 1909.

Kutakov, Leonid Nikolaevich. *Portsmutskii mirnyi dogovor (iz istorii otnoshenii*

Iaponii s Rossiei i SSSR, 1905–1945 gg.) Moscow, 1961.
Lamb, Alastair. *The McMahon line. A study in the relations between India, China and Tibet, 1904–1914*, 2 vols. London, 1966.
Lambton, Ann K. S. *Qajar Persia. Eleven studies.* Austin, 1988.
"Secret societies and the Persian revolution of 1905–6." *St. Antony's papers*, no. 4, *Middle Eastern Affairs*, no. 1 (1959), 43–60.
Lane, David. "The Russian Social Democratic Labour Party in St. Petersburg, Tver and Ashkhabad, 1903–1905." *SS*, XV (1964), 331–344.
Laney, Frank Miller. "The military implementation of the Franco-Russian Alliance, 1890–1914." Ph.D. dissertation, University of Virginia, 1954.
Langer, William L. *The diplomacy of imperialism, 1890–1902*, 2 vols. New York, 1935, 1951.
Laue, Theodore H. von. *Sergei Witte and the industrialization of Russia.* New York, 1963.
Lazzerini, Edward James. "Gadidism at the turn of the twentieth century: a view from within." *CMRS*, XVI (1975), 245–277.
"Ismail Bey Gasprinskii and Muslim modernism in Russia, 1878–1914." Ph.D. dissertation, University of Washington, Seattle, 1973.
Lebedev, Viacheslav Vladimirovich. *Russko-amerikanskie ekonomicheskie otnosheniia, 1900–1917 gg.* Moscow, 1964.
Lee, Dwight Erwin. *Europe's crucial years: the diplomatic background of World War I. 1902–1914.* Hanover, NH, 1974.
Lee, Sidney. *King Edward VII: a biography*, 2 vols. New York, 1927.
LeFeber, Walter. *The new empire: an interpretation of American expansion, 1860–1898.* Ithaca, 1963.
Lensen, George Alexander. *Balance of intrigue: international rivalry in Korea and Manchuria, 1884–1899*, 2 vols. Tallahassee, FL, 1982.
The Russo-Chinese war. Tallahassee, FL, 1967.
Lensen, George Alexander (trans. and ed.) *The D'Anethan dispatches from Japan, 1894–1910. The observations of Baron Albert d'Anethan, minister plenipotentiary and dean of the diplomatic corps.* Tokyo, 1967.
Leont'ev, Viktor Petrovich. *Inostrannaia ekspansiia v Tibete v 1888–1919 gg.* Moscow, 1956.
Lewis, Bernard. *The emergence of modern Turkey.* London, 1962.
Liashchenko, Petr Ivanovich. *History of the national economy of Russia to the 1917 revolution.* New York, 1949.
Lincoln, W. Bruce. *In war's dark shadow. The Russians before the great war.* New York, 1983.
Lindgren, Raymond E. *Norway–Sweden: union, disunion, and Scandinavian integration.* Princeton, 1959.
Lindow, Erich. *Freiherr Marschall von Bieberstein als Botschafter in Konstantinopel, 1897–1912.* Danzig, 1934.
Liu Kwang-Ching. "German fear of a quadruple alliance, 1904–1905." *JMH*, XVIII, no. 3 (Sept. 1946), 222–246.
Livermore, Seward W. "The American navy as a factor in world politics, 1903–1913." *AHR*, LXIII, no. 4 (July 1958), 863–879.
Livezey, William Edmund. *Mahan on sea power.* Norman, OK, 1947.
Lodge, Henry Cabot. *Selections from the correspondence of Theodore Roosevelt and*

Henry Cabot Lodge, 1884–1918, 2 vols. New York, 1925.

Long, James William. "The economics of the Franco-Russian Alliance, 1904–1906." Ph.D. dissertation, University of Wisconsin, 1968.

"Organized protest against the 1906 Russian loan." *CMRS*, XIII (Jan.–Mar. 1972), 24–39.

Lowe, Cedric James and Dockrill, M. L. *The mirage of power*, 3 vols. London,1972.

MacBean, William Alleyne. *Handbook of the Russian army, 1905*, 4th ed. London, 1905.

McCarthy, Mary M. *Anglo-Russian rivalry in Persia*. Buffalo, 1925.

McCullough, David. *The path between the seas: the creation of the Panama Canal, 1870–1914*. New York, 1977.

McDermott, J. "The immediate origins of the Committee of Imperial Defense: a reappraisal." *CJH*, VII (1972), 253–272.

"The revolution in British military thinking from the Boer War to the Moroccan crisis." In Kennedy, Paul M. (ed.) *The war plans of the Great Powers, 1880–1914*. London, 1979, pp. 99–117.

McDonald, David MacLaren. *United government and foreign policy in Russia, 1900–1914*. Cambridge, MA, 1992.

McGeoch, Lyle A. "British policy and the Spanish corollary to the Anglo-French Agreement of 1904." In Baker, Nancy and Brown, Marvin, Jr. (eds.) *Diplomacy in an age of nationalism. Essays in honor of Lynn Marshall Case*. The Hague, 1976, pp. 209–222.

Mackay, Ruddock F. "The Admiralty, the German navy and the redistribution of the British fleet 1904–5." *Mariner's mirror*, LVI (1970), 341–346.

Fisher of Kilverstone. Oxford, 1973.

Mackinder, Halford J. "The geographical pivot of history." *GJ*, XXIII, no. 4 (Apr. 1904), 421–444.

MacMurray, John Van Antwerp. *Treaties and agreements with and concerning China, 1894–1919*, 2 vols. New York, 1921.

Maisky, Ivan Mikhailovich. *Sovremennaia Mongoliia (otchet Mongol'skoi ekspeditsii snariazhennoi Irkutskoi kontoroi Vserossiiskogo tsentral'nogo soiuza potrebitel'nykh obshchestv "Tsentrosoiuz"*. Irkutsk, 1921.

Maksakov, V. (ed.) *Karatel'nye ekspeditsii v Sibiri v 1905–1906 gg*. Moscow, 1932.

Malozemoff, Andrew. *Russian Far Eastern policy, 1881–1904: with special emphasis on the causes of the Russo-Japanese War*. Berkeley, 1958.

Mandelstam, Andrei Nikolaevich. "La politique Russe d'accès à la Mediterranée au XXeme siècle." *Academie de Droit International. Recueil des cours*, XLVII (1934), 603–798.

Manning, Roberta Thompson. *The crisis of the old order in Russia: gentry and government*. Princeton, 1982.

Marder, Arthur J. *The anatomy of British sea power. A history of British naval policy in the pre-dreadnought era, 1880–1905*. New York, 1940.

From the dreadnought to Scapa Flow. The Royal Navy in the Fisher era, 1904–1919, I. London, 1961.

Marks III, Frederich W. *Velvet on iron. The diplomacy of Theodore Roosevelt*. Lincoln, NE, 1979.

Marlowe, John. *Cromer in Egypt*. New York, 1970.

Marrow, Ian E. D. "The foreign policy of Prince von Bülow, 1898–1909." *CHĴ*, IV, no. 1 (1932), 87.

Marsden, Arthur. "Britain and the 'Tunis Base,' 1894–1899." *EHR*, LXXXIX, no. 310 (Jan. 1964), 67–96.

Martin, Bradford G. *German–Persian diplomatic relations 1873–1912*. The Hague, 1959.

Massie, Robert Y. *Nicholas and Alexandra*. New York, 1967.

Masson, Vadim Mikhailovich and Romodin, V. A. *Istoriia Afganistan*, 2 vols. Moscow, 1964–5.

Mathews, Joseph J. *Egypt and the formation of the Anglo-French entente of 1904*. Philadelphia, 1939.

Matsui, Masato. "The Russo-Japanese agreement of 1907: its causes and the progress of negotiations." *MAS*, VI, no. 1 (1972), 33–48.

Matveev, Mikhail Ivanovich. *Studenty Sibiri v revoliutsionnom dvizhenii*. Tomsk, 1966.

Maurice, Frederick. *Haldane, 1856–1928. The life of Viscount Haldane of Cloan, K.T., O.M.*, 2 vols. London, 1937–39.

May, Ernest R. "The Far Eastern policy of the United States in the period of the Russo-Japanese War: a Russian view." *AHR*, LXII, no. 2 (Jan. 1957), 345–351.

Mayer, S. L. "Anglo-German rivalry at the Algeciras Conference." In Gifford, Prosser and Louis, William Roger (eds.) *Britain and Germany in Africa: imperial rivalry and colonial rule*. New Haven, 1967, pp. 215–244.

Mehlinger, Howard and Thompson, John W. *Count Witte and the Tsarist government in the 1905 revolution*. Bloomington, 1972.

"Memorandum 'Russia's relations with India (1900–1917).'" *CAR*, VI, no. 4 (1958), 448–464 (based on O. F. Solov'ev, "K voprosu ob otnoshenii Tsarskoi Rossii k Indii v XIX–nachale XX veka," no. 6 (1958), 96–109.

Merkulov, Spiridon Dionisevich. *Porto-franko i kolonizatsiia Priamurskago kraia russkim naseleniem*. St. Petersburg, 1908.

Meyendorff, Aleksandr Feliskovich. *Correspondence diplomatique de M. de Staal [Egor Egorovich Staal]*, I, *1884–1900*, I, 1883–1888, II, 1889–1900. Paris, 1929.

Meyer, Henry Cord. *Mitteleuropa in German thought and action*. The Hague, 1955.

The military correspondent of "The Times." *Imperial strategy*. London, 1906.

Miliukov, Paul. *Political memoirs, 1905–1917*. Trans. and ed. Carl Goldberg and Arthur P. Mendel. Ann Arbor, 1967.

Milshtein, A. A. "Revoliutsionnye vystupleniia trudiashchikhsia i soldat v 1906–1907 gg. na Dal'nem Vostoke i Vostochnoi Sibiri." In Tikhomirov, M. N., *Sbornik statei po istorii Dal'nego Vostoka*. Moscow, 1958, pp. 316–322.

Mogilevich, A. A. and Airapetian, M. E. "Legenda i pravda o Gullskom intsidente 1904 g." *IZh.*, no. 6 (1940), 41–52.

Monger, George W. *The end of isolation, British foreign policy 1900–1917*. London, 1963.

Morison, Elting E. (ed.) *The letters of Theodore Roosevelt*, 8 vols. Cambridge, MA, 1951.

Moritzen, Julius. "Denmark the buffer state of the north." *AMRR*, XXXII, no. 3

(Sept. 1905), 305–309.

Marrow, Ian E. D. "The foreign policy of Prince von Bülow, 1898–1909." *CHJ*, IV, no. 1 (1932), 63–93.

Muratov, Kh. I. *Revoliutsionnoe dvizhenie v russkoi armii v 1905–1907 gg.* Moscow, 1955.

Murray, John A. "British policy and opinion on the Anglo-Russian entente," 2 vols. Ph.D. dissertation, Duke University, 1957.

"Nakanune russko-iaponskoi voiny". *KA*, no. 63, 1934.

Narochnitsky, Aleksei Leont'evich. *Kolonial'naia politika kapitalisticheskikh derzhav na Dal'nem Vostoke, 1860–1895.* Moscow, 1956.

Nevins, Allan. *Henry White: thirty years of American diplomacy.* New York, 1930.

Newton, Lord [Newton, Thomas Wodehouse Legh]. *Lord Lansdowne: a biography.* London, 1929.

Nicolson, Harold. *Sir Arthur Nicolson, Bart. First Lord Carnock. A study in the old diplomacy.* London, 1931.

Nish, Ian H. *The Anglo-Japanese alliance. The diplomacy of two island empires, 1894–1907.* London, 1966.

— *The origins of the Russo-Japanese war.* London, 1985.

Nol'de, Boris Emmanuilovich. *Dalekoe i blizkoe: istoricheskie ocherki.* Paris, 1930.

Nowak, Karl Friedrich. *Germany's road to ruin.* Trans. W. W. Dickes. New York, 1932.

Ochsenwald, William. *The Hijaz railroad.* Charlottesville, 1980.

Ogg, Frederic A. "European alliances and the war." *AMRR*, XXXIII, no. 3 (Sept. 1905), 295–301.

Okamoto, Shumpei. *The Japanese oligarchy and the Russo-Japanese war.* New York, 1970.

Oppel, Bernard F. "Russo-German relations, 1904–1906." Ph.D. dissertation, Duke University, 1966.

— "The waning of a traditional alliance: Russia and Germany after the Portsmouth Peace Conference." *Central European History*, V, no. 4 (Dec. 1972), 318–329.

Ostal'tseva, Alevtina Fedorovna. "Anglo-frantsuzskoe soglashenie 1904 g. i Anglo-russkie otnosheniia." *Uchenye zapiski Saratovskogo universiteta*, XVI: vypusk istoricheskii (1958), 204–251.

— *Anglo-russkie soglashenie 1907 goda: vliianie Russko-iaponskoi voiny i revoliutsiia 1905–1907 godov na vneshniuiu politiku tsarizma i na peregruppirovku evropeiskikh derzhav.* Saratov, 1977.

— "K voprosu ob imperialisticheskikh protivorechiiakh mezhdu Angliei i Rossiei vo vremia zakliucheniia soglasheniia 1907 g." *Nauchnye doklady vysshei shkoly, istoricheskie nauki*, no. 4 (1958), 143–157.

Oyama, Azusa. *Nihon Gaikoshi Kenkyu.* Tokyo, 1963.

Padfield, Peter. *The great naval race.* New York, 1974.

Paléologue, Maurice. *Three critical years (1904–05–06).* New York, 1957.

Parr, John Francis. *Théophile Delcassé and the practice of the Franco-Russian Alliance 1898–1905.* Fribourg, Switzerland, 1951.

Parsons, Edward B. "Roosevelt's containment of the Russo-Japanese War." *PHR*, XXXVIII, no. 1 (Feb. 1969), 21–43.

Pashukanis, S. A. (ed.) "K istorii Anglo-russkogo soglasheniia 1907 g." *KA*, no.

2–3 (LXIX-LXX) (1935), 3–39.

"Russko-germanskii dogovor 1905 goda, zakliuchennyi v Bërke. Iz telegrammy Vil'gel'ma II k Nikolaiu II." *KA*, V (1924), 5–49.

Pavlovich, Mikhail Lazarovich. "Vneshniaia politika i Russko-iaponskaia voina." In Martov, L., et al. (eds.) *Obshchestvennoe dvizhenie v Rossii v nachale XX-go veka.* St. Petersburg, 1910, II, pt. 1, pp. 1–32.

"Vneshniaia politika Rossii ot Portsmutskago mira do nashikh dnei." In Martov, L., et al. (eds.) *Obshchestvennoe dvizhenie v Rossii v nachale XX-go veka.* St. Petersburg, 1910 (1), IV, pt. 1, pp. 223–278.

Pelcovits, Nathan A. *Old China hands and the Foreign Office.* New York, 1948.

Penson, Lillian. "The new course in British foreign policy, 1892–1902." *TRHS*, XXV (1943), 121–138.

Perkins, Bradford. *The great rapprochement. England and the United States, 1895–1914.* New York, 1970.

Perrins, Michael. "Russian military policy in the Far East and the 1905 revolution in the Russian army." *European Studies Review*, no. 3 (July 1979), 331–349.

Phelps, Dawson. "Izvolskii and Russian foreign policy, 1906–1910." Ph.D. dissertation, University of California, Berkeley, 1931.

Piaskovsky, Anatolii Vladimirovich. *Revoliutsiia 1905–1907 godov v Turkestane.* Moscow, 1958.

Revoliutsiia 1905–1907 godov v Uzbekistane. Tashkent, 1957.

Pierce, Richard A. (ed.) *Russian Central Asia, 1867–1917. A study in colonial rule.* Berkeley, 1960.

Plass, Jens B. *England zwischen Russland und Deutschland: Der Persische Golf in der Britischen Vorkriegspolitik, 1899–1907. Dargestellt nach Englischem Arkhivmaterial.* Schriftenreihe des Instituts für Auswärtige Politik, no. 3. Hamburg, 1966.

Pokrovsky, Mikhail Nikolaevich (ed.) "Tsarskaia diplomatiia o zadachaiakh Rossii na Vostoke v 1900 g." *KA*, no. 5 (18) (1926), 3–29.

Pooley, A. M. (ed.) *The secret memoirs of Count Tadasu Hayashi.* New York, 1915.

Popov, A. L. (ed.) "Stranitsa iz istorii russkoi politiki v Persia." *MZ*, no. 4–5 (1924), 133–164.

"Tsarskaia Rossiia i Mongoliia." *KA*, XXXVII (6) (1929), 3–68.

Popov, A. L. (ed.) "Anglo-russkoe soglashenie o razdele Kitaia (1899 g.)." *KA*, XXV (1927), 111–134.

(ed.) "Anglo-russkoe sopernichestvo na putiakh Irana." *NV*, bk. XII (1926), 126–148.

(ed.) "Anglo-russkoe sopernichestvo v Persii v 1890–1906 gg." *KA*, I (56) (1933), 33–64.

(ed.) "Pervye shagi russkogo imperializma na Dal'nem Vostoke (1888–1903 gg.)." *KA*, LII (1932), 34–124.

(ed.) "Tsarskaia Rossiia i Persiia v epokhu Russko-iaponskoi voiny." *KA*, no. 4 (53) (1932), 3–37.

(ed.) "Zaem 1906 g. v doneseniiakh russkogo posla v Parizhe." *KA*, no. 4–5 (10–11) (1925), 421–432.

Porter, Charles W. *The career of Théophile Delcassé.* Philadelphia, 1936.

Preobrazhensky, E. A. and Romanov, B. A. (eds.) *Russkie finansy evropeiskaia birzha v 1904–1906 gg.* Moscow, 1926.

Price, Ernest Batson. *The Russo-Japanese treaties of 1907–1916 concerning Manchuria and Mongolia.* Baltimore, 1933.

Queen, George Sherman. "The United States and the material advance in Russia 1881–1906." Ph.D. dissertation, University of Illinois, Urbana, 1941.

Quested, Rosemary Y. I. *"Matey" imperialists? The Tsarist Russians in Manchuria 1895–1917.* Hong Kong, 1982.

The Russo-Chinese Bank: a multinational financial base of Tsarism in China. Birmingham Slavonic Monographs. Birmingham, 1977.

Rader, Ronald Ray. "Decline of the Afghan problem as a crisis factor in Russian foreign policy, 1892–1907." Ph.D. dissertation, Syracuse University, 1965.

Raleigh, Sir Thomas (ed.) *Lord Curzon in India. Being a selection from his speeches as viceroy and governor-general of India, 1898–1905.* London, 1906.

Ramazani, Rouhollah K. *The foreign policy of Iran. A developing nation in world affairs.* Charlottesville, 1966.

Rassow, Peter. "Schlieffen und Holstein." *HZ*, CLXXIII, no. 2 (1952), 297–313.

Reichman, Henry Frederick. *Railwaymen and revolution: Russia 1905.* Berkeley, 1987.

Reisner, Igor Mikhailovich (ed.) "Anglo-russkaia konventsiia 1907 goda i razdel Afganistana (po materialam sekretnogo arkhiva byvshego M.I.D.)." *KA*, no. 3 (10) (1925), 54–66.

Renouvin, Pierre. "L'orientation de l'alliance Franco-Russe en 1900–1901." *RHD*, LXXX (July–Sept. 1966), 193–204.

Révoil, Paul. "Journal tenu pendant la Conférence d'Algésiras, 12 janvier–9 avril 1906." *DDF*, 2nd series, IX–2, 857–969.

Rich, Norman. *Friedrich von Holstein. Politics and diplomacy in the era of Bismarck and Wilhelm II*, 2 vols. Cambridge, MA, 1965.

Rich, Norman and Fisher, M. H. *The Holstein papers*, 4 vols. Cambridge, MA, 1963.

Riha, Thomas. *A Russian European: Paul Miliukov in Russian politics.* Notre Dame, 1969.

Ritter, Gerhard. *The sword and the sceptor.* Trans. Heinz Norden, 4 vols. Coral Gables, FL, 1973.

Robbins, Keith. *Sir Edward Grey. A biography of Lord Grey of Falladon.* London, 1971.

Robinson, Henry S. "The Franco-Russian Alliance 1894–1904 with special reference to Great Britain." Ph.D. dissertation, University of London, 1965.

Rolo, Paul Jacques Victor. *Entente Cordiale. The origins and negotiation of the Anglo-French agreements of 8 April 1904.* London, 1969.

Romanov, Boris Aleksandrovich. *Ocherki diplomaticheskoi istorii Russko-iaponskoi voiny, 1895–1907.* Moscow, 1947, 1955.

Russia in Manchuria (1892–1906). Ann Arbor, MI, 1952.

Romanov, Boris Aleksandrovich (ed.) "K peregovoram Kokovtsova o Zaime v 1905–1906 gg." *KA*, III (X) (1925), 3–35.

Ronaldshay, Lord (Earl of) [Zetland, Lawrence]. *The life of Lord Curzon*, 3 vols. London, 1927.

Rosen, Friedrich. *Aus einem diplomatischen Wanderleben*, 4 vols. in 3. Berlin and Wiesbaden, 1931–1959.

"Russlands haltung bei der Morokk-Konferenz von Algeciras. Ein wort zur einführung in die Russischen Algecirasdokumente." *BM*, IX (Mar. 1931), 207–209.

Rosen, Roman Romanovich. *Forty years of diplomacy*, 2 vols. London, 1922.

Rosenbaum, Arthur Lewis. "China's first railway: the imperial railways of North China, 1880–1911." Ph.D. dissertation, Yale University, 1972.

"The Manchuria bridgehead: Anglo-Russian rivalry and the imperial railways of North China, 1897–1902." *MAS*, X, no. 1 (1976), 41–64.

Rothenberg, Gunther E. "The Habsburg army and the nationality problem in the nineteenth century, 1815–1914." *AHY*, III, pt. 1 (1967), 70–87.

Rotshtein, Fedor Aronovich (ed.) "Perepiska V. N. Kokovtsova s Ed. Netslinym." *KA*, IV (1923), 129–156.

Rotshtein, Fedor Aronovich (ed.) "Zakhvat Germeniei Kiao-Chao v 1897 g." *KA*, II (87) (1938), 19–63.

Rozental', Eduard Markovich. *Diplomaticheskaia istoriia Russko-frantsuzskogo soiuza v nachale XX veka*. Moscow, 1960.

"Frantsuzskaia diplomatiia i Anglo-russkoe sblizhenie v 1906–1907 gg. (k voprosu o vkliuchenii Rossii v Antantu)." *ISSR*, no. 5 (1958), 123–136.

Russia. Ministerstvo inostrannykh del. *Dokumenty, kasaiushchiesia zakliucheniia mezhdu Rossiei i Iaponiei obshchepoliticheskago soglasheniia 17 (30) iiulia 1907 goda*. St. Petersburg, 1907.

Ocherk istorii Ministerstva inostrannykh del. 1802–1902. St. Petersburg, 1902.

Protokoly Portsmutskoi mirnoi konferentsii i tekst dogovora mezhdu Rossieiu i Iaponieiu zakliuchennago v Portsmut 23 avgusta (5 sentiabria) 1905 goda. St. Petersburg, 1906 (2).

Sbornik diplomaticheskikh dokumentov kasaiushchikhsia sobytii v Persii s kontsa 1906 g. po 31 dekabria 1911 g. St. Petersburg, I, 1911 and V, 1917.

Pereselencheskoe glavnago upravleniia zemleustroistva i zemledeliia. *Aziatskaia Rossiia*, 3 vols. and atlas. St. Petersburg, 1914.

St. Aubyn, Giles. *Edward VII, prince and king*. New York, 1979.

Schmitt, Bernadette E. "Triple Alliance and Triple Entente, 1902–1914." *AHR*, XXIX, no. 3 (April 1924), 449–473.

Schultz, Lothar. "Constitutional law in Russia." In Katkov, George et al. (ed.) *Russia enters the twentieth century, 1894–1917*. London, 1971, pp. 34–59.

Schwertfeger, Bernhard (ed.) *Zur Europäischen politik 1897–1914*, I, 1897–1904, Zweibund/Englisch-Deutscher Gegensatz. Wilhelm Köhler (ed.) II, 1905–1907, Marokkokrisis/König Edward VII. Bernard Schwertfeger (ed.) V, Revanche-Idee und Panslawismus. Wilhelm Köhler (ed.) Berlin, 1919.

Seeger, Charles Louis. *Recollections of a foreign minister (memoirs of Alexander Iswolsky)*. New York, 1921.

Sergeev, A. A. (ed.) "Vil'gel'm II o Russko-iaponskoi voine i revoliutsii 1905 goda." *KA*, II (9) (1925), 56–65.

ShakabPa, Tsepon W. D. *Tibet: a political history*. New Haven, 1967.

Shatsillo, Kornelii Fedorovich. *Russkii imperializm i razvitie flota nakanune Pervoi mirovoi voiny (1906–1914 gg.)*. Moscow, 1968.

Shaw, Stanford J. and Shaw, Ezel Kural. *History of the Ottoman Empire and modern Turkey*, 2 vols. London, 1977.

Shel'king, Evgenii Nikolaevich [Schelking, Eugene de]. *Recollections of a Russian diplomat: the suicide of monarchies (William II and Nicholas II)*. New York,

1918.

Siebert, Benno Aleksandrovich [Zibert]. *Graf Benckendorffs diplomatischer schriftwechsel*, 3 vols. Berlin, 1928.

Siegelbaum, Lewis H. "Another 'Yellow Peril': Chinese migrants in the Russian Far East and the Russian reaction before 1917." *MAS*, no. 2 (1978), 307–330.

Skrine, Claremont Percival and Nightingale, Pamela. *Macartney at Kashgar: new light on British, Chinese and Russian activities in Sinkiang, 1890–1912.* London, 1973.

Slavin, S. V. "Avantiura Loik de Lobelia [Loicq de Lobel] i Tsarskii dvor." *LS*, no. 1 (1949), 227–241.

Smith, Irving H. "Anglo-Russian relations and the Dogger Bank Incident 1902–1905." MA thesis, McGill University, 1955.

Snesarev, Andrei Evgenevich. *Indiia kak glavnyi faktor v Sredne-aziatskom vopros. Vzgliad tuzemtsev Indii na anglichan i ikh upravlenie.* St. Petersburg, 1906.

Sokol, Edward D. *The revolt of 1916 in Russian Central Asia.* Baltimore, 1954.

Sontag, John P. "Tsarist debts and Tsarist foreign policy." *SR*, XXVII, no. 4 (Dec. 1968), 529–541.

Sorokin, Aleksandr Ivanovich. *Russko-iaponskaia voina 1904–1905 godov (voenno-istoricheskii ocherk).* Moscow, 1956.

Spector, Ivar. *The first Russian revolution: its impact on Asia.* Englewood Cliffs, NJ, 1962.

Spendelow, Howard R. "Russia's lease of Port Arthur and Talien: the failure of China's traditional foreign policy." *PC*, XXIV (1971), 146–169.

Staley, Eugene. "Business and politics in the Persian Gulf; the story of the Wönckhaus Firm." *PSQ*, XLVIII (1933), 367–385.

Stead, Alfred. "Conquest by bank and railway, with examples from Russia and Manchuria." *NC*, LIII, no. 216 (June 1903), 936–949.

Steed, Henry Wickham. *Through thirty years, 1892–1922. A personal narrative*, 2 vols. New York, 1924.

Steinberg, Jonathan. "The Copenhagen complex." *JCH*, I, no. 3 (July 1966), 23–46.

    "The German background to Anglo-German relations, 1905–1914." In Hinsley, F.H. (ed.) *British foreign policy under Sir Edward Grey.* Cambridge, 1977, pp. 193–215.

    "Germany and the Russo-Japanese war." *AHR*, LXXV, no. 7 (Dec. 1970), 1965–1986.

    Yesterday's deterrent. Tirpitz and the birth of the German battle fleet. London, 1965.

Steiner, Zara S. *The Foreign Office and foreign policy, 1898–1914.* Cambridge, 1969.

Stephan, John J. "The Korean minority in the Soviet Union." *M*, XIII, no. 3 (Dec. 1971), 138–150.

Subotich, Dean Ivanovich. *Zadachi Rossii na Dal'nem Vostoke.* Revel, 1908.

Sugawara, Takamitsu. "Japanese interests in Korea and the Yalu issue 1903–1904." MA Thesis, University of Hawaii, 1963.

Sykes, H. R. "Our recent progress in southern Persia and its possibilities." *PCAS*

(1905), 3–28.

Sykes, Percy Molesworth. *A history of Afghanistan*, 2 vols. London, 1940.
A history of Persia, 2 vols. London, 1969.

Synn, Seung Kwon [Sin, Sung-gwon]. "The Russo-Japanese struggle for the control of Korea, 1894–1904." Ph.D. dissertation, Harvard University, 1967.

Szeftel, Marc. "The form of government of the Russian Empire prior to the constitutional reforms of 1905–06." In Curtiss, John Shelton. *Essays in Russian and Soviet history in honor of Geroid Tanquary Robinson*. New York, 1963, pp. 105–119.

Tardieu, André. *La Conférence d'Algésiras. Histoire diplomatique de la crise Marocaine (15 Janvier–7 Avril 1906)*. Paris, 1908.

Tarlé, Evgenii Viktorovich. "Evropa v epokhu imperializma, 1871–1919." In his *Sochineniia*, vol. 5, Moscow, 1958, pp. 21–508.
"Graf S. Iu. Vitte. Opyt kharakteristiki vneshnei politiki." In his *Sochineniia*, vol. 5, Moscow, 1958, pp. 509–566.

Taube, Mikhail Aleksandrovich [Taube, Michael de]. *La politique russe d'avant-guerre et la fin de l'empire des tsars (1904–1917)*. Paris, 1928.

Taylor, Alan J. P. *The struggle for mastery in Europe, 1848–1918*. Oxford, 1954.

Thornton, Archibald Paton. "British policy in Persia, 1858–1890." *EHR*, LXIX, no. 273 (Oct. 1954), 554–579; LXX, no. 274 (Jan. 1955), 55–71.

Tirpitz, Alfred Peter Friedrich von. *My memoirs*, 2 vols. London, 1919.

Townsend, Mary Evelyn. *The rise and fall of Germany's colonial empire, 1884–1918*. New York, 1930.

Treadgold, Donald W. *The Great Siberian migration. Government and peasant in resettlement from emancipation to the First World War*. Princeton, 1957.

Trevelyan, George Macaulay. *Grey of Fallodon. Being the life of Sir Edward Grey afterwards Viscount Grey of Fallodon*. London, 1937.

Tsovikian, K. M. "Vliianie Russkoi revoliutsii 1905 g. na revoliutsionnoe dvizhenie v Turtsii." *SV*, III (1945), 15–35.

Tupper, Harmon. *To the great ocean, Siberia and the Trans-Siberian railway*. London, 1965.

Ukhtomsky, Esper Esperovich. *Pered groznym budushchim i k russko-iaponskomu stolknoveniiu*. St. Petersburg, 1904.

United States. Dept. of State. *Papers relating to the foreign relations of the United States, 1894, 1899, 1900, 1903, 1904, 1905*. Washington DC, 1895, 1900, 1901, 1904, 1905, 1906.

Unterberger, P. F. "Priamurskii kraii, 1906–1910." *Zapiski*, Imperatorskago Russkago Geograficheskago Obshchestva, XIII, 1912.

Urodkov, S. A. "Chitinskoe vooruzhennoe vosstanie 1905 g." *VLU*, no. 8 (1956), 19–39.

USSR Central Archives. *Krasnyi arkhiv*, 73 vols. in 109 issues. Moscow, 1922–41.
Russko-iaponskaia voina: iz dnevnikov A. N. Kuropatkina i N. P. Linievicha. Foreword by M. N. Pokrovsky. Leningrad, 1925.

Valliant, Robert Britton. "Japan and the Trans-Siberian railroad, 1885–1905." Ph.D. dissertation, University of Hawaii, 1974.

Vambery, Arminius. *Western culture in Eastern lands. A comparison of the methods adopted by England and Russia in the Middle East*. London, 1906.

Vetoshkin, Mikhail Kuzmich. *Bol'sheviki Dal'nego Vostoka v Pervoi russkoi revoliutsii*. Moscow, 1947.

Viereck, Peter. "Revolution in values: roots of the European catastrophe, 1870–1952." *PSQ*, LXVII, no. 3 (Sept. 1952), 339–356.

Viskovatov, Vladimir. *Amurskaia zheleznaia doroga* [n.p.], 1908.

Vogel, Barbara. *Deutsche Russlandpolitik: das Scheitern der deutschen Weltpolitik unter Bülow, 1900–1906*. Dusseldorf, 1973.

Vonliarliarsky, Vladimir Mikhailovich. *Moi vospominaniia, 1852–1939 gg*. Berlin, 1939.

Walters, Eurof. "Aehrenthal's attempt in 1907 to re-group the European powers." *SEER*, XXX, no. 74 (Dec. 1951), 213–251.

"Franco-Russian discussions on the partition of Austria–Hungary." *SEER*, XXVIII, no. 70 (Nov. 1949), 184–197.

"Lord Salisbury's refusal to revise and renew the Mediterranean agreements." *SEER*, XXIX, no. 72 (1950), 267–286.

Wells, Samuel F., Jr. "British strategic withdrawal from the Western hemisphere, 1904–1906." *Canadian Historical Review*, XLIX, no. 4 (Dec. 1968), 335–356.

Wertheimer, Mildred S. *The Pan-German League 1890–1914*. New York, 1924.

Westwood, J. N. *Witnesses of Tsushima*. Tallahassee, FL, 1970.

Whigham, Henry James. *Manchuria and Korea*. London, 1904.

The Persian problem: an examination of the rival positions of Russia and Great Britain in Persia with some account of the Persian Gulf and the Bagdad railway. London, 1903.

White, John Albert. "Bezobrazov and the coming of the Russo-Japanese War." *Trudy dvadtsatpiatogo mezhdunarodnogo kongressa vostokovedov. Moscow, August 9–16, 1960*. Moscow, 1963, pp. 433–437.

The diplomacy of the Russo-Japanese War. Princeton, 1964.

"Portsmouth 1905: peace or truce?" *Journal of Peace Research*, VI, no. 4 (1969), 359–366.

Whitney, Henry N. "British foreign policy and the Russo-Japanese War." Ph.D. dissertation, University of Pennsylvania, 1948.

Willetts, Harry T. "The agrarian problem." In Katkov, George, et al. (eds.) *Russia enters the twentieth century*. London, 1971, pp. 111–137.

Williams, Beryl J. "Great Britain and Russia, 1905 to the 1907 convention." In Hinsley, F. H. (ed.) *British foreign policy under Sir Edward Grey*. Cambridge, 1977, pp. 133–147.

"The revolution of 1905 and Russian foreign policy." In Abramsky, C. and Williams, Beryl J. (eds.) *Essays in honor of E. H. Carr*. London, 1974, pp. 101–125.

Williamson, John G. *Karl Helfferich, 1872–1924. Economist, financier, politician*. Princeton, 1971.

Williamson, Samuel R., Jr. *The politics of grand strategy. Britain and France prepare for war, 1904–1914*. Cambridge, MA, 1969.

Witte, Sergei Iul'evich. *The memoirs of Count Witte*. Trans. and ed. Sidney Harcave. Armonk, NY, 1990.

Vospominaniia, 3 vols. Moscow, 1960.

Vospominaniia. Tsarstvovanie Nikolaia II, 2 vols. Berlin, 1922.

Wolf, John B. *The diplomatic history of the Bagdad railroad.* Columbia, MO, 1936.

Wolfe, Bertram D. *Three who made a revolution.* New York, 1948.

Woods, H. Charles. "The Bagdad railway and its tributaries". *GJ*, L, no. 1 (July 1917), 32–57.

Woodward, Ernest L. *Great Britain and the German Navy.* Oxford, 1935.

Yapp, Malcolm Edward. *Strategies of British India: Britain, Iran and Afghanistan 1798–1850.* Oxford, 1980.

Yorck von Wartenburg, Maximilian Graf. *Das Vodringen der russischen Macht in Asien*, 2nd. ed. Berlin, 1900.

Zabriskie, Edward H. *American–Russian rivalry in the Far East: a study in diplomacy and power politics 1895–1914.* Philadelphia, 1946.

Zaionchkovsky, Andrei Medarich. "Franko-russkie otnosheniia do voiny 1914 goda." In Shliapnikov, Aleksandr Gavrilovich, et al. *Kto dolzhnik? Sbornik dokumentirovannykh statei po voprosu ob otnosheniiakh mezhdu Rossiei, Frantsiei i drugimi derzhavami Antanty do voiny 1914 g., vo vremia voiny i v period interventsii.* Moscow, 1926, pp. 11–50.

Zenkovsky, Serge A. *Pan-Turkism and Islam in Russia.* Cambridge, 1960.

Zinov'ev, Ivan Alekseevich. *Rossiia, Angliia i Persiia.* St. Petersburg, 1912.

Index